PAPERS IN THE COLLECTIO

1. **A Victorian History of the Counties of England, A Histor Buckinghamshire, Vol. 2 - Industries Section, William P**

2. **Paper Mills in Buckinghamshire, Alfred H. Shorter, an extract from the Paper Mills and Paper Makers in England 1495-1800.**

3. **Brick makers in Buckinghamshire, Andrew Pike, Buckinghamshire County Museum, Second Edition 1995**

4. **Buckinghamshire Industrial Occupations & Industries, 1841-1951 - David Thorpe, Not previously published,**

PREFACE

The papers in this collection are published here on the occasion of an October 2007 meeting of the Bucks Local History Network which had the theme of Bucks Industrial Heritage. With one exception, they are reprints of material that has been out of print for sometime. The fact that such material has value suggests that there is a need for a new impetus in the study of the history of industry in the county. The statistics of Paper 4 show that there have been a several industries in the county that were far from being simply of local significance. This makes it important for there to be more studies of individual industries, factories and firms in the county. Even the documentation of manufacturers as to who was where and when is very patchy. It would be very desirable for all industries to be covered by studies similar to that published here on brick-making. 2007 has marked the publication of Stanley Freese's *The Watermills of Buckinghamshire* that were so important to a variety of industries

The Buckinghamshire Record Office has a number of important deposits of material that await study and could well prove very useful accounts of individual firms. For instance, records of Nestle in Aylesbury are said to represent the highest standards of book-keeping. Individual firms that have been the subject of books include Hazell, Watson & Watson[1] (although their records have not been explored in any systematic way), and Salmons and Sons at Newport Pagnell. Slough Trading estate has its own history[3] Wolverton works is well documented but even there it would seem there is still scope to explore detailed records further. The conference saw the launch of Brown's study of brewing in the county[4]. This draws in part on records that he personally rescued. These books and others, however, have only touched the surface. There is also a need for more attention to be paid on preserving business records.

[1] *A Century in Print: The Story of Hazels 1839-1939*, Keefe, H.J., 1939
[2] *Long Lease, the Story of Slough Estates 1920-1991*, Cassell, M, 1991.
[3] *Salmons and Sons, the Tickford Coachbuilders*, Mynard, D.C., 2007.
[4] *ABC: A Brewers Compendium, A Directory of Buckinghamshire Breweries*, Brown, M, 2007

Acknowledgements

Paper 1 – The extract is in two parts. Not included is a section on Bells
  a) This information is reproduced from A Victorian History of the Counties of England, A History of the County of Buckinghamshire, Volume II, pages 103-115, by permission of the Executive Editor.
  b) This information is reproduced from A Victorian History of the Counties of England, A History of the County of Buckinghamshire, Volume II, pages 126-129, by permission of the Executive Editor.

Paper 2 – The extract is pages 128-147 from the book which was published by the Paper Publication Society in 1957

Paper 3 – reproduced here in full by permission of the Buckinghamshire County Museum who retains the copywright of text and images.

LIST OF CONTENTS

Front Cover Images
TLH – Hazell's Printing Works, Aylesbury
TRH – Chesham Brewery
BLH – Old Lace Factory, Olney
BRH –Wolverton Works

Reproduced by permission of Buckinghamshire County Council and BRH Milton Keynes Museum

Section dealing with Industries
(pp 103-130 of original, except pp 116-125 Bell-foundries)

BUCKINGHAMSHIRE has never been a manufacturing county, and before the 16th century there were probably no industries but those which supplied the actual wants of the local agricultural population. During the last three centuries the industries carried on in the county, though on a small scale, have been very various. The most interesting are those which may be called cottage industries : lace, straw-plaiting, and chair-seating. Of these, the two latter owe their origin to natural products grown in the county, the wheat-straw being suitable for plaiting, and the beech woods of the Chiltern Hills being famous throughout the history of the county. Chair-making is now perhaps the most important manufacture, and is still peculiarly local in its character, although much of the wood used is not grown in the district. Other trades owe their prosperity to the water-power, arising from the Thames and its tributaries in the south and the Ouse in the north. The chief of these is the manufacture of paper, the mills being grouped for the most part on the streams running into the Thames. In the northern part of the county much of this water-power was lost, owing to the construction of the Grand Junction Canal. Other industries have existed in the county without apparently any dependence on natural commodities or situation. Needle-making, for instance, was a trade carried on for more than two centuries at Long Crendon, where it was difficult to procure wire, and the manufacturers did not attempt to utilize the water that lay close at hand. Silk mills were opened in the early 19th century with the definite object of providing work for the unemployed, and more recently branches of London printing works have been established in the county.

The growth of the town of Slough should be noticed in connexion with the Buckinghamshire industries. Originally quite a small village, it seems to have mainly grown up since the building of the station on the Great Western Railway. Its population is to a great extent industrial, employed in a great variety of undertakings, the chief being perhaps the brick-fields. Until very recent years the means of communication, however, in the county have offered no incentive to the local industries. The roads as a whole seem to have been uniformly bad for many centuries. Each township or parish was responsible for the roads which ran through it, the different land-owners being bound to repair particular pieces.

At the close of the 13th century indulgences were granted to encourage the repair of the roads in the county. In 1292, during the episcopate of Bishop Sutton[1] of Lincoln, such an indulgence was granted to those who were bound to contribute to the repair of Walton Street, in Aylesbury parish, and in the succeeding years similar indulgences[2] were granted for the repair of the bridges at Newport Pagnell and Great Marlow. Presentments in the manorial courts of different obstructions left on the roads were very frequent, and it seems doubtful if the courts were of sufficient authority to have much effect, the same offence coming up in court after court.[3] In the 16th and 17th centuries the justices of the peace superseded the lord of the manor in this duty, but the change seems to have had no effect. In 1634-5 the county was charged with a share of carrying certain timber from Oxfordshire to London. In April the justices wrote that the roads were 'impassable, or at least so foul and unfit for carriages of weight' that the loads must be very small, and therefore they begged that the work might be done later in the summer.[4] In the 18th century a highway rate could be levied on different parishes by order of the justices under an Act of William and Mary instead of the different inhabitants providing labourers for so many days.[5]

The repairs, however, at the close of the century were carried out mainly by gangs of parish labourers, who were underpaid and without supervision. The establishment of turnpike trusts for the repair of the main roads produced some improvement, but of course the by-roads were not affected, and the frequent collection of tolls was often a heavy tax on the farmers of a district. Thus at Aylesbury there was no road out of the town free from toll, and there were no less than seven turnpike trusts, each managing a different road, with a different set of lawyers, officials, and toll-collectors to be paid.[6] The tolls varied slightly under different trusts, but in Buckinghamshire and the neighbouring counties the usual rates were as follows :—[7]

For a horse ridden or led, 1½d.
For a horse drawing any vehicle, 4½d.
A carriage and pair 9d. and so on.
Cattle 10d. a score, and sheep and pigs rather less.

In 1813, in a survey of the county made for the Board of Agriculture, the state of the roads is heavily condemned. The by-roads naturally were the worst ; some were even dangerous, the ruts being so deep that the surveyor reports 'that when the wheels of a chaise fall into them, it is with the greatest danger an attempt may be made to draw them out ; nay, instances may be produced where, if such an attempt is made, the horse and chaise must inevitably fall into bogs.' This actually happened on the road from Risborough to Bledlow, the horse of the surveyor falling into a bog up to his chest.[8] The main roads at the present time are under the control of the County Council. Their course has been dictated from the earliest times by the position of the Chiltern Hills, the roads from London passing in the most cases through the different gaps in the hills. The road from London to Chester passes through before it reaches Buckinghamshire, which it enters at Little Brickhill, and runs north-west, covering the course of Watling Street. The Liverpool road enters the county near Woburn and passes through the town of Newport Pagnell, which owed its prosperity to its being a posting stage on this road. In the south of the county there are two roads to Oxford from London. The one follows the valley of the Thames, the other enters the county near Uxbridge and passes through High Wycombe, going over the Chiltern Hills. From this road a branch road runs up the Missenden valley to Aylesbury and Buckingham, while there is a more direct road to the former town by Tring and Aston Clinton. Other roads of course connect the different towns and villages with one another. The county was better served by water communication than by road. The Thames was used by the manufacturers established near its banks, and the Ouse is navigable throughout its course in Buckinghamshire. The Grand Junction Canal has also supplied a much-needed means of communication for the towns in the centre of the county, which were long without adequate railway service. The main canal passes through Ivinghoe, Fenny Stratford, and Stony Stratford, but is also connected with the three towns of Buckingham, Aylesbury, and Wendover. The Act of Parliament for making the cuts was obtained in 1794. This canal was so much used in the early part of the 19th century that the road from Stony Stratford to Newport Pagnell, along which the commodities sent by canal were distributed in the county, was at many seasons of the year absolutely impassable, being cut up by the heavy wagons.[9] In the early days of railways the Buckinghamshire landowners offered so much opposition to any scheme that the county was badly served by railways for many years. When the London and Birmingham Railway, now the London and North-Western, was surveyed George Stephenson's original plan was to bring the main line down via Aylesbury and Amersham to London, but so much opposition was raised that the line was diverted through the Countess of Bridgewater's land by Berkhampstead and Tring. 'The land,' she is reported to have said to him, 'is already *gashed* by the Canal, and if you take that course you will have no severance to pay, it will disarm opposition, and the position of the locks will be some guide to you in your levels.'[10] Thus the line, when it was opened in 1838, only passed through a small portion of the county by Bletchley and Wolverton. Subsequently several branch lines have been built, opening up the northern part of the county. From Cheddington Junction there is a line to Aylesbury; from Bletchley there are two lines, one by Fenny Stratford to Bedford and Cambridge, and the other to Oxford. The Banbury line passes through Buckingham, leaving the main line at Winslow, and another branch connects Wolverton and Newport Pagnell. In the south the chief railway is the Great Western; the main line, entering the county near Colnbrook and passing through Slough, leaves the county at Maidenhead. It has branches to Eton and Windsor, and to Oxford, via High Wycombe, Princes Risborough, and Thame.

A small line was projected in 1846 by Robert Stephenson, its object being to connect the two great lines, the centre of the county being then practically without railway communications. Part of the scheme was abandoned, and not till 1861 was the Act obtained for the Aylesbury and Buckingham Railway. The project met with opposition of every kind, but finally an arrangement was made for the new line being worked by the Great Western.[11] Afterwards, however, an extension was made bringing the line from Aylesbury to London, the terminus being at Baker Street, and the Aylesbury and Buckingham Railway was bought by the Metropolitan Railway Company. The line is known as the Metropolitan Extension Railway, and a steam tramway is run in connexion with it from Quainton Road to Brill. The Great Central Railway, since its extension to London, also passes through the centre of the county, entering it near Buckingham. It then passes through Quainton Road Junction, Aylesbury, and on to the Marylebone terminus. The Great Western and Great Central Joint Committee have built a new line from Quainton Road, through Princes Risborough and Wycombe, joining the main line near Kingsbury-Neasden and so on to London.

Several industries have sprung up in the county for different reasons during the latter part of the last century. Amongst these may be classed boat-building, on the banks of the Thames. This trade has probably occupied a large number of the riverside population throughout the history of the county. In 1831 there were said to be ten boat-builders and 998 boat-makers or menders,[12] but the trade in its present form has only developed recently. At Eton it dated from the time when the boys at the college began to row—about forty-five years ago.[13] It is now one of the four centres in the country for the building of racing-boats. The industry received a further stimulus about twenty years after the introduction of racing by the popularity of pleasure-boating on the river. A large number of the boats built for this purpose are kept on the Thames for letting on hire, the rest are sold to purchasers in all parts of the country. Recently the demand for punts has brought an increase of trade, which had been decreasing owing to the popularity of motoring and other amusements.[14] A large export trade was at one time carried on by the boat-builders at Eton to most continental countries, but this has been stopped by the establishment of boat-building firms in these countries; boats are still sent to Africa, India, Italy, Portugal, amongst other places. One firm has also extended its business by manufacturing oars and sculls, besides supplying the London County Council with a large number of mahogany boats for use in the London parks. The industry now gives employment to a considerable number of men, whose work is very various, the chief classes being builders, varnishers, decorators, upholsterers and watermen. The wages paid to first-class hands are good, the rate of wages amongst the builders reaching between £3 and £4 a week.

Although the manufacture of paper has been one of the chief industries of Buckinghamshire for so many years, there do not seem to have been any large printing works established until recently. In the second half of the 18th century there was a printer at Aylesbury,[15] and for a short time, in the year 1792, the *Buckinghamshire Herald* was printed there by a man named Norman, and at the present time there are printers in most of the towns of the county. The *Buckinghamshire Standard* is printed at Newport Pagnell, as well as the *Newport Pagnell Gazette*. The *South Bucks Standard* at Wycombe, the *Buckingham Standard* at Buckingham, and the *Bucks Herald* at Aylesbury, are all printed in the towns where they are published. In the last-named town are large printing works owned by Messrs. Hazell, Watson & Viney, Ltd.[16] The firm was founded in London in 1845, but the Aylesbury works were not opened till 1867, when they were started as an experiment in an old silk-mill, with the object of establishing works in the country rather than in London. All kinds of printing are done by the firm, who also are book-binders, printing-ink makers, printers' roller makers, &c. A great many institutions and clubs have been established at Aylesbury for the employees of the firm, who are also shareholders under different schemes, the total value of the shares so held being between £16,000 and £17,000. There are numerous coach and carriage builders in all parts of the county. Their trade appears to be of recent development, since in 1831 only twenty-three men were so employed. The chief centres are at Newport Pagnell, Great Marlow, and Slough. At Slough a large export trade is carried on and this has prevented one firm at least from suffering from the increasing demand for motor cars.[17]

Embrocation is made by two firms in the county, the Line Romanelicum Company at Newport Pagnell and the well-known Messrs. Elliman & Sons, Ltd., at Slough.

Brewing was carried on in Buckinghamshire, as in the rest of England, in nearly every village in mediaeval times, and the industry was supervised as a rule by the lords of the manors or their officials, claiming the right to hold the assize of ale. Owing to the process then obtaining, no large quantities of beer or ale were made, so that the business was carried on a very small scale. At High Wycombe, in the 16th century, there were severe orders against those who brewed selling, or as it was then called 'tippling,' their beer at their own houses.[18] Instead it was to be sent into the town to be sold by the 'tipplers' at the price fixed by the mayor of the borough. The more important breweries, in the modern sense, seem to have been established during the 18th century. At Great Marlow brewing is the most important industry in the town, the chief brewery having been established by the Wethereds in 1758. The same family still carries on the business, which, however, was formed into a company in 1899. The brewery now carried on by the Newport Pagnell Brewery Co., Ltd., has also been established for at least a hundred years. There were also breweries at Buckingham, Bletchley, and Aylesbury, but these are now all in the hands of the Aylesbury Brewery Co., Ltd.

The oldest nursery gardens in Buckinghamshire are the Royal nurseries at Slough, which were founded by Mr. Thomas Brown in 1774.[19] In 1848 they passed into the hands of the late Mr. Charles Turner, and they have remained in his family to the present day. The nurseries have always been noted for 'Florists' Flowers,' the chief kinds grown being carnations, picotees, pinks, roses, auriculas, pelargoniums, dahlias, etc. Roses grown at Slough were specially famous, and Dean Hole described Mr. Charles Turner as 'the king of florists.'[20] At the present day the gardens cover about 150 acres of ground. In the same neighbourhood Messrs. Veitch & Sons, of Chelsea, have opened nurseries at Langley Marish. In 1880, 20 acres of land were purchased, and more has been added till the nursery includes about sixty acres in all. The principal culture is that of fruit trees, roses, and herbaceous plants, but flower and vegetable seeds are also grown there. The nursery is particularly noted for its pears and apples. There are various nurseries in different parts of the county, which have been developed of late years and have profited by the new lines of railway. Of these, the nursery near Claydon was started about fourteen years ago 'to develop a local trade for small orders for ready money.'[21] Tomatoes, bedding plants, and chrysanthemums are grown in large quantities, and cut flowers are also supplied. Fruit of all kinds is grown, and some twelve years ago a Fruit Growers' Association was formed, so that customers living near could obtain the best variety of fruit trees at wholesale prices. To encourage fruit-growing amongst the tenants of Sir Edmund Verney, bart., on whose estate the Claydon Nurseries are situated, compensation for disturbance is given to the cottagers and others who have purchased fruit trees through the Association and have left their cottages within six years after planting. Various other branches of work have also been undertaken, such as fruit-preserving, bee-keeping, and wood-growing. The Claydon Nurseries Company is co-operative so far as the horticultural department is concerned, the profits being annually divided amongst the permanent employees of that branch of the work.

LACE-MAKING

Lace-making for a very long period formed the most important industry of Buckinghamshire. There seems some doubt as to its origin in the county, but tradition attributes it to Queen Katherine of Aragon, who besides holding several manors in Buckinghamshire as part of her dower, also lived for two years at Ampthill in the neighbouring county of Bedford.[1] Thread-lace was made in England as early as 1463,[2] and bone-lace, the original name for pillow-lace, is mentioned in 1577.[3] The type of lace made in England at this time was Flemish, and may have been first brought to England by refugees from Flanders. Pennant[4] speaks ' of the lace-manufacture which we stole from the Flemings,' but Queen Katherine may still, in the first instance, have brought the industry to Buckinghamshire. It seems to have been flourishing by the beginning of the 17th century, since in 1611 men ' who continuallie travelled to sell bone-lace on the Sabbath day ' were presented at an ecclesiastical visitation.[5] A time of depression, however, followed, probably owing to the monopolies granted by James I. In High Wycombe and the neighbourhood there was a great deal of distress in 1623 mainly due to lack of employment, since both the clothing and bone-lace trades were daily becoming more depressed.[6] This depression was, however, merely temporary. Three years later, in the neighbouring town of Great Marlow, Sir Henry Borlase founded a school for twenty-four boys and twenty-four girls, and the latter were to learn to knit, spin, and make bone-lace. The chief centres of the lace industry were Newport Pagnell, or Olney, High Wycombe, and Aylesbury. Fuller, in 1660,[7] specially mentions Olney, but the industry was already widely spread in the county. A few years later Sir Edmund Verney,[8] at Claydon, writes that one of his men had given him some very good lace made by his daughter. She received a guinea, and the lace was made into a cravat of the latest fashion.

The greatest time of prosperity in the industry came, however, in the 18th century, when bone-lace was in great demand. The *Spectator*, when deploring the extravagance of women in their head-dresses,[9] speaks of ' childish Gewgaws, Ribbands and bone-lace.' In 1717 the lace-makers on a large scale, living at Wycombe and in that neighbourhood, petitioned against a decision which forced them to take out licences as petty chapmen or hawkers.[10] One of the chief of these lace-makers was Ferdinando Shrimpton of Penn, who was eight times Mayor of Chepping Wycombe.[11] He and other men of his class kept several hundred workers constantly employed.[12] They went weekly to London, generally on a Monday, and sold their goods to the London milliners at the lace markets held at the George Inn, Aldersgate Street, or in the Bull and Mouth Inn in St. Martin's by Aldersgate. They returned with a stock of thread and silk, which they gave out to their workwomen to be made up according to their orders.[13] In the northern part of the county Newport Pagnell was a sort of staple town for bone-lace,[14] and it was said to produce more lace than any other town in the country.[15] A lace-market was held every Wednesday at which great quantities were sold. Lace-buyers also came round from the London houses about once a month, meeting the lace-makers at some inn, such as the ' Nagg's Head ' at Thame, and there buying their stock.[16]

The Anti-Gallican Society some years before had awarded its first prize for lace shown by Mr. William Marriott, of Newport Pagnell,[17] and in 1761 Earl Temple, the Lord Lieutenant of Buckinghamshire, presented the king, on behalf of the lace-makers, with a pair of fine lace ruffles, made at the same town.[18]

Aylesbury was also noted for the fine quality of the lace made there.[19] In the 18th century the women in the workhouse were employed in lace-making instead of spinning.[20] In 1784 the overseers entered two cloths for lace-pillows in their accounts ;[21] in the same year they paid 4d. to ' four girls cutting off,' and on another occasion Mary Slade received 3s. 7d. to set up lace-making.[22] Lace played a prominent part also in the Parliamentary elections for the borough.[23] No candidate could hope to be successful if he did not promise to uphold the bone-lace industry and denounce the machine-made lace of Nottingham. A lace-pillow was mounted on a pole and carried at the head of processions, and banners were hung with Aylesbury lace, for which enormous prices were paid.

The lace trade flourished in the early part of the 19th century, and its extent is well illustrated by the village of Hanslope.[24] In 1801, 500 people out of a population of 1,275 were employed in lace-making, and both men and women made it their regular employment. No women's labour for agricultural work could be obtained in the county[25] owing to the good wages they were paid for lace-making.

The decline came very quickly after the close of the French wars. The introduction of machine-made lace about 1835[26] and the effects of free trade gradually killed the industry.[27] The quality of the lace made fell off, and in spite of temporary revivals the trade proper became extinct about 1884.[28] The industry, however, lingered on in many parts of the county, and of late years a great effort has been made to bring about a revival. The North Bucks Lace Association was formed in 1897, and is the largest association of the kind. It aims not only at reviving old patterns and improving the quality of the lace made, but also at securing a better price than the workers can obtain for themselves. In other parts of the county various people have interested themselves in the industry, and very beautiful lace is now made, such as the lace in Hughenden Church.

In the south of the county other trades, especially chair-making, afford both an easier and at the same time a better paid occupation for the women, so that there is less lace-making than round Buckingham and Newport Pagnell.

Another difficulty in the way of the revival of the industry is the length of time taken in learning to make lace. It seems probable that after the present generation of workers has passed away no fine, wide lace will be made any more with the object of earning a livelihood. Children, in order to become expert workers, must begin very young and work more hours a day than is possible whilst they are attending school.

In the flourishing days of the industry there were hardly any schools except lace-schools in the county. Sir William Borlase's school at Great Marlow was not continued long, but in 1672 the Aylesbury overseers paid Mary Sutton 5s. to teach the workhouse children to make lace.[29] At Hanslope children were sent to the lace-schools when they were five years old,[30] and both boys and girls could maintain themselves by the time they were eleven or twelve. The hours were very long, and schools were held in small cottages without sufficient light or ventilation. In some parts of the county the children were sent to the lace-schools at four years old. The old woman who kept the principal lace school at Lane End died about a year ago at the age of eighty-six. The schools must have disappeared about thirty to thirty-five years ago, but the children then seem to have had first about an hour's reading lesson, followed by six to seven hours' lace-making.[31] Besides the children, the skilled workers were crowded in large numbers into a small room, with the result that the industry was most unhealthy. As early as 1782[32] Pennant noticed the pale faces of the girls at Newport Pagnell, due to their sedentary state, and three years later a writer in the *Gentleman's Magazine*[33] suggested remedies for this state of things. In the course of a journey in Buckinghamshire and Northamptonshire his attention was drawn to 'the frequent sight of deformed and diseased women in these counties.' He found they were mostly lace-makers, growing deformed and ill from the stooping position in which they worked and from sitting in 'small, low and close' rooms. His recommendations probably had no effect, and in 1797 lace-making in the towns of the hundred of Desborough did not 'induce those habits of neatness and industry which appear highly necessary to render an occupation beneficial to a county.'[34]

The kind of lace made in Buckinghamshire has passed through many variations, but it has always been pillow-lace of one kind or another, the most characteristic lace being pillow-point, or 'half-stitch' as it is called in the county.[35] The earliest Buckinghamshire lace was old Flemish with a wavy and graceful pattern and well-executed ground. Some of the patterns seem to have been worked in with a needle on the net ground. In 1778 point-ground was introduced, and from that time the staple pillow-lace of the county developed. Much of the point-ground was made by men. The principal branch of the trade was 'baby lace' and edgings, mostly used in trimming babies' caps.[36] Point-ground was used, while the patterns were copied from Lille or Mechlin lace.[37] Large quantities were exported to the United States until the outbreak of the Civil War, when the demand ceased rapidly.[38] Other sorts of grounds were made, such as 'wire,' 'double,' and 'trolly.'[39] Fresh kinds of lace were introduced at the outbreak of the French War at the close of the 18th century. Manufacturers undertook to supply French laces, and both true Valenciennes lace and 'French ground' were then made in Buckinghamshire.[40] Early in the 19th century Regency Point came into fashion, a point lace with cloth or toile on the edge. Insertions were also introduced, and made in large quantities. A lace made of worsted of various colours, called Norman lace, suddenly became fashionable,[41] and the demand was great, especially in the United States. The trade dropped, however, as suddenly as it had arisen. In the middle of the 19th century Maltese lace was introduced, resulting in a great recovery in the industry.[42] It was made both of thread and silk,[43] and completely ousted the older Buckinghamshire lace, which could no longer compete with the machine-made article. At the Exhibition of 1862 hardly anything but Maltese lace was exhibited, but a fresh impulse was given to the trade.[44] New kinds of Maltese lace were introduced called 'plaited laces,' but this revival of lace-making came to an end about 1870, the quality of the lace having become worse and worse, both as to pattern and material.[45] The last variety of lace appeared about 1875, and was called Yac lace. It was made from a species of goat's hair dyed to all colours, but the fashion died out very quickly.[46]

Maltese lace-making lingered on in the different villages, and is still made, but the North Bucks Lace Association and kindred societies encourage the older and more characteristic 'Buckinghamshire lace.' Old stores of lace have been sought out and the patterns revived. A good deal of jealousy used to exist with regard to the copying of patterns, and the same feeling has again appeared of late years. The pattern is pricked on a strip of parchment and pinned down to the pillow. It is about ten inches long,[47] and in Buckinghamshire the custom is to have two of these strips, and as one is finished the other is placed below it, the lace-maker thus working round and round the pillow. The lace is made of linen thread, and at the present day there is considerable difficulty in procuring it fine enough and even enough.[48] This was probably a difficulty in earlier times, and silk was used many years before Maltese lace was introduced.[49] Amersham and Great Marlow were specially noted for the black silk lace made there.[50] The bobbins were originally made of bone—hence the name bone-lace; but more frequently they are of wood.[51] The number used varies according to the design, but for a wide pattern as many as 500 may be needed. Old bobbins often show an interesting history of their owner, since it was the custom to inscribe them with names and the dates of various events occurring in her life. Forty years ago it was still the custom to give bobbins, often of intricate workmanship, as love-tokens.[52] The pillow was, however, the costliest part of a lace-maker's implements. It is a hard round cushion, stuffed with straw and well-hammered to make it hard, and covered with 'pillow-cloth.'[53] The making of pillows was almost a monopoly, one family making them for a district.[54] A pillow with all its appurtenances in some cases cost as much as £5 in the early part of the 19th century. In the prosperous days of the industry women could earn very good wages, often making more than their husbands, who were agricultural labourers. In 1794 the average wages of the best lace hands were from 1s. to 1s. 6d. a day,[55] but about the same time in the Thames Valley women only earned 10d. a day and girls about 4d. and 6d.[56] In 1813 the wages given were rather lower, 9d. to 1s. 4d.[57] a day, but good workers at Aylesbury, before machine-made lace killed the trade, could earn 25s.[58] a week, and married women who did not give their whole time to the work often made as much as £1 a week. The workers were sometimes, however, only paid once a month, after the lace-buyers had come round and the local lace-men had sold their store of lace.[59]

At the present day the lace-makers are paid by the hour, and the wages are not high, varying from 1¼d. to 1½d. per hour.[60]

Many old customs existed amongst the lace-makers. St. Catherine was their patron saint, and her festival was kept as a holiday till recent years.[61] The Aylesbury Overseers[62] even gave the lace-makers in the workhouse '3s. to keep Catern,' and special Catern cakes were made to celebrate the holiday.

At Aylesbury a lace-queen was chosen from among the lace-makers and carried round the town on a platform, working on her pillow, and accompanied by a band and a great crowd.[63] Whether these processions were held on St. Catherine's Day is not clear, but more probably they took place during fairs, since the time of year commanded indoor celebrations of the lace-makers' holiday rather than street processions.

In some parts of the county the women, who have lost their employment owing to the decline of the lace trade, have taken to sequin and bead work. This is the case round Princes Risborough, particularly at Lacey Green, Amersham, and near High Wycombe.[64] At Lacey Green bead-work has been done about twenty-five years, and was sent to London, but the demand is lessening, and only an occasional order is now received.

WOODEN WARE AND CHAIR-MAKING

The beechwoods of the Chiltern districts have naturally led to the manufacture of wooden ware for many years. Presumably the 13th-century names, Hubert Turnator, Peter le Turnur, and Bartholomew le Turnur, specify the trade carried on by their bearers, a trade which afterwards obtained a considerable importance, and was and is specially centred at Chesham.[1] In 1725 Defoe[2] mentions the supply of beechwood which was then used for making felloes for 'the great cars of London, cole-carts, dust-carts, &c., which the city laws do not allow to have tyres of iron,' for the billet wood for the king's palaces and similar purposes, and lastly for chairs and turnery ware.

At the close of the 18th century the value of the woods had considerably increased, frequent felling having been found more advantageous to the owners than allowing the trees to come to a considerable size.[3] Even then, however, the wisdom of carrying this new system too far was doubted. The uses to which the wood was put were much the same as in Defoe's time—spokes, felloes, bedsteads, and chairs.[4] Chesham became noted for its turnery ware early in the following century, but in 1862 its wooden ware and turnery trade was declining.[5] There are, however, a considerable number of manufacturers still carrying on the trade in the town and neighbourhood, wooden dairy utensils being a speciality of some makers. Several firms also make brushes of various kinds. Chair-making, though possibly of later development than the wooden-ware manufactory, has outstepped it in importance. Both Defoe and Langley mention chair-making as one of the uses to which the beechwoods on the Chilterns were put, but the industry does not seem to have become of great importance until the 19th century.[6] In 1830 there were said to be only two chair manufacturers in High Wycombe,[7] which has since become the centre of the industry. In 1862 one of the chief manufacturers of the town described the early condition of the business in the following words[8] :—'When I began the trade . . . I loaded a cart and travelled to Luton. All there was prosperous. There was a scramble for my chairs ; when I came home I laid my receipts on my table, and said to my wife : "You never saw so much money before."' The demand for chairs grew rapidly, and the Wycombe chair-makers supplied the chairs for the Crystal Palace, for St. Paul's Cathedral, and many barracks,[9] and a large export trade, especially to the Colonies, was developed in the middle of the 19th century.[10] It was then the boast of Wycombe that it turned out a chair a minute all the year round, or 1,800 doz. per week,[11] that is, over 1,100,000 per annum.

In 1885 there were about fifty chair-makers, large and small, in Wycombe,[12] and at the present day the number has reached nearly a hundred. The trade has, however, suffered a depression of late years, owing to the loss of some of the foreign trade, which has passed into American and Austrian hands, and the competition at home is so severe that some of the work done is unremunerative.[13] Nevertheless nearly every village round Wycombe has its manufactory, employing both men and women, boys and girls.[14]

The falls of timber take place in November and March, when the trees are sold by auction, and the manufacturers lay in their stock of wood.[15] Beechwood forms the greater part of the raw material, but elm is used for the seats, and ash for the bows of Windsor and similar chairs. Oak and walnut are only as a rule procured for special orders.[16]

The manufacturers in 1885 were divided into three classes, which still obtain at the present day. In the first place there are those who have their own steam saw-mills, and turn out the finished article ; then come manufacturers who send their wood to public saw-mills to be cut up into lengths, and afterwards turn out the chair complete ; and lastly, there are smaller men who live in the surrounding villages and supply the manufacturer proper with what is called 'turned stuff,' i.e., with fore-legs, stretchers, and lists of chairs according to pattern. Thus it often happens that only the backs, hind-legs, and seats are made at the factory proper, other parts being sent in from the country. There much of the work is done in the cottages, the wood being turned by hand, after it has come, cut up in lengths, from the saw-mill.

Certain factories in High Wycombe specialize in a particular part of the chair, and turn out nothing but chair-backs, or seats. The seats are made by women and girls, who learn the trade at an early age. When the work is done at home, they can earn about $1\frac{1}{4}d.$ an hour for caning, and rather more for 'matting,' a dirtier and harder process.[17] The greater number of chairs made in this district are, however, seated with cane, not rushes, and the splitting is all done by hand. All kinds of chairs are made, from the common kinds known as Windsor, cathedral, bedroom, kitchen, barrack chairs, to the more elaborate patterns made by the larger manufacturers of High Wycombe. The oak chairs, for instance, made for the judges at the Royal Courts of Justice were manufactured at Wycombe, and, more recently, the mahogany chairs used by the peers and peeresses at the coronation of King Edward VII.[18]

Besides the actual chair-makers there are several firms who make articles used in the manufacture, such as varnish and chair-makers' tools.

Various causes have made paper-making a profitable undertaking in Buckinghamshire. Especially in the Thames Valley, the water-power obtained from the tributaries of the river, the easy means of communication by water, and the nearness to London, all favoured its manufacture, and at the close of the reign of Elizabeth paper-mills had already been established. John Spilman, the queen's jeweller, obtained a licence that he himself, or his deputies, should alone build any paper-mills or collect linen rags in the country,[1] but by 1600 other mills had been erected, and he petitioned for assistance against the paper manufacturers. John Turner, Edward Marshall, and George Friend, had built a mill in Buckinghamshire, but its exact position is not mentioned in Spilman's petition. Other mills must have been built very quickly in spite of his licence. In 1636 there were twelve paper-mills in the county,[2] one of the most important being at Horton, worked by Edmund Phipps. He was chief constable of the county, and seems to have worked his mill with but little consideration for the convenience of his neighbours. In fact the paper-mills seem to have been thoroughly unpopular in the country, owing to the importation of rags, and the consequent outbreaks of the plague. Phipps was presented at an ecclesiastical court in 1635 for working his mill on Sunday all through the year.[3] The next year the mills were stopped owing to the prevalence of the plague, and the paper-masters petitioned for a contribution from the county towards their relief. This made them even more unpopular than before, and the justices of the peace made a counter petition, not only against the rate, but for the destruction of the mills altogether. Some of these mills were already built at High Wycombe,[4] or near the town, and this district became the centre of the paper-making industry in Buckinghamshire. At Horton, Richard West had succeeded Phipps as paper-maker by 1649.[5]

At the close of the 17th century[6] a bill was brought into Parliament for the formation of a company with the monopoly of making white writing and printing paper. Whilst it was before the House of Lords, the mayor, aldermen and inhabitants of Chepping Wycombe petitioned against the formation of such a company, which would ruin their trade. There were then, in 1690, eight paper-mills at High Wycombe; probably they were not all within

the borough itself, but were in the neighbourhood, and fifty families were employed in making paper. The men had mostly been apprenticed to the trade, and if the prohibition against making white paper became law, they would come, for the most part, with their families on the rates. The Wycombe mills were worked by water from the River Wye, but other mills were established on the Loddon, which runs into the Thames between Wycombe and Great Marlow.[7]

In the 18th century paper-making was the most important industry in the county, with the possible exception of lace.[8] In 1797 Thomas Langley wrote :—'The paper manufacture is very flourishing and has experienced every attention its importance so highly deserves.'[9] The paper-mills at Horton and Wyrardisbury (Wraysbury) were worked during the greater part of the 18th century, but for a time were converted into iron or copper mills.[10] Wyrardisbury mills were re-converted into paper-mills early in the 19th century,[11] while in the northern part of the county the manufacture was carried on at Newport Pagnell and at Marsworth,[12] and other mills may have existed on the northern streams. The Marsworth mill was destroyed by the construction of the grand Junction Canal, which took away all the water of the stream, for the reservoirs and canal. In 1831 there were seventy-six paper manufacturers in the county, while 220 men or boys were employed in the trade either as masters or workmen.[13] Since then a mill at Chenies stopped working between 1851 and 1861,[14] and at the present day the chief paper-mills are in the south of the county, the most important being at High Wycombe, Great Marlow, Wooburn, Iver, and Bledlow.

The first paper made in Buckinghamshire was writing and printing paper of good quality,[15] but in 1636–7 complaints were made that the paper would not bear ink on either side, while the price had risen considerably.[16] So little competition was there, that Phipps and his fellow manufacturers seem to have made a great profit on the manufacture of bad paper, while a few

years before they had stopped their mills by combination to bring down the price of rags.

The Wycombe mill-owners claimed to make the best kinds of white writing and printing paper. The price varied from 3s. to 20s. a ream, and the Paper Act of 1690 aimed at preventing their making it over 4s. a ream.[17] Some makers did make this good paper, but the greater part was probably of a cheaper kind, since in mentioning the paper-mills near Wycombe and Marlow in 1725, Defoe[18] said that printing paper was made 'good of its kind and cheap such as generally is made use of in printing our newspapers, journals, &c., and smaller pamphlets, but not much fine or large for bound books or writing.' During the 18th century, however,

many improvements were made in the manufacture. These were due largely to the efforts of Mr. John Bates, a paper-maker at Wycombe Marsh. His chief discovery was a method of producing paper for mezzotints and other engraved plates, which was equal to the French paper for the same purpose, and for this he received the gold medal of the Society of Arts in 1787.[19]

Besides the invention of this special paper, other manufacturers at the close of the 18th century were making only papers *de luxe*. The Rye Mill at High Wycombe, for instance, which has been in existence for certainly a hundred years and probably for longer, has always produced paper of this class for writing, drawing, ledgers, and bank notes.[20]

Several tan-yards used to exist in the county, but they are now closed and there is only one firm of tanners in Buckingham at the present day. So important were the tan-yards of the town of Buckingham that the tanners formed one of the four companies to which all the burgesses of the borough belonged.[1] In 1831,[2] 131 men were employed in the business there, but no other tanneries are mentioned. At Olney, however, the tan-yards must have been working at that time,[3] and it was noted for the excellence of its leather in all parts of the kingdom. Leather tanning seems to have been given up some thirty years ago, when the tan-yard, worked by Mr. Joseph Palmer for oak-bark tanning, was closed. His yard, however, has been purchased within the last few years by Messrs. W. E. & J. Pebody, Ltd., and the works re-constructed, being old-fashioned and disused for many years. The process of chrome tanning is now carried on by the firm at the Olney yard.

The manufacture of boots and shoes, which has developed at Olney during the last twenty years, was not established till after the tan-yard was closed, so that its growth can have no connexion with the tannery.

Boot and shoe-making is also the most important trade of the town of Chesham. One of the chief manufacturers at the present time states that there has been an industry there for many generations, and that it was probably due to the existence of several tan-yards in the town. These latter have been given up a very long time, owing doubtless to the later mode of producing leather by much larger firms in London and other leather centres, and to the large quantity of leather imported. In the 16th century the shoemakers at High Wycombe succeeded in closing the market to 'foreign' shoemakers,[4] but at the close of the reign of Elizabeth a new order was made by the mayor and bailiffs, in which the restriction against showing goods in the market was specially removed from the victualling and shoemaking trades. There is, however, no mention of any particular locality in which shoes were made in any quantity.

Early in the 19th century a great many hands were employed at Chesham in the shoe-making trade, the goods manufactured being sent in the main to the London market.[5] It is curious, however, that shoemaking does not appear among the handicrafts or manufactures of the county in the census of 1831.[6] A few years later the trade was flourishing,[7] and by 1862 it had assumed very considerable proportions, the goods being both sent to London and exported to foreign countries.[8] For many years all the boots and shoes were made by hand throughout, and the work was done in the homes of the workers. This is still the case to the extent that hand-work is produced, but there are few, if any, young 'hand sewn' men in the town. When boots began to be riveted, a number of these men took to that branch of the trade, and the term shoemaker is no longer used, except among the hand-makers, for several hands contribute now in the making of a pair of boots—the riveters, sewers, and finishers and several others all carrying on a specialized part of the work. At one or two factories the welting machine has been introduced and then discarded as not satisfactory for the somewhat stronger classes of boots for which Chesham has become noted. For many years these classes of boots formed the staple of the Chesham factories, and to a large extent this is still the case. The boots, when finished, are sent all over the country and a considerable quantity of them are exported. The conditions of the trade at the present time are said to be good. 'The families engaged in the boot trade here are very well paid and generally occupy good class cottages of the better order; a strike is scarcely ever heard of . . . employers and employed appear to get on very well together. There is no trade union here, from time to time efforts have been made from outside to establish one. There is sufficient demand for labour that an unreasonable employer would find his men leave him.'[9]

A second home industry, which still employs a certain number of people in Buckinghamshire, is the manufacture of straw-plait for hats and bonnets. The manufacture first became important in Italy, Leghorn hats being still famous, but it does not seem to have been introduced into England until the 18th century, when the French War stopped the importation of foreign plait. The industry spread quickly in Bedfordshire, Hertfordshire and Buckinghamshire, where the wheat-straw produced was the most favourable for English plait. In 1768 when Arthur Young visited Dunstable,[1] the manufacture of straw-plait was established, but had not grown to much importance, basket-work being still the chief industry of the neighbourhood. Probably in the neighbouring county of Buckingham there was then no straw-plaiting, but by the end of the 18th century it had spread all over the county.

In 1813 lace and straw-plaiting were the chief industries[2] of the county, occupying so many women and girls that none of them worked in the fields.

When foreign plait was unprocurable, the English article was much used, but the large size of the wheat-straws used made it very inferior to the Italian plait.[3] To overcome this defect the straws were split and the narrow 'splints' used instead of the whole straw. At first this process was done by hand with a pen-knife, but it was tedious and difficult to obtain uniformity in the size of the splints. A straw-splitting machine was then introduced, which greatly added to the success of the industry. It is not certain who was the original inventor, several stories existing as to the first machine made. One of these, however, claims that the honour belongs to a Buckinghamshire man. In an account of straw-plaiting written in 1822, the following story is given[4]:—

Our informant states that his father, Thomas Simmons (now deceased), was residing when a boy, about the year 1785, at Chalfont St. Peter's, Buckinghamshire, and that when amusing himself one evening by cutting pieces of wood, he made an article upon which he put a straw and found that it divided it into several pieces. A female who was present asked him to give it to her, observing that if he could not make money of it, she could. She had the instrument, and gave the boy a shilling. He was subsequently apprenticed to a blacksmith; and on visiting his friends, he found them engaged in splitting straws with a pen-knife. Perceiving that the operation might be better performed by an apparatus similar to that which he had made some time before, he then made some machines of iron on the same principle.

The straw-splitting machine does not seem to have come into general use until about 1815.

The most successful period of the manufacture was during the French War, when foreign plaits were prohibited. The latter were in many ways superior to English plait, but various efforts were made to improve its quality, especially by the Society of Arts.[5] These efforts maintained the industry for a considerable period and it was in a flourishing condition in the middle of the 19th century. Lipscomb, writing at that time,[6] says that at Broughton 'the female population were chiefly employed, formerly in lace-making but more recently in platting straw or chip hats and bonnets' and at High Wycombe lace-making had been almost entirely superseded by straw and chip plaiting.[7]

Very good wages, for the time, were earned at the trade. In 1813 women were able to earn 30s. a week,[8] but this was probably the highest rate obtainable, and in the Aylesbury district 22s. a week were the best wages obtained while the industry was most successful.[9] Ivinghoe and Aylesbury were the chief centres of the manufacture in Buckinghamshire. At the former, the Saturday market was largely for straw-plait, which was still brought to it in considerable quantities in 1862.[10] At Aylesbury a plait-market was established by Mr. Robert Thorpe in 1846[11] and succeeded for a time, but was finally given up owing to the drop in prices that shortly occurred. In 1862 the following places carried on the industry in the county, Bow Brickhill, Great Brickhill, Little Brickhill, Wavendon, Aston Abbots, Drayton Parslow, Hoggeston, Pitstone, Stewkley, Swanbourne, Whitchurch, Amersham, besides the Ivinghoe and Aylesbury districts.[12] The industry had many different kinds of workers, with a great deal of specialization; there were bleachers, cutters, dyers, flatters, stringers, drawers, and packers each doing their own particular work in making the straw-plait.[13]

Although the end of the French War made straw-plaiting less profitable in England than it had been before, it was not till the removal of the import duties on foreign plait, that the real decay of the industry set in. Buckinghamshire seems to have lost the greater part of its trade in this article sooner than the other straw-plaiting counties,[14] but it is still carried on about Ivinghoe and Edlesborough.[15] A rough estimate fixes 500 to 600 as the number of straw-plaiters in Buckinghamshire, but the industry is still declining, the demand being very small. The workers, too, prefer factory or domestic service, for both of which there is a great demand.

In a county possessing but little stone for building, the manufacture of bricks was one of the most important industries. In the rates of wages fixed by the justices of the peace in 1562,[1] only five kinds of artificers are especially mentioned, namely, master carpenters and sawyers, bricklayers, tilers and thatchers. Bricklayers and tilers were to receive 8d. a day in summer and 6d. in winter, and their labourers 6d. and 5d. respectively, though in fact they received much more.

In the 17th century,[2] Sir Ralph Verney started a considerable amount of building, and in his correspondence with his steward there are many details about the brick-fields at Claydon. In 1656 he paid the brick-maker 6s. a thousand for making and burning bricks, 1s. a quarter for burning lime, and 5s. a hundred for making and burning pavements. The year before he had procured brick pavements from the neighbouring villages. They were 9 in. square and there was some difficulty in the carting of them to Claydon. The steward wrote that if Sir Ralph 'take soe great a quantity, as from 12 or 15 hundred together . . . . 6 oxen would not well draw 500 at a loade, for they are not near twice so heavy as brick and an ordinary cart will bring on 5 or 6 hundred of brick at a loade now that wages are good.' The building had to be stopped very soon after this owing to financial straits of the Verneys after the Civil War, but Sir Ralph had already ordered 100,000 bricks to be made and the workmen could not be discharged at once. Two years later, however, in 1658, the building was begun afresh; the brickyard was trenched and as soon as the brickmakers could come, tools, wheel-barrows and moulds were delivered to them by their employer. Bricks and tiles were made at the same period at Brill from the earth of Brill Hills[3] and the brick-fields in the neighbourhood on the line of the Brill Tramway still continue. The earth there was also used for earthenware drain pipes.

Brick-making was carried on in other parts of the county in early times. In 1831,[4] 116 men were employed in the industry either as masters or workmen, and in 1862 there were brick-fields at Fenny Stratford, Whitchurch, Burnham, Chalfont St. Peter and Hillesden.[5] It is curious, however, that the brick-fields at Slough are not mentioned at that date, since they are now the most important in the county and had been established before 1862.

The town of Slough has grown up very recently; the demand for houses there and the facilities for the transportation of bricks have both been made by the building of the Great Western Railway. The brick-fields were started about sixty-three years ago by Mr. Thomas Nash and are now owned by a company formed in 1893 under the name of H. & J. Nash, Ltd. The fields extend into the neighbouring parishes of Langley Marish and Iver, and about fourteen million bricks are made annually, steam-power having been used for the last twenty years.[6]

Buckinghamshire is not famous for any great potteries, but the Brill pottery dates from very ancient times. The first mention of potters there is in 1254,[7] in an inquisition as to rights of gathering wood in Brill Woods. The jurors gave evidence as to the privileges of certain ecclesiastical lords and ended with saying that the potters took small-wood, &c., for their kilns contrary to the forest regulations. The right to dig brick earth in Barnwood Forest was probably theirs from time immemorial, but the lord of the manor of Brill exacted an annual payment of 4s. 6d. known as the 'Claygavel.' This was paid in the 13th and 14th centuries with regularity and is continually entered in the steward's accounts.[8] At the disafforestment of Barnwood in the reign of James I,[9] an allotment of commonable land was made for artificers and cottages, by an order of the Court of Chancery, 'many artificers of Brill having received employment by making brick, tyle, lyme and potts out of the soyle of Brill hills.' A pot was dug up at Long Crendon near Brill, about 1885, containing coins of the period of the Civil War and earlier, and presumably was made by the Brill potters.

More recently the chief pottery works were carried on by a family of the name of Hubbocks, the last descendant being still at Brill at the present time.[10] They were potters for 149 years and the father of the present Mr. Hubbocks owned the last pottery. His kiln is still to be seen, and was used till within three years of his death, which took place about thirty-two years ago. He used the old wheel and fashioned the pots with his finger and thumb. At one time, presumably during the lifetime of the elder Hubbocks, there were seven potteries in Brill, and in 1831 thirty-five men were employed in making earthenware pottery in the county.[11] The industry was, however, not in a flourishing condition a few years later, owing to the increased price of fuel and the cost of carriage,[12] but in 1862, there was still a pottery for the manufacture of brown earthenware. The colour however, seems more generally to have been varying shades of yellow and green, produced by the different kinds of clay from which the pots were made.

Hubbocks made for the most part flower-pots and large pans and jugs, one or two of which are to be seen at Brill, but they bear no date since he only dated his pots at the request of the customer. His stock was bought up some years ago 'for a museum in Oxford.'

An older pot is in the possession of Mr. F. H. Parrott, of 'The Camp,' Kimble. It bears the indented inscription 'M.M. 1764' on its side and on the bottom is written 'John Sheperde, Poter, Brill, Bux.' The pot is of rough red earthenware with a greenish-brown glaze and was found in a cottage at Brill where it was bought by a man at Aylesbury, who sold it to its present owner.

There were other potteries at Coleshill, a hamlet in the parish of Amersham, and at Chalfont St. Peter, in the early part of the 19th century.[13] The latter, which is now called the Beaconsfield Pottery, was established in 1805 by Mr. William Wellins, but changed hands shortly and was bought by Mr. John Swallow, who practically was the real starter of the pottery. It has never assumed very large proportions, and Mrs. M. Saunders & Son, the lessees of the pottery, now chiefly produce flower-pots, stands, chimney-pots and pipes and similar articles.[14] It has, however, continued working to the present day, in spite of the keen competition in the industry.

A pottery of another character existed near Great Marlow until the present year, when it was moved to Staffordshire.[15] The Medmenham pottery was established ten years ago about a mile from the town of Great Marlow, with the object of producing architectural pottery and tiles with individuality in design and execution. To secure this, the works were established in the country, materials from Marlow being used when possible and village workpeople only employed for the most part. It has however, been found impossible to continue the pottery in Buckinghamshire, so far from the main pottery districts. Some of the chief pieces of work accomplished were, however, done while the pottery was still at Marlow, one of the most important being the frieze surrounding the new hall of the Law Society in Chancery Lane.

In 1772 Wyrardisbury mill was tenanted by Jukes Colson, who worked it as an iron mill, but five years later it had been turned into a copper mill by the Gnoll Company.[1] The mill was again sold in 1790, and was tenanted early in the 19th century by George and Thomas Glascott, who were brass-founders. They, however, closed their works in 1820, and the mill has since been converted into a paper-mill. A mill at Horton was also at one time used for iron works, but these were closed early in the 19th century.[2] In 1831 only eleven men were returned as being employed as iron-founders,[3] either as masters or workmen, but thirty-four were employed at copper mills. In the middle of the 19th century several foundries were established. The Castle Iron Works were started at Buckingham in 1857, and were owned by a limited liability company, the shareholders being mostly local people,[4] anxious to improve the trade of the town. The foundry was chiefly occupied in making steam-engines of various kinds. Certain road engines were made there which acquired a considerable amount of importance at the time. In 1858 a road locomotive was built for the Marquis of Stafford, which attained to the speed of twelve miles an hour, and a few years later the foundry produced a steam carriage for export to Belgium, which held three passengers as well as the stoker. It averaged ten miles an hour, but on good roads could attain to sixteen, and its inventor, Mr. Thomas Rickett, the manager of the Castle Iron Works, drove it in 1860 to Windsor, where it was inspected by Queen Victoria.[5] Various machines for agricultural purposes were also made, a locomotive steam cultivator being exhibited at a meeting of the Royal Agricultural Society at Chester in 1858.

Another engineering business, known as the Watling Works, was started at Stony Stratford about the same time as the Castle Iron Works at Buckingham. The position of the little town on the Grand Junction Canal gave it better means of communication, and the business is still carried on at the present day.[6] In 1845 the late Mr. Edward Hayes started the works for general engineering, but gradually the business has become confined to the building of steam yachts, tugs and launches. These are exported to all parts of the world ' for steamers and machinery of various descriptions have been built for the British Admiralty, Crown Agents for the Colonies, the Board of Works, Trinity House Pilots, the Shah of Persia, the Sultan of Morocco,' besides various foreign governments and well-known shipping lines. ' During the late South African War a little steamer destined to work in connexion with the landing of troops and stores actually steamed from the place she was launched, the Old Stratford Wharf, which is a branch of the Watling Works, along the Grand Junction Canal to the Thames and thence to Delagoa Bay, South Africa.' In Stony Strat-

ford it is not an unusual sight ' to see one of these steamers being drawn on large eight-wheel trolleys by a powerful traction engine ' from the Watling Works, where they are built, to the wharf half a mile away, and often followed by its engine and boiler on separate trolleys. In 1861 a display was given at the works of a patent steam windlass for which Mr. Hayes had obtained high honours at an exhibition at Leeds, and the firm have since been equally successful at later exhibitions. The steamers originally built for the river-side work of the Metropolitan Fire Brigade came from the Watling Works, and the present Mr. Edward Hayes has taken out numerous patents for improving steamers, one of the most recent being ' for cheapening and facilitating the exportation of small steamers abroad, making it possible to erect steamers at the site of their work and where only unskilled native labour can be obtained.' Other iron and brass-foundries are worked at the present day at Maidenhead, Horton, Chalfont St. Giles, Looseley Row, Chesham, and Walton (Aylesbury).

At Slough there is also a large firm of manufacturing ironmongers and engineering contractors whose business was established in 1815.[7]

The Wolverton works, belonging to the London and North Western Railway, give employment to a large number of people in the neighbourhood and date from the earliest days of the railway.[8] When it was opened in 1838 as the London and Birmingham Railway the works were started for building engines, and were purely locomotive works until 1865. At that time Wolverton Station was of great importance, all trains stopping there, and descriptions of its magnificence figure largely in accounts of the county written in the middle of the 19th century. Around the station and works sprang up two new villages, New Bradwell and New Wolverton, inhabited entirely by the employees of the railway and tradesmen supplying their needs. In 1840 about four hundred hands were employed, but in the next twenty years the numbers had increased to between 2,300 and 2,400 and the factory contained brass and iron-foundries, shops for erecting, repairing, and fitting engines, and for making boilers, &c.[9]

In 1860, however, a change was decided upon resulting in the conversion of the Wolverton works into carriage works,[10] and the removal of the engine factories to Crewe. The removal took place between 1865 and 1877 and since that time the works have grown beyond recognition, and contain shops for building carriages and all their accessories and also for repairing them, covering in all about eighty acres of land and employing about four thousand five hundred hands.

NEEDLE-MAKING

The village of Long Crendon was long celebrated for an extensive manufactory of needles. There is considerable doubt as to the date of the introduction of needle-making into England, the tradition being that an 'Indian' first brought the art to London about 1545, but that it died out with him.[1] It must, however, shortly have been revived, for it seems to have been brought to Long Crendon about 1560 by one Christopher Greening.[2] In some accounts, a Mr. Damer, a member of a Roman Catholic family, is said to have settled the Greening family in the village in 1650,[3] but this is most probably merely a confusion in the date, since the Greenings had then lived there for nearly a hundred years.

A Christopher Greening lived at Long Crendon in 1558[4]; from 1556 to 1568 he was also churchwarden and drew up, with John Padnoll, the first parish register book preserved there.[5] Another Christopher, the son of John Greening, was born in 1587,[6] and against his name is a later marginal note saying, 'this man first brought out needle-making.[7]' Probably he was the grandson of the first needle-maker, but having the same Christian name, later tradition confused the two Christopher Greenings.

Other accounts say that needles were made in the village before Greening's arrival, but that he was of some importance in the trade and hence its introduction was attributed to him.[8]

The chief family of needle-makers were the Shrimptons, many of whom lived in the neighbourhood of High Wycombe and were officers of the borough.[9] In the 18th century the trade was flourishing. When a sufficient quantity of needles had been made, a journey to London was undertaken by one of the more important manufacturers. He took from seven to ten days, going by the stage-coach from Oxford. The goods had been first conveyed to Tetsworth, where the coach was met and the needle-maker was accompanied by armed men for his protection. This was more especially needed on the return journey, when he brought back a considerable sum of money for the wages of the workmen. A stock of wire was also brought back, part payment for the needles often being made in wire, which was difficult to procure direct from Birmingham. In 1736, the needles were chiefly made in the living rooms of the workers, but later factories were built, one of which is still standing in the village of Long Crendon.[10]

At the beginning of the 19th century the chief manufacturers bore the names of Harris, Shrimpton and Johnson.[11] The processes employed were extremely primitive; everything was done by hand labour, no stamps were used, and the methods of pointing made that part of the trade at least very injurious to the health of needle-makers. The fame of Redditch needles was beginning to grow and the Long Crendon manufacturers felt the pressure of competition in the market. They seem to have taken no steps, however, to meet it or to improve their methods. They never employed the water-power at Notley Mill and were very late in introducing machinery of any kind. In some ways the position of Redditch gave it an advantage over Long Crendon, particularly from being near Birmingham, but the Shrimptons had many opportunities of improving their trade, of which they never took advantage. London merchants offered money so that new machinery might be set up and the workshops improved, but the Crendon manufacturers had been so long without encountering competition that they were utterly unprepared to meet the new conditions of the industry. They seem to have given far more attention to all the pastimes of the countryside, bull-baiting, cock-fighting and boxing, than to their business. Hence the Long Crendon needle-trade gradually died out and the trade in sewing needles was practically lost.

Several makers made a speciality of large needles, however; sail and packing and netting needles were made in considerable quantities, and a revival of the trade took place about 1848. A John Harris had set up for himself and was more energetic in business than others; machinery was also introduced by him and some of the Shrimptons. A London firm, Kirby Beard & Co., started a factory at Crendon, where they had long been customers of the needle-makers. The lack of railway communication, however, proved fatal to their undertaking, and in 1862 they moved to Redditch, taking with them four-fifths of the needle-makers. Almost immediately afterwards the railway was opened to Thame, but it was too late to affect the manufacture at Long Crendon, and even the trade of large needles was obtained by the Redditch makers.

Emigration had, however, been going on slowly for many years; as early as 1824, Jonas Shrimpton journeyed to Alcester, Studley, and Redditch to observe the state of the manufacture there. He advised the Crendon makers to bestir themselves, but nothing, as has been said, was done, and some of the younger men migrated in the next few years. Even in 1861, while Kirby Beard & Co's. factory was still open, the population of the village was declining, the cause being migration of the needle-makers to seek work in other parts of the country.[12]

A considerable amount of wool was grown in Buckinghamshire as early as the 13th century and consequently many men were engaged in the wool trade. The wool grown by the monks at Biddlesden, Ankerwyke, and Notley is mentioned by Pegolotti.[1] Buckingham was a staple town for wool in the time of Edward III, till the staple was removed to Calais. It was then amongst the towns which petitioned Parliament in 1525 for relief, their trade having been destroyed.[1a] In the 17th century Buckingham still seems to have been a centre of the trade, and possessed both a wool hall and wool market, the profits belonging to Christ's Hospital, founded by Queen Elizabeth.[2] In 1731, these profits only amounted to £5 a year.[3] A wool fair was also held at Great Marlow, but it fell into disuse in the first half of the 19th century.

Wool merchants in the 16th century were, however, sternly repressed, no individual being allowed to buy more wool than he could weave himself. In 1577 the 'broggers' of wool were bound over in £100 apiece, 'that neither they nor their heirs shall at any time hereafter buy or bargain any manner of wools that grow or hath grown within the county of Buckingham, but only such quantity of wools as they by themselves or their apprentices shall yearly make in his own mansion house.'[4] The cloth trade never assumed very large proportions in the county, but a certain amount of weaving and fulling was done, presumably for local use.

Early in the 14th century the governing body of the borough of Wycombe tried to attract the trade to their town by remitting a tax on looms.[5] The effort seems to have been successful, and the records of the borough contain many orders with regard to weaving, fulling and dyeing.[6] These trades were gradually limited to the burgesses of the borough, foreigners being forbidden to carry them on without making a heavy payment. Even amongst the town craftsmen there were strict rules for their government.[7] Besides apprenticeship rules, no one man might carry on more than one of the three trades at the same time.[8] Early in the 17th century foreign craftsmen paid 6d. for every loom working, but how often the fine was to be paid was not specified. The increasing strictness of these orders was probably due to the failing condition of the cloth trade. In 1623 this was commented on by the Justices of the Peace and the Mayor of Wycombe[9] and the poor in the town suffered a great deal of misery.

The fullers seem to have suffered even earlier from the loss of their trade. Various fulling mills are mentioned in accounts of the bailiffs of manors in the 14th and 15th centuries,[10] but in the following century, for instance, at Taplow, when the mills were rebuilt in the reign of Henry VIII, certain old fulling-mill stock was found. Many years later a witness, in an inquisition taken in 1613 about these mills, suggested that the name of an eyot or island in the Thames called 'Tenter Eight' took its name from the tentering of cloth.[11] Moreover, at Newport Pagnell a fulling-mill had existed at one time, but it had been converted into a grist mill before 1623. Weaving was still a trade of the town, since George Fynnall, a weaver, gave evidence about the mills at that date.[12] At High Wycombe a fulling-mill, known as Gosham's mill, was working at this time, and was in the hands of a family of the name of Raunce.[13]

Buckinghamshire sheep and rams were famous throughout the 17th century, but more for their size than their wool,[14] and the local cloth trade seems to have gradually disappeared. Sacking was also manufactured in the 17th century. The paupers in the workhouse at Aylesbury[15] were mainly employed in spinning hemp. Their yarn was either sold or sent to the weavers, and afterwards the overseers of the poor sold the manufactured article.[16] Sacking was probably made throughout the 18th century, but in 1831,[17] only forty men were employed in making mats and sacking.

Silk-weaving was carried on in Buckinghamshire for some years during the 19th century. A large mill was established at Tring in 1824 by Mr. William Kaye of Tring Park.[18] It was first worked by Mr. Joseph Kaye, but he afterwards moved to Manchester. On his death the Lancashire factory was given up and his manager Robert Nixon was thus thrown out of employment. He determined to set up a silk-mill at Aylesbury in connexion with the Tring mill and further, made an agreement with the Aylesbury overseers, who were in great need of employment for the parish paupers in the workhouse. The numbers there were rapidly increasing, and the decline of the lace trade left the overseers with no means of giving them work. The latter undertook to build a silk factory on part of the workhouse premises in Oxford Road, and to spend £200 on it, Nixon promising on his part not to employ any hands but paupers chargeable on Aylesbury parish. Forty looms were set up in 1830, but probably women were employed for the most part, since in 1831[19] there were only 30 male silk weavers in the county. The mill afterwards passed into the hands of Messrs. Evans, who had for many years worked the Tring mill.[20] They first bought part of the workhouse premises in 1844, and in 1859, the original parish mill. Soon afterwards 200 hands, mostly girls, were employed, and steam-power had been introduced. In 1885 there were 70 steam looms at the Aylesbury mill. The actual weaving was the only process carried on there, none of the earlier processes being undertaken.

Branches of the Tring and Aylesbury mill were set up near the latter town. At Waddesdon a mill was established in 1843. It stood in the middle of the village, and in 1862 employed some 40 women, but only hand-looms were used. A smaller mill was also worked at Whitchurch.[21]

Silk was manufactured at Wyrardisbury mill[22] about the time that the Aylesbury mill was established, while silk and shawl printing was carried on at the neighbouring town of Horton. The latter works were in the hands of Messrs. Tippets & Co., who employed about 60 persons, but in 1859 a decline of trade made them close their works, and the buildings and stock were sold by auction.

Cotton mills also existed in Buckinghamshire at the close of the 18th century. At Iver and Taplow visitors were appointed by the justices of the peace in 1802 under an Act of 42 Geo III to inspect the cotton mills there.[23] At Amersham another cotton factory was working in 1825;[24] it employed many of the inhabitants but no cotton weavers are returned in the census of 1831.[25]

THE PAPER MILLS AND PAPER MAKERS OF ENGLAND 1495-1800
Alfred H. Shorter

Collection of works and documents illustrating the History of Paper. Vol. VI 1957.
Hilversham, General Editor E.J.Labarre
The Paper Publications Society

Section dealing with Buckinghamshire (pp128-147 of original)

BUCKINGHAMSHIRE

NOTES ON EARLY PAPER MILLS IN BUCKINGHAMSHIRE

1. There was at least one paper mill in Buckinghamshire about the year 1600. It had been set up by John Turner, Edward Marshall and George Frend, who had infringed John Spilman's monopoly of the manufacture of paper in England. The Reverend W. H. Summers, Early Paper Mills in Buckinghamshire, *Records of Bucks.*, VII (1894), 204, quoting *S.P.Dom. Eliz.*, CCLXXVI, 6. This paper mill has not been identified. A statement in 1636 (*S.P.Dom. Ch. I*, CCCXLIV, 40) that paper mills had been erected 'about forty years last past' obviously carries the memory of the establishment of this mill, and may refer to a site or sites on or near the River Colne in South Buckinghamshire and West Middlesex (the districts of Horton, Colnbrook, Poyle and Wraysbury) or (less probably) to sites in the Wye Valley (the districts of High Wycombe, Loudwater and Wooburn). In the light of the evidence at present available, the most probable site of this early mill is Coltnett Mills, Wraysbury (Buckinghamshire, Mill No. 51, below), which was in existence by 1605. This unidentified paper mill has therefore been marked in the Wraysbury area on Fig. 1.

2. By 1636 (*S.P.Dom. Ch. I*, CCCXLIV, 40) there were at least twelve or thirteen paper mills in Buckinghamshire. These almost certainly included mills at High Wycombe, Loudwater, Wooburn (Glory Mills), Horton and Wraysbury. The others have not been identified, but probably they too were in South Buckinghamshire, and have been marked there (without associating them with any known paper mill sites in that area) on Figs. 2 and 3.

3. In several books published in the eighteenth century there is mention of paper mills in the Buckingham district (North Buckinghamshire). In *A new and accurate description of the present Great Roads and the Principal Cross Roads of England and Wales* (c. 1755), 53, it is stated that paper mills were erected on the River Ouse, in the neighbourhood of Buckingham. Similar statements are made on E. Bowen's Map of Buckinghamshire [in *The Large English Atlas* (c. 1750)], in P. Luckombe's *England's Gazetteer* (1790) and in *U.B.D.T.C.M.*, 2 (c. 1791), 394. With the exception of the very doubtful possibility that the evidence given under the heading of Stowe Mill (Buckinghamshire, Mill No. 2, below) is relevant to these statements, there is no evidence to support the assertion that there were paper mills on the River Ouse in the neighbourhood of Buckingham, and the location of these paper mills, if they existed, is not known.

NOTE ON PAPER MILLS IN THE WYE VALLEY OF BUCKINGHAMSHIRE

There are numerous references to unspecified paper mills and to paper makers (including some who must have been owners, proprietors, masters or tenants of paper mills) at, in or of various places in the Wye Valley (from West Wycombe down to the River Thames) in the eighteenth century. In view of the large numbers of mills and paper makers concentrated into such a small district, many complicated problems of identification arise.

References to paper makers and paper mills at West Wycombe strongly suggest that at least three paper mills must have been at work there during most of the eighteenth century, but it is at present impossible to say with certainty with which mill some of the references to paper makers should be connected, or to specify the mill in cases where the sources give no clue as to the exact location and name of the mill, or to be certain of the succession of master paper makers in every case. Even greater difficulties of the same kind arise in dealing with several paper mills lower down the Wye Valley, from High Wycombe to Hedsor. Up to 1800 there are many references to unspecified paper mills at or near High Wycombe, Loudwater and Wooburn, and to paper makers at, in or of those places, which cannot at present be linked with absolute certainty with any particular paper mill.

Having regard to these difficulties, it can only be claimed that the evidence which is given below has been mustered as accurately as possible. In all probability the result does not exaggerate the number of paper mills which were at work in the Wye Valley before 1800.

1. The alternative name, Chipping Wycombe, which often appears in references of the eighteenth century, is here rendered as High Wycombe.

2. As it is part of the parish of High Wycombe, Loudwater must be included in this section of the Appendix. It is probable that if the necessary evidence were available some of the references to paper makers and paper mills which were said to be of or in the parish of High Wycombe should be linked with sites at Loudwater rather than with sites in or adjacent to the town of High Wycombe itself.

3. There is a possibility that the paper makers in Buckinghamshire (John Turner, Edward Marshall and George Frend) who about the year 1600 were contravening John Spilman's monopoly of the manufacture of paper in England, had established their mill or mills in the High Wycombe district. There must have been a paper mill in Wycombe in or before 1636, for it was then stated that it was one of the places in Buckinghamshire to which the infection had been brought with rags used by paper makers. *S.P.Dom. Ch. I*, CCCXLIV, 40.

4. The following references to paper makers of High Wycombe in the seventeenth century cannot be linked with any particular mill.

1639. Matthew Richardson†, paper maker, was a party to a bond. *S.P.Dom. Ch. I*, CCCCXXIX, 23.

1659–60. Will. Harman† and Richard Hyrett, paper makers, were buried. *High Wycombe P.R.* Presumably the latter was the Richard Hyatt, paper maker, whose name is given by T. M. Blagg (ed.), *Index of Wills proved in the P.C.C.*, VIII, 1657–60, Index Library, B.R.S., 61 (1936). His will mentions his mills.

1662. John Carter†, paper maker, was married. G. J. Armytage (ed.), *Allegations for Marriage Licences issued by the Vicar-General of the Archbishop of Canterbury*, 1660–8, Publications of the Harleian Society, XXXIII (1892), 49.

1682. William Adkins†, paper maker, was married. W. P. W. Phillimore and T. Gurney (eds.), *Buckinghamshire P.R., M.*, VI (1910), High Wycombe M.

1685. William Milton†, paper maker, was married. *Ibid.*

1688. William Butcher†, paper maker, was married. *Ibid.*

1699. The recognizance of John Gaddesden†, paper maker, was discharged. W. Le Hardy and G. LL. Reckitt (eds.), *County of Buckingham: Calendar to the Sessions Records*, II, 1694–1705 (published 1936), 227.

5. In 1690 there were eight paper mills in the parish of High Wycombe. H.M.C., Rep. xiii, App., Pt. V, *H. of L. Mss.* 272 (15th May, 1690). These must have included a mill at High Wycombe, Loudwater Mill (worked by WILLIAM RUSSELL), Loudwater Mill (worked by JEREMIAH FRANCIS) and Hedge Mill (EDWARD SPICER); see Mills Nos. 30, 29 and 33, below. In view of the evidence that there was a great increase in the number of paper mills in England during the eighteenth century, we appear to be on safe ground in assuming that at least eight paper mills were at work in the High Wycombe district from 1690, and that there may well have been more in such an important paper making area in the early eighteenth century.

6. The exact location of the following paper makers and paper mills in the High Wycombe district in the eighteenth century is not known.

1755. Ann Gaddesdon†, widow and paper maker, late of Marsworth (Buckinghamshire, Mill No. 4, above) and formerly of Wycombe Marsh, was in debt and in Aylesbury Gaol. *L.G.* (13th May, 1755).

1758. William Gardener†, paper maker, insured houses in the Lower Marsh. *S.F.I.P.* 163112 (14th June, 1758). In 1761 William Gardner†, paper maker, late of High Wycombe, was in the Fleet Prison, London. *L.G.* (26th May, 1761).

1768. John Shrimpton†, paper maker, was married. W. P. W. Phillimore and T. Gurney (eds.), *Buckinghamshire P.R., M.*, VI (1910), High Wycombe M.

1768. John Woldrige†, paper maker, was married. *Ibid.*

1769. John Venable†, paper maker, was married. *Ibid.*

1771. William Lane†, paper maker, was married. *Ibid.*

1772. Richard Evered†, paper maker, was married. *Ibid.*

1772. Jos. Carr†, paper maker, was married. *Ibid.*

1774. Thomas Hatch†, paper maker, was married. *Ibid.*

1776. Thomas Plumridge†, paper maker, was married. *Ibid.*

1777. Joseph Wooster†, paper maker, was a party to the insurance of Glory Mill (Buckinghamshire, Mill No. 35, below). *S.F.I.P.* 384597 (27th May, 1777).

1779. William Mowdey†, paper maker, was married. W. P. W. Phillimore and T. Gurney (eds.), *Buckinghamshire P.R.*, M., VI (1910), High Wycombe M.

1786. John Vowell, stationer, of Leadenhall Street (London), insured his utensils and stock etc. in a paper mill situated at the Upper Marsh (High Wycombe). *S.F.I.P.* 523004 (16th Oct., 1786). The name of J. Vowell, at High Wycombe, is given in lists of paper makers in B.M. Add. Ms. 15054, *Myvyrian Mss.* (1786), and *R.J.A.B.* (1793).

1793. George Dean†, paper maker, insured a dwelling house and tenements. *S.F.I.P.* 615286 (30th May, 1793).

7. Unfortunately the early *Rate Books* of High Wycombe do not specify paper mills or paper makers, but in the entries therein for 1760, for example, it is clear that at least eight mills were in the hands of men who are known from the information given in other sources to have been paper makers at or about that time: GEORGE LANE (two mills), HUGH STRATTON, JOHN SCOTT, JOHN BATES, JOSEPH FRANCIS, WILLIAM DAVIS, and EDWARD SPICER. All these names will be found among the evidence given under mill headings below. It is possible that at least two of the other mills included in the *Rate Book* for 1760 were paper mills; these were in the tenure of JOS. WOOSTER and COMPANY, and ROBERT DAVIS. Joseph Wooster was a paper maker in 1777 (see Glory Mill, Buckinghamshire, Mill No. 35, below), and Robert Davis may have been a paper maker and the predecessor or relative of William Davis, who was the master paper maker at a paper mill at Loudwater in 1763 (see Buckinghamshire, Mill No. 32, below).

8. The *High Wycombe Rate Book* for 1780 contains the names of at least thirteen men who must have been master paper makers at or about that time and who are grouped therein by districts as follows:

High Wycombe 'Foreigns' – GEORGE and JOHN LANE (the 'Foreigns' was a district just outside the town)

Upper Marsh – BASWICK	Loudwater – FRANCIS BLACKWELL
Upper Marsh – HUGH STRATTON	Loudwater – PLAISTOWE
Upper Marsh – RICHARD BARTON	Loudwater – PLAISTOWE (late LANE'S Mill)
Upper Marsh – JOHN SCOTT	Loudwater – WILLIAM DAVIS
Lower Marsh – JOHN BATES	Loudwater – WILDMAN
Lower Marsh – JOHN GOODWIN	Loudwater – RALPH SPICER

All these names will be found among the evidence given under mill headings below. It is possible that at least one other mill included in the *Rate Book* for 1780 was then a paper mill; it was held by THOMAS EDMONDS & CO. In the 1790s Thomas Edmonds held Rye Mill as a paper mill (Buckinghamshire, Mill No. 19, below).

9. At least thirteen or fourteen paper mills must have existed in the High Wycombe – Loudwater district in 1800, for the number of master paper makers there does not decrease up to that year, and fourteen mills in the district can be identified in 1816 in the list of paper mills given in *E.G.L.* (8th Oct., 1816).

10. Some of the mills existed as paper mills throughout the eighteenth century, but there were a few which apparently worked for only part of that time, for example, New Mills (No. 26, below). It is possible, however, that the names of these mills may have changed, and that some of the paper makers who are listed under other mills may have worked there; it is also possible that some of the paper makers named in note 6, above, may have worked these mills, or have been employees there. If that were so, the history of mills such as New Mills may have been longer than that shown below.

11. The paper mills are listed in a sequence going down the Wye Valley from the parish boundary of West Wycombe with High Wycombe.

1.   Apart from the evidence relating to Glory Mill (No. 35, below), the following are the earliest references to paper makers in the Wooburn district. In the absence of more definite information, it is impossible to connect them with particular mills, or to assume that there was more than one paper mill (Glory Mill) in existence in the parish of Wooburn in the seventeenth century. It is possible that these references, and some of those of the eighteenth century under (2) below, should be connected with Glory Mill.

1620.   William Wright†, paper maker, of Wooburn, had the feoffment of a tenement or cottage (5th Nov., 1620). Schedule of documents belonging to Mr E. Bishop, of Wooburn. Information from Miss Cicely Baker, Archivist, Buckinghamshire Arch. Soc., The Museum, Aylesbury.

1662.   The will of Silvanus Hammerton†, paper miller, of 'Wedbourne', was proved. J. H. Morrison, *P.C.C. Wills, Sentences and Probate Acts*, 1661–70 (published 1935), No. 7818.

1696/7.   The recognizance of Thomas Blackwell†, paper maker, of 'Wooborne' was discharged. W. Le Hardy and G. LL. Reckitt (eds.), *County of Buckingham, Calendar to the Sessions Records*, II, 1694–1705 (published 1936), 115.

2.   The exact location of the following paper makers and paper mills in the Wooburn district in the eighteenth century is not known.

1707.   William Church, miller, was required to answer Hugh Stratton†, paper maker. W. Le Hardy and G. LL. Reckitt (eds.), *County of Buckingham, Calendar to the Sessions Records*, III, 1705–12 (published 1939), 112.

1723.   Daniel and Thomas Haydon, millers and paper makers, insured the paper mills in Wooburn. *S.F.I.P.* 31269 (18th Feb., 1723).

1725.   Joseph Massey†, of Wooburn paper mills, is recorded. F. S. Thacker, *Kennet Country* (1932), 312.

1729.   John Bampton†, paper maker, had the feoffment of a cottage. His will is dated 2nd June, 1759. Schedule of documents belonging to Mr E. Bishop, of Wooburn. Information from Miss Cicely Baker, Archivist, Buckinghamshire Arch. Soc., The Museum, Aylesbury.

1744.   William Church†, paper maker, was married. W. P. W. Phillimore and T. Gurney (eds.), *Buckinghamshire P.R.*, M., v (1909), Taplow M. In 1753 William Church†, paper maker, dealer and chapman, late of Wooburn, was bankrupt. *L.G.* (7th Aug., 1753).

1779.   Daniel Dean†, paper maker, is mentioned in the will of Ann Dennis (9th June, 1779). Schedule of documents belonging to Mr E. Bishop, of Wooburn. Information from Miss Cicely Baker.

NOTE ON UNIDENTIFIED PAPER MILLS AT LOUDWATER

The following references to paper making at Loudwater cannot at present be linked with any particular mill.

1784.   Mr Stratkord, paper maker, was mentioned. *R.M.O.G.* (25th Oct., 1784).

1786.   The paper mill of Mr Field was totally consumed by fire. *R.M.O.G.* (14th Aug., 1786).

1782.   Henry Church†, paper maker and shopkeeper, insured a house. *S.F.I.P.* 463873 (22nd Aug., 1782).

1790.   James Duglass†, paper maker, insured a house. *S.F.I.P.* 566714 (4th March, 1790).

Mill No. 1. Newport Pagnell Mill*

1772. Reuben Cotton†, paper maker, of the parish of Newton, was married. Reverend R. F. Bale (ed.), *Bucks. P. R., M.,* IX (1923), Newport Pagnell M. The parish of Newton may have been Newton Blossomville or Newton Longville, in North Buckinghamshire, but no reference to paper making in either of those parishes has been found. The master paper makers at Newport Pagnell are not known. The 'manufactory of paper' there is mentioned in the History and Topography of Buckinghamshire, *Pinnock's County Histories* (c. 1820), 31.

Mill No. 2. Stowe Mill

1676. The 'Paper Mill Meeting' of Quakers is mentioned in *Quaker Minute Book for the Upper Side of Bucks. (1669–90),* transcribed by Beatrice S. Snell, Bucks. Arch. Soc. (1937), 40. From a study of the situation of the 'Meetings' mentioned in this book it seems probable that this reference could be connected with Stowe Mill, but it may be connected with Great Brickhill Mill (Buckinghamshire, Mill No. 3, below) or with an unidentified paper mill in the north of Buckinghamshire or the south of Northamptonshire. The former existence of a paper mill at or near Stowe is strongly suggested, if not absolutely proved, by the occurrence of the name 'Paper Mill Spinney' which is marked near Stowe on O.S. Six Inch Map of Buckinghamshire, Sheet XIII (1885). These are the only known references which may be linked with a paper mill at Stowe.

Mill No. 3. Great Brickhill Mill*

1695. The recognizance of Anthony Holton†, paper maker, was discharged. W. Le Hardy and G. LL. Reckitt (eds.), *County of Buckingham, Calendar to the Sessions Records,* II, 1694–1705 (published 1936), 68. The early proprietors or master paper makers are not known.....

1791. The paper mills were included in property which was for sale and apparently underlet to William Horne and John Franklin. *N.M.* (24th Dec., 1791). These men are not known to have been paper makers, but the latter may have been connected with the paper maker named Franklin who was at Wansford Mill (Northamptonshire, Mill No. 1) about this time.....

1793. WILLIAM WHATLEY must have been the master paper maker at this mill. His name is given in a list of paper makers in *R.J.A.B.* (1793). He was the proprietor or master paper maker at an unnamed paper mill in 1816. *E.G.L.* (8th Oct., 1816). He probably occupied the Great Brickhill Mill from about 1793 until well after 1800.

Mill No. 4. Marsworth Mill

1738. JOHN BUDD, paper maker, insured the mill. *S.F.I.P.* 77857 (9th Aug., 1738). In that year John Budd, paper maker, took an apprentice, John Norwood. *A.G.B.,* 15/176 (1738). These are the only known references to John Budd.....

1747. JOHN GADSDON, paper maker, insured the paper mill. *S.F.I.P.* 109865 (15th Oct., 1747). Only one reference to John Gadsdon has been found.....

1753. Adam Allen†, paper maker, insured houses. *S.F.I.P.* 135726 (9th May, 1753).....

1754. JOHN PYMM, paper maker, insured the paper mill. *S.F.I.P.* 142915 (7th Oct., 1754). Only one reference to John Pymm has been found.....

1755. ANN GADDESDON, widow and paper maker, late of Marsworth and formerly of Wycombe Marsh (Buckinghamshire) was in debt and was in Aylesbury Gaol. *L.G.* (13th May, 1755). Only one reference to Ann Gaddesdon has been found.....

1767. RICHARD WHATLEY, paper maker, insured the paper mill. *S.F.I.P.* 247900 (31st July, 1767).

1793. The name of Richard Whatley, near 'Laton', is given in a list of paper makers in *R.J.A.B.* (1793). This appears to refer to Leighton Buzzard (Bedfordshire), which is not far from Marsworth.....

No reference to paper making at Marsworth at a later date has been found. According to *V.C.H. Bucks.,* II (1908), 111, this mill was destroyed when the Grand Junction Canal was cut; it therefore appears probable that it ceased work *circa* 1795-1800.

Mill No. 5. Ellesborough Mill

1755. EDWARD STUBBLE, paper maker, was buried. *Ellesborough P. R.* Information from the Reverend C. N. White, Rector. In the same year the one-vat, overshot paper mill 'on a small constant spring' was to let. *J.O.J.* (22nd Nov., 1755). These are the only known references to a paper maker and a paper mill at Ellesborough.

Mill No. 6. Long Wick Mill*

1719. JOHN FRANCIS, paper maker, took an apprentice, Rob. Stratton. *A.G.B.,* 7/120 (1719). Only one reference to John Francis has been found.....

1726. Richard Fry, rag merchant at Mr Scales', a jeweller in Green Street, Leicester Fields (London), insured his paper mills at 'Longstock' (Buckinghamshire). *S.F.I.P.* 40763 (3rd Feb., 1726). This appears to refer to Long Wick.....

1743. A cottage in Tile End Green was leased to John Fryer, paper maker. Lease dated 21st July, 1743. In a release (24th Dec., 1756) Fryer is described as 'late of Long Wick and then of Great Marlow'. *A Calendar of Deeds..... preserved in the Muniment Room at the Museum, Aylesbury,* Records Branch of Bucks. Arch. Soc., 5 (1941), 48. Fryer must have left this mill between 1746 and 1756.

1746. JOHN FRYER, paper maker, took an apprentice, George West. *A.G.B.,* 17/195. (1746).....

1762. GEORGE WEST, paper maker, took an apprentice, Ric. Franklin. *A.G.B.,* 23/91 (1762). Only one reference to George West as a master paper maker has been found.....

1766. The paper mill was insured by JOHN TAYLOR and THOMAS HAYDON, paper makers, of Deans Court, St Paul's Churchyard (London). It was in their own occupation. *S.F.I.P.* 234172 (3rd June, 1766). In an advertisement of the paper mill in *J.O.J.* (13th June, 1767) they are described as stationers.

1767. The paper mill was insured by John Taylor and Thomas Haydon, paper makers. It was in the tenure of HENRY WILLIAMS, paper maker. *S.F.I.P.* 250798 (7th Nov., 1767). In 1788 the paper mill was insured by Henry Williams, paper maker, of Saunderton (Buckinghamshire, Mill No. 8, below). *S.F.I.P.* 541176 (20th Feb., 1788). The duration of his tenure is not known precisely, but he may have been in possession of this mill, or Saunderton Mill, or both mills, up to 1800. In 1796 H. Williams was a master paper maker. Meeting of the Master Paper Makers of the whole Wycombe district (4th Feb., 1796), *P.S.M.* He may have been succeeded by JOHN WIL-

LIAMS, who was a master maker in 1799. Meeting of the Paper Manufacturers of the Wycombe district (10th May, 1799), P.S.M. There is, however, a paper watermarked H WILLIAMS 1800 in the Whatman and Balston Archives (see Watermark No. 208 in this book), and this would appear to be connected either with Long Wick Mill or with Saunderton Mill. It is not known whether Henry Williams was in occupation of these mills after 1800. In 1807 Richard Brown†, paper maker, of Long Wick, insured tenements. S.F.I.P. 803010 (10th Apr., 1807). In 1816 Long Wick Mill was held by CHRIST. MAGNAY & CO., paper makers. E.G.L. (8th Oct., 1816).

BUCKINGHAMSHIRE Mill No. 7. North Mill, Bledlow*

1743. North Mill was burnt down. A great deal of paper, and other effects belonging to Mrs Harman, widow, were burnt. R. Gibbs, Buckinghamshire, A Record of Local Occurrences and General Events, Chronologically Arranged (1879), II, 82.

1753. SARAH HARMAN, paper maker, took an apprentice, Rob. Tyler. A.G.B., 19/123 (1753).....

1767. WILLIAM AUSTIN, paper maker, took an apprentice, William King. A.B. (P.R.O., I.R.1), 25/119 (1767). In 1768 the paper mill was insured by Fleetwood Francis, paper maker. It was in the tenure of William Austin, paper maker. S.F.I.P. 265006 (27th Dec., 1768).

1777. Equipment was for sale at the premises of Mr Austin, paper maker, North Mill. J.O.J. (25th Jan., 1777).....

1788. Joseph Francis†, paper maker, insured goods etc. S.F.I.P. 542300 (2nd Apr., 1788).....

1789. JAMES JORDAN, paper maker, took an apprentice, James Smith. A.B. (P.R.O., I.R.1), 34/112 (1789).

1798. John Woodbridge, an apprentice, ran away from James Jordan, paper maker. J.O.J. (20th Oct., 1798). The duration of James Jordan's tenure is not known, and it is not certain whether he occupied the mill after 1800.....

In 1804 WILLIAM JORDAN, paper maker, of Bledlow, insured the stock and utensils in his paper mill. S.F.I.P. 763393 (8th May, 1804).

Mill No. 8. Saunderton Mill*

1769. HENRY WILLIAMS, paper maker, took an apprentice, William Stacey. A.B. (P.R.O., I.R.1), 26/95 (1769). This was probably the same Henry Williams as he who held Long Wick Mill in 1767 (see Buckinghamshire, Mill No. 6, above). There appears to have been a gap in his tenure of Saunderton Mill.....

1785. The paper mill was insured by JOSEPH CHILD, millwright, of High Wycombe. It was in his own tenure. S.F.I.P. 503892 (20th Apr., 1785). This is the only known reference to Joseph Child in connection with this mill.....

1788. The paper mill was insured by Henry Williams, paper maker. S.F.I.P. 541176 (20th Feb., 1788). The duration of his tenure is not known precisely, but he may have been in possession of this mill, or Long Wick Mill, or both mills, up to 1800. In 1796 H. Williams was a master paper maker. Meeting of Master Paper Makers of the whole Wycombe district (4th Feb., 1796), P.S.M. He may have been succeeded by JOHN WILLIAMS, who was a master maker in 1799. Meeting of the Paper Manufacturers of the Wycombe district (10th May, 1799),

P.S.M. There is, however, a paper watermarked H WILLIAMS 1800 in the Whatman and Balston Archives (see Watermark No. 208 in Appendix C), and this would appear to be connected either with Long Wick Mill or Saunderton Mill. It is not known whether Henry Williams was in occupation of these mills after 1800. In 1803 JACOB SIMMONS, paper maker, of Princes Risborough, insured his paper mill. S.F.I.P. 756544 (26th Nov., 1803). This may refer to a second paper mill at Saunderton. In 1815 Saunderton Paper Mill was for sale, and it was stated that Mr Williams was the proprietor. J.O.J. (11th March, 1815). In 1816 there were two paper mills here. JAMES MINTO was the proprietor or master paper maker at Upper Saunderton Mill, and CHRIST. MAGNAY & CO. were at Lower Saunderton Mill. E.G.L. (8th Oct., 1816).

Mill No. 9. Chesham Mill

1768. The paper mill was insured by William Venable, millwright, of High Wycombe. It was in the tenure of GEORGE MOWDAY, paper maker. S.F.I.P. 257516 (31st May, 1768).

1781. The paper mill was for sale. Part had lately been converted into a corn mill. George Mowday was the tenant. J.O.J. (24th Feb., 1781).....

1781. Apparently this was the same corn and paper mill as that in respect of which AARON MOWDAY, paper maker, insured the utensils and stock. S.F.I.P. 452198 (29th Nov., 1781).

1793. Mowday, of Chesham, is named in a list of paper makers given in R.J.A.B. (1793).....

No reference to paper making at Chesham Mill at a later date has been found. It is possible, however, that the watermark A M 1797 (see Watermark No. 107 in this book) is that of Aaron Mowday, of this mill.

Mill No. 10. Weir House Mill*

1770. This was probably one of the paper mills marked in the neighbourhood of Chesham on T. Jefferys' Map of Buckinghamshire (1770). The early proprietors or master paper makers are not known.....

1799. A paper mill was insured by JOHN ALLNUTT, paper maker, of Chesham Waterside. S.F.I.P. 696077 (15th Nov., 1799). That this reference concerns the paper mill at Weir House rather than one of the other mills near Chesham is suggested by the fact that in 1816 John Allnutt was the proprietor or master paper maker at 'Warehouse' Mill. E.G.L. (8th Oct., 1816). He was probably, therefore, in possession of this mill from at least 1799 onwards.

Mill No. 11. Blackwell Hall Mill*

1765. George Street was one of the signatories to a petition concerning the Excise duty (24th May, 1765). Excise and Treasury Correspondence, 1763-8, 134-5. His trade and address are not given in this document, but he was probably already directly interested in paper making in England, and may already have been in possession of this mill. In 1775 George Street, stationer, of No. 2 Bucklesbury, London, insured his paper mill at Chesham in the tenure of JOSEPH ELLIOTT, paper maker. S.F.I.P. 360229 (23rd Oct., 1775).

1777. A similar insurance policy was taken out. S.F.I.P. 391706 (25th Nov., 1777). No later reference to Joseph Elliott, paper maker, at this mill has been found.

1793. The name of George Street is given in a list of paper makers in *R.J.A.B.* (1793). He may already, however, have been succeeded by James Wallis Street, for watermarks I W S are known from 1789 and 1791. (See Watermarks Nos. 164 and 165 in this book.).....

1793. JAMES WALLIS STREET, stationer, of No. 2 Bucklesbury, London, insured a paper mill at Chesham. It was in his own tenure. *S.F.I.P.* 622146 (9th Nov., 1793). He continued to occupy this mill after 1800. In 1803 he again insured the paper mill. *S.F.I.P.* 742368 (15th Jan., 1803).

Mill No. 12. Chesham Bois Mill*

1767. In 1774 a capital paper mill, 'new built about seven years since' was for sale. RICHARD and CHARLES LOOSLEY, paper makers, were bankrupt. *L.E.P.* (14th–16th June, 1774). Richard Looseley was probably the first occupier. In 1769, as a paper maker and miller, he insured the corn and paper mills. *S.F.I.P.* 277429 (16th Nov., 1769). He took out a similar policy in 1771. *S.F.I.P.* 296921 (24th Apr., 1771).

1774. See the details given under 1767, above.....

1775. THOMAS CURTIS, paper maker and miller, insured a corn mill and a paper mill. *S.F.I.P.* 351757 (3rd Apr., 1775).

1793. Thomas Curtis is named in a list of paper makers given in *R.J.A.B.* (1793).....

1793. The paper mill was insured by JOSEPH ELLIOTT, paper maker. *S.F.I.P.* 613010 (27th March, 1793).

1796. Joseph Elliott was a master paper maker. Meeting of Master Paper Makers of the whole district of Hertfordshire (5th Feb., 1796), P.S.M. This paper mill was close to the county boundary of Buckinghamshire and Hertfordshire and therefore it appears to have been included in the Hertfordshire district by the Master Paper Makers, although it was in Buckinghamshire.....

1799. RICHARD ELLIOTT was a master paper maker. General Meeting of Master Paper Makers (12th June, 1799), P.S.M. He continued to occupy this mill. In 1803 Joseph Mack, paper maker, of Hemel Hempstead (Hertfordshire), undertook to keep the peace and be of good behaviour towards Richard Elliott, paper maker, of Chesham Bois, whose mill he had threatened to burn down. *Quarter Sessions Books*, Buckinghamshire Record Office, Aylesbury (Midsummer Session, 1803). Information from Mr L. M. Wulcko, Chalfont St Peter (Buckinghamshire).

Mill No. 13. Chenies Mill*

1741. JOHN DODD, paper maker, took an apprentice, Clement Weeden. *A.G.B.*, 16/53 (1741).

1763. John Dodd, miller and paper maker, insured his goods, utensils and stock. *S.F.I.P.* 205506 (28th Dec., 1763).....

1778. GEORGE DODD, paper maker at Chenies, was mentioned in connection with an advertisement of Sarratt Mill (Hertfordshire). *L.E.P.* (23rd–25th July, 1778). In 1796 George Dodd and George Dodd, junior, were master paper makers. Meeting of Master Paper Makers of the whole district of Hertfordshire (5th Feb., 1796), P.S.M. The mill was in the hands of George Dodd, junior, after 1800. He was a master paper maker in 1801. Letter, Master Paper Makers of Hertfordshire and Buckinghamshire (20th Apr., 1801), P.S.M.

1788. JOHN SHRIMPTON and CHARLES CLARKE, paper makers, insured their utensils, stock etc. in their paper mill. *S.F.I.P.* 543282 (19th Apr., 1788). This is the only known reference to these paper makers, and the last certain reference to this paper mill. It is possible, however, that this mill was continued by a paper maker named Austin, or that there was another paper mill at or near Amersham which was worked by him. In 1777 John Austin, paper maker of Amersham, insured a house. *S.F.I.P.* 380120 (8th Feb., 1777). Presumably this is the – Austin, paper maker, who is named in *R.J.A.B.* (1793).

BUCKINGHAMSHIRE *Mill No. 14. Amersham Mill*

1776. Joseph Gregory, mealman, and AARON MOWDAY, paper maker, insured a corn mill, and a paper mill in Mowday's tenure. *S.F.I.P.* 367298 (6th Apr., 1776). Aaron Mowday, paper maker, insured his goods etc. in the paper mill. *S.F.I.P.* 367300 (8th Apr., 1776). No later reference to Aaron Mowday at this mill has been found.....

Mill No. 15. Francis Mill or Upper Mill, West Wycombe*

1684. Thomas Murrain†, paper maker, was married. W. P. W. Phillimore and T. Gurney (eds.), *Bucks. P. R., M.*, VI (1910), High Wycombe M. A paper mill at West Wycombe is mentioned in extents of the manor between 1686 and 1745. *V.C.H. Bucks.*, III (1925), 139.....

1698. EDWARD CARTOR, miller and paper maker, took an apprentice, John Floid. West Wycombe Apprenticeship Indenture (1698). Information from Mr F. J. Foxall, Verger, West Wycombe. Only one reference to Edward Cartor has been found.....

1700. Recognizances were discharged in respect of Thomas Murrent† and John Beesley†, paper makers. W. Le Hardy and G. LL. Reckitt (eds.), *County of Buckingham: Calendar to the Sessions Records*, II, 1694–1705 (published 1936), 271.....

1712. ALICE MURRIN, widow and paper maker, took an apprentice, John Hobbs. West Wycombe Apprenticeship Indenture (1712). Information from Mr F. J. Foxall. Only one reference to Alice Murrin has been found.....

If the above evidence refers to one and the same paper mill, there must have been two other paper mills in existence at West Wycombe by 1717–25 (Mills Nos. 16 and 17, below). It is not known with which of the three mills the above evidence should be connected, but in view of the fact that JOSEPH FRANCIS held a lease of a paper mill in 1717 (see below) the details have been placed under the heading of his mill.....

1717. A paper mill was in the possession of Joseph Francis, by virtue of a lease. W. Le Hardy (ed.), *County of Buckingham, Calendar of Quarter Sessions Records*, VI (1953), 139.

1718. Joseph Francis, paper maker, took an apprentice, Joseph Marsh. West Wycombe Apprenticeship Indenture (1718). Information from Mr F. J. Foxall.....

1746. FLEETWOOD FRANCIS, paper maker, took an apprentice, Thomas Clisby. *A.G.B.*, 17/214 (1746).

1758. Fleetwood Francis, paper maker, took an apprentice, John Pearce. *A.G.B.*, 21/159 (1758).....

1767. THOMAS FRANCIS, paper maker, took an apprentice, Jonathan Tranton. *A.B.* (P.R.O., I.R.1), 25/123 (1767). (Although in 1770 William Hughes of Eltham (Kent) insured the millhouse in the tenure of Fleetwood Francis, miller and paper maker (*S.F.I.P.* 288325 (27th Aug., 1770)), by that time the business seems to have been taken over by Thomas Francis, who apparently continued as the master paper maker.) In 1775 Thomas Francis, paper maker, insured the utensils and stock in a corn mill and a paper mill. *S.F.I.P.* 362046 (2nd Dec., 1775). At some later date he went into partnership with WILLIAM FRYER. In 1791 Thomas Francis and William Fryer, paper makers, dissolved partnership. The business was to be carried on by Thomas Francis only. *J.O.J.* (19th March, 1791). The mill must have been in his hands after 1800. In 1803 Thomas Francis was a master paper maker in Buckinghamshire, General Meeting of Master Paper Makers (13th June, 1803). P.S.M.....

The above details appear to be connected with the 'Francis Mill' which is marked adjacent to Mill End on T. Jefferys' Map of Buckinghamshire (1770). This mill appears to have been the 'Upper Mill' which was held by JOHN PHELPS in 1816. *E.G.L.* (8th Oct., 1816).

Mill No. 16. Fryer's Mill or Mill End, West Wycombe*

1725. SOLOMON DEAN, paper maker, insured a paper mill at West Wycombe. *S.F.I.P.* 37207 (2nd Nov., 1725).

1741. Solomon alias William Dean, paper maker, took an apprentice, William Low. West Wycombe Apprenticeship Indenture (1741). Information from Mr F. J. Foxall, Verger, West Wycombe.....

1751. JOHN FRYER, paper maker, took an apprentice, William Staples. West Wycombe Apprenticeship Indenture (1751). Information from Mr F. J. Foxall. In 1762 John Fryer took an apprentice, John Fryer (who may have succeeded him at a later date). *A.G.B.*, 23/71 (1762). In 1785 John and ELIZABETH FRYER, paper makers, took an apprentice, Samuel Grange. *A.B.* (P.R.O., I.R.1), 32/164 (1785).

1793. John Fryer is named in a list of paper makers given in *R.J.A.B.* (1793). The duration of his tenure is not known, and he may not have been in occupation of this mill after 1800. In 1801 MICHAEL LEWIS FRYER, paper maker, insured the fixed machinery and utensils in the corn mill and paper mill. *S.F.I.P.* 716697 (21st March, 1801). In 1803 he was a master paper maker in Buckinghamshire. General Meeting of Master Paper Makers (13th June, 1803), P.S.M.....

The above details appear to be connected with the 'Friers Mill' which is marked downstream from 'Francis Mill' on T. Jefferys' Map of Buckinghamshire (1770). This was probably the mill known as 'Mill End' which was occupied by MICHAEL FRYER in 1816. *E.G.L.* (8th Oct., 1816).

Mill No. 17. Ball's Mill or Frog Mill, West Wycombe*

1717. JOHN BUTCHER, paper maker, took an apprentices William Laurence. West Wycombe Apprenticeship Indenture (1717). Information from Mr F. J. Foxall, Verger, West Wycombe.

1727. John Butcher, paper maker, insured a millhouse. *S.F.I.P.* 42127 (8th July, 1727).....

1729. A paper mill at Mill End near High Wycombe was insured by RICHARD FRY, rag merchant, of Sheffield Mills (Berkshire, Mills Nos. 9 and 10). It was in his own occupation. *S.F.I.P.* 48311 (28th July, 1729). This is the only known reference to Richard Fry at West Wycombe, but in the same year he was described as a paper maker of Sheffield Mills. *S.F.I.P.* 47869 (5th June, 1729). He was bankrupt in 1730. *L.G.* (10th Nov., 1730).....

1735. JOHN CROUCH, paper maker, insured a millhouse. *S.F.I.P.* 67091 (22nd May, 1735).

1759. John Crouch, paper maker, took an apprentice, Thomas Barnes. *A.G.B.*, 22/55 (1759).....

1761. Crouch appears to have been succeeded by EDMUND BALL. Although the latter was described as a paper maker of West Wycombe when he insured his mill near High Wycombe in the tenure of William Burnam paper maker (*S.F.I.P.* 139522 (26th Jan., 1754); see Buckinghamshire, Mill No. 22, Bowden Mill, below), it is not known whether he was a master paper maker or a proprietor of a mill at West Wycombe before 1761. In that year he took an apprentice, Zachariah House. *A.G.B.*, 22/198 (1761). In 1776 Edmund Ball, mealman, insured a paper mill and a corn mill. *S.F.I.P.* 367096 (2nd Apr., 1776). From about that time, Vall appears to have let the mill to JOHN GOODWIN. In 1776 John Goodwin, paper maker, of High Wycombe, insured the utensils and stock in the paper mill at Mr Ball's in West Wycombe. *S.F.I.P.* 367097 (2nd Apr., 1776).

1778. Edmund Ball was bankrupt, and the paper mill in the parish of West Wycombe and half a mile from High Wycombe was for sale. It was underlet to John Goodwin. *J.O.J.* (28th March, 1778), and *R.M.O.G.* (6th Apr., 1778).....

1779. John Goodwin, paper maker, of Wycombe Marsh (Buckinghamshire, Mill No. 25, Lower Marsh Mill, below), insured the utensils and stock in the paper mill and corn mill described as 'late Ball's' at West Wycombe. *S.F.I.P.* 414991 (12th June, 1779). He must have continued in occupation of this mill, or Lower Marsh Mill, or both, until after 1800, apparently in partnership with his son after about 1799. In 1796 John Goodwin was a master paper maker. Meeting of Master Paper Makers of the whole Wycombe district (4th Feb., 1796), P.S.M. In 1799 Goodwin and Son were master paper makers. Meeting of Paper Manufacturers of the Wycombe district (10th May, 1799), P.S.M. In 1801 John Goodwin was a master maker. Letter (20th Apr., 1801), P.S.M. In 1803 he was a Deputy for the Master Paper Makers of Buckinghamshire, and Goodwin and Son were master paper makers. General Meeting of Master Paper Makers (13th June, 1803), P.S.M.....

The above details must be connected with 'Balls Mill' which is marked downstream from 'Friers Mill' on T. Jefferys' Map of Buckinghamshire (1770). This was probably the paper mill known as 'Frog Mill' which was occupied by WILLIAM CUBBIDGE from about 1803. In that year he was a master paper maker in Buckinghamshire. General Meeting of Master Paper Makers (13th June, 1803), P.S.M. He may, therefore, have already succeeded John Goodwin at this mill. In 1805 William Cubbidge, paper maker and mealman, insured his paper mill and corn mill. *S.F.I.P.* 784168 (21st Dec., 1805). In 1816 he was the proprietor or master paper maker at Frog Mill. *E.G.L.* (8th Oct., 1816).

Mill No. 18. Ash Mill or Lane's Mill*

1726. JAMES KING, paper maker, insured his goods and stock in a mill in High Wycombe. S.F.I.P. 39666 (20th Sep., 1726). In 1732 Mary Baker, of Chalfont St Giles (Buckinghamshire), insured Ash Mills as a paper mill. S.F.I.P. 57807 (1st May, 1732).

Mary Baker is not known to have been a paper maker.

1737. James King, paper maker, insured Ash Mill. S.F.I.P. 73889 (23rd June, 1737).....

1744. MARY KING, paper maker, took an apprentice, William Hoxwell. A.G.B., 17/111 (1744). Only one reference to Mary King has been found.....

1755. EDWARD KING, paper maker, dealer and chapman, late of the parish of High Wycombe, was bankrupt. L.G. (18th Feb., 1755). Only one reference to Edward King has been found.....

1760. George Lane was assessed for 'late King's Mill'. High Wycombe R.B. (1760). This entry appears to refer to Ash Mill, which was probably the mill marked as 'Lane's Mill' on T. Jefferys' Map of Buckinghamshire (1770). In 1769 GEORGE LANE, paper maker, took an apprentice, John Cox. A.B. (P.R.O., I.R.1), 27/46 (1769).

1777. George Lane was referred to as deceased. S.F.I.P. 387232 (7th Aug., 1777).....

1777. The paper mill was insured by JOHN HEALY, GEORGE LANE and JOHN LANE, paper makers, executors of George Lane, deceased. Ibid. It appears that from then until 1791 George and John Lane were the master paper makers. In 1783 George Lane, paper maker, insured the utensils and stock in a paper mill. S.F.I.P. 480054 (7th July, 1783). In 1788 George and John Lane, paper makers, insured their paper mill. S.F.I.P. 542499 (2nd Apr., 1788).

1791. George Lane, paper maker, dealer and chapman, was bankrupt. L.G. (26th Feb., 1791). The business was carried on by John Lane.....

1791. John Lane, paper maker, insured the paper mill. S.F.I.P. 585234 (30th June, 1791). The mill was in his hands after 1800. In 1803 John Lane was a master paper maker. General Meeting of Master Paper Makers (13th June, 1803), P.S.M.

Mill No. 19. Rye Mill*

1788. The paper mill was insured by THOMAS WHITE, paper maker, of Lepards Court, Baldwin's Gardens (London). S.F.I.P. 539612 (17th Jan., 1788).

1789. The paper mill was insured by Thomas White, paper maker. S.F.I.P. 553600 (27th Jan., 1789).....

1796. THOMAS EDMONDS, mealman, insured his stock and utensils in the paper mill called Rye Mill. S.F.I.P. 656046 (2nd June, 1796). In 1799 Mr Edmonds' paper mill (Rye Mill) was burnt down. H. Kingston, History of Wycombe (1848), facing p. 192. The mill must have been rebuilt almost immediately, and Thomas Edmonds continued to hold it after 1800. A watermark THOS EDMONDS 1801 is in a paper in the Whatman and Balston Archives. Thomas Edmonds was the proprietor or master paper maker at this mill in 1816. E.G.L. (8th Oct., 1816).

Mill No. 20. Upper Marsh Mill*

1760. This was possibly one of the two mills on which GEORGE LANE was assessed in 1760. High Wycombe R.B. (1760). The other was Mill No. 18, above.

1777. George Lane was referred to as deceased. S.F.I.P. 387232 (7th Aug., 1777).....

1778. ROBERT BASWICK, paper maker, insured a paper mill. S.F.I.P. 405114 (2nd Nov., 1778). He was bankrupt in 1779. L.G. (12th Oct., 1779).

1780. — Baswick was assessed for a mill. High Wycombe R.B. (1780).....

1793. The next proprietor or master paper maker at this mill may have been JOSEPH CHILD, whose name is in a list of paper makers given in R.J.A.B. (1793). He was a master paper maker in 1796. Meeting of Master Paper Makers of the whole Wycombe district (4th Feb., 1796), P.S.M. The duration of his tenure is not known, and he may have been followed before 1800 by GEORGE LANE who held this paper mill in 1816. E.G.L. (8th Oct., 1816).

Mill No. 21. Upper Marsh Mill*

1750. A paper mill was in the tenure of HUGH STRATTON, paper maker. S.F.I.P. 120991 (19th Apr., 1750). In 1777 Hugh Stratton, paper maker, insured the utensils and stock in the paper mill; his location is given as Upper Marsh. S.F.I.P. 385246 (18th June, 1777).

1793. — Stratton, Upper Marsh, is in a list of paper makers given in R.J.A.B. (1793). This entry may have been out of date.....

1789. Stratton's successor appears to have been WILLIAM VEARY, paper maker, who insured a paper mill in 1789 S.F.I.P. 559549 (24th July, 1789). This mill was in his hands after 1800. He was a master paper maker in 1803. General Meeting of Master Paper Makers (13th June, 1803), P.S.M. He was the proprietor or master paper maker at this mill in 1816. E.G.L. (8th Oct., 1816).

Mill No. 22. Bowden Mill, Upper Marsh*

1748. WILLIAM BURNHAM and WILLIAM HOLMES, paper makers, of Wycombe Marsh, insured the utensils and stock S.F.I.P. 112965 (26th July, 1748). Only one reference to William Holmes has been found. References to William Burnham occur later.....

1754. EDMUND BALL, paper maker, of West Wycombe, insured a mill near High Wycombe in the tenure of William Burnham, paper maker. S.F.I.P. 139522 (26th Jan., 1754).

1756. Edmund Ball, paper maker, of High Wycombe, insured goods etc. S.F.I.P. 155243 (16th Dec., 1756). This appears to be the last reference to Edmund Ball which may be connected with this mill; later references to Edmund Ball occur in connection with Buckinghamshire, Mills Nos. 17 (above) and 25 (below).....

1758. William Burnham, paper maker, must have continued to hold this mill. In 1758 he took an apprentice, Francis Dennis. A.G.B., 21/127 (1758).

1766. Thomas East, apprentice to William Burnham, paper maker, absented himself. J.O.J. (22nd Sep., 1766).....

1774. RICHARD BARTON, paper maker, insured a paper mill and a corn mill. S.F.I.P. 342375 (19th July, 1774). This mill was in his hands after 1800. In 1803 he was a master paper maker. General Meeting of Master Paper Makers (13th June, 1803), P.S.M. In 1804 Richard Barton, victualler, miller and farmer, insured a paper mill and a corn mill under one roof at Wycombe Marsh. S.F.I.P. 771123 (20th Dec., 1804). He was the proprietor or master paper maker at this mill in 1816. E.G.L. (8th Oct., 1816).

Mill No. 23. Bowden Mill, Upper Marsh*

1760. JOHN SCOTT, paper maker, took an apprentice, John Fulbrook. *A.G.B.*, 22/155 (1760). No change in the name of the proprietor or master paper maker occurs up to 1800, and the mill was in the hands of a John Scott after that date. In 1803 John Scott was a master paper maker in Buckinghamshire. General Meeting of Master Paper Makers (13th June, 1803), P.S.M. In 1805 Bowden's Paper Mill, Upper Marsh, in the occupation of Mr Scott, was burnt down. H. Kingston, *History of Wycombe* (1848), facing p. 192. In 1816 John Scott was still the proprietor or master paper maker at this mill. *E.G.L.* (8th Oct., 1816).

Mill No. 24. Lower Marsh Mill, Wycombe Marsh*

1724. JOHN BATES, paper maker, insured his paper mills. *S.F.I.P.* 33801 (24th Nov., 1724). 'Messrs Bates for Marsh Mill' is an entry in the *High Wycombe R.B.* (1733). No change in the name of the proprietor or master paper maker occurs up to 1800, but it is certain that more than one John Bates worked the mill during that time. In 1756 John Bates the elder and younger (in trust for John Bates, a minor) insured a house. *S.F.I.P.* 151604 (29th March, 1756). The mill was in the hands of John Bates after 1800. In 1803 he was a Deputy for the Master Paper Makers of Buckinghamshire. General Meeting of Master Paper Makers (13th June, 1803), P.S.M....

This mill was probably on the site now occupied by the WYCOMBE MARSH PAPER MILLS, LTD., which are still working in 1957.

Mill No. 25. Lower Marsh Mill (probably Beech Mill)*

1740. WILLIAM GOODWIN, paper maker, insured his mill in Wycombe Marsh. *S.F.I.P.* 85154 (14th Aug., 1740).

1756. John Bates the elder and younger insured a house in the tenure of William Goodwin, paper maker. *S.F.I.P.* 151604 (29th March, 1756).....

1768. JOHN GOODWIN, paper maker, of Wycombe Marsh, insured the utensils and stock in the paper mill. *S.F.I.P.* 259262 (15th July, 1768). This mill was for a time owned by EDMUND BALL who, in 1770, as a paper maker of West Wycombe, insured the paper mill in the tenure of John Goodwin, paper maker. *S.F.I.P.* 280389 (22nd Jan., 1770). In 1778 Edmund Ball, late of West Wycombe, was bankrupt. The notice refers to a paper mill at the Marsh in the parish of High Wycombe. *L.G.* (13th Oct., 1778).

This notice appears to be connected with this mill, rather than with Mill No. 22, above, which Edmund Ball insured in 1754. The mill continued in the occupation of John Goodwin until after 1800. In 1779 he insured his paper mill and utensils and stock in a corn mill and a paper mill. *S.F.I.P.* 408710 (21st Jan., 1779). In 1796 John Goodwin was a master paper maker. Meeting of the Master Paper Makers of the whole Wycombe district (4th Feb., 1796), P.S.M. In 1799 Goodwin and Son were master makers. Meeting of Paper Manufacturers of the Wycombe district (10th May, 1799), P.S.M. In 1801 John Goodwin was a master maker. Letter (20th Apr., 1801), P.S.M. In 1803 he was a Deputy for the Master Paper Makers of Buckinghamshire, and Goodwin and Son were master paper makers. General Meeting of Master Paper Makers (13th June, 1803), P.S.M.

Mill No. 26. New Mills

1725. RICHARD BECK, paper maker, insured a paper mill in the parish of High Wycombe. *S.F.I.P.* 37202 (2nd Nov., 1725).

1733. Richard Beck, paper maker, insured his dwelling houses belonging to but separate from his paper mills called New Mills. *S.F.I.P.* 62602 (Dec., 1733). These are the only known references to paper making at New Mills.

Mill No. 27. Loudwater Mill*

1779. A paper mill was insured by FRANCIS BLACKWELL, paper maker. *S.F.I.P.* 416007 (6th July, 1779). In 1787 Thomas Haydon, gentleman, insured a house in the tenure of Francis Blackwell, paper maker, and a paper mill adjoining. *S.F.I.P.* 527708 (14th Feb., 1787).

1796. Francis Blackwell was a master paper maker. Meeting of Master Paper Makers of the whole Wycombe district (4th Feb., 1796), P.S.M.....

1797. WILLIAM BRIANT, paper maker, insured the standing and going gears in his paper mill. *S.F.I.P.* 669611 (26th Aug., 1797). The duration of his tenure is not known, but he may have held the mill after 1800. In 1807 a notice was given to the creditors of William Bryant, paper maker, late of Loudwater. *L.G.* (14th June, 1807). In 1803, however, JOHN BRIANT was a master paper maker. General Meeting of Master Paper Makers (13th June, 1803), P.S.M. He may have been at this mill.

Mill No. 28. Loudwater Mill*

1762. WILLIAM LOOSLEY, paper maker, insured his goods, utensils and stock in the paper mill. *S.F.I.P.* 191196 (21st July, 1762). This is the only known reference to William Loosley.....

1769. JOHN HOLLIDAY and JOHN SMITH, paper makers, insured their paper mill. *S.F.I.P.* 278010 (2nd Dec., 1769). Only one reference to John Smith has been found.

1775. John Holliday, paper maker, insured his utensils, stock etc. *S.F.I.P.* 349527 (28th Jan., 1775).....

1778. JANE SMITH, paper maker, insured her house, utensils, stock etc. *S.F.I.P.* 393842 (14th Jan., 1778). Only one reference to Jane Smith has been found.....

1778. Robert Hastie, paper maker, was married. W. P. W. Phillimore and T. Gurney (eds.). *Buckinghamshire P.R.*, M., VI (1910), High Wycombe M. It seems that about that time Hastie went into partnership with Plaistowe. In 1780 WILLIAM PLAISTOWE and ROBERT HASTIE, paper makers, insured a paper mill. *S.F.I.P.* 422783 (4th Jan., 1780).

1793. William Plaistowe and — Hastie are named in a list of paper makers given in *R.J.A.B.* (1793).....

1796. MRS ANN PLAISTOWE was a master paper maker. Meeting of the Master Paper Makers of the whole Wycombe district (4th Feb., 1796), P.S.M. She must have continued in occupation of this mill after 1800, for in 1803 she is again recorded as a master maker. General Meeting of Master Paper Makers (13th June, 1803), P.S.M. In 1804 she and WILLIAM DAVIS (executors of the late William Plaistowe) and RICHARD PLAISTOWE, paper makers, insured their paper mill. *S.F.I.P* 761120 (13th March, 1804).

Mill No. 29. Loudwater Mill*

1638. A paper mill called Loudwater Mill was 'newe built'. *S. P. Dom. Ch. I*, CCCCVIII, 148. This may refer to Buckinghamshire, Mill No. 30 or Mill No. 33, below. The early proprietors or master paper makers are not known.....

1690. JEREMIAH FRANCIS was one of the 'ancient paper makers' who petitioned against the Parliamentary Bill concerning the Company of White Paper Makers. H.M.C., Rep. xiii, App., Pt. V, *H. of L. Mss.* 272 (15th May, 1690).

1717. The paper mills, corn mills and house of Jeremiah Francis, paper maker, of Loudwater, were burnt down. Evidence was given by Henry Blackwell†, papermaker . W. Le Hardy (ed.), *County of Buckingham, Calendar of Quarter Sessions Records*, IV, 1712–18 (1951), 186.....

1744. JOSEPH and JOHN FRANCIS, paper makers, insured the paper mill. *S.F.I.P.* 98536 (31st March, 1744). This is the only known reference to John Francis.....

1752. Joseph Francis, paper maker, insured his paper mill in the tenure of GEORGE LANE. *S.F.I.P.* 133304 (25th Nov., 1752). In 1760 Joseph Francis was assessed for the mill (*High Wycombe R.B.* (1760)), but at a later date it may have passed to William Francis†, paper maker, of Loudwater. He died in 1775. *R.M.O.G.* (31st July, 1775).

1777. George Lane died in or shortly before 1777. He is referred to as deceased in *S.F.I.P.* 387232 (7th Aug., 1777).....

1780. A mill in the possession of — Plaistowe (probably WILLIAM PLAISTOWE, paper maker, who had another mill here: see Mill No. 28, above) was described as 'late Lane's Mill' in the *High Wycombe R.B.* (1780).

1793. William Plaistowe's name is in a list of paper makers given in *R.J.A.B.* (1793).....

1796. MRS ANN PLAISTOWE was a master paper maker. Meeting of the Master Paper Makers of the whole Wycombe district (4th Feb., 1796), P.S.M. She must have continued in occupation of this mill, or Mill No. 28 above, or both mills, until after 1800. In 1803 she is again recorded as a master maker. General Meeting of Master Paper Makers (13th June, 1803), P.S.M. She was probably succeeded by RICHARD PLAISTOWE who, with her, was a party to the insurance of Mill No. 28, above, in 1804. *S.F.I.P.* 761120 (13th March, 1804). In 1816 Richard Plaistowe, paper maker, occupied two paper mills at Loudwater. *E.G.L.* (8th Oct., 1816).

Mill No. 30. Tredway Mill, Loudwater

1682. Early references to WILLIAM RUSSELL, paper maker, may be connected with this mill. William Russell, paper maker, of Loudwater, was married in 1682. W. P. W. Phillimore and T. Gurney (eds.), *Buckinghamshire P.R., M.*, VI (1910), High Wycombe M. In 1690 he was one of the 'ancient paper makers' who petitioned against the Parliamentary Bill concerning the Company of White Paper Makers. H.M.C., Rep. xiii, App., Pt. V, *H. of L. Mss.* 272 (15th May, 1690).

1694. William Russell's recognizance was discharged. W. Le Hardy (ed.) *County of Buckingham, Calendar to the Sessions Records*, I, 1678–94 (1933), 507.....

1726. WILLIAM TURNER insured a paper mill in the parish of High Wycombe. *S.F.I.P.* 39048 (24th June, 1726). His trade is not given.

1762. William Turner, millwright, insured his paper mill and corn mill called Tredways Mills, in the tenure of JOHN SPICER. *S.F.I.P.* 193117 (11th Oct., 1762). John Spicer may have been a paper maker at that time. In 1763 he took over Two Waters Mill (Hertfordshire, Mill No. 9). *S.F.I.P.* 204815 (29th Nov., 1763).....

No reference to paper making at this mill at a later date has been found.

BUCKINGHAMSHIRE Mill No. 31. Overshots Mill, Loudwater*

1766. JOHN BATES, junior, paper maker, insured a paper mill, and a corn mill in the tenure of John Ball, miller. *S.F.I.P.* 23036 (25th Jan., 1766). In 1767 John Bates, paper maker, of Wycombe Marsh, insured a house at Loudwater in the tenure of JOHN NASH, paper maker, and the paper mill adjoining. *S.F.I.P.* 243164 (26th Feb., 1767). This is the only known reference to John Nash. In the same policy John Bates also insured a corn mill, adjoining the paper mill, in the tenure of John Ball, miller. In 1760 and 1780 John Ball was assessed for Overshot Mill. *High Wycombe R.B.* (1760 and 1780). This must have been the corn mill, adjoining the paper mill of the same name.....

1769. John Bates, paper maker, of Wycombe Marsh, insured a house at Loudwater in the tenure of JOHN WILDMAN, paper maker, and the paper mill adjoining. *S.F.I.P.* 269315 (22nd Apr., 1769). From that time up to 1799 at least, John Wildman was the master paper maker. In 1775 he insured the utensils and stock in his paper mill. *S.F.I.P.* 352125 (10th Apr., 1775). In 1783 John Bates, paper maker, of Wycombe Marsh, insured his house in the tenure of John Wildman, paper maker, and mills at Loudwater. *S.F.I.P.* 480255 (11th July, 1783). John Wildman was a master paper maker in 1796. Meeting of the Master Paper Makers of the whole Wycombe district (4th Feb., 1796), P.S.M. The duration of his tenure of this mill is not known, but he was probably still there in 1799, when those indebted to the estate of William Fellows of Wooburn were asked to pay debts to James Fellows of Wooburn or John Wildman in the parish of Wycombe. *J.O.J.* (20th Apr., 1799). In 1803 Overshots Paper Mill was insured by William Davis and Thomas Crouch, paper makers. *S.F.I.P.* 748419 (5th May, 1803). The master paper maker here at that time was probably THOMAS CROUCH. In 1812, as a paper maker, he insured Overshot Paper Mill. *S.F.I.P.* 868812 (30th March, 1812). William Davis was probably the master maker at Mill No. 32, below.

Mill No. 32. Loudwater Mill*

1763. The paper mill was insured by WILLIAM DAVIS, paper maker. *S.F.I.P.* 196523 (4th Feb., 1763). In 1782 William Davis, paper maker, took an apprentice, James Bugg. *A.B.* (P.R.O., I.R.1), 31/174 (1782). In 1789 James Bugg†, paper maker, insured tenements. *S.F.I.P.* 557780 (3rd June, 1789). His name is in lists of paper makers given in B.M. Add. Ms. 15054, Myvyrian Mss. (1786), and in *R.J.A.B.* (1793). He may therefore have been a master paper maker, possibly working for William Davis. The latter's name is, however, also given in these sources, and in 1796 he was a master paper maker. Meeting of the Master Paper Makers of the whole Wycombe district (4th Feb., 1796), P.S.M. He was still a paper maker in 1803 and 1804 (see Mills Nos. 31 and 28, above), and may still have been at this mill.....

This mill appears to have been on the site of the present Snakeley Mills, which are still working in 1957, under the firm of T. B. FORD, LTD.

1690. EDWARD SPICER, paper maker, was at this mill. Jenkins, 176, quoting *House of Commons Journal*. Edward Spicer was one of the 'ancient paper makers' who petitioned against the Parliamentary Bill concerning the Company of White Paper Makers. H.M.C., Rep. xiii, App., Pt.V, *H. of L. Mss.* 272 (15th May, 1690). In 1694 his recognizance was discharged. W. Le Hardy (ed.), *County of Buckingham, Calendar to the Sessions Records*, I, 1678–94 (1933), 507. No change in the name of the proprietor or master paper maker at this mill is known up to 1762.

1762. A notice referred to the estate of Edward Spicer, late of the parish of High Wycombe, paper maker. *J.O.J.* (27th Feb., 1762).....

1767. A notice referred to the sale of furniture belonging to Ralph Spicer, paper maker, of Hedge Mill. *J.O.J.* (28th Feb., 1767). The partnership between GEORGE GROVE and RALPH SPICER, paper makers, was dissolved, and Ralph Spicer was to continue on his own account at Hedge Mill. *J.O.J.* (19th Dec., 1767). In 1781 Ralph Spicer, paper maker, took an apprentice, William Thompson. *A.B.* (P.R.O., I.R.1), 31/12 (1781).

1786. William Davis, paper maker, of High Wycombe, and Stephen Gage, gentleman, of Bisham (Berkshire), executors of Ralph Spicer, deceased, insured a paper mill in the parish of High Wycombe. *S.F.I.P.* 523743 (31st Oct., 1786).....

1791. There was mention of RALPH SPICER, paper maker, of High Wycombe. *R.M.O.G.* (28th March, 1791). It appears that in the 1790s he went into partnership with STEPHEN SPICER and FREEMAN GAGE SPICER. In 1799 the three men were master paper makers. Meeting of Paper Manufacturers of the Wycombe district (10th May, 1799), P.S.M. In that year, as paper makers of Loudwater, they insured their stock and utensils in their paper mill. *S.F.I.P.* 693658 (17th Sep., 1799). They probably continued to hold this mill after 1800. In 1801 F. G. Spicer & Co. were master paper makers. Letter from Master Paper Makers of Buckinghamshire and Hertfordshire (20th Apr., 1801), P.S.M. In 1803 R., S. and F. G. Spicer were master makers. General Meeting of Master Paper Makers (13th June, 1803), P.S.M. In 1816 Freeman Gage Spicer and Stephen Spicer were the proprietors or master paper makers at this mill. *E.G.L.* (8th Oct., 1816).....

This mill is still working in 1957, as a box board mill under the firm of G. H. HEDLEY, LTD.

1764. SARAH PELTZER and GILBERT BECK, paper makers, insured the Wire Mill and the paper mill, separate. *S.F.I.P.* 210175 (30th June, 1764). This is the only known reference to Sarah Peltzer and Gilbert Beck.....

1786. WILLIAM HOWARD, paper maker, at the Wire Mills, insured goods etc. *S.F.I.P.* 519037 (14th June, 1786). The paper mill was in his hands after 1800. In 1803 William Howard was a Deputy for the Paper Makers of Buckinghamshire. General Meeting of Master Paper Makers (13th June, 1803), P.S.M. In 1805 an estate called Claptons in Wooburn was for sale. It included a wire mill, and a paper mill let to Mr Howard. *J.O.J.* (13th Apr., 1805).

1627. The paper mills were devised to RICHARD KING on lease (10th Dec., 1627). In 1645 he was in arrears with the rent and was ordered to make over paper and equipment in satisfaction. Bill of Complaint of Edmund Waller, of Gregories near Beaconsfield (Buckinghamshire). P.R.O., Chancery Proceedings: Series II (1642–60); C.3/466/35. Information from Mr J. S. Milne, General Manager at Glory Mill, and P.R.O. From the above evidence it appears that Richard King was the proprietor or master paper maker up to 1645, but his immediate successors are not known.....

1756. A paper mill and a corn mill called Glory Mills were insured by GEORGE GROVE and RALPH SPICER, paper makers. The mills were in their own tenure. *S.F.I.P.* 150908 (12th Feb., 1756).

1767. The partnership between George Grove and Ralph Spicer, paper makers, was dissolved, and George Grove was on his own account at Glory Mills. *J.O.J.* (19th Dec., 1767).....

1777. Joseph Wooster, of High Wycombe, John Church, of Harefield (Middlesex) and George Grove, all paper makers, insured the paper mill in the tenure of George Grove. *S.F.I.P.* 384597 (27th May, 1777). This is the only known reference to Joseph Wooster and John Church at this mill.

1781. George Groves, paper maker, late of Wooburn, was a fugitive from debt, and was in the Kings Bench Prison (Surrey). *L.G.* (11th Sep., 1781).....

1786. JOHN GROVE, paper maker, insured the utensils and stock in his mill. *S.F.I.P.* 517169 (8th Apr., 1786).

1793. In a list of paper makers given in *R.J.A.B.* (1793), Messrs Grove, Glory Mill, were deleted and transferred to Stoke Mill (Surrey, Mill No. 9 or No. 10).....

circa 1791. Freeman Spicer was a paper maker in the High Wycombe district. *U.B.D.T.C.M.*, 3 (c. 1791), 266. He may have been at this mill then. In 1798 FREEMAN GAGE SPICER and STEPHEN SPICER, paper makers, insured their corn mill and paper mill called Glory Mills. *S.F.I.P.* 676580 (26th March, 1798). The paper mill was in their hands after 1800. They were the proprietors or master paper makers at this mill in 1816. *E.G.L.* (8th Oct., 1816).....

This mill is still working in 1957, under the firm of WIGGINS, TEAPE & CO. (1919) LTD.

1759. JOHN FELLOWS, maltster, miller and paper maker, of Beaconsfield (Buckinghamshire), insured his stock of rags and paper in a paper mill adjoining a corn mill in Wooburn. *S.F.I.P.* 170911 (13th Oct., 1759). Only one reference to John Fellows has been found.....

1761. WILLIAM FELLOWS, miller and paper maker, insured his stock in the corn and paper mills. *S.F.I.P.* 185913 (17th Nov., 1761).

1796. There was mention of William Fellows, senior, mealman and paper maker, deceased, late of Wooburn. *J.O.J.* (3rd Dec., 1796).....

1799. A notice referred to the estate of William Fellows, paper maker and mealman. Debts were to be paid to James Fellows or John Wildman. *J.O.J.* (20th Apr., 1799). John Wildman was at Overshots Mill, Loudwater (Buckinghamshire, Mill No. 31, above), and JAMES FELLOWS was probably at this Wooburn Mill. He was a master paper maker in 1799. Meeting of the Paper Manufacturers of the Wycombe district

(10th May, 1799), P.S.M. The mill must have been in his hands after 1800. In 1802 James Fellows, paper maker, of Wooburn, took an apprentice. *A.B.* (P.R.O., I.R.1), 39/16 (1802). In 1803 he was a Deputy for the Paper Makers of Buckinghamshire. General Meeting of Master Paper Makers (13th June, 1803), P.S.M. . . . .

This mill appears to have been on the site of the present Soho Mills, which are still working in 1957, under the firm of THOMAS & GREEN, LTD.

Mill No. 37. Core's End Mill*

1777. John Butler†, paper maker, of Core's End, insured property. *S.F.I.P.* 381974 (29th March, 1777). Only one reference to John Butler in connection with Core's End has been found. . . . .

1791. WILLIAM EAST, paper maker, of Wooburn, took an apprentice, John Allnutt. *A.B.* (P.R.O., I.R.1), 35/13 (1791). William East must have continued to work this mill after 1800. He was a master paper maker in 1803. General Meeting of Master Paper Makers (13th June, 1803), P.S.M. In 1811 there were for sale the utensils in a paper manufactory, the property of Mr East, who was leaving the Fuller's Mill, Core's End. *R.M.O.G.* (16th Sep., 1811).

Mill No. 38. Core's End Mill* (probably that which was later known as Prince's Mill)

1785. JOHN HOWARD, paper maker, insured the utensils and stock in his paper mill at Wooburn. *S.F.I.P.* 501404 (1st Feb., 1785). The mill was in his hands after 1800. In 1816 John Howard was still the proprietor or master paper maker at this mill. *E.G.L.* (8th Oct., 1816).

Mills Nos. 39 and 40. Egham's Green Mills (two mills)*

1763. BARTHOLOMEW REVELL, paper maker, of Wooburn, insured a paper mill at Two Waters (Hertfordshire, Mill No. 9). *S.F.I.P.* 204815 (29th Nov., 1763).

1764. Bartholomew Revell, paper maker, insured the goods, utensils and stock in the paper millhouse. *S.F.I.P.* 212122 (15th Sep., 1764). . . . .

1765. Henry Ravall, paper maker, of Wooburn, was a surety for the appearance of John Spicer. *Hertfordshire County Records, Calendar to the Sessions Books*, VIII, 1752–99, 117. . . . .

1778. HENRY REVELL, paper and millboard maker, of Egham's Green, insured his paper mill and millboard mill, separate. *S.F.I.P.* 399639 (27th June, 1778). This is the only known reference to two such mills in one and the same tenure at Egham's Green up to the year 1800.

1793. Henry Revell is named in a list of paper makers given in *R.J.A.B.* (1793). The duration of his tenure is not known. It is probable that by 1800 or shortly afterwards he was succeeded by WILLIAM PEGG, who was the proprietor or master paper maker at a paper mill at Egham's Green in 1816. *E.G.L.* (8th Oct., 1816).

The duration of Rance's tenure is not known, but it is probable that by 1800, if not considerably earlier, he had been succeeded by HARRY PEGG, of Egham's Green, who, as a millwright and paper maker, had already insured the utensils and stock in a paper mill at Shiplake (Oxfordshire, Mill No. 9) (*S.F.I.P.* 435826 (20th Nov., 1780)). In 1803 Harry Pegg, senior, was a Deputy for the Master Paper Makers of Buckinghamshire. General Meeting of Master Paper Makers (13th June, 1803), P.S.M. In 1816 HENRY PEGG was the proprietor or master paper maker at a paper mill at Egham's Green. *E.G.L.* (8th Oct., 1816).

Mills Nos. 42 and 43. Bourne End Mills (two mills)**

1719. BOWEN WHITLEDGE, citizen and stationer, insured his 'Brown Board Mill' in Bourne End. *S.F.I.P.* 13020 (5th Jan., 1719). Perhaps John Whitlidge, paper maker, was connected with this mill at a later date. His name is given in a specimen entry in *Instructions for Officers who survey Paper Makers and Paper Stainers in the Country* (1778), 14. Only one reference to John Whitlidge has been found, and his location is not known. . . . .

1775. THOMAS and SARAH WILDMAN, paper makers and millboard makers, insured the utensils and stock in a paper mill and a millboard mill. *S.F.I.P.* 352122 (10th Apr., 1775). This is the only known reference to Sarah Wildman. In 1795 Thomas Wildman was one of the signatories to a petition by several manufacturers of millboards, praying that a drawback of the duty might be granted on the exportation thereof. *Excise and Treasury Correspondence, 1793–5* (memorial of 6th May, 1795). He was probably still a paper maker and a millboard maker.

1796. Thomas Wildman was a master paper maker. Meeting of Master Paper Makers of the whole Wycombe district (4th Feb., 1796), P.S.M. . . . .

1798. EADY WILDMAN, paper maker, insured her paper mill and pasteboard mill adjoining. *S.F.I.P.* 679507 (13th July, 1798). It is probable that both mills continued to be in her tenure after 1800. In 1807 Mrs Wildman was assessed for a paper mill and a millboard mill. *Wooburn R.B.* (1807). Information from the Reverend C. G. Hester, Vicar of Wooburn. It appears certain from the above evidence that there were two mills in the Wildmans' tenure from at least 1775 to 1807. In 1816 Eady Wildman was a proprietor or master paper maker at a mill at Bourne End. *E.G.L.* (8th Oct., 1816). . . . .

It is possible that one of the above mills at Bourne End was

on the site of the present board mill, Jackson's Lower Mill, which is still working in 1957, under the firm of JACKSON'S MILLBOARD AND FIBRE CO., LTD.

Nos. 44 and 45. Hedsor Mills (two mills)**

1724. ROBERT MOORER, paper maker, insured two paper mills and a corn mill in the parish of Hedsor. *S.F.I.P.* 33198 (1st Oct., 1724). Only one reference to Robert Moorer has been found. . . . .

1757. ROBERT LUNNON, paper maker, insured the utensils and stock in his mill and in his New Mill, separate. *S.F.I.P.* 157871 (17th June, 1757). In the same year Robert 'London', paper maker, took an apprentice, George Tucker. *A.G.B.*, 21/98 (1757). . . . .

1766. John Lunnon, paper maker, of 'Hedsworth', was married. W. P. W. Phillimore and T. Gurney (eds.), *Buckinghamshire P.R.*, M., VIII (1912), Chesham M., 94. From about that time one paper mill was worked by Robert Lunnon and the other by JOHN LUNNON. In 1768 Robert Lunnon, paper maker and miller, insured a corn and a paper mill, and at the same time John Lunnon, paper maker, insured his paper mill, in his own tenure. *S.F.I.P.* 258488 and 258489 (30th June, 1768). . . . .

One paper mill remained in the tenure of Robert Lunnon until after 1800. In 1770 Robert Lunnon, paper maker, pasteboard maker and miller, insured the corn mill and paper mill, and the raghouse adjoining the paper mill in the tenure of John Lunnon. *S.F.I.P.* 282640 (26th March, 1770). Robert Lunnon and Robert Lunnon, junior, were master paper makers in 1803. General Meeting of Master Paper Makers (13th June, 1803), P.S.M.

At some time between 1770 and 1781 John Lunnon's paper mill appears to have passed to ANN LUNNON, then to RICHARD LUNNON.

1781. Ann Lunnon, paper maker, insured her paper mill, in her own tenure. S.F.I.P. 441950 (10th Apr., 1781). Only one reference to Ann Lunnon has been found.....

1796. Richard Lunnon was a master paper maker. Meeting of Master Paper Makers of the whole Wycombe district (4th Feb., 1796), P.S.M. At some time between then and 1806 he was joined by WILLIAM LUNNON, and they took over both paper mills. In 1806 Robert Lunnon, paper maker, insured his house, and Richard and William Lunnon, paper makers, insured their first and second paper mills. S.F.I.P. 788659 and 788660 (27th March, 1806). In 1816 Richard and William Lunnon were the proprietors or master paper makers at a mill then described as 'Bourne End'. E.G.L. (8th Oct., 1816). This appears to refer to one of the above paper mills.

Mills Nos. 46 and 47. Marlow (two mills)★★

1747. 'The several corn and paper mills' at Marlow were mentioned. *Universal Magazine of Knowledge and Pleasure* (1747), I, 245. The earliest proprietor or master paper maker is not known.....

1756. John Fryer† was a paper maker of Great Marlow, late of Long Wick (Buckinghamshire). *A Calendar of Deeds..... preserved in the Muniment Room at the Museum, Aylesbury.* Records Branch of Bucks. Arch. Soc., 5 (1941), 48.....

1759. John Farmer†, paper maker, of Great Marlow, was married. W. P. W. Phillimore and T. Gurney (eds.), *Buckinghamshire P.R., M.,* VIII (1912), Chesham M., 86.....

1769. Thomas Rickett, miller, insured the paper mill, and a house in the tenure of Sarah Bark†, paper maker. S.F.I.P. 266213 (20th Jan., 1769).

In 1776 THOMAS RICKETT, paper maker and mealman, insured his paper mill, a new paper mill and a corn mill. S.F.I.P. 367098 (2nd Apr., 1776). This is the first known reference to the second paper mill at Marlow.

1783. A similar policy was taken out. S.F.I.P. 479260 (21st June, 1783).....

1796. EDWARD WRIGHT was a master paper maker. Meeting of Master Paper Makers of the whole Wycombe district (4th Feb., 1796), P.S.M. In 1798 Thomas Ricketts was deceased and there were for sale two paper mills and a corn mill in the possession of MESSRS WRIGHT. *J.O.J.* (20th Jan., 1798).

1798. Edward and JOSEPH WRIGHT, paper makers, took an apprentice, Francis Pepper. A.B. (P.R.O., I.R.1), 37/200 (1798).....

1799. Joseph Wright & Co. were master paper makers. Meeting of Paper Manufacturers of the Wycombe district (10th May, 1799), P.S.M. As far as is known, the mills were in the hands of this firm after 1800. In 1813 Joseph Wright was a master paper maker. Meeting of Master Paper Makers (6th July, 1813), P.S.M. In 1816 one paper mill at Marlow was held by Edward and Joseph Wright, and another by FRANCIS PEPPER. E.G.L. (8th Oct., 1816).

Mill No. 48. Taplow Mill★

1767. WILLIAM BURNHAM, paper maker, insured the paper mill. S.F.I.P. 247942 (4th Aug., 1767).....

1771. The paper mill was insured by Samuel Harding and Giles Cobsell. S.F.I.P. 300127 (20th July, 1771). They are not known to have been paper makers. The mill was probably in the tenure of ANN BURNHAM, paper maker. In 1778 Ann Burnham & Co., paper makers, took an apprentice, William Barnet. A.B. (P.R.O., I.R.1), 30/14 (1778). The mill was then to be let or sold. Ann and William Burnham were the occupiers. R.M.O.G. (1st June, 1778).

1780. The equipment was for sale. William Burnham was on the premises. R.M.O.G. (17th July, 1780).....

1781. The mill was insured by a cotton merchant, and was described as 'late a paper mill'. S.F.I.P. 446525 (27th July, 1781). It appears to have become a cotton mill and was probably the 'new-erected cotton mill' mentioned in *M.M.* (1st Oct., 1782). It had reverted to paper making by 1810; in that year an apprentice absconded from J. B. WISE. R.M.O.G. (8th Jan., 1810). In 1815 Joseph Beeby Wise, paper maker, was bankrupt. L.G. (3rd Oct., 1815).....

This mill was probably on the site of the present paper mill, which is still working in 1957, under the firm of NEW TAPLOW PAPER MILLS, LTD.

Colnbrook (doubtful)

1636. There may have been a paper mill here, held by HENRY HARRIS. Jenkins, 169. Harris was one of those who petitioned the Privy Council for relief from paying rent during the closure of the paper mills in Buckinghamshire and Middlesex. *S.P. Dom. Ch. I*, CCCLXXVII, 60.....

1686. In or about 1686 the COMPANY OF WHITE PAPER MAKERS had entered into a seven years' contract for the services of a skilled paper worker (Daniel Juilhard) and had, apparently, installed him as head of their mill at or near Colnbrook. (The French ambassador gave the location as 'Cobroc'.) R. H. George, A Mercantilist Episode, *Journal of Economic and Business History*, III (1930–1), 267. No paper mill site at Colnbrook has been found, and the reference may possibly be connected with one of the mills in the parish of Stanwell (Middlesex, Mills Nos. 6 and 7), which is near Colnbrook, rather than with that place itself. ....

1690. In 1688 John Slocombe of 'Colebrooke' was one of the petty constables and tithingmen. W. Le Hardy (ed.), *County of Buckingham, Calendar to the Sessions Records*, I (1933), 254. His trade is not given. In 1690 John Slocombe was one of the 'ancient paper makers' who petitioned against the Parliamentary Bill concerning the Company of White Paper Makers. H.M.C., Rep. xiii, App., Pt.V, *H. of L. Mss.* 272 (15th May, 1690). Possibly this was the same man.....

No definite reference to paper making at Colnbrook at a later date has been found.

Mill No. 49. Thorney Mill★

1699. Robert Beaver†, paper maker, was married. W. P. W. Phillimore and T. Gurney (eds.), *Buckinghamshire P.R., M.,* VIII (1912), Iver M., 11. (Thorney mill was in the parish of Iver.) The early proprietors or master paper makers are not known. The following paper makers are among those mentioned in the Iver Parish Records of the eighteenth century, but it is not known which of them worked the mill. Some names were found in *Bucks. P.R., M.,* VIII (quoted above); other information has been supplied by the Reverend J. J. Cresswell, Vicar of Iver. The following list simply gives the years when the paper makers' names appear in the *Iver P.R.*

1701. John Hill† (and various dates up to 1723).

1702. Robert Beaver† (and various dates up to 1720).

1708. William Barton† (and various dates up to 1727).

1708. William Goodsheart† (and various dates up to 1713).

1711. Thomas Silous†. 1711 James Goodchild† (and various dates up to 1730).

1715. John Ballinger† (and various dates up to 1727).

1715. John Carter† (and various dates up to 1732).

1719. William Blackwell†, James Shelloe† and Henry Light†.

1719. Samuel Broughall † (and again in 1732).

1720. Garret Light†. 1720 Derrick Willis† (and again in 1727).

1722. William Knight† and Thomas Knight†.

1726. Mary Light†.

1729. Jacob Johnson†.

1741. John Urlin†.

1752. Edward Parker†.

1754. William Wild†....

1759. WILLIAM FORRESTER paid rates on property which appears to have been the paper mill. *Iver Churchwardens' Accounts*. Information from Mr H. L. White, Iver. In 1761 the name of RICHARD ABROOK first appears in these *Accounts*, next to that of Forrester, but he is not mentioned therein after 1762. In 1764 the paper mill was insured by William Forrester and Richard Abrook, paper makers. *S.F.I.P.* 266046 (12th Jan., 1764). The name of Richard Abrook is in lists of paper makers given in B.M. Add. Ms. 15054 (1786), Myvyrian Mss., and in *R.J.A.B.* (1793). It therefore appears that he was the master maker here until the 1790s. In 1796 a master maker of that name was at Frogmore Mill (Hertfordshire, Mill No. 10), and Richard Abrook may have moved there from Thorney Mill. William Forrester was still the proprietor; he was assessed in 1800. *Iver Churchwardens' Accounts*. The next proprietors or master paper makers were JOHN and NICHOLAS MERCER, who in 1802 insured their paper mill. *S.F.I.P.* 731578 (15th Apr., 1802).

Mill No. 50. Horton Mill*

1635. A presentment was made in the Ecclesiastical Court at Aylesbury against EDMUND PHIPPS, gentleman, complaining that his paper mill went for the most part on every Sunday throughout the year. The Reverend W. H. Summers, Early Paper Mills in Buckinghamshire, *Records of Bucks.*, VII (1894), 207, quoting *S. P. Dom. Ch. I*, CCXCVI, 17.

1636. Edmund Phipps was a Paper Master in this district. Richard Gunn† was one of his men. It was stated that Mr Bulstrode (Phipps' landlord) had employed labourers of Horton Mill when they were thrown out of work because of the closing of paper mills in Buckinghamshire. Summers, *op. cit.*, 208-9, quoting a letter from Justices of the Peace in Buckinghamshire and Middlesex (*S. P. Dom. Ch. I*, CCCXLIV, 40). Edmund Phipps was a petitioner to the Privy Council for relief from paying rent during the closure of the paper mills. *S. P. Dom. Ch. I*, CCCLXXVII, 60.....

1649. Richard West† was a paper maker. G. W. J. Gyll, *History of the Parish of Wraysbury*..... (1862), 198 and 213.

1657. The will of Richard West†, senior, paper maker, was proved. T. M. Blagg (ed.), *Index of Wills proved in the P.C.C.*, VIII, 1657-60, Index Library, B.R.S., 61 (1936).....

1663. Thomas West†, paper maker, was married. G. J. Armytage (ed.), *Allegations for Marriage Licences issued by the Vicar-General of the Archbishop of Canterbury, 1660-8*, Publications of the Harleian Society, XXXIII (1892), 91.....

1680. The will of Timothy West†, paper maker, was proved. C. H. Ridge (ed.), *Index of Wills proved in the P.C.C.*, X, Index Library, B.R.S., 71 (1948).....

1687. John West may have been the master paper maker. His name is given in a warrant (10th March, 1687) issued on behalf of the Company of White Paper Makers. Overend, 205.

1690. John West was one of the 'ancient paper makers' who

1699. The recognizance of George Glanvile†, paper maker, was discharged. W. Le Hardy and G. LL. Reckitt (eds.), *County of Buckingham, Calendar to the Sessions Records*, II, 1694-1705 (published 1936), 227.....

There appears to be no clue as to who were the master paper makers during the first half of the eighteenth century, but according to G. W. J. Gyll, *History of the Parish of Wraysbury*..... (1862), 262, the following paper makers are mentioned in the *Horton P.R.*, Bu.

1738. William Gibbon†.

1742. Thomas Lavender†.

1746. Thomas Chely†. 1746. Mr West†.

In 1744 Colthrop Mill (Berkshire, Mill No. 12) was leased to Joseph Lane†, paper maker, late of Horton. Lease (2nd Jan., 1744/5), D/EB x T7, in the Berkshire Record Office, Shire Hall, Reading. Information from Mr P. Walne, County Archivist.....

1758. The paper mill was in the tenure of WILLIAM PEARSON. Gyll, *op. cit.*, 199.

1764. William Pearson, paper maker, insured property. *S.F.I.P.* 207842 (27th March, 1764). It appears that by that time the paper mill was being worked by THOMAS and JAMES PEARSON.....

1763. Thomas and James Pearson, paper makers, insured the utensils and stock in the paper mill. *S.F.I.P.* 204962 (6th Dec., 1763). In 1765 Thomas Pearson, paper maker, insured goods. *S.F.I.P.* 216796 (4th Feb., 1765). From about that time the paper mill appears to have been worked by James Pearson only. In 1767 he insured tenements in the occupation of Francis Davis†, Stephen Rutter† and John West†, paper makers. *S.F.I.P.* 243706 (20th March, 1767).

1768. James Pearson, paper maker, was bankrupt. *L.G.* (29th Dec., 1768). No further reference to James Pearson carrying on this mill has been found, but in 1782 a dividend in respect of James Pearson, paper maker, was reported. *L.E.P.* (20th-23rd Apr., 1782).....

1769. HALLARD COOKSEY, paper maker, of Braces Leigh (Worcestershire), insured the utensils and stock in his paper mill at Horton. *S.F.I.P.* 272733 (3rd Aug., 1769). Only one reference to Hallard Cooksey has been found.....

1786. Horton Corn Mills were described as formerly a paper mill and late a leather mill. *R.M.O.G.* (8th May, 1786). Apparently the mill was soon reconverted to paper making.....

1787. The paper mill was insured by THOMAS HODGSON and RICHARD BLOXAM, paper makers, of 425 The Strand (London). *S.F.I.P.* 532933 (3rd July, 1787). This is the only known reference to Richard Bloxam at this mill.

1794. The paper mill was for sale, late the property of Thomas Hodgson, paper maker. *R.M.O.G.* (14th July, 1794).....

1795. The paper mill was part of the effects of WILLIAM LOVATT, paper maker, of New Mills, Henley (Oxfordshire, Mill No. 8). *L.G.* (10th March, 1795). This is the only known reference to William Lovatt at this mill.....

1795. The paper mill was insured by WILLIAM ARMSTRONG, paper maker, of Colnbrook (Buckinghamshire). It was in his tenure. *S.F.I.P.* 640296 (7th Apr., 1795). The duration of his tenure is not known, and it is not known whether he occupied the paper mill after 1800.....

In 1806 BENJAMIN BUTLER, paper maker, insured the utensils and stock in his paper mill. *S.F.I.P.* 784881 (17th Jan., 1806).

Mill No. 51. Coltnett Mills, Wraysbury*

1605. *j molendinum papir* was held by HENRY BOULSTROWDE. *V.C.H. Bucks.*, III (1925), 321, quoting *Ld. Rev. Misc. Bks.*, CCX, L.R. 2/210, P.R.O., 474. Boulstrowde is not known to have been a paper maker, but he may have been connected with the Mr Bulstrode who was Edmund Phipps' landlord in 1636 (see Horton Mill, No. 50, above). No other early proprietor or master paper maker at this mill is known.....

1659. The will of Richard Crawley†, paper maker, was proved. T. M. Blagg (ed.), *Index of Wills proved in the P.C.C.*, VIII, 1657–60, Index Library, B.R.S., 61 (1936).....

1687. Nicholas Mercier may have been the master paper maker. His name, connected with Wraysbury Mill, is given in a warrant (10th March, 1687), issued on behalf of the Company of White Paper Makers. Overend, 205.....

1699. The recognizance of Richard Heritage†, paper maker, was discharged. W. Le Hardy and G. LL. Reckitt (eds.), *County of Buckingham, Calendar to the Sessions Records*, II, 1694–1705 (1936), 227.....

1725. John Leader† (who died in 1731) and James Meeres† were paper makers at Wraysbury. G. W. J. Gyll, *History of the Parish of Wraysbury*..... (1862), 72.....

1730. The several paper mills, commonly called Coltnet Mills, were to be let or sold. They were late in the possession of THOMAS WATKINS, paper maker. *Daily Journal* (27th Nov., 1730). Only one reference to Thomas Watkins at this mill has been found.....

1732. The paper mill was insured by JOHN CROWDER and WILLIAM PEARSON, paper makers. *S.F.I.P.* 59511 (9th Dec., 1732). In 1737 William Pearson, paper maker, took an apprentice, William Gill. *A.G.B.*, 15/128 (1737).

1762. MARY and John CROWDER, of Wraysbury, and William Pearson, of Horton, paper makers, insured their paper mill and corn mill under one roof. *S.F.I.P.* 194450 (11th Dec., 1762). This is the only known reference to Mary Crowder.....

1766. John and THOMAS CROWDER, of Wraysbury, and SARAH PEARSON, of Windsor, millers and paper makers, insured their paper mill and corn mill under one roof. *S.F.I.P.* 237510 (29th Sep., 1766). This is the only known reference to Thomas Crowder and Sarah Pearson.....

1769. Joseph Bullock insured the paper mill house. It was in the tenure of JOHN BERRY, paper maker and flock maker. *S.F.I.P.* 266937 (14th Feb., 1769). This is the only known reference to Joseph Bullock and John Berry. The former is not known to have been a paper maker.....

The site of this mill was put to other uses from about 1772 to about 1844, when paper making recommenced. G. W. J. Gyll, *History of the Parish of Wraysbury*..... (1862), 71–2. The site was probably that now occupied by the Wraysbury Paper Mills, which are still working in 1957, under the firm of ISAAC WARWICK & CO. LTD.

GAZETTEER OF BUCKINGHAMSHIRE BRICKYARDS

Andrew Pike
Buckinghamshire County Museum 1980 & 1995

INTRODUCTION

Brickmaking has a long history in Buckinghamshire. Although there is building stone available, in particular cornbrash (a shelly limestone) or oolitic limestone, and used in the construction of many churches, it is not generally of good quality since it tends to weather badly. Indeed it was often limewashed, even externally, to help prevent erosion. Flint was also used in the Chilterns for churches and other buildings. In medieval times and probably earlier, most houses were of timber. Wichert was a unique building material in the Haddenham area of the county. It is a hard, chalky earth which is mixed with straw and water. Provided it is kept dry with stone footings and thatched or tiled roofs it becomes very hard and lasts a long time. The basic material of brick, clay, - is, however, widely available across the whole county.

Bricks were made and used extensively by the ancient Egyptians and also by the Greeks and Romans throughout their empires. Flue tiles, used in the heating systems of Roman buildings, have been found on several Roman sites in Buckinghamshire, as have "tegulae" and "imbrices", the principal types of Roman roof tile. Roman bricks were much thinner than modern ones. Several wedge-shaped bricks (voussoirs), used for constructing arches or vaulted roofs, were found at the extensive Roman site at Stantonbury (Woodfield 1989). No Roman brick or tile works have yet been discovered in Buckinghamshire, although bricks and tiles were made in kilns at nearby Harrold in Bedfordshire in the fourth century (Cox 1979).

After the end of the Roman period in Britain in the early fifth century, brick and tile manufacture effectively ceased, only being reintroduced, possibly from the Low Countries, in the tenth or eleventh century. There are no early references to brick making in Buckinghamshire although it may have taken place at Brill and elsewhere from the thirteenth century. Whilst strictly outside the scope of this publication, the important tile making centres at Penn and Little Brickhill are worthy of note. At Penn, the fourteenth century saw the production of high quality, glazed floor tiles with a variety of animal and geometric designs. The works supplied many churches in Buckinghamshire and surrounding counties; large mounts were also supplied to Windsor Castle between 1344 and 1357. Successful though the Penn works undoubtedly were, they do not appear to have survived beyond the end of the fourteenth century. Two tile kilns were excavated at Little Brickhill in 1929 and again in 1968 (Mynard 1975). These produced decorated floor tiles in the fifteenth and sixteenth centuries. During restoration of Great Linford church, Milton Keynes, in 1980 a pavement made of Little Brickhill tiles was discovered. It was conveniently dated by a brass of Robert Hunt in the church recording Hunt's bequest of a new floor in about 1473. The fifteenth century brickworks at Slough which supplied vast quantities of bricks for Henry VI's new foundation of Eton College lie outside the modern area of Buckinghamshire.

The Tudor period brought prosperity to many parts of the country, including Buckinghamshire, and much new building. A tile kiln, used in the fifteenth century mainly for making roof tiles, was discovered and excavated at Leyhill, near Chesham in 1987. A pottery kiln, subsequently built of brick within the tile kiln, indicates that bricks were being made nearby in the 1400s (Farley and Lawson, 1990). An early use of brick is Chenies Manor House, built in the fifteenth century. In 1534 a contract was drawn up between a London brickmaker and St. Mary College of Winchester at Oxford for the supply of bricks "whereof 800,000 shall be made at Tingewick in the county of Buckingham in three kilns or clamps" (Harvey 1975). The old manor house at Stoke Poges was rebuilt in brick in 1555. Work by J. Chenevix

A Penn Tile

Trench has shown that bricks were being used for building houses in Coleshill from the sixteenth century. A tile maker is recorded here in 1615 (Trench 1983). Mr. Trench has also discovered a brick kiln at Glory Farm, Penn, which he believes operated in the early seventeenth century.

As brick became more widely used and fashionable, many estates operated their own brickyards. In February 1658 Sir Ralph Verney ordered the trenching of the brickyard at Claydon. The brickmaker was paid 6 shillings a thousand for making and burning bricks, and Sir Ralph had tools, wheelbarrows and moulds delivered to the "brickmen" (Verney 1894). A brickmaker on the Temple estate at Stowe is mentioned in 1665 and local brickmaking featured prominently in Sir Richard Temple's rebuilding of his great mansion at Stowe in brick during 1676. Brickmaking also took place on the Shardeloes Estate at Wycombe Heath in 1750. West Wycombe Estate also had its own brickyard. For a large building project a brick kiln or clamp would have been constructed specifically for the manufacture of bricks. The building of Winslow Hall in about 1700 necessitated the construction of a kiln locally to manufacture the bricks, which cost from 14 to 18 shillings per thousand. Likewise Chicheley Hall was built with 86,900 locally made bricks in 1719. Excavations near the site of Salden House, Mursley in 1967, located ten clamps which provided bricks for the house in about 1580. Even as late as 1830 bricks were being made in a specially constructed kiln for Quainton's tall tower mill. The clay pit is still visible behind the mill.

The late seventeenth and eighteenth centuries heralded the "great rebuilding" of town centres in newly fashionable styles with brick, being used almost exclusively. In many instances, such as in Church Street, Aylesbury, this meant a refacing in brick of an earlier timber-framed building. It also led to some impressive new civic buildings such as Amersham's Market Hall (1682), Aylesbury's County Hall (completed 1740) and High Wycombe's Guildhall (1757). Hedgerley, in south Buckinghamshire, became an important brickmaking centre in the eighteenth century. Bricks and tiles of fine quality were made there and sent down the river to London for some of the new buildings in the City. Hedgerley bricks are much praised by Isaac Ware in his Complete Body of Architecture (1756) and were said to be virtually impervious to fire. They were often known as Windsor bricks or fire bricks.

The Industrial Revolution and the great increase in population in the late eighteenth and nineteenth centuries, together with much improved communications (turnpike roads, followed by canals and railways) led to the need for more housing in Britain's expanding towns and villages. During the nineteenth century, almost every village with a suitable clay supply seems to have operated a brickworks. By the early twentieth century over 170 brickworks were, or had been, in existence in Buckinghamshire. A few, like those at Calvert and Bletchley, developed into large concerns, supplying much of southern England with bricks; others fulfilled a purely local need, perhaps only manufacturing bricks for a short season each year. By about 1940 most of the small brickyards had closed and more recent changes in construction methods have led to the closure of even the large works at Calvert and Bletchley (Newton Longville). Only two small works in the Chilterns are still in operation today as memorials of this once flourishing industry.

The former extent of brickmaking in Buckinghamshire is obvious from the many visible remains. Several clay pits remain, often as ponds. Some, like those at Calvert, have become large lakes used for water-sports and as a nature reserve. The pock-marked landscape of Brill Common serves as a reminder that clay, both for brickmaking and pottery manufacture, was extracted from here over a long period. Elsewhere, parts of kilns can be seen. At Cadmore End a complete downdraught kiln with a range of ancillary buildings remain; two large downdraught kilns survive almost intact beside the canal at Great Linford; Stewkley and Woburn Sands both have remains of a Scotch type kiln. The tall chimneys which once dominated Bletchley have all but disappeared.

The work of brickmakers was a skilled one. Brickmaking in the neighbouring County of Bedfordshire has been described in detail by Cox (1979). The process may be summarised as follows.

Traditionally, the clay was dug during the winter to enable it to be broken down by frost. Brickmaking would then begin in the late spring and continue through to the autumn, although smaller brickyards often operated on an even more seasonal basis - perhaps just for a few weeks after harvest. The weathered clay was puddled either by workers treading it or in a pug-mill, a barrel-like structure containing a series of blades. The resulting soft, paste-like clay was then put into a mould - a rectangular, wooden box frame. The moulds were then placed on wooden racks inside "drying hacks", wooden tent-shaped structures, which allowed the bricks to be "cured" or to dry out before firing. Bricks were formerly fired in clamps in the open air; they were stacked on edge over a fire of charcoal or turf and the pile covered by underfired bricks from a previous firing in order that the heat could be retained. The heat would be gradually increased to allow the bricks to dry out slowly. After three days, the fire would be allowed to go out, although the bricks inside the clamp or kiln would take ten days or so to cool down sufficiently to be removed.

Clamps were often used where bricks were being produced for a specific project such as the building of a large house. In time, when brickworks supplied a wider clientele, permanent kilns were constructed. These were initially updraught or "Scotch" kilns, rectangular structures with a series of fireholes in each side wall and a "wicket" or door in the end door through which the bricks could be loaded and unloaded. The fire was started at the bottom and the heat circulated through the bricks. A roof of wooden planks could be removed to speed up the cooling process.

The Ruined Pug-Mill at Stewkley

The nineteenth century brought many changes to brickmaking. Pug-mills were improved. Extrusion machines gave a far better texture to the clay and allowed it to be automatically cut up into brick shapes by a system of wires.

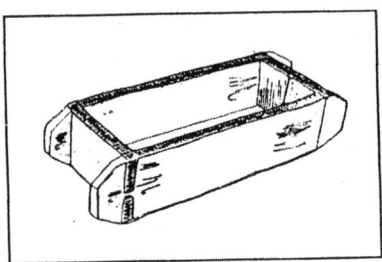

A Brick Mould

The drying-out process was also speeded up. Tile-making machines and many other mechanical processes meant that huge numbers of bricks could be produced for an ever increasing market. A new type of kiln - the downdraught or "Hoffman" kiln - was introduced by the Austrian Frederick Hoffman in the 1850s. Such kilns could be either rectangular or circular (the surviving kilns at Great Linford are good examples of the circular downdraught kiln). A domed roof meant a more even temperature; the heat passed up through the kiln's walls and was then drawn through openings in the floor by means of tall chimney situated alongside the kiln. Further improvements led to kilns made up of several chambers of differing temperatures so that unfired bricks could be placed in one chamber, other bricks could be fired in another and more, still, could be cooling down in a third. The savings in fuel costs and the speeding up of brick production were enormous. The kilns in the Bletchley area and at Calvert were of the Hoffman type.

Bricks themselves could be coloured by the addition of various minerals. In the mid nineteenth century "frogs" - rectangular hollows in the top of bricks - became commonplace. They gave a good key for the mortar in bricklaying, and also made the brick lighter. Perforated bricks were sometimes made for the same reasons. "Flettons" - bricks made from the deeper deposits of the Oxford clay - had displaced most other bricks by the turn of the nineteenth and twentieth centuries. The moisture content of the clay was such that it did not have to be cured or dried. In addition, the clay contained enough combustible material so that the bricks were virtually self-firing with enormous saving of fuel. Flettons were the main product of the large Bletchley and Calvert works operated by the London Brick Company and were the mainstay of the vast house building programmes of southern England and the Midlands in the 1920s and 1930s (Markham 1975).

The first edition of this booklet was the result of research carried out by Philip Chaundy in 1979 as part of an employment scheme based at the Buckinghamshire County Museum. In 1980 an exhibition on the small brickyards of Buckinghamshire was mounted by the Museum and the gazetteer compiled by the present author in conjunction with Rosemary Ewles.

The principal sources of information have been Kelly's (and other) Trade Directories and the various editions of Ordnance Survey 6-inch and 25-inch maps. Published histories of the county including Sheahan and the Victoria County History have been consulted, together with other printed sources (see BIBLIOGRAPHY). Several sites have been visited on the ground.

Most of the brickworking sites lie on private property; there can be no guarantee of access and permission should always be sought before visiting.

Further information would be gratefully received by staff of the Archaeology Section, County Museum Technical Centre, Tring Road, Halton, Aylesbury, Bucks HP22 5PJ.

ACKNOWLEDGEMENTS

Thanks are due to the many landowners and tenants who have allowed Museum staff access to their land to record and examine sites on their properties and who have often provided additional information.

Many retired brickmakers have given valuable information and have, in many cases, allowed their reminiscences to be recorded on tape. The assistance of staff at the two remaining brickworks in the county, Dunton Bros. and Messrs. H.G. Matthews, is gratefully acknowledged. The help and interest of the staff of the County Record Office is also much appreciated. The line drawings in the text are by Sally Cutler.

USING THE GAZETTEER

Entries are arranged in alphabetical order of place, with a cross-reference from the parish name if different. Places beginning with 'Great', 'North', etc are entered under those prefixes; thus 'Great Missenden' is so entered and not under 'Missenden, Great'.

Each brickworks in any one place is separately numbered, usually in chronological order of date of operation and is followed by a site name and a 6-figure National Grid reference.

A number in square brackets prefixed by 'CAS' refers to information held in the County Sites and Monuments Record at Buckinghamshire County Museum.

This is followed by the earliest reference to the works on maps, followed by each relevant directory entry with the name of the operator.

Next, comments and descriptions of the works in published sources, or from former owners or employees and information resulting from site visits are given.

Finally details of product samples, photographs and other records held by the Museum or elsewhere are provided. Numbers in round brackets refer to Museum accession numbers.

A directory entry by itself indicates that the brickworks has not been located on the ground or from maps. Grid references in square brackets [ ] are conjectural.

ABBREVIATIONS

BCM	Buckinghamshire County Museum.
BRO	Buckinghamshire County Record Office, Aylesbury.
CAS	Buckinghamshire Sites and Monuments Record, c/o County Museum.
MKAU	Milton Keynes Archaeology Unit.
NGR	National Grid Reference.
OS	Ordnance Survey.
Posse Comitatus	Beckett, I. F. W. (ed.) 1985 'The Posse Comitatus', *Buckinghamshire Record Society* **22.**
Recs Bucks	*Records of Buckinghamshire* Volumne 1 (1848) -
VCH	*Victoria History of the County of Buckingham* I-IV and Index 1905-1928.

Basden, E.B. 1966, and 1967, 'Pennlands Brick and Tile Works', *Buckinghamshire Rural Studies Association Journal.*

Beckett, I. F. W. (ed.) 1985, 'The Buckinghamshire Posse Comitatus', *Buckinghamshire Record Society 22.*

Bonnell, D. G. R. and Butterworth, B.1950, 'Clay building bricks of the United Kingdom', *Ministry of Works National Brick Advisory Council Paper 5.*

British Brick Society Information 1970-

Brunskill, R. W. 1990, *Brick building in Britain.* London , Gollancz.

Brunskill, R. and Clifton-Taylor, A.1977, *English Brickwork.* London, Ward Lock

Bryant, A. 1825, *Map of the County of Buckingham, from an Actual Survey in 1824.* London, Bryant.

Clifton-Taylor, A. 1972, *The Pattern of English Building.* London, Faber & Faber.

Cole, N. & Dawson W. 1967, *Echoes of the Past.* Wolverton.

Cox, A. 1979, *Survey of Bedfordshire Brickmaking, a History and Gazetteer.*

Directories:-

Pigot & Co, 1830 *National & Commercial Directory ... of Buckinghamshire.*

Pigot & Co.,1842 *Royal, National & Commercial Directory & Topography of... Buckinghamshire.*

Kellys' , 1847 *Directory of Buckinghamshire* & 1863-1864, 1883-1924, 1928-1939

Musson & Craven, 1853 *Commercial Directory of the County of Buckingham.*

Edward Cassey & Co.,1865 *History, Topography & Directory of Buckinghamshire.*

J.G. Harrod & Co., 1876, *Royal County Directory of ....Buckinghamshire.*

Town & County Directories Ltd., 1926 *Buckinghamshire South Survey District Trades Directory.* & 1949

Aubrey & Co. 1940 *Bedfordshire, Bucldnghashire & Oxfordshire Directory,*

Farley, M. and Lawson, J. 1990, ' A Fifteenth-Century Pottery and Tile Kiln at Leyhill,Latimer, Buckinghamshire', *Recs Bucks 32, 35-62.*

Gibbs, R. 1885, *A History of Aylesbury.* Aylesbury, R. Gibbs.

Green, A. H. 1864, *Memoirs of the Geological Survey, Sheet 45, Banbury...and Buckingham.* London, HMSO

Groves, J. 1984, *Identifying medieval and post-medieval bricks.* London, Museum of London.

Hammond, M. D. P. 1977, 'Brickkilns: An illustrated survey', *Industrial Archaeology Review 1, 171-192.*

Harvey, J. 1975, *Medieval Craftsmen.* London, Batsford.

Hillier,R. 1981, *Clay that Bums: A History of the Fletton Brick Industry.* London, London Brick Company.

Jefferys, T. 1788, *The County of Buckingham, Surveyed in 1766, 1767 and1768.* London, Sayer.

Lloyd, N. 1925, *A History of English Brickwork.* London, H.G.Montgomery.

Markham, Sir F. 1975, *A History of Milton Keynes & District*, Volume 2. Luton, White Crescent Press.

Miller A. 1950, ' Clay brickmaking in Great Britain: a survey of the methods used', *Ministry of Works National Brick Advisory Council Paper 6.*

Moore N. J. 1991, 'Bricks' in Blair, J. and Ramsey N. (eds.) *English medieval industries: craftsmen, techniques, products.* London, Hambleden Press.

Moreton, C. 0. 1929, *Waddesdon & Over Winchendon.* London, S.P.C.K

Mynard, D. C. 1975, 'The Little Brickhill Tile Kirns and their Products', *Journal of the British Archaeological Association,* Third Series, 38, 55-80

Parker, T. J. 1915, *Quainton Fifty Years Ago.* Aylesbury, G.T. De Fraine.

Plaisted, A. H. 1925, *The Manor and Parish Records of Medmenham,* London, Longmans, Green.

Records of Buckinghamshire Volume 1 (1848) - present

Rice, M. (ed.) 1980, *A South Bucks Village - The History of Hedgerley.* Hedgerley Historical Society.

Searle, A. B. 1911, *Modem Brickmaking.* London, Benn.

Sheahan, J. J. 1862, *History and Topography of Buckinghamshire.* London, Longmans, Green.

Sherlock, R. L. (ed.) 1960, *British Regional Geology: London and the Thames Valley.* London, HMSO.

Sherlock, R. L. (ed.) 1922 , *Memoirs of the Geological Survey, Sheet 238, Aylesbury and Hemel Hempstead.* London, HMSO.

Sherlock, R. L. and Noble, A. H. (eds.) 1922, *Memoirs of the Geological Survey, Sheet 255, Beaconsfield.* London, HMSO.

Smith T. P. 1985 , 'The medieval brickmaking industry in England, 1400-1450', *British Archaeological Reports 138.*

Tomlinson C. (ed) 1854, [Articles on brick and bricklaying], *Cyclopaedia of Useful Arts* Volume 1. London, Virtue.

Trench, J. C. 1983 , 'The Houses of Coleshill: The Social Anatomy of aSeventeenth Century Village', *Recs Bucks 25, 61-109.*

Turner, Rev. J. M., *Notes from the Annals of Akeley.* Buckingham, Walford.

Vernacular Architecture Volume 1 (1980) - present.

Victoria History of the County of Buckingham I - IV and Index (1905-1928). London, Constable/St.Catherine's Press.

Verney, M. M. 1894, *Memoirs of the Vemey Family* Volume 3. London, Longmans, Green.

Vince, J. N. T. January 1968, *Brickmakers of Langley and Stewkley',* Bucks Life

Walker, F. 1884, *Brickwork: A Practical Treatise.* London.

Ward, W. H. & Block, K. S. 1933, *History of the Manor and Parish of Iver.* London, M.Seeker.

Wight, J. A. 1972, *Brick building in England: From the Middle Ages to 1550.* London, John Baker.

Woodfield, C. with Johnson, C. 1989 'A Roman site at Stanton Low, on the Great Ouse, Buckinghamshire', *Archaeological Journal 146, 135-278.*

Woodforde, J. 1976, *Bricks to build a house.* London, Routledge & Kegan

AKELEY

1. SP 713 381 N.E. of village. [CAS 4174].

'Akeley Pottery', 'Brickfield', 'Kilns', 'Lime Kiln'
(OS 6", 1st edition, 1880/85).

Directories:

1877-1911	Watts, Robert, brick and tile manufacturer, potter and farmer.
1841	Census records 'John Basford (20), brickmaker, John Church (40) brickmaker, Brick Kiln; William Hunt (35), brickmaker, Brick Kiln', Akeley.
1861	Census records 'James Holton (42), agricultural labourer and brickmaker, Akeley'.

'Akeley possessed a flourishing brickyard and pottery ... but owing to severe competition and lack of railway facilities they have long been obliged to close down. Specimens of the Akeley potters' are are still to be see in many of the houses and the bricks are so well made that they might easily have given rise to that proverbial expression which may indeed be applied to Akeley - "every man is a brick"', (Turner, n.d., 36).

Visible features: pits. (Field visit, 1980).

Product samples: bricks, roof tile and stamped floor tile. (BCM 1980.8).

2. In BCM collection (1980.121) is a vegetable forcing jar marked 'SAUNDERS AKELEY POTTERIES' but no further information is known about Saunders either from directories or from local inhabitants.

AMERSHAM

1. SU 992 973 Amersham Common [CAS 2032]

'Brick works' (OS 6", 1st edition 1883)

Directories:

1830	Andrew, William, Amersham Common, brick and tile maker.
1842	Andrew, Thomas & Co., Amersham Common, brick and tile make.
1853	Andrew, John, Amersham Common, brick and tile maker.
1883-1903	Smith, H., Amersham Common, brick maker.

2. SP 945 998 Copperkins Lane [CAS 5718] 'Brick works, kilns' (2 kilns marked) (OS 25", 1925).

Directories:

1928-1931	Rust & Ratcliffe, Copperkins Lane, brick and tile maker (office Chesham).
1935-1949	Allied Brick & Tile Works Ltd., Copperkins Lane.

Apparently in use till 1950s. Site used by army in World War II to store vehicles. Known as 'Darlington Brickworks'. Directories 1899-1926, 1940-1949 show George Darlington had an office in Amersham, High Street; (other information from R. Nash, Weedonhill Farm, Feb. 1990).

3. (*see also* LEYHILL 3)

Directories:

1830	Woodhams, Wicken, brick maker.
1842	Woodhams, Wm. James, brick and tile maker.

ASTON ABBOTTS

'Brickfield' (1663) (BRO Parish Index Cards).

AYLESBURY

1. SP 822 143 Cambridge Street, Cambridge Close [CAS 5782].

'Brickfield' (OS 6", 1st edition, 1878/84).

Directories:

1830-1853	Read, Joseph, Cambridge Road, brick make and lime burner.
1864-1887	Hill, J., Cambridge Road, coal and lime merchant, brick and tile manufacturer.
1891-1911	Webster & Cannon, 42 Cambridge Street, builders... brick and tile manufacturers.
1915-1920	Ward & Cannon, 36 & 38 High Street, builders... brick and tile manufacturers.
1924	Webster & Cannon, 42 Cambridge Street, builders... brick and tile manufactures.
1939	Aylesbury Brick Works (Webster & Cannon), 42 Cambridge Street.
1940	Webster & Cannon, 42 Cambridge Street.

Description of "disastrous fire" May 1750 which began at brickfield in Cambridge Street, later know as Read's but at the time of the fire was occupied by James Lee (Gibbs, 1885, 604-605).

Notes conviction of James Wilson, brickmaker employed by Joseph Read, at Quarter Sessions, Jan 1832. (*Bucks Herald*, 7 Jan 1832).

Ward & Cannon,

36 & 38, HIGH STREET,

And L. & N.-W. Railway Station,

COAL AND COKE MERCHANTS,

BUILDERS' MERCHANTS,

And BRICK MANUFACTURERS.

Works: BIERTON, near AYLESBURY.

Truck Loads of Coal sent to any Station.

LOWEST QUOTATIONS FREE.

Advertisement from the Aylesbury Directory 1911-12

Visible features: Site now occupied by retail warehouses (Field visit, 1980).

2. Notes J.P.s' treaty with Henry Bayley of Aylesbury, brickmaker, to supply bricks for the building of Aylesbury Gaol, 1722, at 17s. (85p) per 1000, plus 18s (90p) per load of lime (Le Hardy W. (ed.) 1958 *Calendar of the Bucks Sessions Records*, 5 (1718-1724: Midsummer Session, 12 July 1722).

3. 'Freeman, Joseph, Aylesbury with Walton, Whitehall Street, brickmaker' (Index of Poll, 31 July 1839, for the Hundred of Aylesbury, extracted by G. Marjorie de Fraine).

BEACONSFIELD (*see also* CHALFONT ST PETER; WOOBURN)

1. SP 924 899 East of Holtspur Farm [CAS 1470].

'Brick kilns' (Bryant, 1825) 'Brick works, kiln' (OS 1st edition 1875/83).

Directories:

1847	Rance, Joseph, Holtspur Heath, brick and tile maker.

Visible features: none. Site now covered by housing and a service road. (Field visit, 1980).

Directories:

1891	Child, William High Street, builder and contractor, undertaker, brick and tile manufacturer.
1895	Child, William & Son, builder and contractor, undertaker, brick and tile manufacturer.

BELLINGDON

1. SP 946 050 Bellingdon Brick Works [CAS 5345].

'Works' (OS 6", 2nd edition, 1899) 'Brick Works' (OS 6", 1981).

Directories:

1899-1903	Bellingdon Brick Co.
1931-1939	Matthews, H.G. brickmakers.
1948-1949	Bellington Brick Yard.

These works are still in operation and were acquired by Mr. H.G. Matthews (father of the present owner) in 1923, having been operated since 1891 by J. Mead. Facing bricks - *Chesham Multies* - are made with a moulding machine and various *specials* are made by one hand moulder. Three oil-fired Scotch kilns produce 40-50,000 bricks a week, costing £90 per 1,000 (1979). Clay stocks have been supplemented by the acquisition of the former Froghall Brickyard at Bottrells Lane (*see* CHALFONT ST. GILES 1) from which clay is transported to Bellingdon (Information from T.G. Matthews, Bellingdon, 1979).

Brick samples, hand brick moulds, two barrows (BCM 1978.21; 1980.150; 1980.225; 1981.412).

2. SP 934 060 Gyles Court [CAS 5346].

Operated from 1936 to 1962 by Dunton Bros., producing hand-made multi facing bricks in coal-fired Scotch kilns.

3. SP 947 051 Bloomfield Farm [CAS 5347].

'Brick works' (OS 6", 2nd edition, 1990).

Directories:

1899-1935   Baker, J., brickmaker.

1939   Baker, William, brickmaker.

Operated from 1899 to 1960, producing hand-made multi-facing bricks in coal-burning Scotch kilns. (Information from T. G. Matthews, Bellingdon, 1980).

4. SP 965 060 Hog Lane [CAS 4565].

'Works' (OS 6", 1960).

Operated by S. T. Brown from 1926 to 1939, producing hand-made multi-facing bricks in coal-fired Scotch kilns. (Information from T. G. Matthews, Bellingdon, 1980).

5.

Directories:

1891-1895   Howard, John, beer retailer and brickmaker.

John Howard was the father of Samuel Howard who opened his own yard at Prestwood in 1895 (*see* PRESTWOOD 1). It may have been situated near the later yard operated by Dunton Bros. (*see* BELLINGDON 2). (Information from John Howard, Portsmouth, 1979 and BCM tape no. 4).

BIERTON

1. SP 839 158 Brick Kiln Lane [CAS 1045].

'Brickfield: kiln' (OS 6", 1st edition 1878/84).

Directories:

1864-1865   Bonham, J., farmer, coal merchant and brick-maker.

1877-1883   Bonham Bros., brickmakers.

1887-1895   Bonham, George, grocer, baker, brickmaker. Post Office.

Visible features: Various large ponds/pits. No structures.

BLETCHLEY (*see also* FENNY STRATFORD; NEWTON LONGVILLE; SIMPSON; WATER EATON)

1. SP 869 335 Duncombe Street, by railway station [CAS 6087].

'Brickfield', 'Kilns', 'Clay Pit' (OS 25", 1st edition, 1881).

Directories:

1883-1891   Clarke, Wm., Ed., Bletchley Station, brick-maker and carriers.

'Robert Holdom opened his own brickyard in the 1870s in Duncombe Street', (Markham, 1975, 290).

An 1864 directory entry under Fenny Stratford indicates that Holdom had an office in the High Street.

Visible features: possible remains of clay pits. No structures.

2.

Directories:

1895-1928   Yirrel, Thomas, brick and tile maker.

BOLTER END (*see also* LANE END)

1.

Directories:

1899   Harris, Harry, Old Peacock P.H., brick and tile maker, Bolter End, Lane End.

BOOKER

1. SU 836 913 Junction of Cressex road and Gibson Road.

'Brickfield Cottages' (OS 25", 1921).

Directories:

1911   Gibson & Son, brickmakers.

BOTLEY (*see also* LEYHILL) [CAS 5351].

1. SP 984 025 Shepherd's Farm.

Operated by Mr. Saunders from 1927 to 1948, producing hand-made multi-facing bricks in coal-fired Scotch kilns. (Information from T. G. Matthews, Bellingdon, 1980).

BOW BRICKHILL

1. SP 897 355 Caldecotte [CAS 6008].

During the laying of a pipeline a pile of brick and tile wasters in partly fired clay was found. No structure was visible, but the site was almost certainly a clamp fired kiln of 17th/18th century. The field is called 'Kiln Furlong Ground' on a 1791 Estate Map. (Field visit, MKAU, 1980).

BRADENHAM (*see* WALTERS ASH)

BRILL

1. SP 654 144 Brill Common [CAS 2498].

'Kilns & Brickfield' (OS 6", 1st edition, 1878/85).

Posse Comitatus, 1798, records James Norcott, James Norcott Snr, William Norcott, brickmakers.

Directories:

1847   Norcot, William, tile maker.

1853   Norcot, Jane, tile maker.

1864   Norcot, Mrs. J., brick and tile maker.

1865   Norcot, Jane, brick and tile maker.

Visible features: the only building remaining on the site is a brick cottage. (Field visit, 1979).

Brill Common (from OS 6 inch Map, 1885)

Ridge tile inscribed 'W. Norcott Brill 1839' fro barn at Cuddington. (BCM 1979.502).

2. SP 650 143 Brill Common [CAS 0796].

'Kilns and Brickfield' (OS 6", 1st editio 1878/85).

Directories:

1864-1864   Holme, T., brickmaker.

1876-1895   Home, Thomas, brick and ti maker.

1899-1903   The Cross Roads Brick and Ti Co.

Visible features: 2 kilns remain on this sit converted into garages for houses. One was updraught kiln, the other a downdraugl although the chimney no longer exists. (Fie visit, 1979).

Photograph of site and of Thomas Hume (BCN Also know as Poore's Brickworks.

Two floor tiles stamped 'T. Home' (BC 1979.340-341).

3. SP 652 141 Brill Common [CAS 4652].

'Kiln' (OS 6", 1st edition, 1878/85).

Posse Comitatus, 1798, records William Gibbo brickmaker. Gibbons (or Gibbins, Gubbins) said to have started the kiln later bought by Ni (P. Chaundy, BCM, from local information).

1891 Nixey, Andrew, High Street, miller (wind), corn dealer and brickmaker.

Visible features: nothing remains of this site. This site was called Nixey's Kiln. (Field visit, 1979 and local information).

4.   SP 655 149 Brill Common [CAS 4192].

'Kilns and Brickfield' (OS 6", 1st edition, 1878/85).

Visible features: site is now a private house and garden. The house is probably substantially the main works building. (Field visit, 1978).

5.   SP 653 143 North Hills [CAS 2497].

A subterranean brick structure, possibly a brick kiln, was discovered here by local inhabitants in 1976. (I. Rodger, Brill, 1976).

6.   SP 653 144 Brill Common [CAS 4651].

'Building, Kiln & Pottery, owner and occupier John Meads' (Brill Tithe Map, 1839).

'Kiln', 'Brickfield' (OS 25", 1st edition 1880).

Visible features: none. (Field visit, 1979).

7.   SP 665 152 North of Brill, adjacent to Wotton Road [CAS 4176].

'Brill Brick and Tile Works' (OS 6", 2nd edition, 1900).

Directories:

1895-1899   Brill Brick and Tile works, the Grove (Ralph A. Jones, Managing Director).

1903   Brill Brick and Tile works (W.J.W. Patterson, Secretary).

1907-1911   Brill Brick and Tile Co. Ltd., (John Uff, Secretary).

A large-scale brickyard. In the early years of this century it was making a full range of products by the Fletton process, employing up to 100 men.

According to one local informant it was largely the cause of the other smaller yards in Brill closing down. It had a spur to the Brill Tramway which connected with the main London line at Quainton Road. It closed in 1911 and was demolished shortly afterwards. (Information from J. Brown, Brill, 1979; BCM tape no. 6).

Visible features: none. Site is now used for light industry. (Field visit, 1979).

Photographs of workers and of site, c. 1900 (BCM).

8.   SP 656 148 Bottom of Brill Common [CAS 4653].

This is the approximate site of a short-lived works opened in 1922 which lasted only one season. It was formed by subscription shares of £1 among some of the unemployed of Brill of which there were about eighty after World War I. It closed due to financial difficulties. (BCM tape no. 6. J. Brown, Brill, 1979).

brickmaker, cottage on Brill Hills Common (4 bays) with lime and coal houses and brick kiln. Term 14 years. Rent £6 10s 0d £6.50' (BRO, ref. D/HO, p3, 25).

10.   SP 666 140 Kiln Yard Field [CAS 5263] 'Kiln Yard, occupier George Fuller' (Brill Tithe Map, 1839).

No indications, in a pasture field, of what kiln, if any, was located here. (Field visit, 1983)

11.   SP 655 141 Temple Street [CAS 5293].

Excavations in 1983 located a large two-phase kiln. The later kiln seems to have been designed as a triple-flued rectangular structure with raised floor. Roof tiles, including crested ridge tiles, as well as pottery, were produced in this kiln in the early 16th century. (Yeoman, P. A. St. J. 1988 'Excavation of an early Post-medieval kiln at Temple Street, Brill, 1983', *Recs Bucks* 30, 123-155).

12.   Reference to Robert Mooswell paid 10 shillings in 1465/6 for 2 loads of brick and carriage from Brill, probably to build the great central chimney stack of Tackley's Inn, Oxford/ (Gee E. A. 1952 'Oxford Masons 1370-1530', *Archaeological Journal* 109, 120).

BUCKINGHAM

1.

Directories:

1830-1842   Adams, Mathew, Well Street, brickmaker and lime burner.

2.

Directories:

1830-1842   Holdom, Samuel, Prebend End, brickmaker and lime burner.

3.   SP 692 333 Lenborough Road, Prebend End [CAS 5130].

'Brickfield', 'Limekilns' (OS 6", 1st edition, 1880/850.

Directories:

1842-1842   Cherry, John, Prebend End, brickmaker and lime burner.

1853   Cherry, J., Prebend End, brick and tile maker.

1876   Emerton, Edward, Lenborough Road, brick and tile merchant,

1883-1887   Emerton, Edward, Lenborough Road, brickmaker.

Visible remains: none. Site now allotments (Field visit, 1982).

4.

Directories:

1864-1865   Adcock, E., High Street, brickmaker.

Site of 19th century brick kiln. (Field visit, 1974, and local information).

6.   Dancer, Mary, brick and tile maker, Buckingham.

Turnham, John, brick and tile maker, Buckingham.

(*Universal British Directory of Trade, Commerce and Manufacture, 1793*, **2**).

BUCKLAND COMMON

1.   SP 918 075 Buckland Wood Farm [CAS 1822].

'Brick Field', 'Kilns' (OS 6", 1st edition 1877/84).

'Job Brown, brickmaker, Buckland Common (Index of Poll, 31 July 1839, for the Hundred of Aylesbury, extracted by G. Marjorie de Fraine).

Directories:

1864-1865   Gomm, G., farmer and brickmaker.

A works owned by the Rothschilds operating from about 1850 to 1900, making hand-made multi-facing bricks in coal-fired Scotch kilns (Information from T. G. Matthews, Bellingdon 1980).

2.   SP 923 070 Between Buckland Common and Cholesbury [CAS 1234].

Directories:

1907-1924   Fincher, H., brickmaker.

Operated from 1900 to 1961, making ordinary facing bricks and 'specials' - brickettes and 'water-table' bricks for window-sills - in three Scotch kilns. (BCM tape no. 2: interview with A Horn, Buckland Common, who worked here from 1923 until after the World War II).

BURNHAM

1.   SU 949 873 Harehatch Lane [CAS 4750] 'Brick kiln' (Bryant, 1825).

OS 6" maps show an extensive quarry in the same area. (OS 6", 1st edition, 1875/83 and later editions).

2.   SU 939 855 Dorney Wood [CAS 4661]

'Brick works' (OS 6", 1st edition, 1875/82).

Directories:

1899   Dorney Wood Brick Work (Henry Gilbert Hogarth).

1903   Dorney Wood Brick Works (T Berridge).

Visible features: Remais of clay pits and a well Across the road. at SU937 856, is the site of another brickworks, apparently active in early 20th century. A brick chimney base, remains of a kiln and a pugmill, together with several pits remain. (National Trust Survey 1992). (Field visit 1980).

3. SU 924 839 Poyle Farm [CAS 1551]
'Poyle Brick Works; kilns; chimneys' (OS 25",
1932).

Directories:

1895-1903   Almond, George, builders'
material merchant and
brickmaker.

1931-1940   Almond, George William,
Britwell Road, timber merchant
and brick manufacturer.

G.W. Almond, Lent Rise, Burnham, describes
finding fragments of Iron Age pottery from his
brickworks at Poyle Farm, near the store sheds.
(*Recs Bucks* 1943, **14**, 174-183, and BCM
Records).

Visible remains: no remains of the site which has
reverted to farm land and buildings (Field visit,
1980).

4. SU 925 817 Newtown.

'Brick works' (OS 25", 1st edition, 1875).

5. SU 927 816 Lent Rise.

'Brick works' (OS 25", 1st edition, 1875).

6. SU 945 845 East Burnham Common
[CAS 4740].

'Kiln' (1808 map, J. Field, copy at BCM).

1810 Court Roll of Allards Manor refers to brick
kiln on East Burnham Common (Corporation of
London Record Office).

Earthenware sherds and a brick stamped *B* found
in side of quarry in area of NGR (BCM
1980.273). (Field visit, 1980).

7. SU 943 845 Kiln Wood [CAS 4741].

'Kiln Close' (1808 map, copy at BCM).

A deep quarry in the wood with mud compacted
tile and vitrified brick in its sides indicates the
former existence of brick and tile works.

CADMORE END

1. SU 793 989 Cadmore End Common
[CAS 2469].

'Brick and Tile Works' (OS 6", 1st edition,
1876/83).

The brickyard of the Parmoor Estate and
operated as such until taken over by the Piercey
Brothers after the World War I. During that
period, eight or nine people worked there, making
bricks and tiles (lime had formerly been burnt
there), using one downdraught kiln, and one
Scotch kiln. The yard functioned until c. 1939
when the clay was worked out. (Information from
Mr. Randall, High Wycombe, who worked at the
site c. 1926-1933, and Mr. Lloyd-Jones, Kiln
Cottage, Cadmore End, 1977).

Visible features: downdraught kiln, foundations of
downdraught kiln, pay office, foreman's house and
workers' cottages. Also pits in vicinity. (Field
visit, 1977).

Kilns report and photograph of kiln in operation
(BCM).

2. SU 796 932 Cadmore End Common.

'Brick and Tile Works' (OS 25" 1st edition,
1881).

Drawing of downdraught kiln,
Cadmore End

CALVERT

1. SP 685 243 Calvert Brickworks

'Calvert Brick Works' (OS 25", 1938).

Directories:

1903-1920   Itter, Arthur, W., Calvert Brick
Works.

1924-1935   Itter Ltd., Calvert Brick Works.

'In 1936 ... the London Brick Company acquired
Itter's Brick company at Calvert. These had
started in a humble way in 1890 and had been
changed over to Fletton methods around 1900.
Now the most productive brickworks in
Buckinghamshire, 9,000,000 bricks are produced
a week', (Markham, 1975. 295-297).

Brickworks closed in 1991. (Field visit, 1991).

CALVERTON

1. SP 810 391 North of Brickkiln Farm
Watling Street [CAS 3985].

'Wolverton Brick Kilns' (Bryant, 1825)

'Brickfield', 'Kiln', (OS 6", 1st edition,
1881/85).

Directories:

1865   Bailey, Richard, Calverton
Common, brick and tile, drain
manufacturer.

Visible remains: none. Area now covered by
warehousing. (Field visit, 1991).

2. SP 813 384 Two Mile Ash [CAS 5783].

'Brickfield', 'Kilns' (OS 6". 1st edition, 1880/85).

'Works Disused' (OS 6", 1958).

Directories:

1883   Gilks, Geo., brick merchant,
Two Mile Ash.

Visible remains: a series of small ponds/pits. No
structures.

CHALFONT ST. GILES (see also CHALFONT ST. PETER)

1. SP 977 942 Froghall, Bottrells Lane [CAS
2039]

'Brick and Tile Works' (OS 6", 1st edition,
1878/83).

Directories:

1853   Kirby, Joseph, farmer and brick
and tile manufacturer, Frog Hall
Kiln, Amersham.

1864-1876   Kirby, J., Froghall, brickmaker.
1883   Kirby, Henry, Thomas, Froghall,
brickmaker.

1887-1931   Kirby, Edward, brickmaker.

1935   Kirby, Edward & Son, Froghall.

1939   Kirby, Edward & Son, Three
Households.

Daniel Kirby (41), tile, lime and oven tile burner,
Chalfont St. Giles Village Street. (1861 Census
Returns).

The kiln at Froghall was built in 1783. The yard
closed in June 1978, having up to this time been
run by the Kirby family (*see also* CHALFONT
ST. GILES 2 and CHALFONT ST. PETER 2 for
other yards run by the Kirby family). Bricks were
always made, but the most important produce was
tiles for lining bakers' ovens to which the clay at
the site was particularly suited. There were about
ten men making oven tiles until 1952, after which
sales declined with the closure of small baking
firms. The yard then concentrated on
brickmaking. After closure the site was acquired
by H.G. Matthews (*see* BELLINGDON 1) for
clay stocks. (Information from Joseph and
Kenneth Kirby, BCM tape nos 2, 21).

Visible features: Scotch kiln, making sheds, pug
mill (installed 1932), pits. (Field visit, 1979).

Series of photographs taken before closure
(BCM). Product samples, moulds, hack covers,
kiln rakes (BCM 1977.557 & 571). Kiln report by
J.K. Major, 1977 (BCM)

'Hat-Cap' Covers over drying bricks, Froghall

2. SU 987 922 South of Narcott Farm.
'Brickworks', 'Kiln' (OS 25", 1924).

Finished bricks at Froghall

Kirby's acquired this site, known as 'The
Klondike Brickworks', early this century when
another yard they owned (Austenwood,
CHALFONT ST. PETER 2) ran out of clay.
Product: bricks and plain tiles. The site was
closed down c. 1936. (Information from Kenneth
Kirby, BCM tape no. 2).

2.

Directories:

1883   Smith, Harry, brick and tile
maker.

CHALFONT ST PETER

1. SP 967 900 Durrants Heath, south of Jordans [CAS 2562].

'Brick kiln' (Bryant, 1825) 'Pottery' (Stampwell, Mumford and Laters Green Estate Map, 1838) 'Brick and Tile works' (OS 6", 1st edition, 1875/83).

Directories:

1847 — Swallow, John, brick and tile maker and pot kiln.

1853 — John Swallow, earthen ware and brick manufacturer, Durrent's Heath.

1853 — Robert Swanner, potter.

1864-1865 — Swallow, J., Pitlands Wood, brick and drainpipe maker.

1931-1935 — Saunders, M. & Son, Pottery, Pottery, bricks and tiles and sanitary ware manufacturers.

'Thomas Saunders, brickmaker, Old Highway House, Chalfont St. Giles'. Also Thomas Saunders (44) tile maker; Alfred Saunders (16) kiln labourer "Brick", born Amersham; Albert Saunders (13) brickmaker's assistant, born Chalfont St. Giles. (1861 Census Returns).

A pottery existed at Chalfont St. Peter in early 19th century. Now called Beaconsfield Pottery it was established in 1805 by Mr. William Wellins but changed hands shortly and was bought by Mr. John Swallow who practically was the real starter of the pottery. Never assumed large proportions and Mrs M. Saunders and Sons, lessees, now produce flower pots, chimney pots, etc., (*VCH Bucks* 2, 115).

According to A.F. Boddy, who worked there from 1914 until its closure during the World War II, there were two updraight kilns and a downdraught kiln (built 1905), a steam pug mill, and a tile-making machine. Apart from thrown pottery, the yard made about 250,000 bricks per year which represented about one-tenth of total production. In 1914 it was employing eighteen men (BCM tape no. 4).

Some of the original shed survive; also the outline of a circular kiln, embedded in the drive. (Field visit, 1978).

2. TQ 000 894 Austenwood [CAS 5880].

'Brickworks' (OS 25", 1st edition, 1876).

Directories:

1883 — Coleman, Joseph, Austenwood, brickmaker.

1887-1895 — Kirby, Edward, Austenwood, brick manufacturer.

1899-1903 — Coleman, Joseph, builder and brick and oven tile manufacturer. Assistant overseer.

The Austenwood site made bricks as its chief product and was forced to close due to lack of clay. Site now built over. (Information from Joseph and Kenneth Kirby, BCM tapes nos. 2, 21).

3. TQ 015 926 Kiln Wood [CAS 2821].

'Liberties kiln' (Jefferys, 1788).

In the area of Kiln Wood are several pits, although no evidence of a kiln survives (Field visit, 1978).

CHARTRIDGE (see also BELLINGDON; CHOLESBURY)

1. [SP 932 036] Portobello

Directories:

1847 — Lane, Thomas, brickmaker, 'Portobello'.

A few small pits are shown on OS 6", 1st edition, 1874/83 in the vicinity of the *Portobello Arms* public house.

CHEDDINGTON (see IVINGHOE)

CHEPPING WYCOMBE (see HAZLEMERE)

CHESHAM (see BOTLEY; LEY HILL; LYE GREEN)

CHICHELEY

1. SP 915 467 Swansriver. [CAS 4767].

'Brickfield', 'Kilns' (OS 6", 1st edition, 1881/85).

Directories:

1853 — Jackson, Joseph, Chicheley Green, brick and tile manufacturer.

1882 — Coales, Francis, farmer and brickmaker.

1887-1895 — Tayler, W.R., farmer and brickmaker.

1899 — Tayler, Geoffry, brickmaker.

The first directory entry, at Chicheley Green, is shown by Bryant to correspond with the area now known as Swansriver. OS map shows a brickfield of some size with several sheds and at least two kilns. The yard closed c. 1900. (Information from Mrs. B. Sapwell, Swansriver, whose father worked at the yard).

Photograph of works on Thickthorn and Grange Farms, including brickyard workers, c. 1880s. (BCM).

The bridge carrying the road over the never-completed railway at Filgrave (SP 8843 4828) was built with Chicheley bricks. It was always known as Coales Bridge since the railway company went bankrupt before they could pay Coales for it! (J. Coales to D.C. Mynard (MKAU) 1980).

2. ?SP 904 460 Chicheley Hall [CAS 4861]

Accounts re building of Chicheley Hall mention in Jan 1719/20 the brickmaker Sam Burgen receiving £30 12s 6d (£30.62) for "making and burning 86900 of bricks at 5s 6d (27p) per 1000" & for lime] (Tanner J.D. 1960 'The Building of Chicheley Hall', *Recs Bucks* 17, 45, 46).

Considerable quarrying is evident in pasture field north of the former vicarage (now Chicheley House) suggesting brickmaking and clay extraction took place here. (Field visit, 1980).

CHILTON

1. SP 691 114 Brick Kiln Corner [CAS 1681].

18th century Estate Map marks field at NGR.

'Brick Kiln Corner' (BRO, ref. ID/BMT/55R).

Shallow depressions in the field may be the result of clay extraction for a brick kiln. (Field visit, 1982).

CHOLESBURY (see also BELLINGDON; BUCKLAND COMMON),

1. SP 927 078 Shire Lane [CAS 1235].

'Works' (OS 6", 1960).

This yard was run by Duntons and operated from 1946 to 1960. (Information from Harry James, foreman at H.G. Matthews' brickworks, Bellingdon, and T.G. Matthews, Bellingdon, 1980).

2. SP 930 076 Shire Lane [CAS 0413] 'Works' (OS 6", 1960).

Directories:

1948-1949 — Brown Ltd., Shire Lane.

This yard operated from 1946 until the 1970s although the site has now been completely levelled. (Information from H. Thatcher and Dunton Bros. employees, BCM tape no. 1, 1979).

3. SP 926 063 Oak Lane [CAS 5258]

Directories:

1948-1949 — Harrowell Brick Co. Ltd.,

These works operated from 1928 to 1939 and made multi-facing bricks in coal-fired Scotch kilns. (Information from T.G. Matthews, Bellington, 1980). ∎

COLESHILL

1. SU 958 957 Coldharbour Farm [CAS 2031].

'Brick kilns' (Bryant, 1825) 'Brick and tile works' (OS 25", 1st edition, 1883).

Directories:

1847 — Pearce, Thomas, brick maker.

1853 — Pearce, Thomas, Cold Harbour Farm, brickmaker.

2.

Directories:

1887 — Lewin, George, cattle dealer and brick maker.

3.

Directories:

1891 — Lane, Stephen, brickmaker and wheelwright.

4.

Directories:

1891-1895 — Rogers, Hy. Alfred, brickmaker.

5. 'Jas Kirby, brickmaker, born Froghall. (1861 Census Returns).

6. A tile-maker, Hugh Wingrave, is recorded at Coleshill in 1615. (Trench J. C. 1983 'The Houses of Coleshill', *Recs Bucks* **25**, 86)

DORTON (*see also* WOTTON UNDERWOOD)

1.

Directories:

1864-1865 Foot, W., brickmaker.

DRAYTON BEAUCHAMP

1. [SP 915 087] Oaken Grove

Directories:

1864-1865 Bull, George, Oaken Grove, farmer and brick maker.

No evidence on maps of a brickworks at Oakengrove Farm, which is at NGR.

EDLESBOROUGH

1.

Directories:

1864 Peppiat, J., Greyhound, brick maker.

ELLESBOROUGH

1. SP 850 056 Brick-Kiln Cottage [CAS 5198].

'Brick-Kiln Cottage' (OS 6", 1st edition, 1874/83; OS 25", 2nd edition, 1899).

Site of cottage marked by a low rectangular bank, sought of which is a large pit and remains of a well. Probably the site of a small brickworks, the pit providing the clay. Some purplish bricks visible in vicinity. (Field visit, 1982).

FAWLEY

1. [CAS 1939].

References to a hothouse and cowhouse built 1807-1816 of bricks made on the Fawley estate in a 'cross-kiln' (Tyack G. 1982 'The Freemans of Fawley and their Buildings', *Recs Bucks* 1982, **24**, 141).

FENNY STRATFORD (*see also* BLETCHLEY, WATER EATON)

1. SP 870 350 Watling Street, north side [CAS 6056].

'Brick Field' (OS 6", 1st edition, 1880/85).

'In 1876 yet another brickworks came into existence at Foxhole, Bletchley, where John Munday, a timber merchant, purchased the hand-made bricks and built houses with them in Albert Street and around', (Markham, 1975. 290). Closed by 1898, and houses erected fronting on to Watling Street. Houses have now been demolished and the site is now derelict. The ground is uneven and parts of it are waterlogged. No remains of original kilns or other buildings are visible above ground. (Information from E. Legg, Bletchley, 1963.

2. [SP 882 347] White Hart.
'Samuel Bragg had a small brickyard east of the canal down by the White Hart, Fenny Stratford, which changed hands in the late 1860s', (Markham 1975, 290). No trace of a brickworks in the vicinity of the White Hart at NGR. (Field visit and OS 6", 1977).

FINGEST & LANE END (*see* BOLTER END: CADMORE END: LANE END: WHEELER END)

FULMER

1. SU 988 869 Duke's Kiln [CAS 5048]
'Kiln'; 'Brick & Tile Works' (OS 6" 1st edition, 1875/83).

No remains of any structures on the site, now partly destroyed by M40 motorway. A terrace of houses adjacent is called *Duke's Kiln Cottages*. The irregularity of the land may be the result of quarrying. (Field visit, 1981).

GREAT AND LITTLE HAMPDEN

1. SP 831 015 Ironbeech Kiln [CAS 5080]
'Ironbeech Kiln' (Jefferys, 1788; Monks Risborough Inclosure Map, 1839, at B.R.O; OS 6", 1st edition, 1877/85).

No evidence has been found to indicate the type of kiln. The site is occupied by a later 17th/18th century cottage, with brick and tile fragments in the garden, perhaps indicating a brickworks. A pit nearby is probably a clay pit. (Field visit, 1988).

2. [SP 828 032] Green Hailey
Hampden Estate Records contain references to Green Hailey Kiln, 1752. (BRO).

GREAT AND LITTLE KIMBLE

1. SP 814 085 South of Marsh [CAS 0918].

'Brick Field', 'Kiln' (OS 6", 1st edition, 1877/85).

Directories:

1864-1865 Carter, D., brickmaker and farmer.

No remains of a kiln or associated structures exist, although two sheds in the garden of *The Willows* may be contemporary with the brickworks. Three bungalows now occupy the site. (Field visit, 1979).

GREAT AND LITTLE WOOLSTONE

1. SP 870 396 West of Little Woolstone alongside Grand Union Canal [CAS 6085].

'Brickkiln' 'Old Brickkiln' (OS 25", 1st edition, 1881)

Directories:

1853-1864 Forster, Alfred, farmer and brick and tile manufacturer.

'Little Woolstone had a brick and tile manufactory for years'. (Markham, 1975, 290).

2. SP 870 383 Alongside Canal, Great Woolstone [CAS 6084].

'Brick Field'; Kiln (OS 25", 1st edition, 1881).

No remains; site partly built on, partly open space.

GREAT HORWOOD

1. SP 767 292 Between Great Horwood and Winslow [CAS 5132].

'Kiln; Brick Field' (OS 6", 1st edition, 1878/85).

Directories:

1883-1887 Buckingham, Edmund, brick and tile manufacturer.

1891 Buckingham John, brick and tile maker.

1895 Buckingham, John, brick and tile maker and miller (wind and steam).

1903 Buckingham, John, The Kilns, brick and drain pipe manufacturer.

Visible features: none. Former pits have been infilled and converted to pasture (field visit 1982).

GREAT LINFORD

1. SP 860 416 Adjacent to canal, south-west of village [CAS 6023].

'Old kilns' - 3 marked (OS 25", 1925).

Directories:

1911 Read, John, brickmaker.

The yard, which appears to have operated from the 1880's until World War I, was owned by George Price & Son of Newport Pagnell [*see* NEWPORT PAGNELL directory entries]. Information from the late Mr. Walter King of Newport Pagnell, who worked both at this yard and at Price's other yard, confirms that the directory entry refers to 'Jack Read', who lived in the brickyard cottage and oversaw the kilns. Most of the bricks produced at this site went to the building of Wolverton and New Bradwell, being transported by barge along the canal. The brickyard had a steam navvy to dig the clay and was considered one of the most modern pits in the area when it was opened. (*Milton Keynes Gazette*, 14 January 1977).

Photograph of one of the kilns being constructed. (BCM).

The two surviving circular downdraught kilns are scheduled as an Ancient Monument.

2. SP 855 427 Railway Terrace [CAS 6070].

Directories:

1842 Sheppard, Richard, brick maker and lime burner.

The works were said to be near the site of Railway Terrace. No remains (MKAU).

3.

Directories:

1830 Keeps, Labrum & Taylor, Great Linford Wharf, brick maker and lime burner.

GREAT MARLOW (*see* MARLOW)

GREAT MISSENDEN (*see also* HYDE HEATH; PRESTWOOD; THE LEE)

1.

Directories:

1883	Woollams, Harry, builder, undertaker and brickmaker.
1887-1891	Ford, John, brickmaker.

GRENDON UNDERWOOD

1. SP 692 193 South of village, at Kingswood.

'Brick Field' (OS 25", 1st edition, 1880).

Directories:

1853	Heritage, Thomas, brick and tile manufacturer.
1883-1887	Hammond, W., brickmaker and shopkeeper.
1899-1903	Daniel, W., brickmaker.
1907	Wellings, William, Crossroads, shopkeeper and brickmaker.

The brickfield at NGR is the only one visible on maps and on the ground in Grendon Underwood, so probably the various directory entries refer to the one site.

HADDENHAM

1. SP 753 103 Haddenham Low [CAS 4745].

'Brick Kiln' (Bryant, 1825); 'Brick field; kiln' (OS 6", 1st edition, 1877/85).

Brick kiln demolished by Mr. Field in 1940s. Made two-inch land drains (many have been dug up near the farm), roof tiles and bricks. A lake to the south of Haddenham Low Farm was the former brick pit. Near the brick kiln was a lime kiln and both were apparently exclusively for the use of the Westlington House Estate. (Information from J. T. Field, Haddenham Low, and field visit, 1980).

2.

Directories:

1847	Cox, Edwin Wm., farmer and brickmaker.

3.

Directories:

1863	Butcher, Thomas.
1864	Butcher, Edwin, farmer and brick maker.

4.

Directories:

1864-1865	Roads, Francis, farmer and brick manufacturer.

5.

Directories:

1891-1895	Sims, John, brickmaker.

HARDWICK

1. SP 806 204 Bushmead Road [CAS 5604].

'Brick & Tile Kilns' (Bryant, 1825); 'Kiln, Brickyard' (OS 25", 1st edition, 1880).

Directories:

1864	Howard, J., brick, tile and drain pipe manufacturer.

Visible features: none: site now occupied by a house and garden (Field visit, 1987).

HARTWELL

1. SP 804 125 Aylesbury Road [CAS 4094].

'Brickfield and Kilns' (OS 1st edition, 1877/85).

Directories:

1887	Locke, John, brick and tile maker.
1891-1931	Locke, R.W. brick and tile maker.

Similar entries under Aylesbury show that the offices were at Castle Street, later Buckingham Street, Aylesbury.

A large brickfield with three kilns, several pits and associated buildings. (OS 25", 1921).

Visible features: none. (Field visit, 1972).

38 AYLESBURY DIRECTORY.

P.O. Telephone No. 8. Telegrams—"LOCKE, Aylesbury."

R. W. LOCKE,

Brick, Tile, and Lime Manufacturer,

Building Material Merchant.

COAL MERCHANT,

AYLESBURY.

OFFICE—*18, Buckingham Street, Aylesbury.*

BRICK WORKS—*Hartwell, Aylesbury.*

SAND PITS—*Stone, Aylesbury.*

COAL DEPÔT—*London and North-Western Railway, Aylesbury.*

ESTABLISHED 1830.

Advertisement from the Aylesbury Directory 1911-12

HAZLEMERE

1. SU 884 950 Biblelands Society, Amersham Road [CAS 2426].

'Brick kiln' (Jeffreys, 1788)

'Brick kiln' (Bryant, 1825)

'Brickworks' (OS 6", 1st edition, 1885).

Thomas Floyd brickmaker Chepping Wycombe. (Posse Comitatus, 1798).

Directories:

1907-1920	Tilbury, Thos., Oakengrove Fm., brickmaker.

Area known as *The Kiln*. During construction of new buildings on site for Biblelands Society, vitrified bricks were observed. Many clay pits in area. (Field visit, 1974).

HEDGERLEY

1. SU 958 872 Pennlands Farm, Hedgerley Dean [CAS 2822].

'Brick kiln' (Bryant, 1825) 'Brick and tile works' (OS 6", 1st edition, 1877/85).

Directories:

1853	Piner, William, brick manufacturer.
1915	Piner, Frank, brick and tile maker.
1920	Kewlay, Richard, brick and tile maker.
1924	Kewlay, A.W.R., brick and tile maker.

'Hussey, William (28), brickmaker, Hedgerly Dean' (1861 Census Returns).

Directory entries for Piner, William and Henry, in 1847, 1853, 1864, 1865 under Gerrards Cross suggest they had an office or yard there.

Closed c. 1936. The Piner family were connected with Pennland as long ago as 1421. Certainly a Hedgerley brick was well known in the early 18th century. Main products were finest quality sand-faced buildings bricks, rubbing bricks, oven tiles and crown bricks for bakers' ovens: roofing and paving tiles. (Basden, 1966, 1967) (*see* Introduction).

Remains of a square Scotch kiln, a round lime kiln and a pottery kiln making flower-pots survived until the mid-1970s but have now been covered over by a new farmyard, although fragmentary flue holes of the pottery kiln are still visible. Mr. Healy remembers a kiln full of unfired pots at the time of the 1st World War. There was a pug mill originally driven by a horse, but later two pug mills were operated by a steam engine. There are remains of large quarries in the vicinity. A signpost on the A355 road to the farm still reads *Pennlands Kiln*. (Field visit, 1980, and information from Mr. Healy, Pennlands Farm).

2. SU 963 869 Andrew Hill [CAS 4747].

'Brick and Tile Works' (OS 6", 2nd edition, 1900).

These works were managed by the Saunders family, landpipes, flower-pots and some bricks were produced (Rice, 1980, 67).

Remains of the brick kiln survive in the garden of the house now standing on the site, incorporated in a garden feature. Nearby is a stamped floor-tile with the initials *H.H,* also a brick stamped *CSH* in deep frog which could refer to a member of the Healy family, known to have been brickmakers in the vicinity. (Field visit, 1980, and information from Mr. Healy, Pennlands Farm).

3.   SU 963 871 Andrew Hill [CAS 4746].

'Brick and Tile Works' (OS 6", 1st edition; 1875/83); 'Kiln' (OS 6", 2nd edition 1900).

Length of walling in road bank on E. side of Andrew Hill Lane is probably part of the kiln. Near the kiln site shown on OS maps many earthenware flower-pot sherds, field drain-pipe fragments etc were noted. That flower-pots were probably made is suggested by the *Potters Arms*, a former public house just north of the kiln. Samples of flower pots, field drain pipes and bricks (one inscribed *P* (?)) collected (BCM 1980.275; 1981.139). (Field visit, 1981).

HIGH WYCOMBE (*see also* BOOKER; HAZLEMERE)

1.   [SU 865 930] Paul's Row.

Directories:

1853   Burnham, William, brick and tile manufacturer, Paul's Row.

No evidence on maps for a brickworks. NGR to Paul's Row.

2.   [SU 861 934] 121-123 Oxford Road.

Directories:

1891   Looseley, R.W., 121 & 122 Oxford Road, brick and tile manufacturer.

1895   Looseley & Son and Pearce, 121, 122 and 123 Oxford Road, brick and tile manufacturer.

No evidence on maps for a brickworks. NGR to Oxford Road.

3.   [SU 856 935] Victoria Street.

Directories:

1948/9 Brick Bakers & Factories Ltd.,

No evidence on maps for a brickworks. NGR to Victoria Street.

4.   Reference in 1734 to Lord Shelburne's brick kiln which was apparently near Keep Hill (*Recs Bucks* 1897 **8**, 63).

HILLESDEN

1.   SP 669 301 Hillesdenwood Farm [CAS 1535].

'Brick Field', 'Kiln' (OS 25", 1st edition, 1880).

'Brickworks' (OS 6", 1900).

'Extensive brick and tile works, carried on by Mr. John Page', (Sheahan, 1862, 281).

A small brick building on site of kiln (as marked on OS 25" (1880) may be associated with the works. The site is very overgrown. The works had closed by about 1920. (Field visit, 1991).

HITCHAM

1.   SU 919 847.

'Part of Brick Field' (*Survey of the Parish and Manor of Hitcham*, 1770, BRO).

HUGHENDEN (*see also* HAZLEMERE; PENN; WALTERS ASH)

1.   [SU 892 973] Wycombe Heath.

References, in the 18th century, to the Shardeloes Estate brick kiln on Wycombe Heath, and large tract of land centred approximately at NGR, as shown on Jefferys, 1788 (Drake MSS, BRO).

HYDE HEATH

1.   SP 920 013 Chesham Road [CAS 0195].

'Brickworks' (OS 6", 2nd edition, 1900).

Directories:

1853   Kirby, Joseph, brick manufacturer.

1895   Mead, Abel, brickmaker.

1915   Mead, Jesse, brickmaker (also office: 176 Berkhamstead Road, Chesham).

1931-1939 Reed, Albert, Plantation Road, builder and contractor, timber merchant and brick maker.

While the works were operated by Albert Reed, a large double kiln was built and various innovations such as indoor drying were instituted, but they never re-opened after World War II. Eight brickmakers were employed (1928-1930) and ordinary facing bricks made. (BCM tape nos. 1 and 5: interview with H. Thatcher, who worked at the site, 1928-1930).

A chalk mine existed here in 1897, owner: A. Mead (*Report of H.M. Inspector of Mines*).

Visible remains: none. Various shallow pits are visible in the vicinity. (Field visit, 1979).

IVER

1.   TQ 044 805 Iver Court.

'Iver Court Brickworks' (OS 25", 1932).

Directories:

1827-1926 Reed, Edward Baron, Brickmaker.

1928-1940 Reed, E.B. & Co. Ltd., Iver Court Brickworks, brickmaker.

2.   [TQ 030 802] Shredding Green [CAS 5134].

Reference in 1725 and 1727 to Richard Bigg, brickmaker, and his kiln at Shredding Green (Ward & Block, 1993, 182, 193).

Directories:

1887   Mead, W. Shredding Green, brick maker and farmer.

1895-1911 Mead, William & Co. Ltd., brickmakers and farmer.

Although the site of Mead's brickworks is unknown, BCM records list prehistoric artefacts from Mead's Bridge Pit at NGR. Also *Mead's Cottages* are shown nearby on OS 6", 1960.

3.   [TQ 018 804] Parsonage Farm.

Directories:

1903-1907 Gibbons, Benjamin, Parsonage Farm, Shredding Green, brickmaker.

Although the site of Gibbons' brickworks is unknown, a small pit is shown on OS maps at NGR, adjacent to Parsonage Farm, Shredding Green.

4.   [TQ 043 805] Iver Court Farm.

Directories:

1895-1903 Studds, W. & J., Iver Court, farmers and brickmakers.

1907   Studds, Alfred, Iver Court Farm, farmer and brickmaker.

This site must have been near the Iver Court Brickworks (see Iver 1) and was, perhaps, a smaller concern represented by one of the numerous pits shown in the vicinity of the NGR above on OS maps.

5.   TQ 036 805 South-West of Iver village.

Directories:

1928   Everlasting Tile Co. Ltd.,

1931   Everlasting Tile, Concrete Products and Granite Supplies Ltd.

1935-1939 Everlasting Tile Co., concrete tile makers.

BCM records list prehistoric artefacts from the Everlasting Tile Company works at NGR. A works is shown here, but not marked as such, on OS 6", 1960.

6.   TQ 029 836 (approx) Iver Heath [CAS 5135].

Reference in 1741 to Richard Bigg, brickmaker and his brickworks at the coney warren at Iver Heath, formerly Warren Farm, now Ensbys] (Ward & Block, 1933, 193-194 and field visit, 1982).

IVINGHOE

1.   SP 927 182 Foxons Farm [CAS 5036].

'Brickfield' (OS 6", 1st edition, 1877/1884 'Old Kiln' (OS 6", 1960).

Directories:

1883   Ivinghoe and Horton Brick & Tile Co. (Foxen, Jasper, Foreman).

1887-1891 Ivinghoe & Horton Brick & Tile Co.

1895-1920 Foxon, T., brickmaker.

A small local yard making yellow-coloured bricks. The site is now occupied by a bungalow. No remains. (Information from J. Hawkins, Pitstone, 1979). Site was also dug for coprolites (*Recs Bucks* 1990, **32** 76-90).

.ACEY GREEN

.   SP 829 002 East of village [CAS 4398].

Brick Kiln' (Princes Risborough Inclosure Map, 810, BRO).

Reference to Lacey Green Kiln, 1752. (Hampden Estate Records, BRO).

Visible remains: none. The lane from Lacey Green village, passing near the site, is called Kiln Lane. Clay pits, now filled in, are remembered locally. (Field visit, 1979, and local information).

LANE END

1.   SU 802 909 Moore Common [CAS 4642].

'Brick works' (OS 6", 1st edition, 1876/83).

The site is now occupied by *Boundary House*, next to a property called *Old Kiln*.

Considerable terracing and quarrying are evident in the garden of *Boundary House*.

The brick kiln was demolished in the 1920s, some of the bricks being used in the construction of the house. There is also a chalk well, almost certainly pre-dating the brickworks, in the garden. (Information from S.J. Smith, Bolter End, and other local inhabitants, and field visit, 1980).

2.   SU 806 920 Handleton Common, adjacent to playing field [CAS 4665].

'Brick works' (OS 6", 2nd edition, 1900).

A brickyard worked by Edwards, which closed c. 1914, said to have had two bottle kilns. It was a one-man concern. (Information from S.J. Smith, Bolter End, 1979).

No remains of kiln, although much broken brick and tile are evident in the garden of a bungalow now occupying the site. Two circular areas of burning have been discovered in the garden, probably the site of the kiln. (Field visit, 1980).

No directory entries for Lane End, but *see also* BOLTER END.

LATIMER (*see* LEYHILL)

LAVENDON

1.   SP 929 542 NE of Uphoe Manor [CAS 5067].

'Brickfield', 'Limekiln' (OS 6", 1st edition, 1881/85).

Visible remains: none, although site is very overgrown (Field visit, 1981).

LEYHILL

1.   SP 986 023 Joiners Close [CAS 5612]: see Introduction

2.   SP 987 017 South of Leyhill Common [CAS 5348].

'Cowcroft Brickkiln', 'Brickfield', 'Clay Mills' (OS 6", 1st edition, 1873/83).

Directories:

1924, 1928   Rust & Ratcliffe Ltd., brick and tile makers.

1926   Rust & Ratcliffe Ltd., Cowcroft Brick and Tile Works.

1928   Steward, Wm. John, brick and tile makers.

1931-1939   Steward & Partners Ltd., Cowcroft Brick Works.

This yard had four kilns and made bricks and a full range of specials and tiles. It closed in the 1970s due to exhaustion of the clay pits. Latterly it was owned by Dunton Bros. Ltd. (BCM tape no. 2: interview with Dunton Bros. employees, January 1979).

3.   SP 987 012 South-East of Cowcroft Wood [CAS 5350].

'Brickworks' (OS 6", 1976).

This yard was opened in 1959 by Dunton Bros. Ltd. and still makes facing bricks (Chesham multies) and specials, using three oil-fired kilns. About ten people are employed, using a clay digger, a chain loader, roller crushers and a brick-making machine which produces 7,000 bricks per day. Six hand makers used to be employed. Clay resources are estimated to be good for another fifteen years. (BCM tape no. 1: interview with Dunton Bros. employees, 1979).

4.   SP 983 017 South-East of St. George's Church, Cowcroft Wood [CAS 5349].

'Brick Field', 'Brick Kiln' (OS 6", 1st edition, 1873/83).

This yard made tiles and closed many years ago. (Information from H. James, foreman at H.G. Matthews & Sons, Bellingdon, 1980).

No directory entries for Leyhill appear to correspond with this, but note: 1847 Woodhams, Wicken, Botley, brickmaker and farmer.

LITTLE BRICKHILL

1.   SP 907 327 West of village [CAS 1577].

Brickmaking and a tile-house are recorded in the 15th century (VCH 4, 299).

Two kilns were excavated in 1930 and again in 1968. Floor and roof tiles were made here in the late 15th and 16th centuries. The floor tiles were influenced by the famous decorated tiles made at Penn (*see* PENN 4) and were used in several churches in North Buckinghamshire and surrounding counties. Part of a pavement of Little Brickhill tiles, dated by a memorial brass to 1473, has been discovered in Great Linford church (*see* Introduction). Roof tiles from Brickhill were used in the repair of Wing church in 1527 and 1530. Bricks were used in the construction of the kilns and brick fragments were found during the excavation - probably made on site. (Mynard, D. C. 1975 'The Little Brickhill Tile Kilns and their Products', *Journal of the British Archaeological Association* 3rd series **38**, 55-80)
Fragments of bricks were found in excavations of the tile kilns and bricks were used in the tile kilns' construction. (Information from D.C. Mynard, MKAU).

LITTLE HORWOOD

1.   SP 799 322 About 1 mile north-east of village [CAS 5794].

'Kiln and Brickfield' (OS 6", 1st edition, 1878/85).

Directories:

1883-1895   Gunthorpe, Joseph, brick, tile and pipe maker.

1907-1915   Gunthorpe, J.J., brick maker.

Visible remains: 2 ponds probably represent former clay pits. No kiln structures survive. (Field visit, 1991).

LITTLE MISSENDEN (*see* PENN)

LITTLEWORTH

1.   SP 881 232 Soulbury Road, Chesterfield Crescent [CAS 1011].

'Brickfield and Kiln' (OS 6", 1st edition, 1879/85).

Directories:

1876-1887   Truman, George, brickmaker.

1892-1903   Webster & Cannon, brickmakers.

1907-1939   Faulkner, L.B., brickmakers.

'In the beginning of 1849 Rev. Richard Harris commenced the present extensive brick and tile works here. The soil is a blue clay. bricks, draining pipes, tiles, etc., are made here', (Sheahan, 1862, 783).

Visible features: none. Site now built on. (Field visits, 1977, 1980).

LONG CRENDON

1.   SP 697 082 South of village on Thame Road [CAS 1014].

'Brick Field and Kiln' (OS 6", 1st edition, 1878/85).

Directories:

1876-1883   Sims, Joseph, brickmaker.

1887-1891   Sims, John, brickmaker.
1899-1903   Brick & Tile Works (W. Blane, Manager).

Visible features: none, although extensive quarrying has taken place in adjacent wood. (Field visit, 1980).

LYE GREEN

1.   SP 975 030 South of Lye Green, by Brockhurst Farm [CAS 5164].

'Works Disused' (OS 6", prov. edition 1960).

Directories:

1948-1949   Brockhurst Brick Works.

MAIDS MORETON

1.

Directories:

1847   Barford, John, brickmaker.

No indication of the site of the brickworks although remains of quarries (e.g. at SP 702 361 and 711 and 357) may be possible areas. (OS maps and field visit, 1979).

MARLOW

1. SU 861 872 North-East of Marlow town centre [CAS 5055].

'Brickworks' (OS 6", 2nd edition, 1900).

'Thomas Webb, brickmaker, Great Marlow' (Posse Comitatus, 1798).

Directories:

| 1876 | Webb, James Alfred, Field House, Gt. Marlow, brickmaker. |
| 1911-1939 | Burnham and Marlow Brick Co. Ltd., Newtown, Newtown Road. |

Burnham and Marlow Brick Company made mainly yellow and multi-coloured stock bricks and some red facing bricks. A kiln and clamps were both used for firing. (BCM tape no. 3: interview with R. Ives of Marlow who worked as an engineer at the site in the 1930s).

2. SU 824 868 Marlow Common [CAS 4659].

'Brickworks' (OS 6", 1st edition, 1875/83).

No remains of the works survive, the site now being part of the terraced gardens of *Monks Corner*. Several pits in the immediate vicinity. It would seem likely that the works were operated by one of the brickmakers listed 5-8 below. (Field visit, 1980).

3. SU 825 870 Marlow Common [CAS 4660].

'Brick kiln' (OS 6", 1st edition, 1875/83).

No remains of the yard survive; the site being occupied by a modern house, 'Old Kiln House'. Several pits in the immediate vicinity. It would seem likely that the site was operated by one of the 'brickmakers' listed 4-8 below. (Field visit, 1980).

4. SU 834 869 Bovingdon Common.

'Brickworks'; 'kiln' (OS 25", 1st edition, 1876).

Directories:

| 1877 | Hewett, H.R., Bovingdon Green, brickmaker and lime burner. |
| 1883 | Hewett, H.R., High Street, Gt. Marlow, brickmaker and lime burner. |

5.

Directories:

| 1830 | Allum, Thomas William, High Street, brickmaker and lime burner. |

6.

Directories:

1830	Corby, Thomas, High Street, brickmaker and lime burner.
1842	Corby, Thomas & Son, High Street, brickmaker and lime burner.
1847	Corby, Thomas, brickmaker and

7.

Directories:

| 1853 | Hickman, Thomas, West St., Great Marlow, brick and tile manufacturer and shopkeeper. |

8.

Directories:

| 1891-1895 | Butler, T.B. High Street, Great Marlow, coal merchant, brick and tile and lime manufacturer. |

9. SU 825 867 Marlow Common [CAS 4757].

'Medmenham Pottery' (OS 2nd edition, 1900).

'A business opened in 1897 and closing around 1906. Although mainly producing 'art pottery' it also made unglazed terracotta ware, such as architectural decoration, tiles, mouldings, etc., Examples of the products may be seen on houses at Monks Corner, Marlow Common, and Westfield. Medmenham', (Plaisted, 1925, 314-5).

MEDMENHAM (*see also* MARLOW)

Part of a frieze at Monk's Corner made at the Medmenham Pottery

Tiles from Medmenham Pottery at BCM (1955.24; 1993.135)

1.

Directories:

| 1847 | Sawyer, Edmund, brickmaker. |

MENTMORE

1. SP 916 215 Adjacent to railway near Whaddon Farm [CAS 4766].

'Brick field', 'Kiln' (OS 6", 1st edition, 1879/85).

Directories:

| 1928-1931 | Leighton Buzzard Brick Co. Ltd., brickmakers, Ledburn. |

Apparently the brickyard for the Mentmore Estate, a receipt book for which, covering the years 1888-1898, is at BRO. The products printed on each receipt are as follows:

    Slop building bricks
    Machine building bricks
    2" draining pipes
    2 1/2" draining pipes
    3" draining pipes
    4" draining pipes
    Plain tiles.

Visible remains: site is very overgrown, although a waterfilled pit remains. Several derelict wooden sheds may be former drying sheds. Other structures may also be associated. (Field visit, 1981).

MIDDLE CLAYDON

1. SP 711 257 North-West of Claydon House [CAS 4489].

'Brick Field'; 'Brick and Tile Works'; 'Kiln' (OS 25", 1st edition, 1878).

Directories:

1864	Marshal, J., brickmaker.
1887-1907	Daniels, Williams, brick and tile maker.
1911-1915	Cox, Albert John, brick and tile maker.

'In a country witιout stone, brick making is one of the most important outdoor industries at Claydon (Feb. 1656): the brickyard is to be trenched and the brickmaking will come as soon as the weather permits... In 1656 the brickmaker is paid 6 shillings a hundred for making and burning "pavements".' (Verney, 1894, 132).

Although there is no documentary evidence to link the 17th century site with that at NGR, its proximity to Claydon House and the apparent absence of old workings elsewhere in the vicinity suggests they could be associated. (Field visit, 1979).

MURSLEY

1. SP 829 298 Salden House Farm [CAS 1533].

Excavations in 1967 located a row of ten brick clamps, which produced bricks identical to those used in the construction of Salden House in about 1580. The clamps were fired with locally-produced charcoal. (Information from Dr. P.N. Jarvis, Bletchley).

NAPHILL (*see* WALTERS ASH)

NASH

1. SP780 333 [CAS 4758].

Field at NGR is called 'The Brickyard' (Information from R. Unwin, Nash 1970).

NEWPORT PAGNELL

1. SP890 424 Broughton Road [CAS 4429].

'Brick Kilns', 'Brick Field' (OS 6", 1st edition, 1881/86).

Directories:

1830	Yates, William, London Road, brickmaker and lime burner.
1899-1903	Price, George Osborne, The Green, corn cake, coal, lime merchant, and brickmaker.
1907-1915	Price, G.O., corn cake, coal, lime merchant and brickmaker.

In the early years of this century the yard made bricks using an extrusion machine and drainage pipes. There was one kiln and the clay was dug by hand. Bricks from this site were used to build the Bury Street School and houses in Bury Street, Greenfield Road, Bury Avenue and Lovat Street, Newport Pagnell. George Prince also owned the much more modern yard at Great Linford. (Information from Walter King, who worked at the yard).

2.   SP 887 437 Chicheley Street [CAS 4878].

Directories:

1842   Mundy, Edward Miller, Shipley Wharf and Tickford End, brickmaker and lime burner.

1847   Goodman, Daniel, Tickford End, brickmaker.

1847   Ward, John, Tickford End, brick and tile maker.

1853   Rose, James, Tickford End, bricklayer, builder, brick and tile maker.

1853   Ward, John, Tickford End, brick and tile maker.

1864   Rose, J., Clay Lane, brick and pipe maker.

'The ancient craft of brickmaking was carried on in Tickford for centuries. The area abounds in clay and several pits have been worked over the years. Chicheley Street (Clay Lane) has produced large quantities and seams are intermixed with gravel over the whole district. Many of the houses were built of bricks produced in their own garden. The mechanisation of this industry killed the local craft, and all the pits are now closed', (Cole, 1967, 48).

'In 1851 James Rose of Clay Lane built Great Woodstone Rectory.....at a cost of £611', (Markham, 1975, 290).

Mr. Baylis of Tickfordfield Farm, Newport Pagnell, points out remains of extensive clay digging at NGR and recalls remains of brickworks existing in the early 20th century. (Field visit, 1980).

3.   SP 872 437 Old Shipley Wharf [CAS 5809].

Directories:

1830   Clarke, Shipley Wharf, brickmaker and lime burner.

1842   Mundy, Edward Miller, Shipley Wharf, brickmaker and lime burner.

'Newport had three principal brickyards, in Clay Lane, in the Brickfield along the Broughton Road, and at Shipley Wharf in Green End until 1859 when the clay 'gave out', (Markham, 1975, 289).

Shipley Wharf was at NGR. No remains of a brickworks except for a possible pit at SP 871 438. (Field visit, 1991).

4.

Directories:

1830   Walker, Richard, brick kilns, brickmaker and lime burner.

NEWTON LONGVILLE (*see also* BLETCHLEY; FENNY STRATFORD; WATER EATON)

1.   SP 852 325 North of Newton Longville near former Bletchley-Oxford railway line [CAS 5793].

'Brick Field' (OS 6", 1st edition, 1880/85)
'Brick Works' (OS 6", 1977).

Directories:

1847   Eitter, William, brick and tile maker.

1883   Gilkes, Geo., brickmaker.

1887-1895   Read, Charles, brickmaker.

1899   Read, John Thornton, brickmaker.

1903   Read, T., brickmaker and tile manufacturer.

1907-1915   Read and Andrews, brickmakers, Bletchley Steam Brick Works, manufacturers of all kinds of wire cut bricks .. noted for the celebrated red wire cut bricks.

1920-1931   Bletchley Bricks Co., manufacturers of all kinds of wire cut bricks.. noted for the celebrated red wire cut bricks.

1935-1939   London Brick Co. and Forders Ltd., brickmakers.

1940   Read & Andrews, The Bletchley Steam Brickworks.

1948-1949   Bletchley Brick Co. Ltd.,

'Just after 1890 John Thornton Read and his father, Thomas, opened a small traditional plastic brickworks on a five-acre site half a mile north of Newton Longville, and employed about a dozen men. Later Richard Andrews joined them and the firm of Read & Andrews made steady progress. Around 1919 Read & Andrews were joined by W.T. Lamb & Sons, and the Bletchley Brick Company was formed in 1923 with a capital of £60,000. They changed over to the Fletton methods in 1924. The works were acquired by the London Brick Company and Forders in 1929. In the 1930s the new works were erected on the opposite side of the Newton Road. The old site is now allotment gardens and a lake. Close by can be seen the remains of the great kilns that were the pride and joy of John Thornton Read. Nowadays [1975] the Bletchley brickworks make 4$^1/_4$ million bricks per week and employ 375 men', (Markham, 1975, 291-297).

Works closed Autumn 1990; of the original site one wall of one of the kilns survives, with five stoke-holes visible. Of the later works, two chimneys and various buildings survive. (Field visit, 1991).

NORTH CRAWLEY

1.

Directories:

1847   Dudley, John, brickmaker and farmer.

2.

Directories:

1864   Cave, J., beer retailer and brick and tile maker.

1865   Cave, James, Wren Park Brickworks, builder and contractor, brick and tile maker, and potter.

3.   SP 917 442 Newport Road; [CAS 4811].

'Brick field' (OS 6", 1st edition, 1881/86).

Directories:

1876-1887   Armstrong, W., farmer and brickmaker.

1891   Armstrong, W.N., farmer and brickmaker.

Although no connection has been found between the known site of a brickworks and Armstrong's works, the two are contemporary with each other.

Visible remains: a partly infilled clay pit in the NW corner of the site survives. (Field visit, 1980).

OLNEY

1.

Directories:

1830   Raban, John, High Street, brickmaker and lime burner.

2.

Directories:

1830   Todd, John Bridge Street, brickmaker and lime burner.

1847   Todd, John, Olney Ovens, beer retailer and brickmaker.

3.

Directories:

1847   Lord, Joseph, Dagnel Lane, brickmaker and maltster.

4.

Directories:

1864   Talbot, C., Market Place, farmer and brick manufacturer.

5.   SP 889 541 Olney Hyde [CAS 4995].

'Brick Field', 'Kiln' (OS 25", 1st edition, 1882).

Directories:

1876-1903   Talbot, William, The Hyde, farmer and brick and tile manufacturer.

Visible features: waterfilled clay pits. Site very overgrown. (Field visit, 1981).

6.   SP 881 541 Pasture Farm [CAS 5047].
'Brick Field', 'Brickkiln' (OS 25", 1st edition, 1881/85).

[Probably worked by one of OLNEY 1-4 above, the directory entries referring to offices in the town].

Visible features: waterfilled clay pits at SP 881 541 and 881 540. Much broken brick including overfired and mis-shapen bricks and drainage tiles are visible at the kiln site. (Field visit, 1981).

PADBURY

1. SP 712 299 Norbury, to west of village [CAS 5785].

'Brick field', 'Kilns', 'Clay pit' (OS 25", 1st edition, 1880).

Directories:

1853-1876	Foxley, Thomas, brick and tile make.
1883-1887	Foxley, William, brickmaker.
1891-1899	Foxley, Mrs R. brickmaker.
1903-1907	Foxley, Frank, brickmaker.

Visible features: remains of clay pit. Site very overgrown. Sample brick at BCM (1989.15).

PENN (*see also* TYLERS GREEN)

1. SU 925 954 Penn Street [CAS 2824].

'Brick and Tile Works' (OS 25", 1st edition, 1876).
Visible features: none. Cottages on the site predate the works. (Field visit, 1983).

2. SU 937 945 Glory Farm [CAS 2931].

A brick kiln was found during construction of a swimming-pool. The bricks were 1.75 inches thick. The sides of the kiln were built up of layers of roof tiles. The structure was dated to the early 17th century (information from J. Chenevix Trench, Coleshill, 1977).

3. SU 914 964 Wycombe Heath [CAS 5871].

Reference to the Shardeloes Estate brick kiln, 1750 and the making of "tyles, bricks, coping bricks" there (Shardeloes Estate Account Book 1747-68 at BRO).

Wycombe Heath was centred at NGR; a number of clay pits are visible in the vicinity. (Field visit, 1992).

4. SU 908 934 (approx.) [CAS 4244].

An important tileworks existed at Penn during the 14th century, making inlaid and patterned floor tiles as well as roof tiles. Several churches and houses were supplied as well as Windsor Castle (10,000 floor tiles were supplied in 1352 for the Warden's Hall at St George's, Windsor, at a cost of 6 shillings a thousand). (Hohler, C. 1941 'Medieval Pavingtiles in Buckinghamshire', *Recs Bucks* **14**, 1-49.

PRESTWOOD

1. SP 859 014 Aldridge Grove, Honor End Lane [CAS 5056].

Directories:

| 1903-1939 | Howard, Samuel, Kiln Lodge, brickmaker. |

A large brickyard started in 1895 by Samuel Howard initially employing about seven men. There were seven kilns and the yard produced both machine- and hand-made high grade facing bricks, and specialist bricks, including those made to match old bricks for repairs to buildings. In 1939 about eighty men were employed at peak periods. Temporarily closed in 1940, it was re-opened in 1949 by John Howard and finally closed in the 1950s. (Written information from John Howard of Portsmouth, 1979; BCM tape no. 4: interview with Mr. E. Buckland, 1979).

Description of the geology of the brickyard (Sherlock, 1922, 41).

The Pugmill at Howard's Brickyard, Prestwood, in about 1927

Photographs (BCM).

Visible features: site levelled. (Field visit, 1979).

2. SP 869 012 Kiln Common, Prestwood [CAS 2193].

'Brickworks'; 'Kiln; 'Claypit' (OS 25", 1st edition, 1877).

Directories:

| 1876-1907 | Groom, Solomon, shopkeeper and brickmaker. |

A small yard, burning bricks and lime. Solomon Groom died in 1907: his grave is in the Strict Zion Methodist Chapel graveyard, adjacent to his former yard, the older part of which is built from his bricks. The yard lost labour to Howard's brickyard when it opened in the 1890s (*see* PRESTWOOD 1 above). (Information from Mrs Hall, E. Buckland and Miss Groom, Prestwood, 1979).

The yard was originally worked by William Avery, prior to Groom (information from D.J. Keen, Preswood, 1980).

Visible features: site now developed. (Field visit, 1978).

Photographs (BCM).

3. Between Kiln Lane and Greenlands Lane.

Directories:

| 1877 | Essex, Elisha, brickmaker. |

Local residents (*see* PRESTWOOD 2) remember it as a small yard with one kiln.

4. SP 865 009 Nanfans.

In a meadow opposite the southern gates of Nanfans, near the present footpath to Stoney Green, were the remains of a brick kiln, defunct before 1850 (information from D.H. Keen, Prestwood, 1980).

In a corner of this field a depression may represent an old clay pit (information from Mrs L.M. Head, Wendover, 1985).

5. Entries in Great Hampden Parish Register from mid 17th to late 18th centuries refer to Tibbals of Prestwood, brickmakers. Hampden Estate Records and Lee Papers (BRO) refer to bricks supplied by Timothy Tibbals for Hampden House, 1740-1762 (also William Floyd)

and accounts from James Tibals for bricks and lime, 1683, and from Delafield for bricks, 1684 (information from Mrs L. M. Head, Wendover, 1985).

PRINCES RISBOROUGH

1. Nathaniel Winfield, brickmaker (Posse Comitatus, 1798).

QUAINTON

1. SP 732 192 Doddershall, NW of Quainton Road [CAS 4310].

'Kilns', 'Brick Field' (OS, 1st edition, 1878/85).

Directories:

| 1881-1895 | Hammond, James, Railway Arms P.H., brick and tile maker. |

'The Oxford clay ... was at one time well exposed in the Doddershall brickyard. The yellow bricks from this yard have been used in building the farmhouse by Raghall Station and various cottages at Westcott', (Moreton, 1929, 6-7).

Visible features: only pits remain. (Field visit, 1979).

Sample brick (BCM 1980.334).

2. SP 747 203 Behind windmill in centre of village [CAS 4184].

'Old Brick kiln' (OS 25", 1899).

'The brick kiln where bricks for the windmill were made and pits from which clay was dug may even now be seen behind the mill', (Parker, 1915, 8).

Visible features: possible outline of kiln and clay pits visible in field. (Field visit, 1978).

ROWSHAM (*see* WINGRAVE)

SALDEN (*see* MURSLEY)

SEER GREEN

1. 'Jesse Saunders (36), brickmaker, Seer Green'. (1861 Census returns).

SLAPTON

1. SP 931 202 Between village and Grand Union Canal.

'Brickfield' (OS 6", 1st edition, 1879/85).

Directories:

| 1847 | Howard, James, brickmaker. |
| 1877 | Foxon, James, brickmaker. |

'There are extensive works for the manufacture of bricks, draining tiles, etc here' (Sheahan, 742).

SOULBURY

1. SP 906 287 (area) Bragenham [CAS 5126].

Documents re brick-and-tile kiln in Soulbury, 1720 (Gurney 'Wills' in Bedfordshire County Record Office).

Documents of 1764 include account of bricks carried from "Bragnam Kiln" to Little Linford (BRO ref D/KN10).

Document of 1806 describes brick kiln for making and drying bricks at Kiln Piece near Kiln Farm and Bragenham Wood (Bedfordshire County Record Office).

'Kiln' at NGR (Bryant, 1825).

Extensive brick and tile works, the property of Colonel Hanmer (Sheahan, 748).

Exact site of works not located; hollows near Kiln Farm probably represent clay pits. (Field visit, 1981).

2.   SP 880 261 Brick Kiln Furlong [CAS 5128].

'Brick Kiln Furlong' at NGR (Lovett Estate Map, 1769, in BRO).

Possible indication of a brickworks.

STEEPLE CLAYDON   (see CALVERT)

STEWKLEY

..   SP 856 249 Wing Road [CAS 5786].

'Kiln and brick field' (OS 6", 1st edition, 1879/85).

Directories:

1877   Cole, W., farmer and brickmaker.

1883-1887   Griffin, Edward W., brick, tile and pipe maker.

Disused kiln and drying shed, behind cottage, extant in c.1920. *The Croft* built of bricks from works (R. Dickens, Stewkley, 1980).

Chimney at Hedges' Brickworks, Stewkley

account books/ledgers for works survive (M. Griffin, Bierton).

ponds (clay pits) remain. (Field visit, 1991).

2.   SP 848 250 Dunton Road, behind 'Kilnholm' [CAS 0622].

'Kiln' (OS 2", 1822) 'Brickfield and Kiln' (OS 1st edition, 1879/85).

Directories:

1864-1865   Hedges and Grace, brick, tile and draining pipe manufacture.

1876-1935   Hedges, J., The Warren, brick tile and pipe maker.

1939   Hedges, Hedley, J., brick and tile maker.

Made hand and later, wire-cut bricks, drainage pipes and tiles. It was owned and run by the Hedges, a local farming family. (BCM tape no. 3: interview with E. Keen, Stewkley, 1979).

Visible features: pits, chimney, ruined sheds and pug mill. (Field visit, 1979-1980).

Vince (1968).

Product samples BCM (1979.242-243).

3.   SP 846 248 Dunton, adjacent to Old Brick Farm [CAS 0620].

'Brickfield and Kilns' (OS 6", 1st edition, 1879/85).

Directories:

1864   Bliss, D., blacksmith, brick and tile and draining pipe manufacturer.

1876-1899   Bliss, J., brick, tile and drainpiper maker.

1903-1907   Bliss, Mrs. E.

1911-1924   Bliss, A.

Made bricks, drainage tiles and was able to make large diameter foot pipes on a special extrusion machine. Also some artistic modelling, date plaques, etc., in the early years of this century. (Vince, 1968; information form Mr. F. Keen, Stewkley, 1979, BCM tape no. 3).

Visible features: ruined Scotch kiln with five fire holes. Ruined sheds. Pits. (Field visits, 1979, 1980).

Drawing of a decorative brick made at Bliss' Brickworks, Stewkley

STOKE GOLDINGTON

1.   SP 839 486 East of village [CAS 0052].

'Brick field; kilns' (OS 6", 1st edition, 1881/85).

'Brick Works (Disused)' (OS 25", 1925).

Directories:

1864-1865   Bird, J., farmer, brickmaker and maltster.

1876-1891   Smith, Thomas, brick and tile merchant builder.

1899-1907   Bull, G. & Co., brick and tile makers.

Substantial remains of a Scotch kiln, with 3 firing chambers and 8 fireholes. A long shed may be a former drying shed. Buildings adjacent to the main street may have been offices. 2 large pits are probably former clay pits. (Field visit, 1981).

Product samples BCM (1981.126).

STOKE HAMMOND

1.   SP 882 294 Adjacent to Bell Inn [CAS 5759].

'Large piece of ground used as brickyard ... excellent strata of brickearth and a brick clamp therein' (Sale Notice, May 1820, BRO).

Site was at NGR: no remains (H.O. Allen, Stoke Hammond, 1991).

STOKE MANDEVILLE

1.   William Pedder, brickmaker (Posse Comitatus, 1798).

STOKENCHURCH

1.   SU 747 967 [CAS 5903].

Reference in 18th-19th centuries to chalk dug for use in Stokenchurch brick-kiln belonging to the Clerkes (*VCH Oxon* **8**, 33).

A brick kiln in *Kiln Close* is shown on Stokenchurch Tithe Map, 1842, where Kiln Farm is today (Starey C. J. H. and Viccars P. G. 1992 *Stokenchurch in Perspective,* 16).

STOKE POGES

1.   Reference in c. 1532 to "Wyllm Hudson and Wyllm Martin of Stoke" making and burning bricks within the King's park at Hampton Court and being paid 2s. 10d. per 1000 bricks. Indicates skilled workers being brought to Hampton Court for its rebuilding and, presumably, a brickworks at Stoke Poges (Musty J. 1990 'Brick Kilns and Tile Suppliers to Hampton Court Palace', *Archaeological Journal* **147**, 412).

STONE

1.   SP 792 126 [CAS 0659].

Slight evidence of clay extraction and brick manufacture, perhaps associated with Hartwell House. (Field visit, 1984).

STONY STRATFORD (see also CALVERTON; THORNBOROUGH)

1.

Directories:

1842   Wilkinson, George, Brickkilns, brickmaker.

2.

Directories:

1847   Freeman, Thomas, High Street,

3.

Directories:

1853   Hailey, Alfred, Wolverton Road, builder, contractor.. and brick and tile manufacturer.

STOWE

1.   SP 665 373 Boycott Manor [CAS 4896].

'Brick Field', 'Brick Kiln', 'Lime Kiln', 'Smithy' (OS 6", 1st edition, 1880/85).

Since there are no directory entries for Stowe, it is likely that these works were a private concern of the Stowe Estate.

No remains; former pits now landscaped into a water garden. (Field visit).

2.   SP 654 379 Hill Gate Spinney.
'Old Brick kiln' (OS 25" 1st edition, 1881).

3.   The Temple Family Papers Box III (Henry E. Huntingdon Library, California, USA) contain an agreement between Sir Richard Temple & Thomas Holding of Sysham [sic], Northants, brickmaker, Dec. 1665.

Stowe Repair Box 32 (also in Henry E. Huntingdon Library) contains miscellaneous papers on kilns, forestry, timber etc., 1770-1880.

TAPLOW

1.   SU 932 874 Wooburn Common.

'Brick Field' (Survey of the Parish & Manor of Hitcham, 1770) .

OS maps show quarries in vicinity.

THE LEE

1.   SP 901 051 Swan Bottom.

'Brickfield' (OS 6", 1st edition 1874/83).

Directories:

1876   Beeson, Charles.

2.   Deed of 1736 refers to James Hawkes of Great Missenden, brickmaker, and a cottage and

land adjoining, on Lee Common ('Calendar of Deeds' 1941 *Bucks Record Society* **5**, 41).

Various clay pits exist near Lee Common (formerly in Great Missenden parish) (OS 25", 1st edition, 1874/83).

THORNBOROUGH

1.

Directories:

1842   Boneham, Samuel, brickmaker and lime burner.

2.

Directories:

1842   Foxley, Thomas and John, brickmaker and lime burner.
1847-1865   Foxley, Thomas, brick and tile maker.

Similar directory entries under 'Stony Stratford' show that the offices were there.

3.   SP 735 325 Coombs [CAS 4905].

'Brick Field; kilns, clay pits' (OS 6", 1st edition, 1880/85) 'Works (Disused)' (OS 6", 1958).

Directories:

1876-1887   Bell, Robert, brickmaker, lime burner and farmer.

1891-1895   Bell, Robert, The Coombs, brickmaker, lime burner and farmer.

1900-1903   Chapman, Lewis John, The Coombs, brickmaker, lime burner and farmer.

Remains of a large clay pit survive. (Field visit, 1981).

TINGEWICK

1.   SP 652 330.

'Brick Field; Lime kiln' (OS 6", 1st edition, 1880/85).

Directories:

1876   Sharman, Amos, brick and tile maker.

Site now a cemetery (OS 6", 1959 and field visit, 1981).

2.   SP 657 328 Stockleys Lane [CAS 5536].

During development, the probable remains of a brick kiln - large pieces of brickwork, kiln lining and fragments of brick - were exposed. No actual remains of a kiln. 19th century? (Information from A. Houghton-Brown, Tingewick, 1986).

3.   Notes a brickmakers' contract of 1534 between a London brickmaker and St. Mary College of Winchester, Oxford, for the supply of bricks to be made at Stanton St. John, Oxon and 300,000 to be made at Tingewick, Bucks, in three kilns or clamps (Harvey, J. 1975 *Medieval Craftsmen*, 197-198).

TURVILLE

1.   SU 754 896 Southend.

'Brick Works'; 'Brick-kiln'; 'Quarry'; 'Clay Pit'.

TURWESTON

1.   'John Foxly, brickmaker' (Posse Comitatus, 1798).

Directories:

1853-1864   Foxley, James, brick and tile manufacturer.

No evidence on ground or on maps for brickworks. (Field visit, 1982).

TYLERS GREEN (*see also* PENN)

1.

Directories:

1903-1915   Wheeler, George, brickmaker and builder.

No evidence on ground or on maps for brickworks.

TYRINGHAM-WITH-FILGRAVE

1.   SP 880 489 Filgrave [CAS 1356].

'Brick & tile works on an extensive scale have been established at Filgrave nearly three years [1862]' (Sheahan, 626). 'No longer in existence' (*VCH Bucks* **4**, 482).

Area of burning exposed in ploughsoil was probably site of kiln (D.C. Mynard, MKAU, 1964).

UPPER WINCHENDON

1.   SP 734 143 Decoy Farm [CAS 5407].

'Brick kiln Yard', at NGR (Moreton, 1929).

Evidence of ground disturbance and a pond may mark the site of a small brickworks and clay pits (Field visit, 1977).

WALTERS ASH

1.   SP 836 982 West of Walters Ash [CAS 4782].

'Brick and Tile Works' (OS 6", 1st edition, 1874/85).

Directories:

1847-1853   West, Frederick, brickmaker.

1876   Free, Thomas, stone cutter, brick and lime kiln.

1876   West, Frederick, Naphill, coal, brick and lime merchant.

1883   Free, Thomas, stone cutter and brickmaker.

1887-1891   Free, Thomas & Sons, stone cutter and brickmaker.

This yard seems to have been worked by West and Free - no other yard is shown on contemporary maps in the vicinity. Although no structures survive, the ground is still uneven and pitted. (Local information and field visit, 1979).

2.   SP 838 984 North of Walters Ash [CAS 4783].

'Brickfield' (OS 6", 2nd edition, 1900) 'Works' (OS 6", 1922).

Directories:

1911-1949   Bristow, T. & Bros., brick and stone merchants.

This yard was very close to Brown's yard (*see* WALTERS ASH 3) and closed at the same time - about 1950. The site has now been built on by the RAF. (Field visit, 1979, and local information).

3.   SP 837 985 North of Walters Ash [CAS 4784].

'Works' (OS 6", 1922).

Directories:

1911-1920   Brown, James, brickmaker.

1924-1949   Brown Bros., Wells Brickfield, brickmakers, multi-coloured wall facings.

ьnis yard was very close to Bristow's yard (*see* WALTERS ASH 2) and closed at the same time - about 1950. The site has now been built on by the RAF. (Field visit, 1979, and local information).

WARRINGTON (*see* OLNEY)

WATER EATON (*see also* BLETCHLEY)

1.   SP 871 313 Slad Farm [CAS 6089].

'Brick   Works' (OS 6", 1977).

Directories:

1935-1939   Bletchley Flettons Ltd., brick manufacturers.

1948-1949   Flettons Ltd., Skew Bridge.

'In 1933 A.E. Lamb commenced the building of a new works at Skew Bridge, Slad Farm, the third largest works in the area.   A new company, Bletchley Flettons, was formed.   The new installations were bought by the London Brick Company and later christened 'Jubilee   Works'. Nowadays [1975] the Jubilee Works produce

1,300,000 bricks per week and employ ninety men', (Markham, 1975, 294-297).

Bases of 2 kilns remain; site derelict. (Field visit, 1991).

2.   SP 884 339 Between River Ouzel and Grand Union Canal.

'Kiln;   Brickfield' (OS 25", 1st edition, 1881) [CAS 6080]

Directories:

1847   Clarke,   Gregory   Odle... brickmaker and maltster.

1853-1891   Clarke, Gregory, Ton Yard Wharf, London Road, brick and tile maker.

[Similar directory entries under Fenny Stratford show the offices were in the High Street there].

'In   Fenny Stratford the most prominent brickmaker around 1820-1870 was a man of many activities Gregory Odell Clarke, who set up business as a coal, timber, slate and iron merchant, and brick and tile maker, at Ton Yard Wharf, London Road. Clarke's brickworks were originally confined to the rear of Watling Terrace between the river Ouzel and the canal, but they were extended before 1869 to include the land behind the canal wharf. Following his death, the works were run by his son, William Edward Clarke. By 1877 Clarke had brickworks, coal wharves and offices at Simpson, Water Eaton, Woburn Sands and Ridgmont', (Markham, 1975, 290).

Site is now part of a recreation park. (Field visit and OS 6", 1977).

3.   SP 893 331 Water Eaton Road, South Side.

'Brick   Field; Kiln' (OS 25", 1st edition, 1881) [CAS 6081].

Perhaps one of Clarke's new works, following his expanding business from about 1877; (*see* WATER EATON 2 above).

Site now built over; no visible remains of works.

4.   SP 870 327 Home Farm [CAS 6088].

'Works'   (OS 6", 1958).

Directories:

1935-1939   Flettons Ltd.

'Water   Eaton Works, created in 1929 for Flettons Ltd., whose main works were at Whittlesea, Peterborough. This works was built on Home Farm, Water Eaton and was capable of producing 60 million bricks per annum and about two hundred men were employed up to the war years...   Around 1970 Milton Keynes Development Corporation bought up Flettons Ltd., partly for housing development and partly for park space', (Markham, 1975, 294, 297).

Site now landscaped as "Blue Lagoon Park", 1990, clay pits becoming lakes. No structures. (Field visit, 1991).

WATER STRATFORD

1.   Lease of brick kiln and quarry, 1828 (document PR219 in BRO).

WENDOVER

1.   References in March 1688/9 to a brick kiln on Birche's peece, Wendover] ('Calendar of Deeds' 1941 *Bucks Record Society* 5, 69).

WEST WYCOMBE (*see also* WHEELER END)

1.   SU 820 962 Hearnton Wood.

'Brick   kiln' (Map of the Manor of West Wycombe, 1767, in possession of Sir Francis Dashwood Bt, West Wycombe Park).

Visible features: a mass of flint tumble and brick, presumably remains of the kiln.   Pits are still visible to the north and south of the site. (Field visit, 1973).

2.   'William   Carr, tile maker aged 60' (1851 Census Returns).

WHADDON

1.   SP 810 347 Whaddon Park [CAS 5667]. Area of dry crumbly fired clay, with several fragments of poorly fired brick, noted in a

ploughed field. An oval-shaped area probably represents a brick clamp site. (Field visit, 1988).

WHEELER END

1.   [SU 802 930].

Directories:

1842   Bigg, John, brickmaker and lime burner.

No indication of brickworks on maps, but quarry indicated (OS 6", 1st edition, 1876/83) and marked 'Old   Quarry' (OS 25", 1921) at NGR. Also *Brickmakers Arms* public house in vicinity.

WHITCHURCH

1.   SP 806 204 Bushmead Road [CAS 4308].

'Kiln   and Brick Field' (OS 6", 1st edition, 1873/83).

Directories:

1830   Denchfield, Richard, brickmaker and farmer.

1864-1865   Grace, W.

1876   Beasley, Anthony, brickmaker.

1883-1895   Beasley, George, brickmaker.

1899-1903   Cannon, T., brickmaker.

1907   Cannon, John, brickmaker.

1911   Cannon,   Thos. John Nash, builder,   brickmaker   and undertaker.

A small yard with one updraught kiln (approx. seven fire holes). One lime kiln. Made bricks and tiles and burnt lime. By the 1920s it was solely making bricks and burning lime; clay was dug on site but sand and limestone were quarried from pits to the north of the village, on the Oving road. Although output was small, only about 50,000 bricks a year in the 1920s, the Whitchurch product was held to be a high quality facing brick. Closed in the early 1930s. (Information from Arthur Adams, Whitchurch, who worked at the yard as a clay digger in the 1920s).

Visible features: foundation of lime kiln, shed, pits. (Field visit, 1980).

Workers at Whitchurch Brickyard in about 1910

Photograph c. 1910 (BCM).

WING (*see* LITTLEWORTH)

WINGRAVE

1.   SP 851 193 Rowsham Barn [CAS 2988].

'Rush   Dean Brick Kilns' (Bryant, 1825) 'Brick Field and Kiln' (OS 1st edition, 1879/85).

Visible features: pits. (Field visit, 1980).

WINSLOW

1.

Directories:

1842   Staniford, Richard, High Street, lime burner and brickmaker.

2.

Directories:

1864   Allen, T., High Street, builder and brick and tile maker.

3.   SP 767 272 Tinkers End [CAS 5069].

'Kiln', 'Brickfield' (OS 6", 1st edition, 1878/85).

Directories:

1877   Clarke, John, brick and tile maker, Tinkers End.

1883-1891   Clark, Robert, brick and tile maker, Tinkers End.

No visible remains except for amorphous earthworks in pasture field. (Field visit, 1981).

4.   SP 769 285 North of railway station [CAS 5069].

'Brick Works' (OS 6", 2nd edition, 1900).

Directories:

1877   Buckingham, W., brick and tile make, Railway Wharf.

1883   Foxley, William, Railway Wharf, brickmaker.

1903-1907   Ridgway, William, brickmaker.

Kiln finally demolished in 1970s. Buckingham started the works c.1868, carrying on till early 1900s. (Information from A.H. Wigley, Winslow, 1980).

5.   SP 767 279(?) Norden [CAS 5091].

[Describing building of Winslow Hall, c.1700]. 'Some bricks provided locally, from John Stutsbery, subsidised to the extent of £20 "for building ye middle kiln in Norden"' (*Recs. Bucks* 1926 **11**, 412ff).

Norden was at NGR. At SP 767 279 a circular line of bricks may be a kiln; remains of quarrying nearby. (Information from A.H. Wigley, Winslow, 1980 and field visit, 1981).

6.   Propectus of the 'Buckingham Brick & Tile Co. Ltd', 1928 proposing to set up a brickworks on the Roddimore Estate (SP 7729). Not all the 580,000 shares on offer were taken up and the project was abandoned. (Information from A.H. Wigley, Winslow, 1980).

WOBURN SANDS

1.   SP 923 364 North of railway, between railway and the Wavendon road. [CAS 4833].

'Brick Field', 'Kilns' (OS 6", 1st edition, 1880/85).

'Fullers Earth Works' (OS 6", 2nd edition, 1900).

Later maps show the site as a series of waterfilled pits.

No structures survive; site now developed. (Field visit, 1980).

2.   SP 925 363 Station Road, south of station [CAS 4834].

'Brick Field', 'Kiln' (OS 6", 1st edition,

Directories:

1920-1924   Dudley & Sons Ltd., brick and tile manufacturers.

1928-1939   Dudley, C. & Sons Ltd., Station Road, roofing tile manufacturers.

1940   Dudley, Charles, Station Road.

No features visible; site now developed. (Field visit, 1980).

3.   SP 927 360 Station Road, east side [CAS 4835].

'Brick Field', 'Kiln' (OS 6", 1st edition, 1880/85).
No features visible; site now developed. (Field visit, 1980).

4.   SP 921 362 South of railway, west of station [CAS 4836].

'Brick works' (OS 6", 2nd edition, 1900) 'Brick works (disused)' (OS Prov. edition, 1952).

Directories:

1920-1924   Eastwood & Co. Ltd., brickworks

1940   Fletton Brick Co., Station Road.

This was the site of Eastwood's works. (Information from Miss M. Jackson, Wavendon).

Copy of photograph of works, c. 1900 (BCM).

A length of wall of a Scotch kiln with 6 stoke holes visible survives; also waterfilled pits. (Field visit, 1990).

WOLVERTON (*see* CALVERTON: STONY STRATFORD)

WOOBURN (*see also* BEACONSFIELD; TAPLOW)

1.   SU 909 890 White Pit Lane, Wooburn Green [CAS 4756].

'Brick Works' (OS 2nd edition, 1900).

Various brickmakers including Andrew/Andrews, Hughes, Smith, recorded in Posse Comitatus, 1798.

Directories:

1847   Andrews, John, Green, brick & tile manufacturer.

1915   Nash, Fred, Wooburn Green, brickmaker.

2.   SU 908 870 Niplands, Hawks Hill [CAS 1175].

'Limekiln'; 'Kiln'; 'Brickworks' (OS 6", 1st edition, 1875/82; 1914 edition).

Directories:

1876,1883   Billinghurst, Mrs. Rosa, Chequers, brick & lime works.

1847   Wethered, William, Common, brickmaker.

1887   Lynn, William, Common, Niplands Kiln, brick, lime & tile manufacturer.

1891   Lyne, William, Common, Niplands kiln, brick kiln.

'Niplands, where there was a kiln for bricks and tiles in the eighteenth century' (*VCH* 3, 107).

Wooburn Enclosure Map, 1803, shows *Niplands* in area of NGR above, although a brickworks is not shown here.

Slight remains survive of the lime kiln. The remainder of the site has been levelled for a recreation area. (Field visit, 1978).

3.

Directories:

1853   Pegg, William, paper, brick and tile manufacturer.

WOODHAM

1.   SP 707 186 North of Akeman Street near former Akeman Street Station.

'Works' (OS 6", Prov. edition, 1942).

Directories:

1939   Woodham Brick Co. Ltd., brickmakers.

Brickworks consisted of four Hoffman type kilns erected in 1937. There were also pug mills and two rotary grinders and a sandblaster. The material was lifted onto overhead hoppers and then dropped into six brickpressing machines each forming two frogged bricks at each pressing. The works were demolished in the 1970s and the site is now used for light industry. (Information from Dr. P.N. Jarvis, Bletchley).

WOTTON UNDERWOOD

1.   SP 683 177 South-East of Tittershall Wood [CAS 4646].

'Brick and Tiles Works' (OS 6", 1st edition, 1878/80).

Directories:

1865   Foot, William, brick and tile maker.

Visible features: none. (Field visit, 1980).

2.   SP 699 144 West of Hill Farm, Ashendon [CAS 0038].

'Brickfield'; 'Kiln'; 'Limekiln' (OS 25", 1st edition, 1880).

Situated just inside the parish boundary. Perhaps associated with Hill Farm.

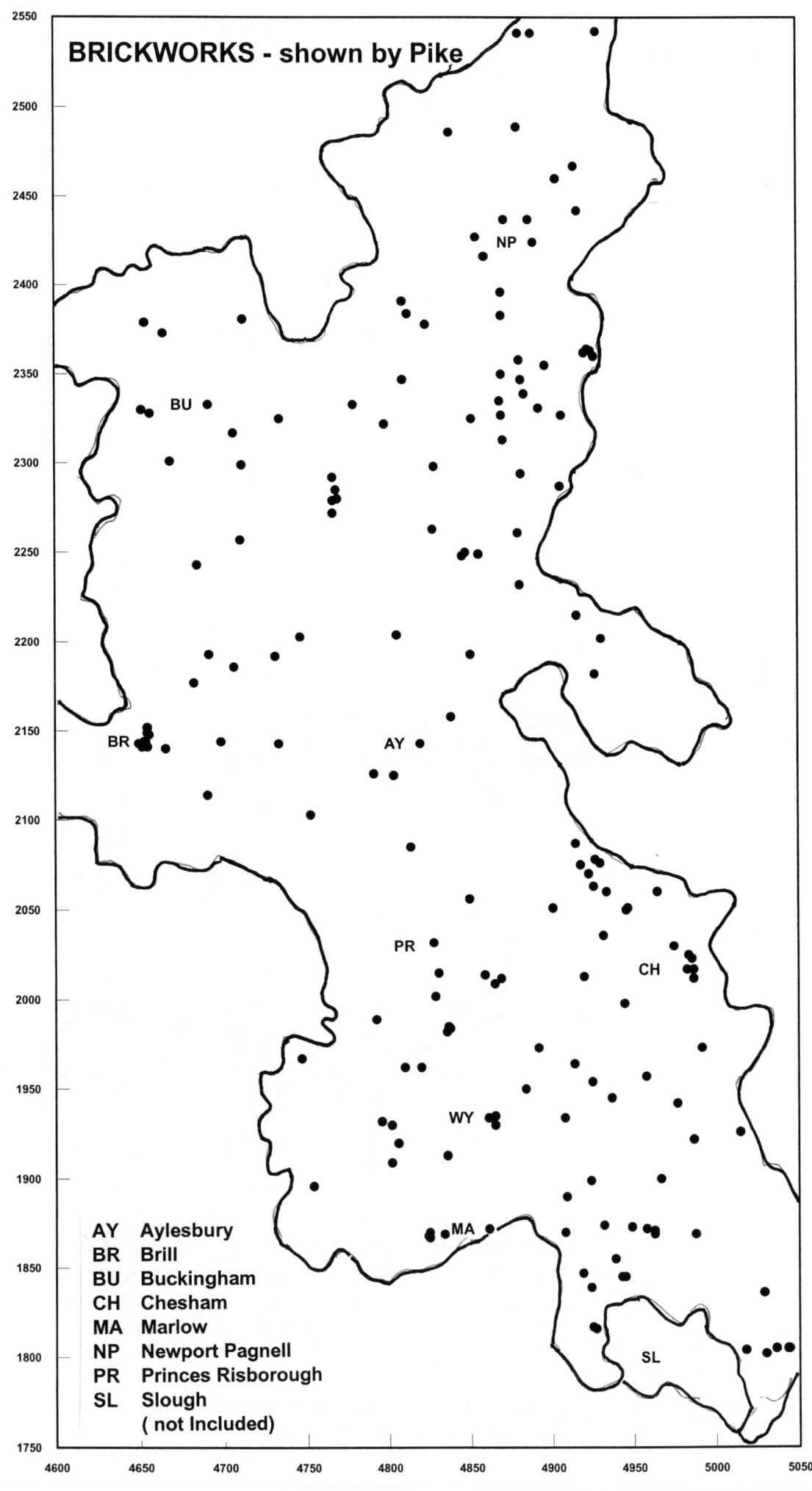

BRICKWORKS - shown by Pike

AY	Aylesbury
BR	Brill
BU	Buckingham
CH	Chesham
MA	Marlow
NP	Newport Pagnell
PR	Princes Risborough
SL	Slough
	(not Included)

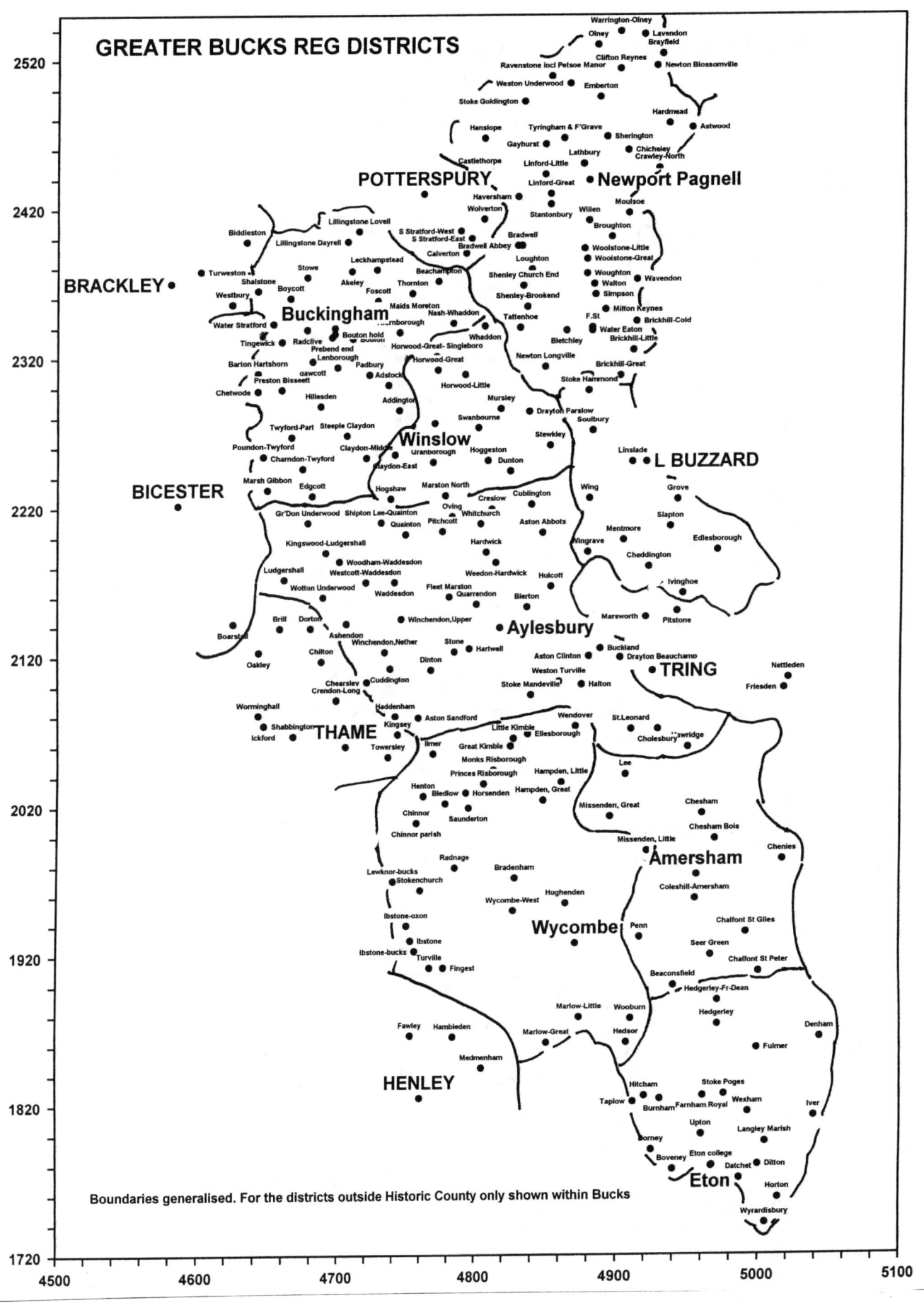

GREATER BUCKS REG DISTRICTS

Boundaries generalised. For the districts outside Historic County only shown within Bucks

The 1851, 1861 & 1871 Censuses published figures by Registration District (see below).
This map shows the boundaries of the areas.

BUCKINGHAMSHIRE INDUSTRIAL OCCUPATIONS & INDUSTRIES 1841-1951

Statistical materials for a cross-sectional study & an examination of change

DAVID THORPE

This paper provides, through a series of tables, graphs and maps, information from which a detailed statistical picture of the county's industries can be obtained. It is part of a project that is examining change in the overall occupational structure of the county. It is published on the occasion of the Bucks Local History Networks' Conference on Bucks Industrial Heritage in October 2007.

The material has been drawn from the published Reports of each census from 1841 to 1951. These reports are now available in 'image form' on the invaluable web-site, 'www.histpop.org,' *Histpop - The Online Historical Population Reports'*. (This site is an AHDS History project, funded as part of the JISC Digitisation programme and is hosted by the UK Data Archive at the University of Essex). This site goes far beyond the basic population reports with a wealth of textual and statistical material that provide an in-depth view of the economy, society (through births, deaths and marriages) and medicine during the nineteenth and early twentieth centuries. It contains 200,000 pages of census and registration material for the British Isles supported by numerous ancillary documents from The National Archives, critical essays and transcriptions of important legislation that provide an aid to understanding the context, content and creation of the collection. It should be noted that the original census tables are difficult to consult in that they frequently extend over several pages

Two sites contain data from many of these reports in machine-readable format. The first is *'Vision of Britain Through Time'* but this does not house much material at a local level on occupations (1841 summary and 1951 Occupations. The other *'The Great Britain Historical Database'* is limited to those with a University access. Since the objective here has been to convert the census data into 'information' by comparing figures for Buckinghamshire with national figures and for areas within Bucks with the rest of the county and similar ones elsewhere it was found easier to rely on the original tables. Data for 1851 at Registration District level has been provided by David Gatley of the University of Staffordshire

Text is kept to a minimum as the intention is not to provide a reasoned account of change but is designed only to aid an understanding of the tables, graphs and maps. As the 1851 Census provided far more data than 1841 the notes on 1851 (pages 53-74) include an explanation of much of the approach. 1851 is used as base to describe the evolution of the county's industries to 1951. Special attention is also given to 1921, a census that provided more information than its predecessors. This year is also useful as it captures the structure of the county's industries before the full effect of the Slough Trading Estate, and other inter-war developments, changed much of the structure of the county's industries.

The presentation of material is designed to assist those with who want to focus on a given census (perhaps exploring local detail from the Enumerators' Books), a particular industry overtime or a part of the country.

One technicality needs special explanation. In order to assess the relative importance of an industry calculations have been made of LOCATION QUOTIENTS. These are calculated as follows:

(Percentage of the local population in a given occupation)
times 100 divided by
(Percentage of the national population in a given occupation)

Local Abbreviations

AM	Amersham		**BU**	Buckingham
ET	Eton		**HE**	Henley
WY	Wycombe		**TH**	Thame
AY	Aylesbury		**PO**	Potterspury
WI	Winslow		**LB**	Leighton Buzzard
NP	Newport Pagnell			

Higgs has warned that who seek to use the censuses should be aware of the processes of their construction and that the information in the census is not necessarily in the form that modern historians assume. This cautionary note is one that has been constantly in mind when preparing the pages that follow. Higgs book, *Making Sense of the Census Revisited, the Census records for England and Wales 1801-1901* should be consulted by those who might use these pages. In particular, his chapter, 'Occupations in the Census', ought to be required reading. Woollard's article on the internet *The Classification of Occupations in the 1881 British Census* found at <u>privatewww.essex.ac.uk/~matthew/work/occlass.htm</u> is an another very useful introduction to the problems that arise when using the censuses

Given the array of material that follows it is worth starting with a single graph that shows, as far as possible, changes in the number employed in the major occupations/industries in the county. Given that were changes in the geographical definition this can only be an approximate expression of change. It should be noted that figures for some industries have yet to be established for 1951.

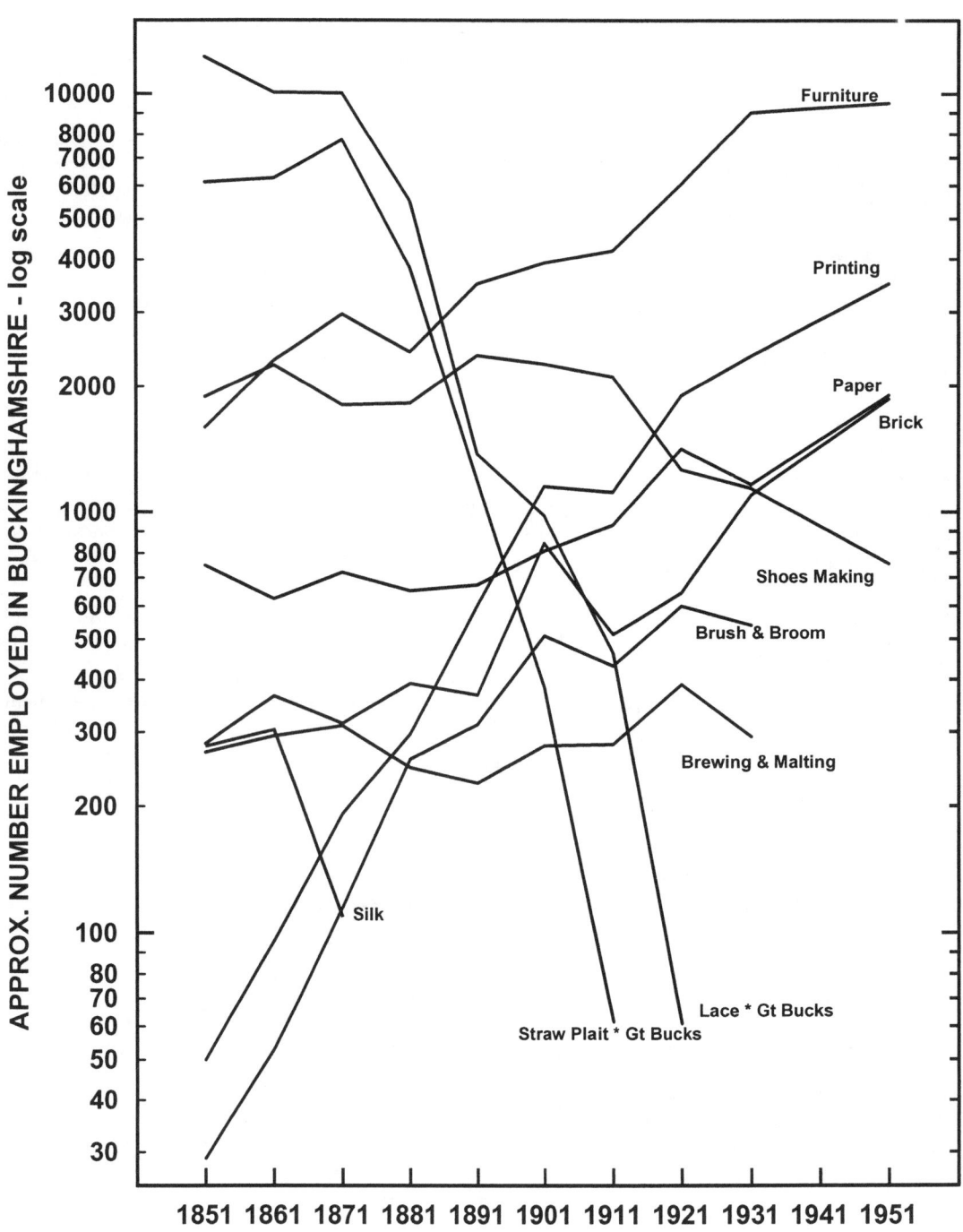

INDUSTRIAL OCCUPATIONS IN 1841

Those who have studied the Census enumerators' books, and nineteenth century directories, are aware that in the period many people had more than one occupation. The Census tabulations of occupations had to ignore such complex arrangements. The tables that follow both for 1841 and later years are only an approximation of the structure of employment.

The 1841 census provided the first generally reliable count of the number of persons in different occupations, although at a local level the information with one exception was printed in a form that makes comparisons between counties difficult. The information was published for historic counties, certain boroughs and a mix of administrative units in the industrial counties. In Bucks only for the Borough of Buckingham were local figures given.

A national table provides comparison between counties and a total for England & Wales for 16 categories of employment. It emphasises Bucks agricultural role with nearly twice the proportion employed in the county in that industry as in England & Wales as a whole. There was, however, a higher proportion of females in commerce, trade & manufacture in the county than in the country but a lower proportion in domestic service. This last activity was more important in the county amongst the male population. This may have been in part the result of living-in 'servants' in farms being classed as domestic servants.

	Number in Buckinghamshire					Bucks Percentage of England & Wales				
	Male 20+	Male <20	Female 20+	Female <20	Total	Male 20+	Male <20	Female 20+	Female <20	Total
Commerce, trade & manufacture	11188	1422	5310	1744	19664	0.635	0.443	1.348	1.089	0.746
Farmers & graziers	2256	40	169		2465	0.980	1.481	0.874		0.977
Agricultural labourers	15681	2702	341	136	18860	2.023	1.716	1.196	1.473	1.943
Gardeners, nurserymen, florists	545	20	6	1	572	1.245	0.895	0.550	0.794	1.211
TOTAL Agriculture	18482	2762	516	137	21897	1.761	1.701	1.054	1.464	1.724
Labourers	2345	294	552	23	3214	0.484	0.345	0.552	0.315	0.475
Army	50	5			55	0.161	0.077			0.146
Navy	186	8			194	0.207	0.106			0.199
Clerical Profession	311				311	1.511				1.511
Legal Profession	70				70	0.491				0.491
Medical Profession incl females	104				104	0.559				0.559
Other educated	371	21	237	14	643	0.453	0.196	0.781	0.760	0.515
Government civil service	65	1	8	1	75	0.484	0.457	1.538	6.667	0.529
Parish, town church officers	132		13		145	0.660	0.000	0.706	0.000	0.653
Domestic servants	1830	1248	3702	1870	8650	1.214	1.487	0.771	0.641	0.859
Independent	928	32	2018	106	3084	0.767	0.617	0.645	0.739	0.681
Alms, prisoners, paupers	616	366	598	266	1846	0.939	1.299	0.991	1.142	1.041
Total above	36678	6159	12954	4161	59952	0.935	0.866	0.907	0.819	0.912
Total with above occupations	36668	6164	12959	4161	59952	0.935	0.864	0.906	0.819	0.912
	10	-5	-5	0	0					
Others	2782	30868	30205	32176	96031	1.155	1.043	0.979	1.011	1.015
Total	39450	37032	43164	36337	155983	0.948	1.009	0.956	0.985	0.973

The full county table provides information for 288 different occupations, although 99 of these had fewer than 5 individuals in them. In the national abstract those in commerce and trade were divided 'as far as possible' into manufacture as opposed to commerce and trade. Such a division reveals that Bucks had 0.832% of those in the former class and only 0.684% in the latter, figures both well below that of the county's share of the total population (0.973%). Moreover, 74% of those in manufacturing in Bucks were female.

Full figures for the substantial manufacturing industries in Bucks show considerable differences in the employment of those aged under 20 compared with England & Wales as a whole.

	Number in Buckinghamshire					% of Total England & Wales				
	Male 20+	Male <20	Female 20+	Female <20	Total	Male 20+	Male <20	Female 20+	Female <20	Total
Lace maker	45	45	3448	902	4440	0.84	4.20	23.90	15.95	16.77
Straw plaiter	21	130	617	564	1332	4.70	26.53	10.82	17.84	13.59
Chair maker	398	62	7	1	468	9.85	10.63	2.93	2.33	9.54
Paper maker	274	22	29	8	333	7.18	3.75	3.22	2.06	5.85
Brick & tile maker	135	15			150	0.95	0.59	0.00	0.00	0.87
Silk manufacture	28	36	29	51	144	0.16	0.56	0.16	0.43	0.27
Cabinet maker	71	17	4		92	0.35	0.45	0.21	0.00	0.35
Turner	68	10		1	79	1.33	1.10	0.00	5.00	1.29
Basket maker	48	7	1		56	0.98	1.34	0.37	0.00	0.98
Mat maker	41	6	4		51	6.50	6.74	3.81	0.00	6.12

The figures for Buckingham Borough, an area that was far larger than the town, reveal a town with little manufacturing

	Number in Buckingham Borough					Buckingham % Bucks County				
	Male 20+	Male <20	Female 20+	Female <20	All	Male 20+	Male <20	Female 20+	Female <20	All
Military	10				10	11.8	0.0			11.0
Government	16		3		19	7.1	0.0	13.0	0.0	7.6
Professional	43		12	2	57	5.1	0.0	3.6	11.1	4.6
Commerce	392	65	35	18	510	4.1	7.3	3.1	9.8	4.3
Labourers	93	8	4		105	4.5	2.7	1.2	0.0	3.8
Domestic Service	31	39	109	58	237	1.7	3.1	2.9	3.1	2.7
Agriculture	258	45	1	1	305	1.4	1.6	0.2	0.7	1.4
Manufacturing	36	5	21	11	73	2.3	1.3	0.5	0.7	0.9
Total Occupied	879	162	185	90	1316	2.5	2.9	1.8	2.4	2.4
Trade not specified	5	1	1		7	3.4	0.7	5.6	0.0	2.1
Independent	34		86	4	124	3.7	0.0	4.3	3.8	4.0
Alms people	27	42	40	40	149	5.3	12.6	6.8	15.1	8.8
Vagrants prisoners	10		1		11	2.9	0.0	0.8	0.0	2.2
'Residue'	76	669	894	814	2453	2.7	2.2	3.0	2.5	2.6
Total	1028	873	1207	948	4056	2.6	2.4	2.8	2.6	2.6

For the county as a whole individual occupations are shown on the graph below.

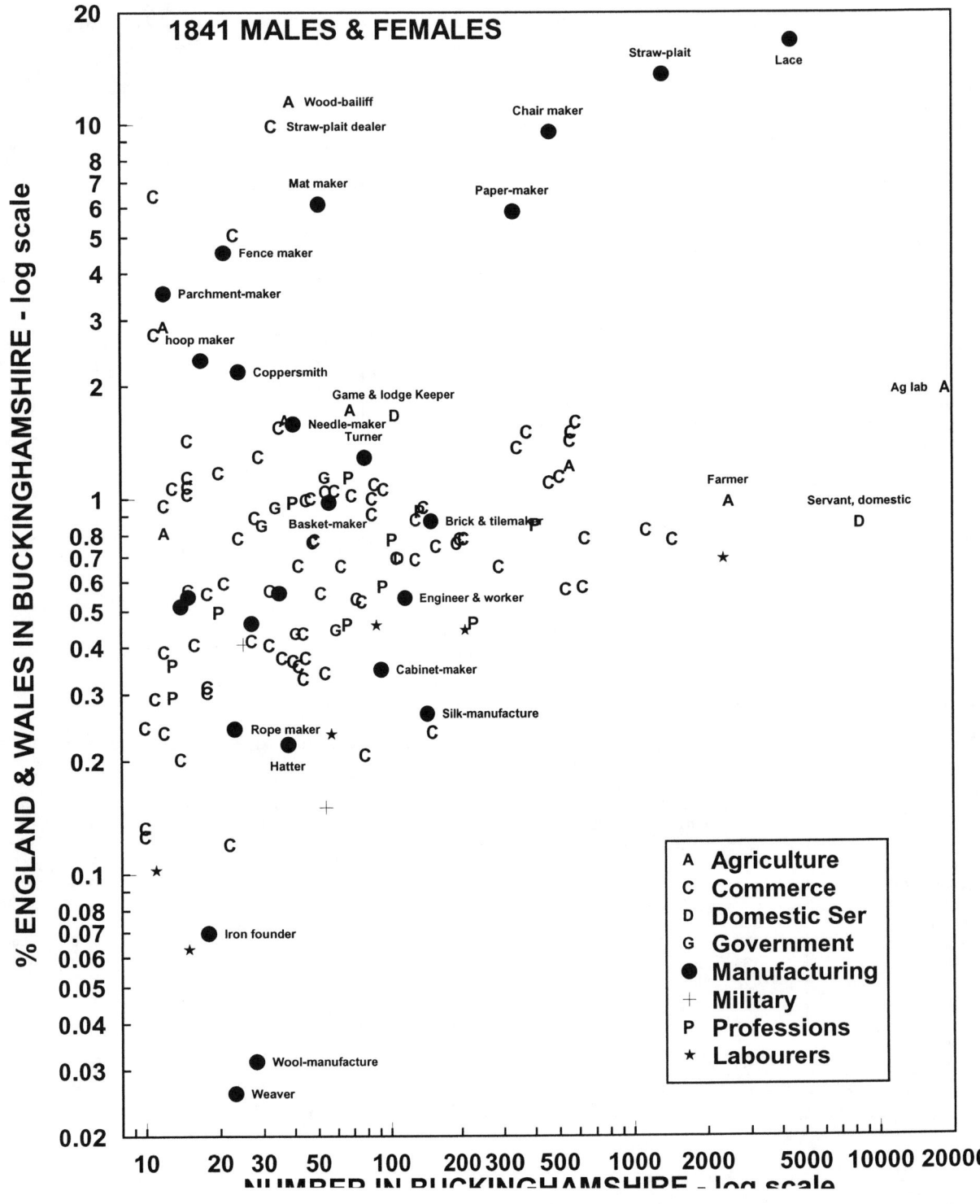

INDUSTRIAL OCCUPATIONS IN 1851

The first Census to provide full information on occupations was 1851 (1841 had provided some information but with less precision). Figures for 322 male and 198 female categories were published for Registration Counties and Districts, although for the latter only those aged 20 or more (of these 280 and 136 were present in Greater Bucks amongst those aged 20+)

The use of the registration geography is a problem for a study of Buckinghamshire as many Bucks parishes were in Registration Districts (RDs) in other counties. For example, Hambleden lay in Henley RD and Brill in Thame RD both in Oxfordshire, Stony Stratford and Wolverton in Potterspury RD in Northamptonshire, and Wing and Ivinghoe in Leighton Buzzard RD in Bedfordshire. To allow for these losses the county figures below are given for a 'Greater Bucks' area by including the whole of these RDs even though this brings into the account Henley, Thame, Leighton Buzzard and parts of Salcey Forest. To exclude these RDs would mean that very significant features in Buckinghamshire's industrial character would be missed (especially the Wolverton Works and the core of the straw plaiting area).

The basic figures are in the tables on pages 59-61. Graphs on pages 62-63 show the importance of various occupations in Greater Bucks amongst those aged 20+.

The graphs and the tables provide information on the two ways of measuring significance: the absolute number employed in each occupation and the number relative to the total number of persons in each area. The latter is measured either as the percentage of the England & Wales total in the occupation found locally or by a 'location quotient'. 'Location quotients'(LQ) are calculated by dividing the percentage that were locally in an occupation by the percentage that were in that occupation nationally, expressing the result in index form so that a quotient of 100 means that the local significance of the industry was precisely the same as the national significance. For example if 2% of area's adult population were found in a given industry and the national percentage was 4% the LQ would be 50% and if the national proportion was 1% the LQ would be 200.

Using Location Quotients as the measure of significance, certain male occupations in Bucks in RDs were rated very highly nationally:

a) **Wycombe RD** – chairmakers 1st, papermakers 1st, others in horticulture 1st (water-cress?), sawyers 2nd, others in Arboriculture 5th

b) **Potterspury RD** - engine & machine makers 1st, railway drivers 1st, boilermakers 2nd, other design & draughtsmen 2nd, blacksmiths 4th, mechanic, manufacturer, & shopmen 6th

c) **Leighton Buzzard RD** – others in cane & straw 1st (mainly straw plaiting), canal service 5th.

d) **Thame RD** –Needlemakers 3rd

e) **Amersham RD** – sawyers 1st, chairmakers 2nd, others in horticulture 3rd, turners 5th.

f) **Winslow RD** – cattle & sheep dealers 2nd, butchers 5th, others in harness 5th.

g) **Henley RD** – Others in arboriculture 2nd, others in wood 7th

h) **Newport Pagnell RD** – other messengers 2nd

i) **Aylesbury RD** - Paupers (without stated occupations) 2nd

j) **Eton RD** – gardeners in domestic service 5th

These figures for Potterspury point to a problem in using 'occupation' types in measure the importance of industry as each trade employed in the Railway works was separately distinguished (see below). More generally, both in Bucks and nationally, the census reported large numbers of labourers without any indication of what their work was. In Bucks they seem to be have been found in towns rather than in villages.

Equivalent figures for female occupations in Bucks in RDs were:

a) **Wycombe RD** – dealers in furniture (includes workers) 1st, embroiders 2nd, lace makers 6th, paper makers 6th

b) **Potterspury RD** – lace makers 6th

c) **Leighton Buzzard RD** – straw plaiting 1st,

d) **Thame RD** – none

e) **Amersham RD** – Bonnet makers 3rd

f) **Winslow RD** – lace makers 2nd, wine merchants 2nd, midwives 5th

g) **Henley RD** – arborculture 7th

h) **Newport Pagnell RD** – lace makers 1st

i) **Buckingham RD** – clothiers 4th, builders 5th

A major feature of 1851 was the influence that lace making and straw plaiting had on female employment. In 1851 most adult women were not in 'work' Indeed, nationally this applied to 67% and in Buckinghamshire RC to 59% of the total. The lowest proportions locally were found in the Winslow RD (45%) and Leighton Buzzard RD (44%), while in Eton RD (66%), Thame RD (67%), Buckingham RD (68%) and Henley RD (69%) the proportion was near to the national average. Winslow and Leighton Buzzard (and to a slightly lesser extent Newport Pagnell RD (49%)) were special. Nationally, only 9 RDs had more adult females at work than 56% (Luton (75%), Foleshill, Nuneaton, Coventry, Hinckley, Leigh, Yeovil, Worcester and Nottingham.

Of those females who were at work in the county there were proportionally fewer in agriculture than the country as a whole (6.5%). The only exceptions amongst the RDs were Buckingham RD (10.3%), Thame RD (9.2% and Henley RD

(9.1%). The county's special character lay in the high proportion that were occupied in secondary or industrial activity with Leighton Buzzard RD (81%) and Winslow RD (76%) having nearly twice the national average. Leighton Buzzard ranked 12th in the country in this respect behind some of the districts mentioned above but also Keighley, Oldham, Saddleworth, Bradford and Ashton under Lyme. Absolutely there may not have so many women employed in 'industry' in Buckinghamshire than in the new seats of industrial England but proportionately they were on a par with these areas.

It is now recognised that in 1851 an agricultural county like Buckinghamshire had a wide mix of industries to support the farming population. It was a time before a large degree of specialisation in industry had occurred and many local crafts provided goods for a local market. A consequence of this is that it would be a mistake to concentrate solely on the special industries. Pages 64 and 65 show how Bucks RDs compared with others in tailoring, shoemaking, sawyers, watchmakers, wheelwrights and saddlers. In most of these activities most of the Bucks RDs were within minus 40% or plus 50% of the national average, as were most RDs in the country.

The figures for the special key industries are illustrated in pages 66-74.

a) **Lace-making** – The extent of the South-Midland lace making area is shown to be limited to a oval shaped area with Market Harborough in the north, Wycombe and Henley in the south and at its widest Banbury in the west and St Neots in the east. The Honiton area in the Devon failed to match this area in the intensity of local employment. However, machine lace making in the Nottingham area had become of such importance that it totalled 23% of adult female lace makers compared with 27% in Greater Bucks, 29% in adjacent South Midland areas and 10% in Devonshire/Dorset, and with only 12% elsewhere (these figures rather exaggerate the importance of Bucks and Beds as two thirds of total female employment in the industry was adult compared with only 56% in Northants and Devon and 60% in Nottinghamshire. Locally it might be noted that amongst the RDs Bedford had 2,515 employed in the industry, Newport Pagnell 2,204 and Wycombe 2,010.

b) **Straw plaiting** - the South-Midlands were the only area to be significant for straw plaiting. This high degree of concentration can be seen from the fact that Leighton Buzzard Rd had a LQ of 13,296 compared with the LQ of 5,279 at Newport Pagnell for lace-making (i.e. straw-plaiting on this measure was 2.5 times as concentrated as lace-making). Bucks was on the western end of the area which stretched eastwards through Hertfordshire to Saffron Walden and Halstead in north Essex. Even more than in lace-making juvenile labour was especially important. In Bucks only 20% of female employed were adults, 51% in Bedfordshire and 47% in Hertfordshire

		all	<10	10-14	15-19	<20	<10	10-14	15-19	<20
			Number by age				Percentage of total			
Lace fem	Bucks	10487	621	1424	1349	3394	5.9	13.6	12.9	32.4
	Beds	5734	354	893	721	1968	6.2	15.6	12.6	34.3
	Northants	10322	754	2124	1658	4536	7.3	20.6	16.1	43.9
	Notts	9724	285	1561	2089	3935	2.9	16.1	21.5	40.5
	Devon	5478	259	968	1168	2395	4.7	17.7	21.3	43.7
Straw fem	Bucks	2922	321	669	1349	2339	11.0	22.9	46.2	80.0
	Beds	10054	1282	1899	1772	4953	12.8	18.9	17.6	49.3
	Herts	8753	708	1439	1618	3765	8.1	16.4	18.5	43.0
Straw	Bucks	505	206	153	31	390	40.8	30.3	6.1	77.2
	Beds	2290	689	596	321	1606	30.1	26.0	14.0	70.1
	Herts	1143	344	341	147	832	30.1	29.8	12.9	72.8

c) **Chair making** – 1851 was early in the development of the growth of the Wycombe furniture industry but even so the area accounted for 18% of the number of adult chair-makers (66% of the total were adults). The figures for other occupations in the industry were small. In London there appears to have been about twice the number in the industry as in the population.

Males Only	Cabinet Makers	Turners	Chair Makers	French Polishers	Total	Cabinet Makers	Turners	Chair Makers	French Polishers	Total
	Number of Males 20+					Percentages				
London	8300	1317	1631	1591	12839	33.4	23.8	34.6	64.2	34.2
Wycombe & Amersham	25	42	835	20	922	0.1	0.8	17.7	0.8	2.5
Other	16544	4164	2248	867	23823	66.5	75.4	47.7	35.0	63.4
Total	24869	5523	4714	2478	37584	100.0	100.0	100.0	100.0	100.0

d) **Paper making** – The figures suggest Wycombe and Watford industries were only 63% of the size of that in Kent. Kent's extra size was largely due to the employment of large numbers of women In Kent there were also more children employed.

		Wycombe, Amersham, Eton	Watford, Hemel Hempstead	Maidstone	London	Other	All
Males 20+	No	368	220	640	207	3216	4651
Females 20+	No	188	187	895	30	1885	3185
Total 20+	No	556	407	1535	237	5101	7836
Males 20+	%	7.9	4.7	13.8	4.5	69.1	100.0
Females 20+	%	5.9	5.9	28.1	0.9	59.2	100.0
Total 20+	%	7.1	5.2	19.6	3.0	65.1	100.0
Males*	% adult	73.9	64.9	75.3	81.8		76.0
Females*	% adult	77.0	71.2	68.6	75.0		68.0

* using county average figures

1851 WOMEN aged 20+

Column groups: columns 10-14, 15-19, %<20 fall under "Bucks reg county"; columns AM–LB fall under "REGISTRATION DISTRICTS – number of women".

1851 WOMEN aged 20+	E & W	Greater Bucks	Bucks R county	Gt Bucks /10000 ew	Per 10000 Gt Bucks	10-14	15-19	%<20	AM	ET	WY	AY	WIN	NP	BU	HE	TH	PO	LB
TOTAL	5,099,584	56,395	39,852	111	10,000	2,325	2,638	27	5,191	5,962	9,098	6,329	2,511	6,606	4,155	4,968	4,201	2,979	4,395
Lace-Maker	32,230	8,721	7,093	2,706	1,546.4	1,424	1,349	28	556	23	2,010	927	748	2,204	625	191	654	700	83
Straw Plait Manufacture	17,409	2,984	1,323	1,714	529.1	669	609	49	549	1	101	421	176	70	5	3	4	2	1,653
Milliner	178,441	1,431	1,037	80	253.8	35	297	24	146	144	231	184	79	160	93	113	73	71	137
Shoemakers-Wife	84,910	750	556	88	133.0	-	4	1	124	60	143	99	20	84	26	62	63	27	42
Seamstress	50,172	458	293	91	81.2	8	41	14	36	32	121	33	14	32	25	89	9	19	30
Straw Hat & Bonnet Maker	14,787	221	155	149	39.2	3	30	18	11	9	38	36	14	28	19	7	9	19	45
Shoemaker	21,265	216	182	102	38.3	20	57	30	45	13	28	40	14	24	18	6	5	15	8
Paper Manufacture	3,380	195	188	577	34.6	13	48	24	10	61	117	-	-	-	-	7	-	-	-
Silk Manufacture	42,591	90	88	21	16.0	51	51	54	33	-	-	51	-	3	-	-	-	1	1
Embroiderer	1,777	80	80	450	14.2	23	47	47	-	1	79	-	-	-	-	9	-	1	1
Bonnet Maker	5,166	61	50	118	10.8	-	11	18	35	3	-	5	-	4	3	-	-	1	1
Oth in Deal in Wood Furnit	1,611	61	60	379	10.8	68	66	69	-	-	60	-	-	-	-	-	6	-	1
Labourer-Undefined Branch	5,810	25	19	43	4.4	1	6	27	-	7	9	-	-	2	1	13	-	-	1
Staymaker	9,143	21	7	23	3.7	-	-	-	1	3	-	2	-	1	-	-	-	1	1
Knitter	1,767	19	15	108	3.4	2	1	17	-	-	-	4	-	10	-	1	-	1	1
Tailor	13,475	14	12	10	2.5	-	1	8	3	1	5	-	1	1	1	1	1	1	1
Glover-Material Not Stated	16,464	14	12	9	2.5	1	1	-	-	1	1	3	-	-	7	1	1	1	1
Cap-Maker	2,789	12	9	43	2.1	1	2	25	2	3	5	-	-	1	-	1	1	1	2
Stationer	905	12	7	133	2.1	1	1	13	-	-	2	-	-	1	-	4	1	1	1
Cabinet-Makers,Uphols	3,873	11	7	28	2.0	1	1	13	1	5	-	1	-	-	-	2	1	-	-
Others in Cane,Rush,Straw	867	11	5	127	2.0	2	1	38	1	-	-	3	-	-	-	1	-	-	5
Blacksmith	557	10	6	180	1.8	-	-	-	2	2	-	-	-	-	2	3	1	-	-
Othr Work,Dealers in Iron,	3,707	9	8	24	1.6	-	1	-	3	4	1	1	-	-	1	1	-	1	-
Undefine Mech,Manuft,,	1,618	9	6	56	1.6	-	7	54	-	-	1	2	-	2	1	1	-	-	1
Hose,Stocking Manufacture	17,377	8	7	5	1.4	-	-	-	-	4	-	-	3	-	-	-	-	-	-
Other Dealers in Silk	2,315	8	6	35	1.4	-	2	25	5	-	1	-	-	1	-	-	-	-	2
Harness Makers	536	6	4	112	1.1	-	-	-	-	1	1	-	-	-	-	1	-	-	2
Umbrella,Parasol,Stick	1,210	5	2	41	0.9	-	-	-	-	-	2	1	-	-	1	1	-	-	2
Others Prov.Dress	5,227	5	3	10	0.9	-	-	-	-	-	2	-	1	1	-	-	5	-	-
Needle Manufacture	1,214	5	0	41	0.9	-	-	-	-	-	-	-	-	-	1	-	1	-	-
Implements	108	4	1	370	0.7	-	-	-	-	1	-	-	-	-	-	-	-	-	-
Thread Manufacture	372	4	4	108	0.7	-	-	20	-	4	-	-	-	-	4	-	-	-	-
Tobacco-Pipe Makers	684	4	4	58	0.7	1	-	-	2	-	-	-	-	-	-	2	2	-	-
Hosier,Haberdasher	1,838	3	1	16	0.5	-	-	-	-	1	-	-	-	-	1	-	-	-	-
Publications Other	2,523	3	3	12	0.5	-	-	-	-	3	-	-	-	-	-	-	-	1	-
Toy Maker,Dealer	641	3	3	47	0.5	-	-	-	-	-	-	1	-	-	1	-	-	-	-
Dyer,Scourer,Calenderer	557	3	1	54	0.5	-	-	-	-	-	-	1	-	-	-	1	-	-	-
Ropemaker	1,150	3	1	26	0.5	-	-	-	1	-	-	-	-	-	-	2	-	-	-
Hemp Manufacture	412	3	2	73	0.5	-	-	-	-	-	2	-	-	-	-	1	-	-	-
Other in Flax,Cotton	1,768	3	3	17	0.5	-	-	-	1	-	2	-	-	-	-	-	-	-	-
Other Coalworkers	838	3	3	36	0.5	-	2	40	-	-	2	1	-	1	-	-	-	-	-
Hatter	2,404	2	1	8	0.4	1	1	67	-	-	-	1	-	1	-	-	-	-	-
Furrier	1,462	2	2	14	0.4	1	2	60	-	-	-	-	-	-	-	1	-	-	-
Clothier	229	2	2	87	0.4	-	-	-	-	-	2	-	-	-	-	-	-	-	-
Fancy Goods Manufacture	961	2	2	21	0.4	1	1	50	-	-	-	1	-	-	-	-	-	-	-
wood tool makers	332	2	2	60	0.4	-	-	-	-	-	-	-	-	-	-	-	-	-	-
Other Hemp Workers	2,013	2	2	10	0.4	-	-	-	-	-	-	-	-	-	-	-	-	-	-
Flax,Linen Manuft	6,460	2	1	3	0.4	-	1	50	-	-	-	1	-	1	-	-	-	1	-
Stone Quarrier	643	1	2	16	0.2	-	-	-	-	-	-	-	-	-	-	-	-	-	-
Goldsmith,Silversmith	826	2	2	24	0.4	-	-	-	-	1	1	1	-	-	-	-	-	-	-
Shawl Manuft.	190	1	0	53	0.2	-	-	-	-	1	-	-	-	-	-	-	-	-	-
Rag Gatherer,Cutter,Dealer	713	1	0	14	0.2	-	-	-	-	-	-	-	-	-	-	-	-	-	-
Artifical Flower-Maker	1,516	1	0	7	0.2	-	-	50	1	-	-	-	-	-	-	-	-	-	-
Other Work Dealer Wool	3,612	1	0	3	0.2	-	-	-	-	-	-	-	-	-	-	1	-	-	-
Oil & Colourman	643	1	1	16	0.2	-	-	-	-	-	1	-	-	-	-	-	-	-	-
Dealers wood utensils	99	1	1	101	0.2	-	-	-	-	-	-	-	-	-	-	1	-	-	-
Cotton Manufacture	110,869	1	1	0	0.2	-	-	-	-	-	-	-	-	-	-	-	-	-	1
Lint Manufacture	117	1	1	85	0.2	-	-	-	-	-	-	-	-	-	-	-	-	-	-
Earthenware Manufacture	5,581	1	1	2	0.2	-	-	-	-	-	-	1	-	-	-	-	-	-	-
Salt Makers,Dealers	58	1	1	172	0.2	-	-	-	-	-	-	1	-	-	-	-	-	-	-
Other Deal in Mixed Metals	2,141	1	1	5	0.2	-	-	-	-	1	1	-	-	-	-	-	-	-	-
Nail Manufacture	6,603	1	0	2	0.2	-	-	-	-	-	-	-	-	-	-	-	-	1	-

1851 MEN aged 20+	E & W	Greater Bucks	Bucks R county	Gt Bucks per 10000 E & W	Per 10000 Gt Bucks	Bucks reg county			REGISTRATION DISTRICTS -number of men										
						10-14	15-19	%<20	AM	ET	WY	AY	WI	NP	BU	HE	TH	PO	LB
	4,717,013	52,409	36,718	111	10,000.0	8,170	7,312	30	4,671	5,483	8,452	6,076	2,407	5,922	3,707	4,705	3,991	2,866	4,129
Labourer-Undefined	274,079	2,927	2,058	107	558.5	243	398	24	467	340	547	164	8	352	180	281	328	167	93
Shoemaker	173,932	1,700	1,271	98	324.4	82	279	22	265	147	284	199	67	198	111	129	111	88	101
Carpenter,Joiner	133,675	1,375	945	103	262.4	17	127	13	111	195	190	143	65	152	89	150	82	81	117
Chair-Maker	4,714	875	848	1,856	167.0	149	265	33	119	9	716	4	-	-	-	8	17	-	2
Blacksmith	75,998	802	515	106	153.0	12	76	15	88	58	129	75	33	83	49	86	54	97	50
Tailor	96,633	683	492	71	130.3	22	69	16	64	94	96	79	32	82	45	51	42	39	59
Sawyer	27,824	664	516	239	126.7	9	52	11	124	35	214	41	18	54	30	72	17	34	25
Wheelwright	23,495	398	283	169	75.9	5	46	15	51	45	66	42	17	45	17	35	33	18	29
Paper Manuft.	4,651	386	370	830	73.7	59	71	26	23	66	279	-	2	-	-	13	-	3	-
Other in Cane,Rush,Straw	2,874	377	115	1,312	71.9	153	31	62	24	18	11	39	17	5	1	3	1	-	258
Brickmaker	21,707	322	230	148	61.4	15	37	18	29	34	26	59	13	37	32	50	14	9	19
Miller	26,413	303	197	115	57.8	6	16	10	22	31	56	27	6	37	18	38	18	28	22
Engine & Machine Maker	34,797	249	41	72	47.5	1	7	16	2	15	5	4	1	9	5	6	2	198	2
Brewer	16,128	240	173	149	45.8	1	11	6	31	30	57	25	4	17	9	29	6	9	23
Saddler	12,594	159	119	126	30.3	7	16	16	22	15	31	12	6	20	13	14	9	8	9
Maltster	9,812	124	80	126	23.7	-	4	5	10	7	14	15	5	20	9	14	5	8	17
Cabinet-Makers,Upholsterer	24,869	98	67	39	18.7	1	10	14	4	17	21	14	1	5	5	15	4	6	6
Basket-Maker	6,078	88	67	145	16.8	3	10	16	8	5	17	12	-	24	1	8	4	2	7
Watchmaker	14,020	87	67	62	16.6	-	9	12	9	12	11	7	2	17	9	7	7	1	5
Cooper	13,520	84	56	62	16.0	1	8	14	4	5	6	14	6	14	7	11	5	6	6
Other In Timber	2,213	75	51	339	14.3	5	4	15	17	13	18	-	-	1	2	16	3	4	1
Others Prov.Dress	2,882	66	52	229	12.6	1	1	4	-	6	25	7	1	10	3	1	4	-	9
Turner	5,523	64	45	116	12.2	9	13	33	28	1	14	1	-	1	-	2	3	14	-
Millwright	6,446	59	49	92	11.3	-	6	11	5	8	30	1	-	3	2	3	1	2	4
Iron Manuft	49,005	59	26	12	11.3	-	5	16	2	8	8	6	-	1	1	12	1	20	-
Other Hemp Workers	3,760	53	38	141	10.1	3	6	19	-	-	-	1	1	35	1	9	-	5	1
Tanner	6,924	50	40	72	9.5	6	5	22	2	-	4	4	7	15	8	6	-	-	4
Currier	9,739	48	29	49	9.2	-	1	3	5	2	4	6	1	5	6	3	6	3	7
Mechanic,Manuft.,Shopman	7,892	48	12	61	9.2	3	5	40	-	2	-	-	-	8	2	4	-	32	-
Needle Manuft.	1,884	46	1	244	8.8	-	-	0	1	-	-	-	-	-	-	-	45	-	-
Printer	16,034	45	36	28	8.6	2	12	28	2	3	9	15	1	3	3	3	2	2	2
Silk Manufacture	31,042	40	37	13	7.6	42	9	58	9	-	-	26	-	-	2	3	-	-	-
Whitesmith	7,615	40	29	53	7.6	2	9	28	2	9	6	6	-	6	-	9	1	1	-
Boiler-Maker	4,857	40	1	82	7.6	-	-	0	-	-	-	-	-	1	-	2	-	37	-
Brazier	3,391	35	26	103	6.7	1	2	10	3	6	4	2	5	4	2	1	2	3	3
Earthenware Manuft.	14,943	33	24	22	6.3	3	5	25	19	-	2	1	-	-	2	5	1	2	1
Ropemaker	7,794	31	23	40	5.9	4	2	21	3	-	15	3	-	2	-	4	-	4	-
Tinman	5,897	30	21	51	5.7	-	-	0	4	1	4	5	-	5	2	3	4	1	1
Lace-Maker	5,579	26	19	47	5.0	12	10	54	-	-	4	2	1	11	1	-	1	6	-
Brush & Broom Maker	6,053	24	23	40	4.6	3	3	21	11	8	-	1	-	2	1	1	-	-	-
French Polisher	2,478	24	23	97	4.6	3	6	28	-	1	20	-	1	1	-	1	-	-	-
Leather -Other	1,790	22	16	123	4.2	1	-	6	-	-	14	-	-	2	-	4	1	1	-
Others In Dealing In Furniture	3,655	22	21	60	4.2	-	1	5	17	2	2	-	-	-	-	1	-	-	-
Other Workers In Tin	4,814	21	14	44	4.0	-	-	0	4	-	3	-	-	6	1	-	1	6	-
Woolstapler	1,642	19	13	116	3.6	-	2	13	1	-	1	-	1	3	7	-	6	-	-
Other Workers In Flax,Cotton	5,882	19	18	32	3.6	-	-	0	1	2	2	1	2	8	2	1	-	-	-
Hatter	11,297	16	12	14	3.1	-	1	8	1	3	2	5	-	1	-	1	-	-	3
Other Wood Tool Makers	3,675	16	16	44	3.1	-	-	0	10	-	6	-	-	-	-	-	-	-	-
Tobacco-Pipe Makers	2,707	16	12	59	3.1	-	-	0	-	9	3	-	-	-	-	-	-	-	4
Umbrella,Parasol,Stick Maker	10,684	14	12	13	2.7	-	1	8	4	-	4	-	1	2	1	-	1	-	1
Boat,Barge Maker	2,378	14	10	59	2.7	-	-	0	-	6	3	-	-	1	-	3	-	-	1
Other Dealers In Mixed Metals	6,008	14	9	23	2.7	-	-	0	3	2	1	-	2	-	1	2	-	3	-
Lath-Maker	1,377	13	11	94	2.5	-	1	8	2	1	5	1	-	2	-	1	-	-	1
Others Dealing In Wood Utensils	1,347	13	13	97	2.5	2	1	19	13	-	-	-	-	-	-	-	-	-	-
Goldsmith,Silversmith	7,915	13	13	16	2.5	-	-	0	-	2	3	-	-	3	1	1	2	1	-
Coppersmith	1,211	12	8	99	2.3	-	3	27	1	3	4	-	-	-	-	1	-	3	-
Glover-Material Not Stated	3,505	10	7	29	1.9	-	-	0	2	-	-	3	-	-	2	1	-	1	1
Stationer	3,101	9	9	29	1.7	2	-	18	1	6	1	1	-	-	-	1	-	-	-
Water Providers,Dealers	1,503	9	8	60	1.7	-	2	20	1	1	4	-	-	2	-	1	-	-	-
Grinder	1,599	9	5	56	1.7	-	-	0	1	-	-	1	-	2	1	-	-	2	2
Dyer,Scourer,Calenderer	8,162	8	6	10	1.5	-	-	0	1	1	2	-	-	1	1	1	-	1	-
Woollen Cloth Manuft	54,977	8	6	1	1.5	-	-	0	-	1	-	2	-	-	3	-	-	-	2
Limestone Quarrier,Burner	4,390	8	3	18	1.5	-	-	0	1	-	1	-	-	-	1	-	1	1	3

1851 MEN aged 20+	% Males in each category											Location Quotient E & W average =100										
	AM	ET	WY	AY	WI	NP	BU	HE	TH	PO	LB	AM	ET	WY	AY	WI	NP	BU	HE	TH	PO	LB
Total Industry	35.52	23.98	35.81	17.99	13.75	22.53	18.88	24.10	21.30	33.98	22.06	100	67	101	51	39	63	53	68	60	96	62
LabourerUndefined	10.00	6.20	6.47	2.70	0.33	5.94	4.86	5.97	8.22	5.83	2.25	172	107	111	46	6	102	84	103	141	100	39
Shoemaker	5.67	2.68	3.36	3.28	2.78	3.34	2.99	2.74	2.05	3.07	2.83	154	73	91	89	75	91	81	74	73	75	66
Carpenter,Joiner	2.38	3.56	2.25	2.35	2.70	2.57	2.40	3.19	2.05	2.83	2.83	84	125	79	83	95	91	85	112	73	100	100
ChairMaker	2.55	0.16	8.47	0.07				0.17	0.43		0.05	2549	164	8477	66				170	426		48
Blacksmith	1.88	1.06	1.53	1.23	0.85	1.40	1.32	1.83	1.35	3.38	1.21	117	66	95	77	85	87	82	113	84	210	75
Tailor	1.37	1.71	1.14	1.30	1.33	1.38	1.21	1.08	1.05	1.36	1.43	67	84	55	63	65	68	59	53	51	66	70
Sawyer	2.65	0.64	2.53	0.67	0.75	0.91	0.81	1.53	0.43	1.19	0.61	450	108	429	114	127	155	137	259	72	201	103
Wheelwright	1.09	0.82	0.78	0.69	0.71	0.76	0.46	0.74	0.83	0.63	0.70	219	165	157	139	142	153	92	149	166	126	141
Paper Manuft.	0.49	1.20	3.30	0.08				0.28	0.10	0.10		499	1221	3348					280	84	106	
Other in Cane,Rush,Straw	0.51	0.33	0.13	0.64	0.71	0.08	0.03	0.06	0.03	0.31	6.25	843	539	214	1053	1159	139	44	105	41	68	10255
Brickmaker	0.62	0.62	0.31	0.97	0.54	0.62	0.86	1.06	0.35	0.98	0.46	135	135	67	211	117	136	188	231	76	174	100
Miller	0.47	0.57	0.66	0.44	0.25	0.62	0.49	0.81	0.45	6.91	0.53	84	101	118	79	45	112	87	144	81	937	7
Engine & Machine Maker	0.04	0.27	0.06	0.07	0.04	0.29	0.13	0.13	0.05	0.31	0.05	6	37	8	9	6	21	18	17	7	92	163
Brewer	0.66	0.55	0.67	0.41	0.17	0.34	0.24	0.62	0.15	0.28	0.56	194	160	197	120	49	84	71	180	44	105	82
Saddler	0.47	0.27	0.37	0.20	0.25	0.34	0.35	0.30	0.23	0.28	0.22	176	102	137	74	93	126	131	111	84	134	198
Maltster	0.21	0.13	0.17	0.25	0.21	0.08	0.24	0.32	0.13	0.21	0.41	103	61	80	119	100	162	117	143	60	40	28
CabinetMakers,Upholsterer	0.09	0.31	0.25	0.23	0.04	0.41	0.13	0.17	0.10	0.07	0.15	16	59	47	44	8	315	26	60	19	54	132
BasketMaker	0.17	0.09	0.20	0.20		0.29	0.03	0.15	0.18	0.03	0.17	133	71	156	153		97	21	132	78	12	41
Watchmaker	0.19	0.22	0.13	0.12	0.08	0.24	0.24	0.23	0.10	0.21	0.12	65	74	44	39	28	82	82	50	59	73	51
Cooper	0.09	0.09	0.07	0.23	0.25	0.02	0.19	0.34	0.13	0.21	0.15	30	32	25	80	87	36	66	82	44	297	52
Other In Timber	0.36	0.24	0.21			0.17	0.05	0.02	0.08	0.14	0.02	776	505	454			276	115	725	160		357
Others Prov.Dress		0.11	0.30	0.12	0.04		0.08	0.04	0.10	0.49	0.22		179	141	189	68	14	132	35	164	417	
Turner	0.60	0.02	0.17	0.02		0.05		0.08	0.08	0.07		512		260	14		37	39	36	64	51	71
Millwright	0.11	0.15	0.35	0.02		0.05		0.06	0.03	0.70	0.10	78	107	9	12		2	3	47	18	67	
Iron Manuft	0.04	0.15	0.09	0.10		0.02	0.05	0.26	0.03	0.17		4	14		10			34	25	2	219	30
Other Hemp Workers					0.04	0.59	0.03	0.19			0.02			32	21	52	741		240			66
Tanner	0.04	0.04	0.05	0.07	0.29	0.25	0.22	0.13	0.15	0.10	0.10	29	18	32	45	198	173	147	87	73	51	82
Currier	0.11	0.04	0.05	0.10	0.04	0.08	0.16	0.06		1.12	0.17	52	22	23	48	20	41	78	31		667	
Mechanic,Manuft.,Shopman						0.14	0.05	0.09				54		31			81	32	51			
Needle Manuft.	0.02	0.15	0.24			0.05	0.08	0.06	1.13			13	16	141	73	12	15	24	19	2823	21	14
Printer	0.04	0.02	0.17	0.25	0.04		0.05	0.06	0.05	0.07	0.05	29	16	260	65			8	10	15		
Silk Manufacture	0.19			0.43		0.10				0.70		27	102	44	61		63		118	16	22	
Whitesmith	0.04	0.16	0.07	0.10		0.02		0.04	0.03	0.17				9			16		41		1254	
BoilerMaker						0.07		0.02	0.05	0.10	0.07		152	66	46	289	94	75	30	70	146	101
Brazier	0.06	0.11	0.05	0.03	0.21		0.05	0.02	0.03	0.07	0.02	89		7	5			17	34	8	22	8
Eartheware Manuft.	0.41		0.02	0.02		0.03	0.05	0.11		0.14		128		107	30	35	20		51	80	84	
Ropemaker	0.06	0.02	0.18			0.08	0.05	0.09	0.10	0.03	0.02	39	18	38	66	79	68	43	51	80	28	19
Tinman	0.09		0.05	0.08		0.19	0.03	0.06	0.03	0.21		68	15	40	28		157	23	51	21	177	
LaceMaker		0.15	0.05	0.03	0.04	0.03		0.02				184	114	450	13		26	21	17			169
Brush & Broom Maker	0.24	0.02	0.24	0.02		0.02	0.03	0.02					35	436		79	32		40		92	11
French Polisher			0.17			0.03						470	47	31	73		89	8	224	66		48
Leather Other			0.04					0.09	0.03	0.03		84		35	65				27	25	21	
Others In Dealing In Furniture	0.36	0.04	0.04		0.04	0.10	0.08	0.06	0.03	0.21	0.05	62	29	34	61		99	26		432	205	
Other Workers In Tin	0.09		0.01		0.08	0.05	0.05	0.02	0.15			17	23	19	13	119	146	542	126	11		83
Woolstapler	0.02		0.02	0.02		0.14						9	29	10	34	67	108	43	33		82	30
Other Workers In Flax,Cotton	0.02		0.02	0.08		0.02	0.03	0.02			0.07	275		91			7		73			
Hatter	0.21	0.16	0.07									38	286	62	46	18	20	12	13		21	
Other Wood Tool Makers			0.04					0.02	0.05	0.10	0.10			21	5	289			83	30	408	169
TobaccoPipe Makers	0.09	0.02	0.05		0.04	0.03					0.02			70								11
Umbrella,Parasol,Stick Maker		0.11	0.04			0.02	0.03	0.06	0.03			50	217	9	30	18	33	12				48
Boat,Barge Maker	0.06	0.04	0.01	0.02	0.08	0.03		0.04				147	29	203	56	65	116	21	33	25	82	
Other Dealers In Mixed Metals	0.04	0.02	0.06				0.08	0.02				975	62	21		73	30	16	73			83
LathMaker	0.28		0.04			0.05	0.03	0.02		0.03	0.02		22	184	66				13		21	
Others Dealing In Wood Utensils		0.04	0.04					0.05	0.05	0.10		83	213	21	25				83	30		33
Goldsmith,Silversmith	0.02	0.05	0.05	0.05			0.05	0.02	0.03	0.03		58	166	18	66		106		29		47	
Coppersmith	0.04	0.11	0.01	0.02		0.03		0.02		0.10	0.02	33	57	149	25		100	73	67			143
GloverMaterial Not Stated	0.02	0.02	0.05			0.03			0.15	0.03		67						80			206	4
Stationer	0.02	0.02		0.02		0.03	0.03	0.02		0.07	0.05	63	11	14	49		10	16	12		20	
Water Providers,Dealers	0.02	0.02	0.02	0.03		0.02	0.03	0.02		0.03		12	2	13	3			7				78
Grinder																						
Dyer,Scourer,Calenderer																						
Woollen Cloth Manuft																						
Limestone Quarrier,Burner	0.02	0.01	0.01			0.03	0.03	0.03		0.03	0.07	23		13			29			27	37	78

61

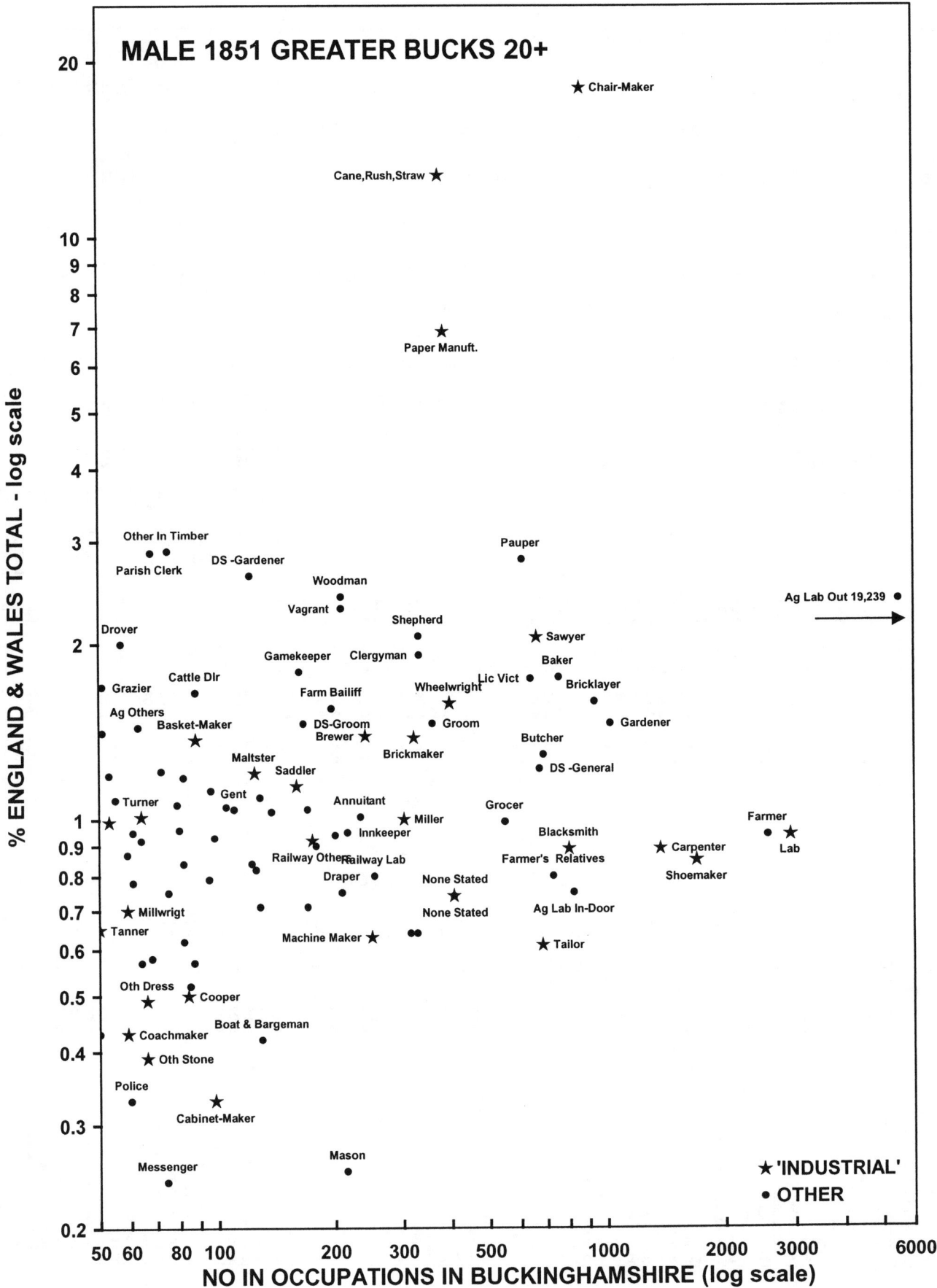

MALE 1851 GREATER BUCKS 20+

% ENGLAND & WALES TOTAL - log scale

NO IN OCCUPATIONS IN BUCKINGHAMSHIRE (log scale)

★ 'INDUSTRIAL'
● OTHER

Chair-Maker
Cane,Rush,Straw
Paper Manuft.
Other In Timber
Parish Clerk
DS -Gardener
Pauper
Ag Lab Out 19,239
Woodman
Vagrant
Shepherd
Drover
Sawyer
Gamekeeper
Clergyman
Baker
Grazier
Cattle Dlr
Wheelwright
Lic Vict
Bricklayer
Ag Others
Basket-Maker
Farm Bailiff
Groom
Gardener
DS-Groom
Brewer
Butcher
Brickmaker
DS -General
Maltster
Saddler
Gent
Annuitant
Grocer
Turner
Miller
Blacksmith
Innkeeper
Railway Others Railway Lab
Farmer's Relatives
Carpenter
Farmer
Draper
None Stated
Shoemaker
Lab
Millwrigt
None Stated
Ag Lab In-Door
Tanner
Machine Maker
Tailor
Oth Dress
Cooper
Boat & Bargeman
Coachmaker
Oth Stone
Police
Cabinet-Maker
Messenger
Mason

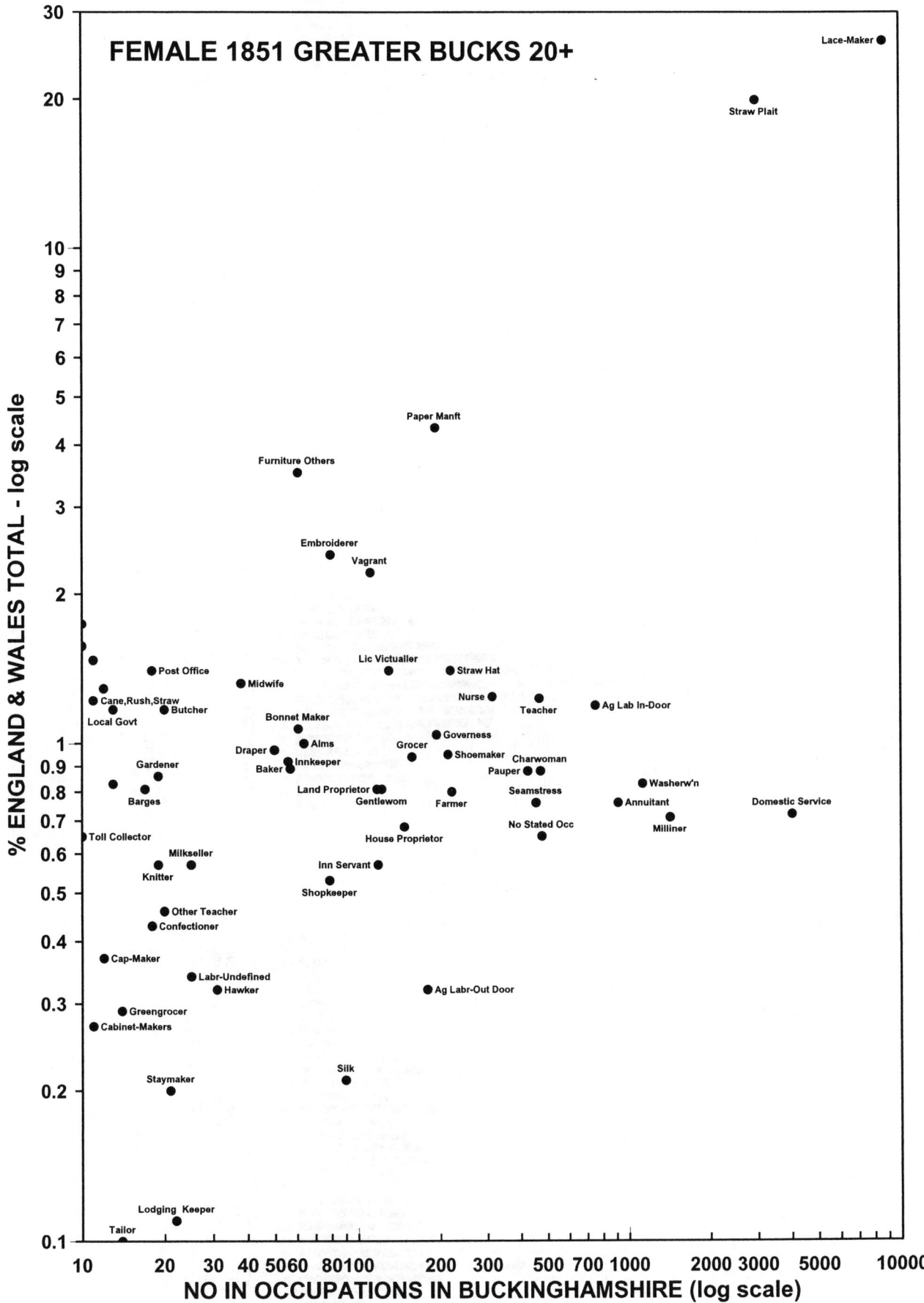

FEMALE 1851 GREATER BUCKS 20+

X-axis: NO IN OCCUPATIONS IN BUCKINGHAMSHIRE (log scale)

Y-axis: % ENGLAND & WALES TOTAL - log scale

Data points: Lace-Maker, Straw Plait, Paper Manft, Furniture Others, Embroiderer, Vagrant, Lic Victualler, Straw Hat, Post Office, Midwife, Cane,Rush,Straw, Butcher, Nurse, Teacher, Ag Lab In-Door, Local Govt, Bonnet Maker, Governess, Gardener, Draper, Alms, Grocer, Shoemaker, Charwoman, Baker, Innkeeper, Pauper, Washerw'n, Barges, Land Proprietor, Gentlewom, Farmer, Seamstress, Annuitant, Domestic Service, Toll Collector, House Proprietor, No Stated Occ, Milliner, Milkseller, Knitter, Inn Servant, Shopkeeper, Other Teacher, Confectioner, Cap-Maker, Labr-Undefined, Hawker, Ag Labr-Out Door, Greengrocer, Cabinet-Makers, Staymaker, Silk, Lodging Keeper, Tailor

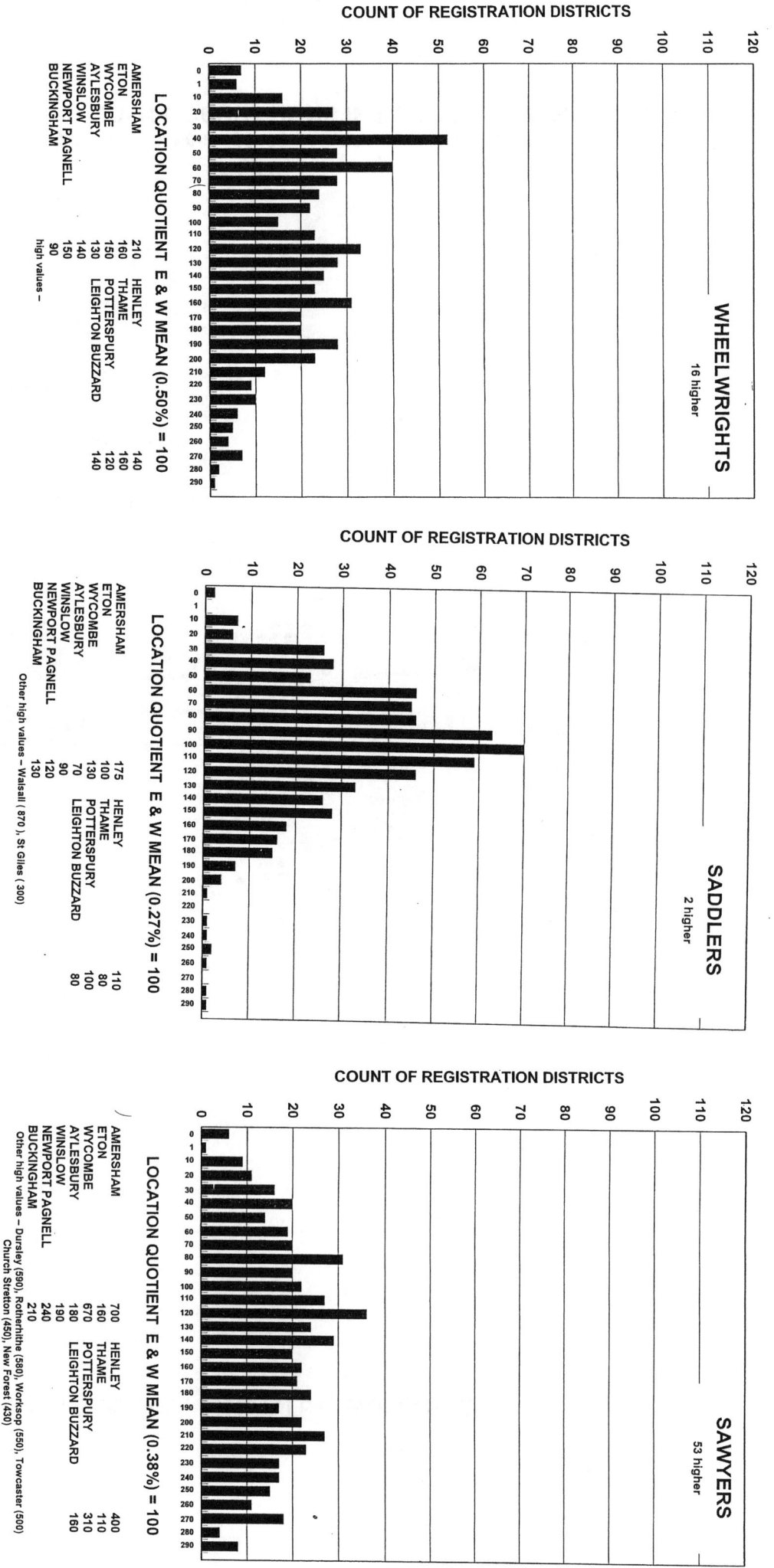

COUNT OF REGISTRATION DISTRICTS

WHEELWRIGHTS

16 higher

LOCATION QUOTIENT E & W MEAN (0.50%) = 100

AMERSHAM	210	HENLEY	140
ETON	160	THAME	160
WYCOMBE	150	POTTERSPURY	120
AYLESBURY	130	LEIGHTON BUZZARD	140
WINSLOW	140		
NEWPORT PAGNELL	150		
BUCKINGHAM	90		

high values –

COUNT OF REGISTRATION DISTRICTS

SADDLERS

2 higher

LOCATION QUOTIENT E & W MEAN (0.27%) = 100

AMERSHAM	175	HENLEY	110
ETON	100	THAME	80
WYCOMBE	130	POTTERSPURY	100
AYLESBURY	70	LEIGHTON BUZZARD	80
WINSLOW	90		
NEWPORT PAGNELL	120		
BUCKINGHAM	130		

Other high values – Walsall (870), St Giles (300)

COUNT OF REGISTRATION DISTRICTS

SAWYERS

53 higher

LOCATION QUOTIENT E & W MEAN (0.38%) = 100

AMERSHAM	700	HENLEY	400
ETON	160	THAME	110
WYCOMBE	670	POTTERSPURY	310
AYLESBURY	180	LEIGHTON BUZZARD	160
WINSLOW	190		
NEWPORT PAGNELL	240		
BUCKINGHAM	210		

Other high values – Dursley (590), Rotherhithe (580), Worksop (550), Towcaster (500)
Church Stretton (450), New Forest (430)

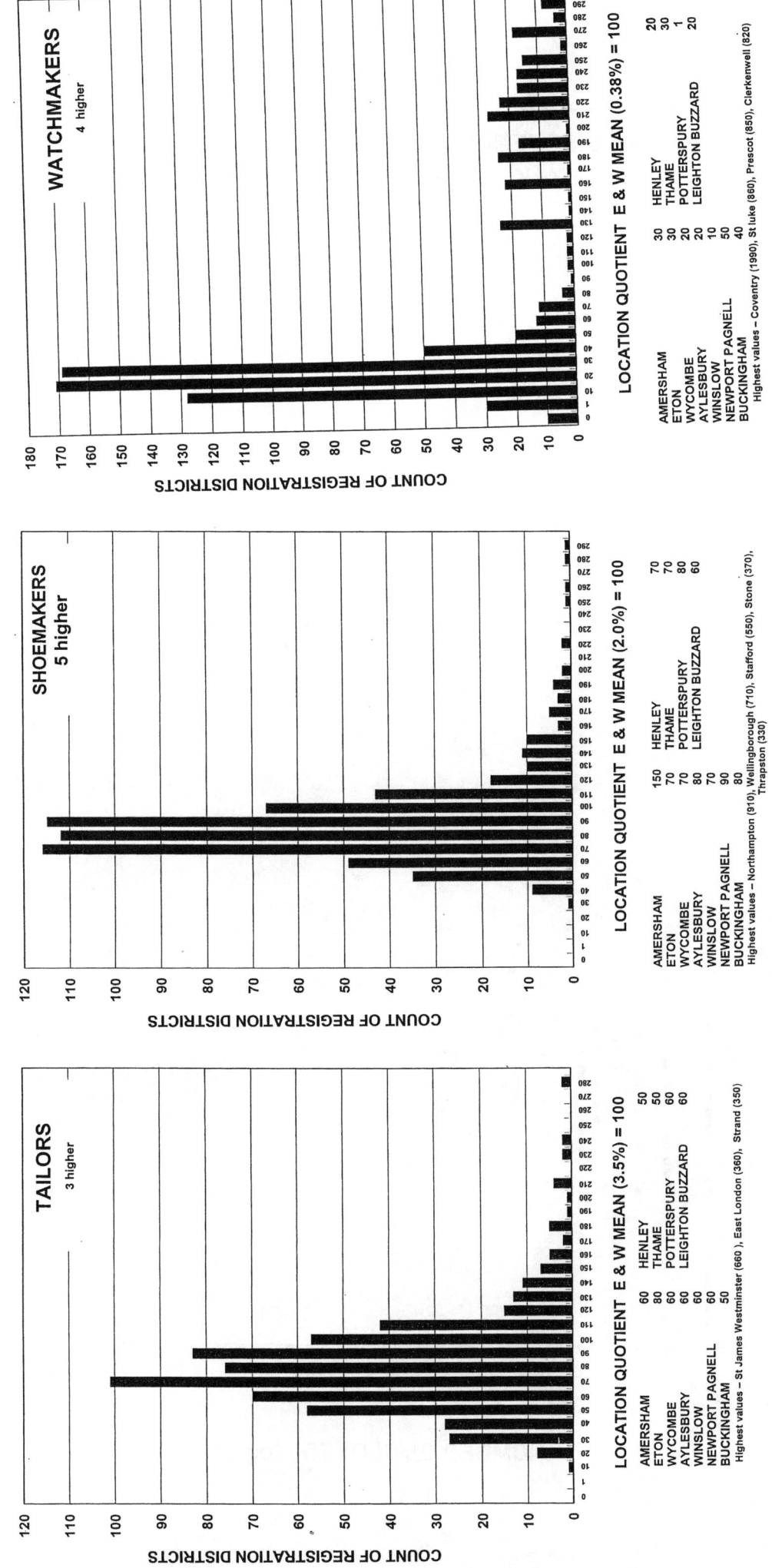

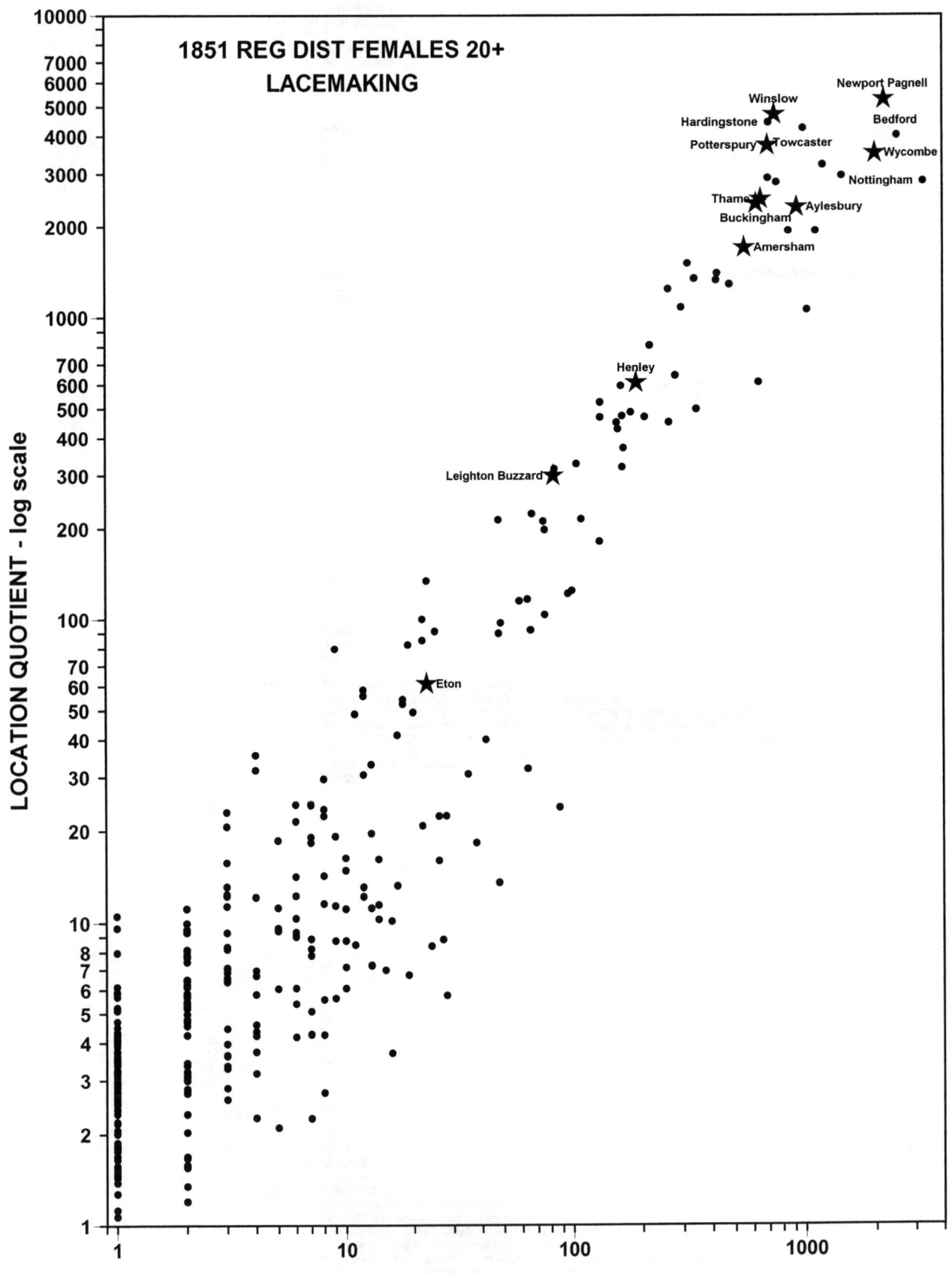

NUMBER EMPLOYED - log scale

LOCATION QUOTIENT - log scale

1851 REG DIST FEMALES 20+
LACEMAKING

Newport Pagnell
Winslow
Bedford
Hardingstone
Potterspury Towcaster
Wycombe
Nottingham
Thame
Aylesbury
Buckingham
Amersham
Henley
Leighton Buzzard
Eton

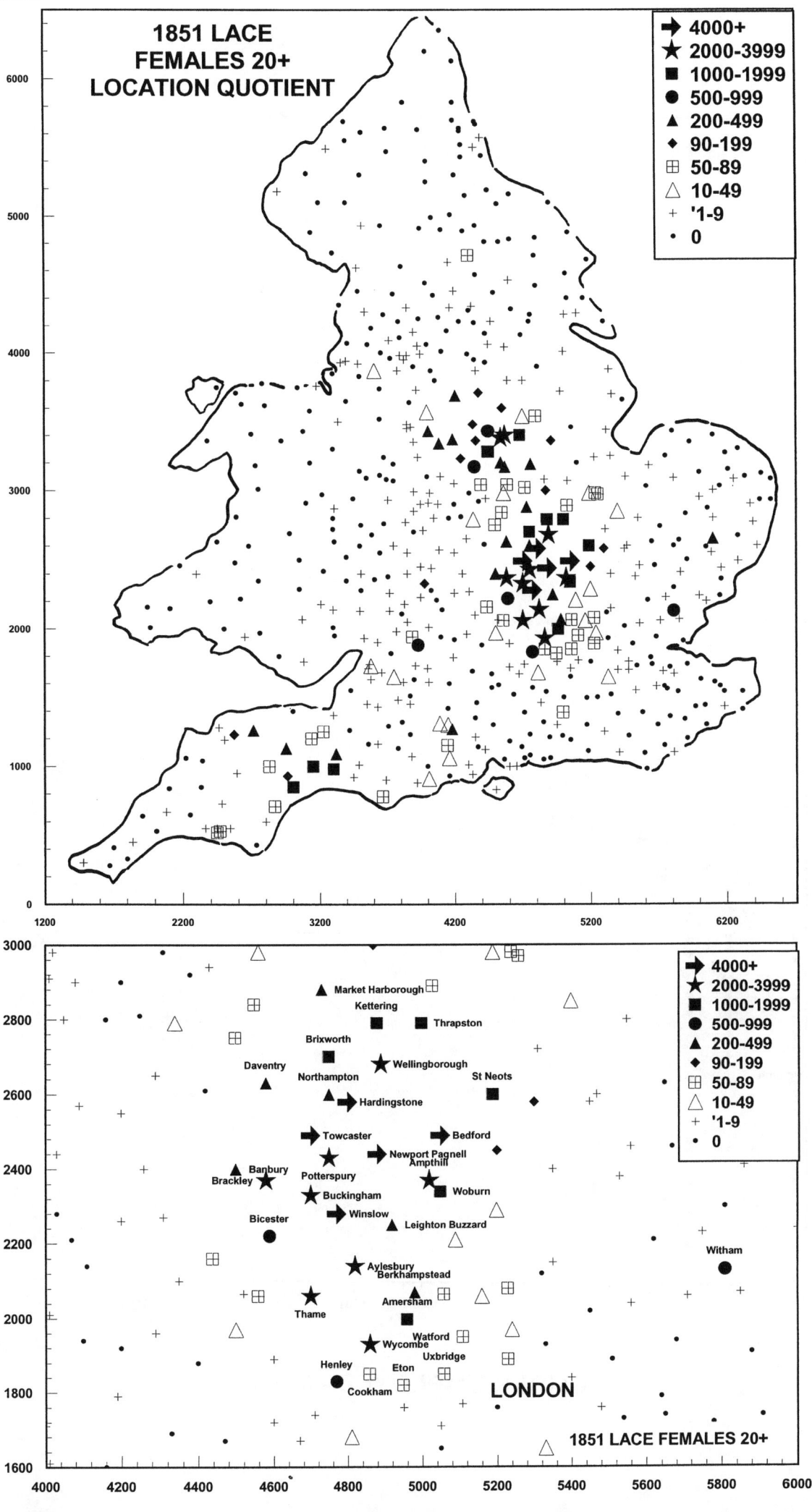

1851 LACE
FEMALES 20+
LOCATION QUOTIENT

Legend (upper map): 4000+, 2000-3999, 1000-1999, 500-999, 200-499, 90-199, 50-89, 10-49, '1-9, 0

Legend (lower map): 4000+, 2000-3999, 1000-1999, 500-999, 200-499, 90-199, 50-89, 10-49, '1-9, 0

Market Harborough, Kettering, Thrapston, Brixworth, Daventry, Northampton, Wellingborough, St Neots, Hardingstone, Towcaster, Bedford, Newport Pagnell, Ampthill, Banbury, Potterspury, Brackley, Buckingham, Woburn, Bicester, Winslow, Leighton Buzzard, Witham, Aylesbury, Berkhampstead, Thame, Amersham, Watford, Wycombe, Uxbridge, Henley, Eton, Cookham, LONDON

1851 LACE FEMALES 20+

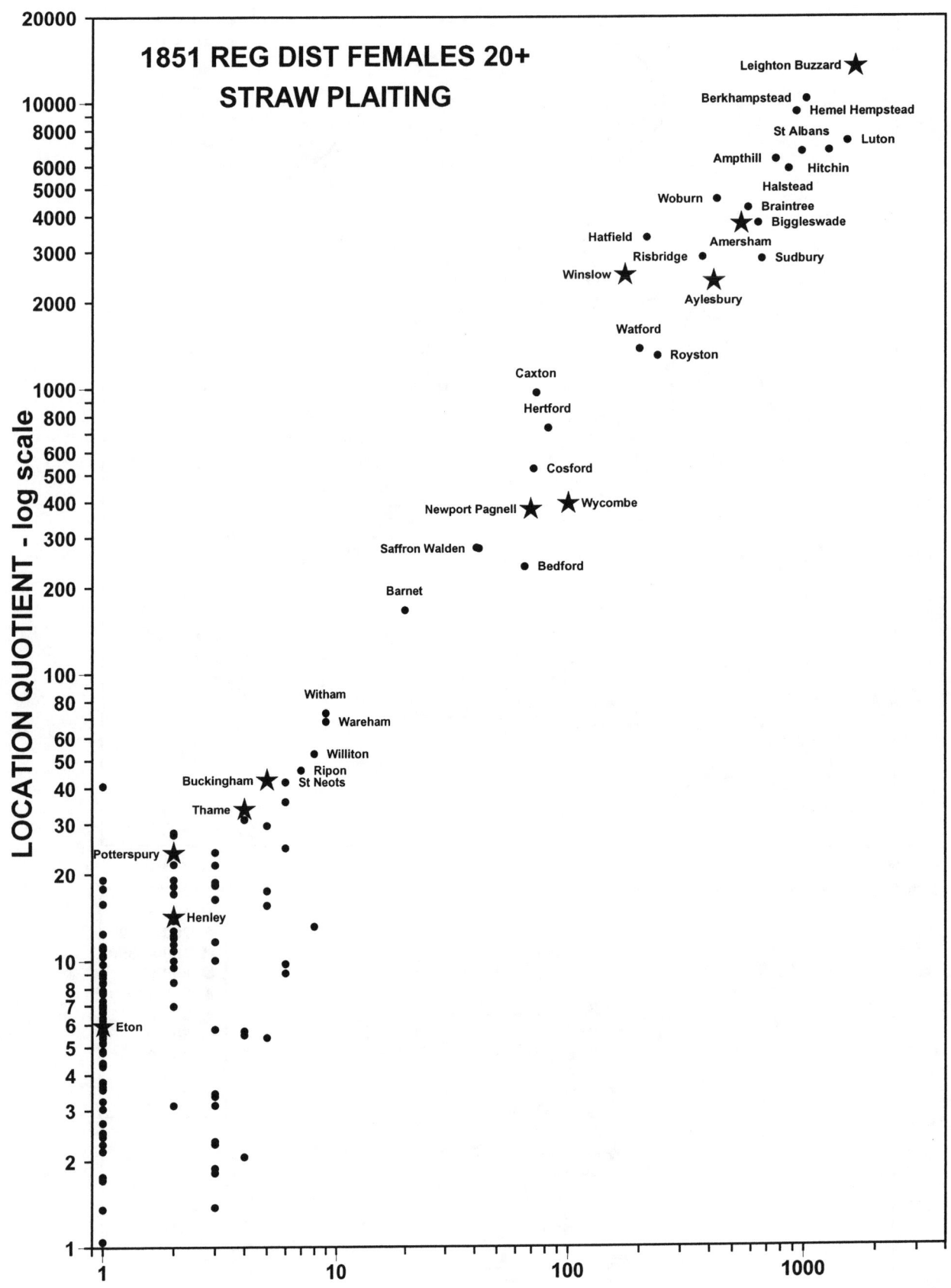

1851 REG DIST FEMALES 20+
STRAW PLAITING

LOCATION QUOTIENT - log scale

NUMBER EMPLOYED - log scale

Leighton Buzzard
Berkhampstead
Hemel Hempstead
St Albans
Luton
Ampthill
Hitchin
Halstead
Woburn
Braintree
Biggleswade
Hatfield
Amersham
Risbridge
Sudbury
Winslow
Aylesbury
Watford
Royston
Caxton
Hertford
Cosford
Newport Pagnell
Wycombe
Saffron Walden
Bedford
Barnet
Witham
Wareham
Williton
Ripon
Buckingham
St Neots
Thame
Potterspury
Henley
Eton

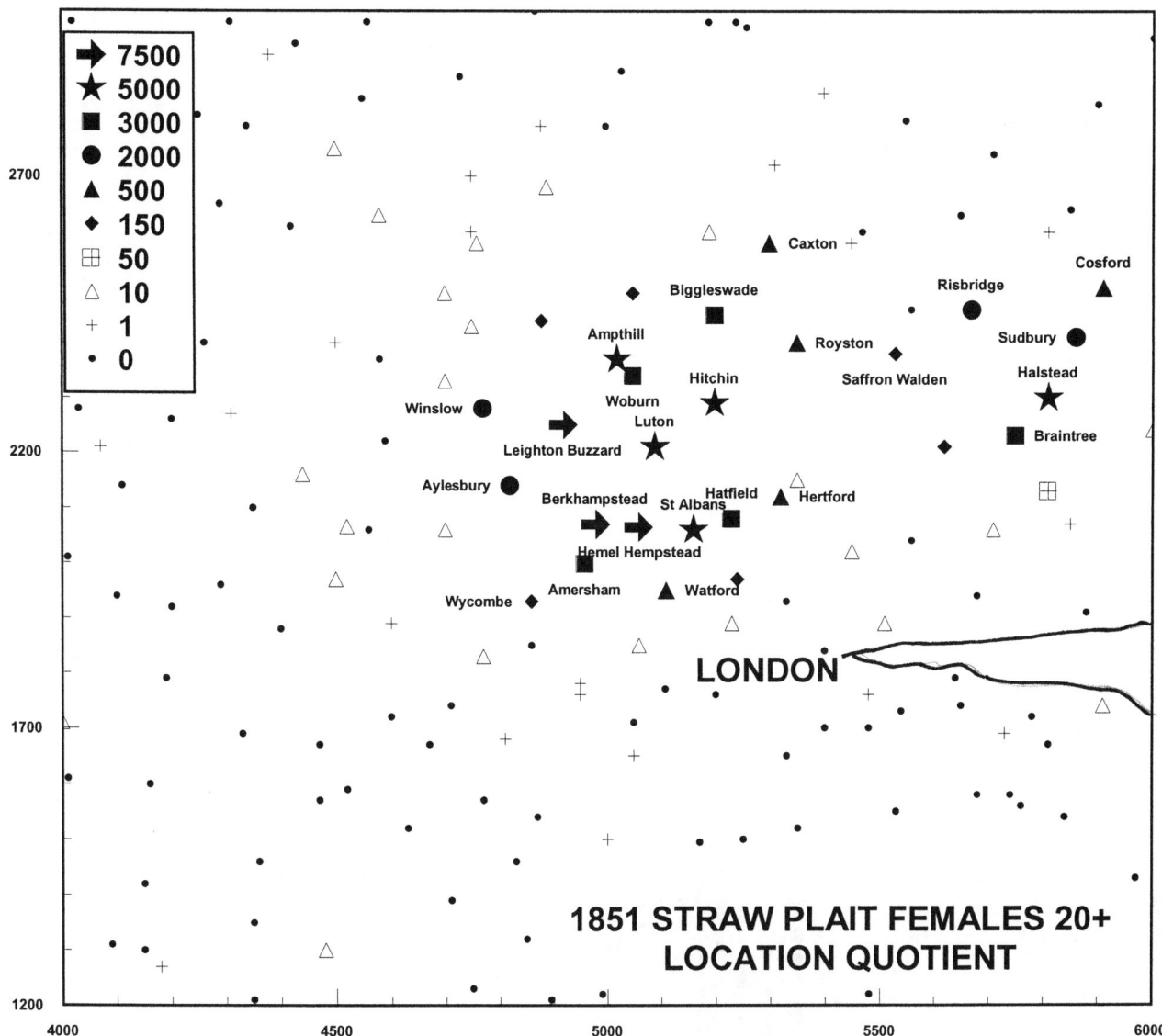

1851 STRAW PLAIT FEMALES 20+
LOCATION QUOTIENT

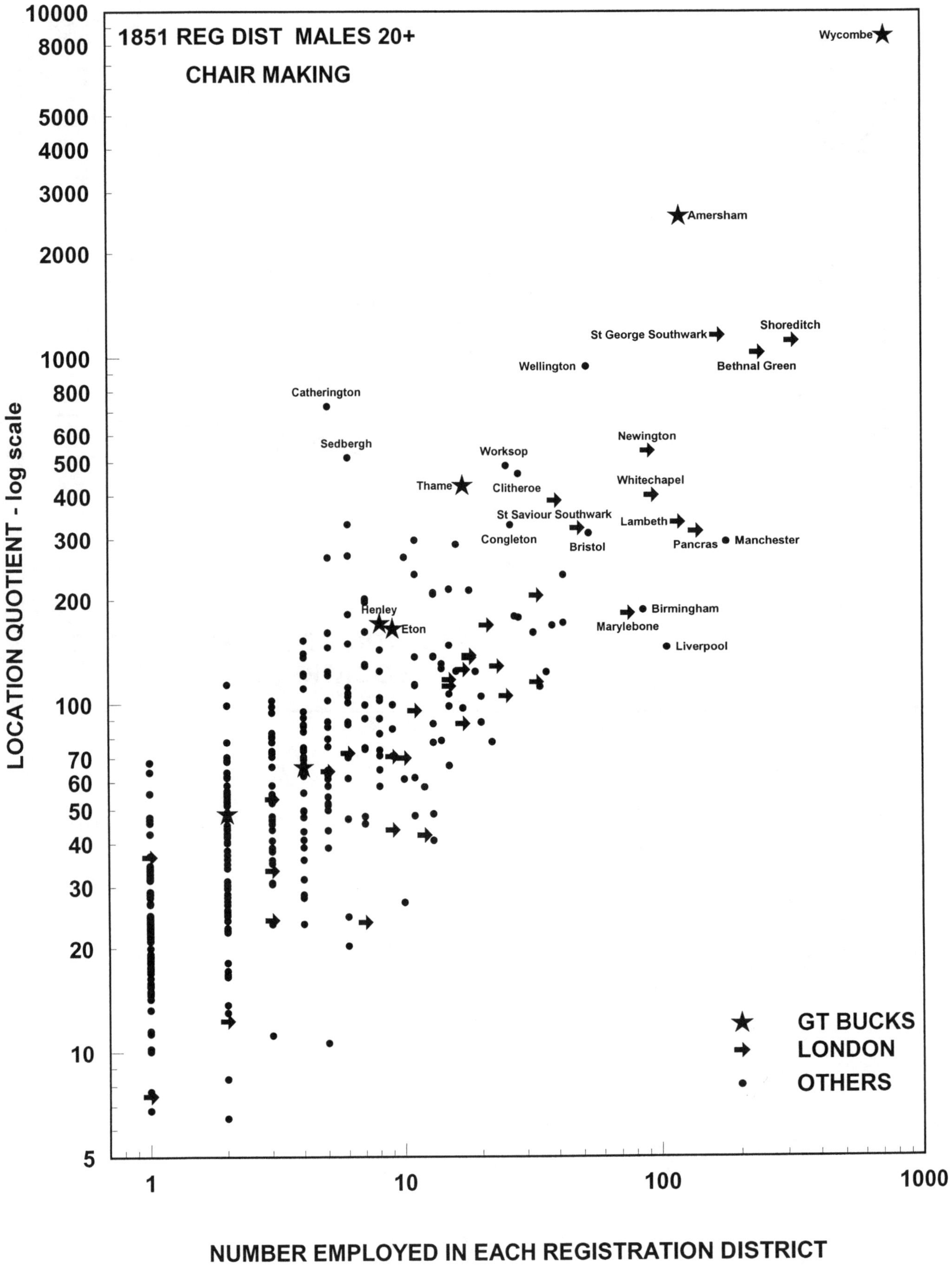

1851 REG DIST MALES 20+
CHAIR MAKING
Wycombe
Amersham
St George Southwark
Shoreditch
Bethnal Green
Wellington
Catherington
Sedbergh
Worksop
Newington
Thame
Clitheroe
Whitechapel
St Saviour Southwark
Lambeth
Congleton
Bristol
Pancras
Manchester
Henley
Eton
Birmingham
Marylebone
Liverpool
GT BUCKS
LONDON
OTHERS
LOCATION QUOTIENT - log scale
NUMBER EMPLOYED IN EACH REGISTRATION DISTRICT
10000
8000
5000
4000
3000
2000
1000
800
600
500
400
300
200
100
70
60
50
40
30
20
10
5
1
10
100
1000

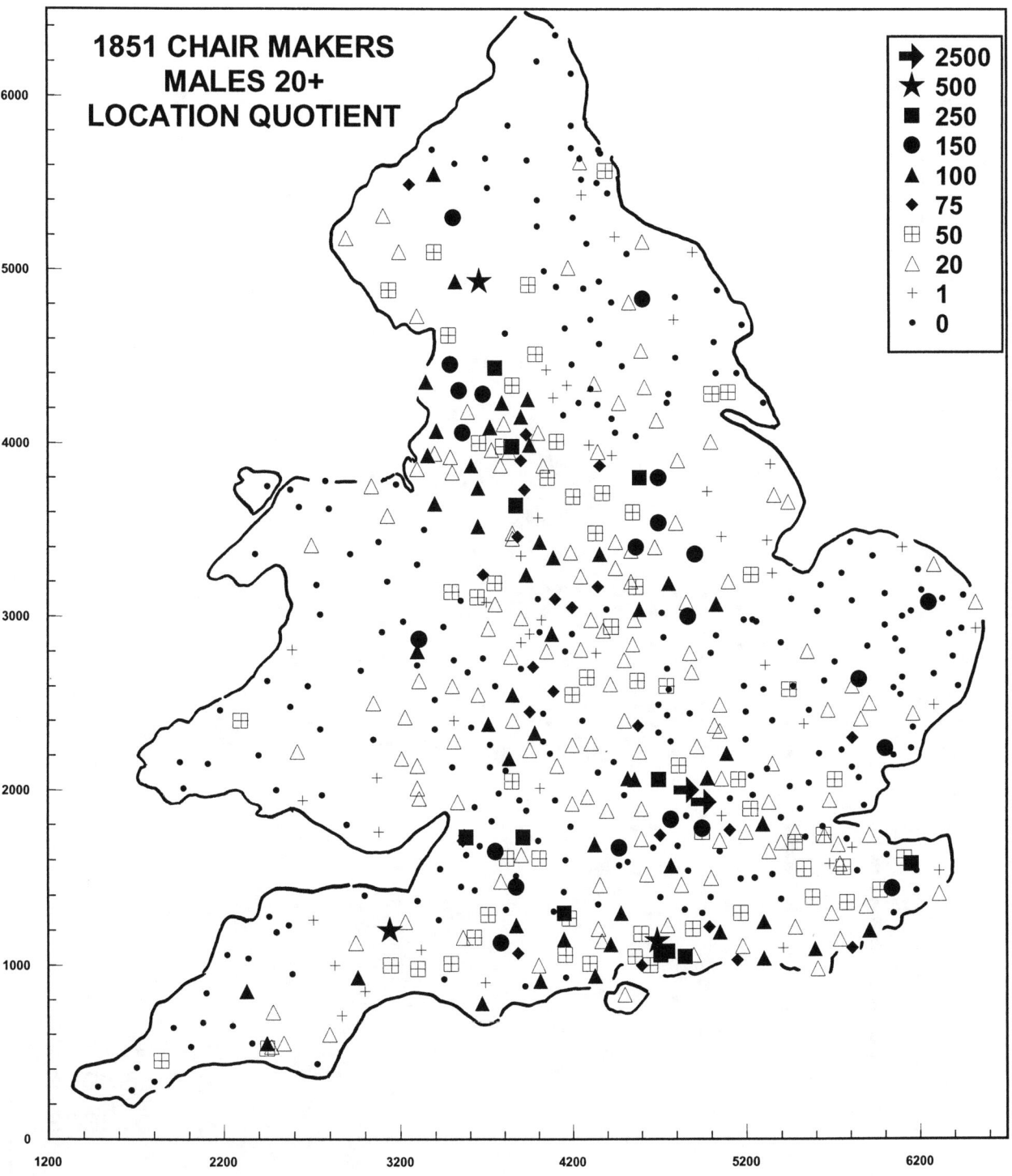

1851 CHAIR MAKERS
MALES 20+
LOCATION QUOTIENT

➡	2500
★	500
■	250
●	150
▲	100
◆	75
⊞	50
△	20
+	1
·	0

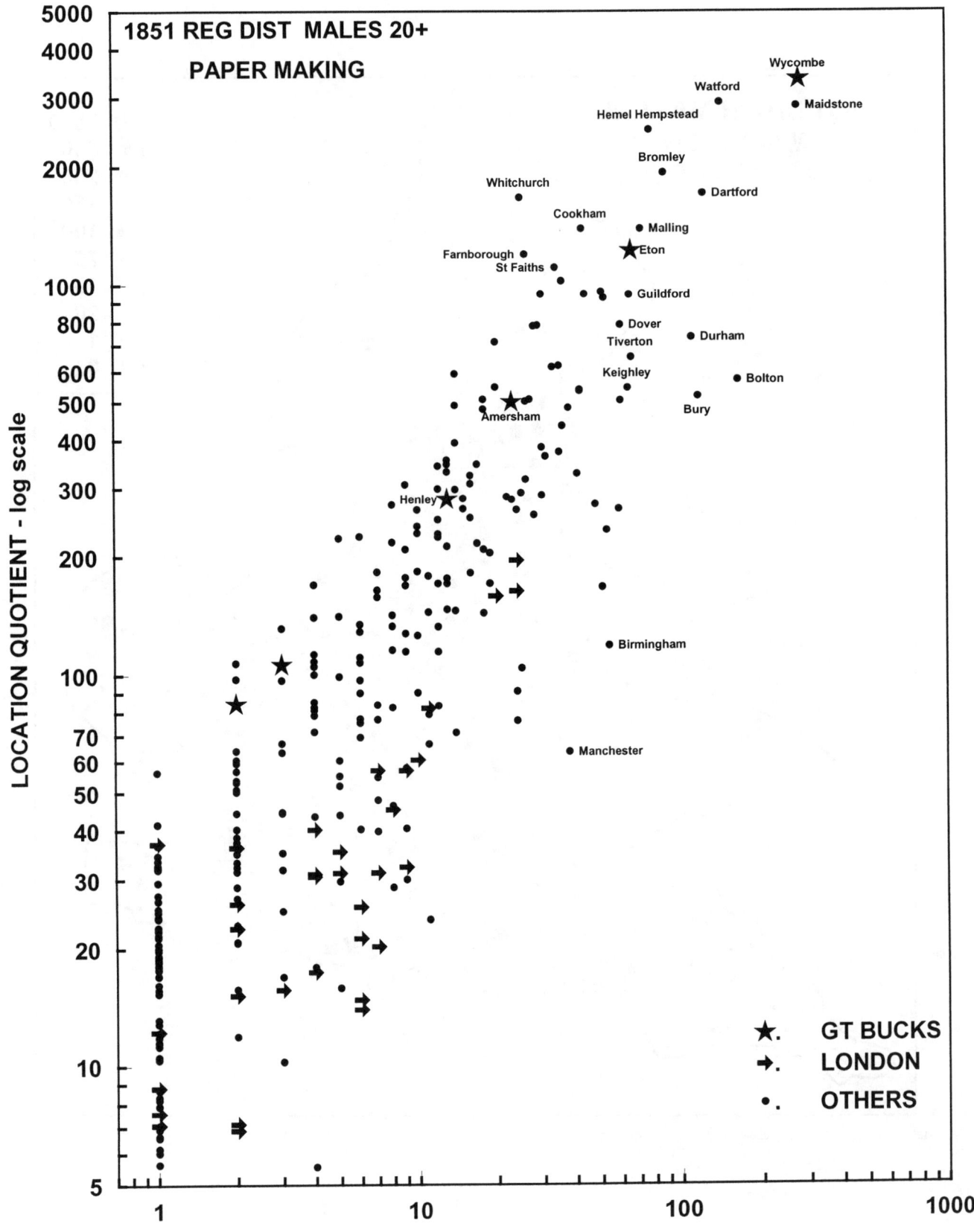

1851 REG DIST MALES 20+

PAPER MAKING

X-axis: NUMBER EMPLOYED IN EACH REGISTRATION DISTRICT - log scale

Y-axis: LOCATION QUOTIENT - log scale

Legend:
- ★. GT BUCKS
- ➔. LONDON
- •. OTHERS

Labelled points: Wycombe, Watford, Maidstone, Hemel Hempstead, Bromley, Dartford, Whitchurch, Cookham, Malling, Farnborough, St Faiths, Eton, Guildford, Dover, Tiverton, Durham, Keighley, Bolton, Bury, Amersham, Henley, Birmingham, Manchester

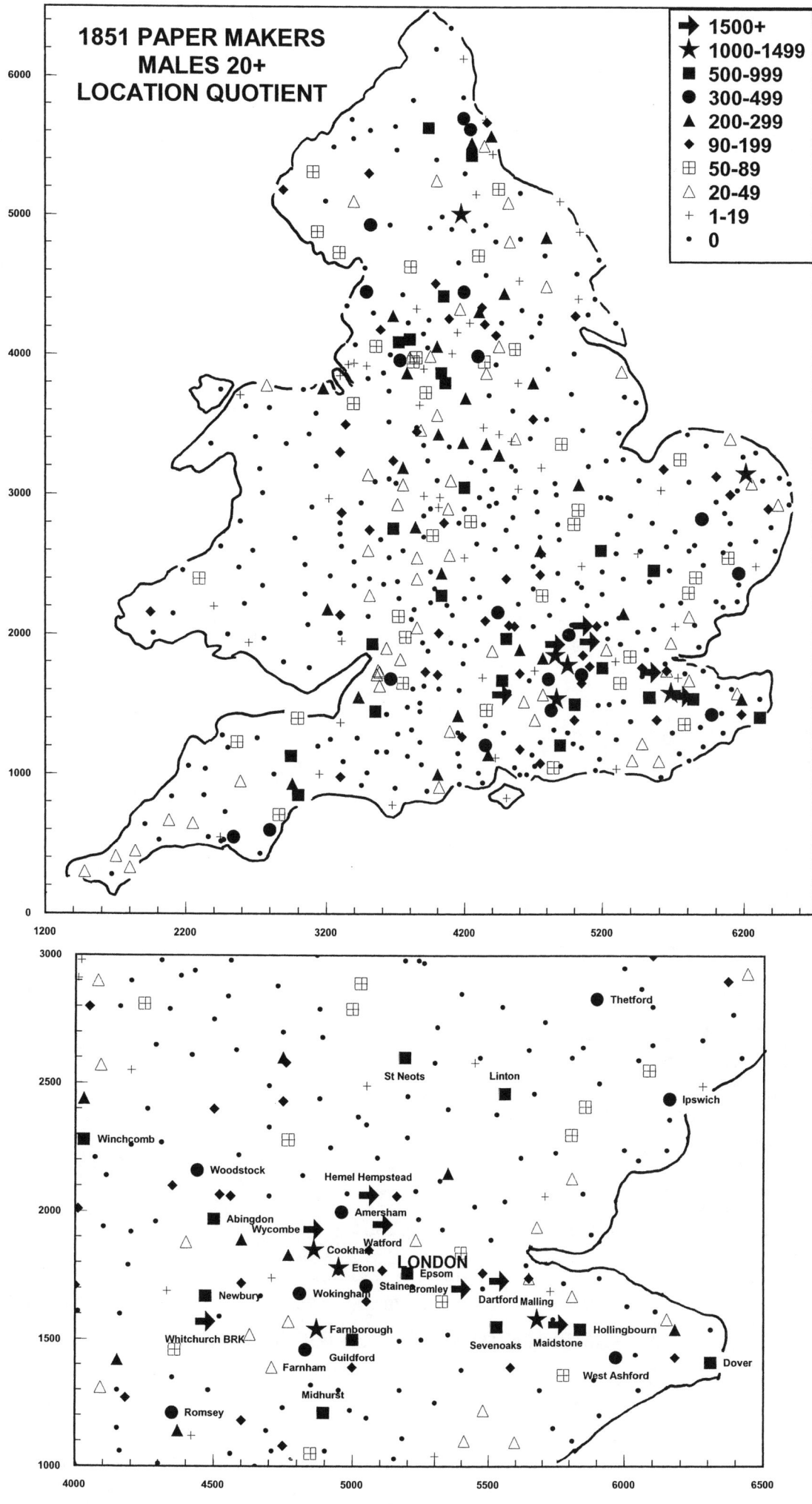

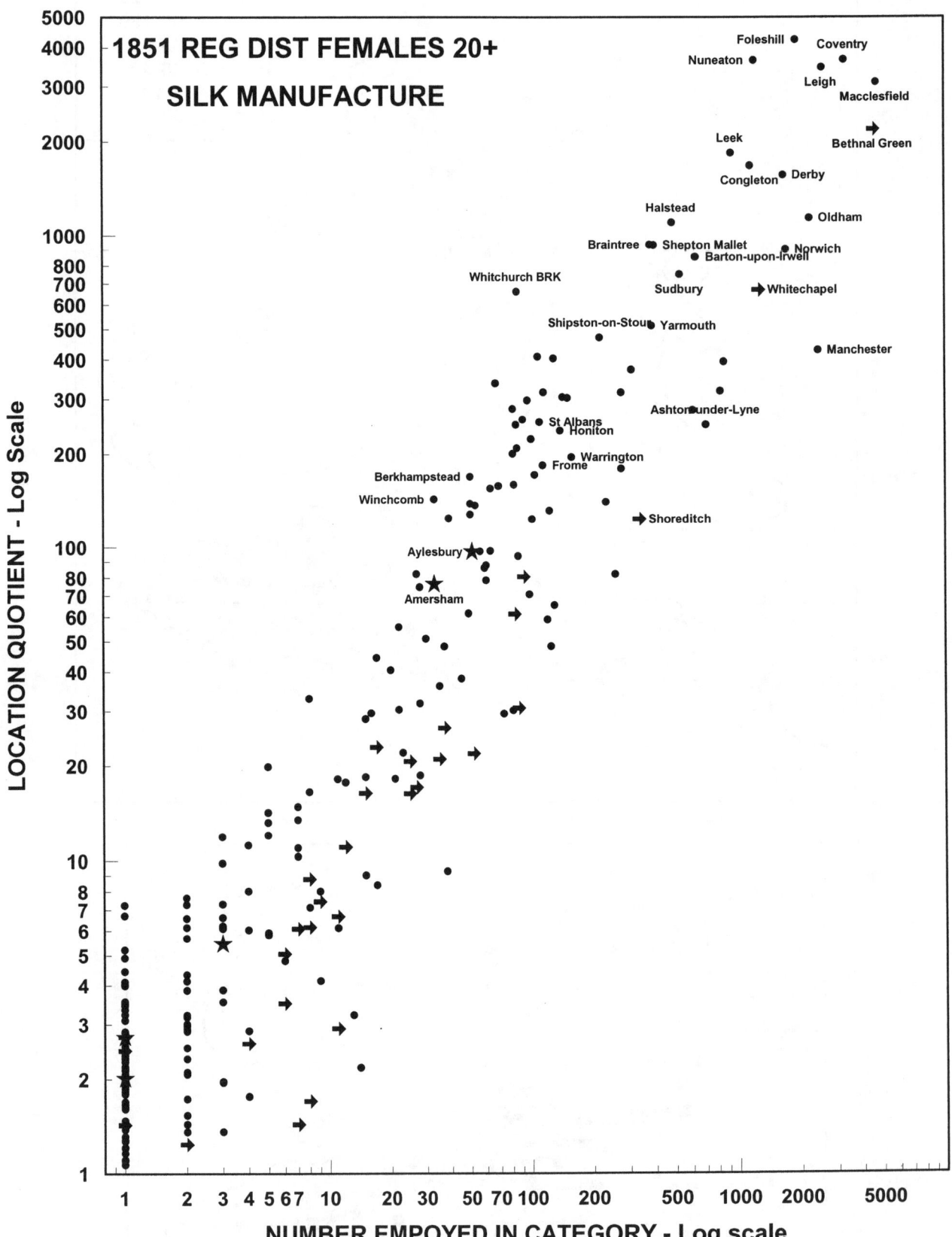

1851 REG DIST FEMALES 20+
SILK MANUFACTURE

Chart — X-axis: NUMBER EMPOYED IN CATEGORY - Log scale; Y-axis: LOCATION QUOTIENT - Log Scale

Labelled points: Foleshill, Coventry, Nuneaton, Leigh, Macclesfield, Leek, Bethnal Green, Congleton, Derby, Halstead, Oldham, Braintree, Shepton Mallet, Norwich, Barton-upon-Irwell, Whitchurch BRK, Sudbury, Whitechapel, Shipston-on-Stour, Yarmouth, Manchester, St Albans, Honiton, Ashton-under-Lyne, Warrington, Frome, Berkhampstead, Winchcomb, Shoreditch, Aylesbury, Amersham

KEY INDUSTRIAL OCCUPATIONS IN 1861

The information published in 1861 was in much the same format as in 1851. This applied both to the level of local detail given and the occupational categories used for classification. In 10 years there were changes both nationally and locally. It is sufficient here simply to consider the key industrial occupations. Lace-making can be seen to have begun its major decline. Straw plaiting, however, saw a substantial increase in employment. Employment in paper-making perhaps as a result of improved efficiency fell, most notably in WycombeRD. A dramatic increase in chair-making took place with numbers of males employed nearly increasing by 50%. Employment in brick-making nearly doubled especially in Eton ED where brick fields were opened up to serve both a local market in Slough and London. The small silk industry (total employment in 1851 was 93 males and 194 females and in 1861 77 and 248 showed a modest growth. Shoemaking grew although the figures for females need to be considered with care for in both years the census identified 'shoemakers' wives' as a category – not shown below but totalling 750 in 1851 and 854 in 1861.

REGISTRATION DISTRICTS 20+

1851		AM	ET	WY	AY	WIN	NP	BU	Bucks RC	HE	TH	PO	LB	Gt Bucks	Bucks RC	% <20
Adults	Male	4,671	5,483	8,452	6,076	2,407	5,922	3,707	36718	4,705	3,991	2,866	4,129	52,409	All	
Adults	Female	5,191	5,962	9,098	6,329	2,511	6,606	4,155	39852	4,968	4,201	2,979	4,395	56,395	Incl <20	
Lace	Male	-	-	4	2	1	11	1	19	-	1	6	-	26	53	64.2
	Female	556	23	2,010	927	748	2,204	625	7093	191	654	700	83	8,721	10487	32.4
Straw Plait	Male	24	18	11	39	17	5	1	115	3	1	-	258	377	505	77.2
	Female	549	1	101	421	176	70	5	1323	2	4	2	1,653	4,307	2922	54.7
Paper	Male	23	66	279	-	2	-	-	370	13	-	3	-	386	501	26.1
	Female	10	61	117	-	-	-	-	188	7	-	-	-	195	249	24.5
Chairmaking	Male	119	9	716	4	-	-	-	848	8	17	-	2	875	1285	34.0
	Female	na	na	na	na	na	na	na	na	na	na	na	na	na	na	na
Other Furniture	Male	na	na	na	na	na	na	na	0	na	na	na	na	na	na	na
	Female	-	-	60	-	-	-	-	60	-	-	-	1	61	220	72.7
Brickmaking	Male	29	34	26	59	13	37	32	230	50	14	9	19	322	283	18.7
Silk	Male	9	-	-	26	-	-	2	37	3	-	-	-	40	93	60.2
	Female	33	1	-	51	-	3	-	88	-	-	1	1	90	194	54.6
Shoemaking	Male	265	147	284	199	67	198	111	1271	129	111	88	101	1,700	1635	22.3
	Female	45	13	28	40	14	24	18	182	6	5	15	8	216	260	30.0
1861		AM	ET	WY	AY	WIN	NP	BU	0	HE	TH	PO	LB	0		
Adults	Male	4571	5761	8946	6078	2338	6499	3568	37761	4671	3895	3279	4298	53,904		
Adults	Female	5060	6461	9325	6603	2487	6930	3912	40778	5101	4118	3133	4781	57,911		
Lace	Male	2	-	6	-	-	12	1	21	-	-	2	-	23	42	50.0
	Female	442	13	1686	737	512	2016	764	6170	142	548	857	44	7,761	8459	27.1
Straw Plait	Male	12	-	6	11	9	-	-	38	-	-	-	79	117	157	75.8
	Female	598	5	197	508	219	116	2	1645	1	1	4	1929	3,580	2976	44.7
Paper	Male	12	63	213	1	-	1	-	290	20	-	-	-	310	376	22.9
	Female	7	36	128	-	-	-	-	171	2	-	-	-	173	253	32.4
Chairmaking	Male	132	7	1054	12	-	-	1	1206	42	17	-	-	1,265	1783	32.4
	Female	4	-	132	1	-	-	-	137	3	1	-	-	141	409	66.5
Other Furniture	Male	2	26	18	20	1	10	8	85	19	1	2	8	115	99	14.1
	Female	0	10	5	2	-	-	1	18	6	1	-	-	25	18	0.0
Brickmaking	Male	34	84	34	51	24	52	18	297	52	20	13	29	411	365	18.6
Silk	Male	8	-	1	17	-	-	-	26	1	-	-	-	27	75	65.3
	Female	23	-	1	68	-	-	-	92	-	-	-	-	92	248	62.9
Shoemaking	Male	282	155	333	207	65	251	121	1414	130	92	107	109	1,852	1882	24.9
	Female	65	16	72	39	7	39	29	267	5	12	20	35	339	376	29.0
% Change 51/61		AM	ET	WY	AY	WIN	NP	BU		HE	TH	PO	LB	Gt Bucks		
Adults	Male	-2.1	5.1	5.8	0.0	-2.9	9.7	-3.7	2.8	-0.7	-2.4	14.4	4.1	2.9		
Adults	Female	-2.5	8.4	2.5	4.3	-1.0	4.9	-5.8	2.3	2.7	-2.0	5.2	8.8	2.7		
Lace ##	Male	-	-	50.0	-	-	9.1	0.0	10.5	-	-	-66.7	-	21.1		
	Female	-20.5	-43.5	-16.1	-20.5	-31.6	-8.5	22.2	-13.0	-25.7	-16.2	22.4	-47.0	-11.0		
Straw Plait	Male	-50.0	-	-45.5	-71.8	-47.1	-	-	-67.0	-	-	-	-69.4	-69.0		
	Female	8.9	400.0	95.0	20.7	24.4	65.7	-60.0	24.3	-50.0	-75.0	100.0	16.7	20.0		
Paper	Male	-47.8	-4.5	-23.7	-	-	-	-	-21.6	53.8	-	-	-	-16.2		
	Female	-30.0	-41.0	9.4	-	-	-	-	-9.0	-71.4	-	-	-	-11.3		
Chairmaking	Male	10.9	-22.2	47.2	200.0				42.2	425.0	0.0	-		49.2		
	Female															
Other Furniture	Male															
	Female	-	-	-91.7	-	-	-	-	-70.0	-	-	-	-100.0	-59.0		
Brickmaking	Male	17.2	147.1	30.8	-13.6	84.6	40.5	-43.8	29.1	4.0	42.9	44.4	52.6	78.7		
Silk	Male	-11.1	-	-	-34.6	-	-	-	-29.7	-66.7	-	-	-	-27.0		
	Female	-30.3	-	-	33.3	-	-	-	4.5	-	-	-	-	2.2		
Shoemaking	Male	6.4	5.4	17.3	4.0	-3.0	26.8	9.0	11.3	0.8	-17.1	21.6	7.9	8.9		
	Female	44.4	23.1	157.1	-2.5	-50.0	62.5	61.1	46.7	-16.7	140.0	33.3	337.5	56.9		

Wycombe - it is tempting to believe the reduction was a switch to the furniture industry. However even though in both years embroiderers were identied seperately (79 in 1851 & 50 in 1861) there were also 389 adults in 1861 shown as 'cotton manufacture' incl those under 20 perhaps over 600. So far the location of these women has not been determined. In 1861 a factory was established at Little Marlow that according to Sheahan employed 200 females -the census suggests a smaller enterprise)

INDUSTRIAL OCCUPATIONS 1871-1891

The three censuses 1871, 1881 and 1891 used occupational categories that were similar. Only in 1871 were limited local figures published. In none of the censuses is it possible to construct a Greater Bucks area, figures are limited to the Registration County. There follow two tables for 1871 and a two part table that combines 1881 and 1891.

The first table provides all the local information given in 1871. It is limited to those aged 20+ and shows for each Registration District the number and percentage in 15 major categories of employment.

The second table gives county wide figures for that year, with the industries ranked in order of their size in the county. The table lists the number in each occupation, the Bucks location Quotient (LQ) for that activity and the overall importance in the county's population aged 10+ (in this it assumes that all those at work were aged 10+).

The 1881 and 1891 table shows industries in order of the census listing but provides Location Quotients for both years and the absolute percentage change in the county for those occupations with at least 25 persons

1871 20+

	AM	ET	WY	AY	WI	NP	BU	HE	TH	PO	LB	Gt Bucks	E & W	
MALES no	4716	6283	9596	6405	2284	6655	3530	4787	3834	3056	4542	55688	5866168	
Government	51	87	70	93	19	69	37	68	35	25	36	590	92536	
Defence	15	51	47	22	5	19	12	33	3	10	12	229	114491	
Professional	114	220	185	157	50	152	83	142	84	78	91	1356	173476	
Personal Service	210	575	360	254	68	206	148	463	164	127	166	2741	200220	
Commerce	96	84	125	136	29	73	50	47	53	47	88	828	201563	
Transport	55	250	161	124	32	163	65	73	54	85	124	1186	401086	
Agriculture	1776	2242	3116	3044	1278	2826	1778	2109	2225	978	1878	23250	1084182	
Animal Workers	92	107	120	121	58	146	79	78	79	54	130	1064	82352	
Industries Gen	556	851	2265	646	184	866	283	573	287	642	443	7596	902415	
Textiles	519	307	464	357	108	405	183	181	140	145	333	3142	651464	
Food	252	379	586	375	120	345	189	340	205	171	325	3287	332801	
Animal Substances	35	5	27	12	4	39	11	20	4	10	13	180	40107	
Veg Substances	229	147	691	109	27	80	44	157	34	43	79	1640	115184	
Minerals	179	380	348	228	106	594	126	255	130	233	320	2899	854326	
Labourers	521	552	1007	708	189	658	433	214	327	399	492	5500	594826	
Rank	16	46	24	19	7	14	9	34	10	9	12	200	25139	
FEMALES No	5157	7239	10171	6953	2494	7222	3931	5278	4027	3137	5230	60839	6463645	
Government	8	7	3	6	3	5	5	12	5	2	8	64	5552	
Professional	93	161	148	95	38	116	58	136	85	36	67	1033	94555	
Wives	2863	4175	5321	3596	1252	3247	2173	3107	2474	1734	2158	32100	4014044	
Personal Service	564	1537	1005	943	224	679	429	886	463	304	453	7487	901606	
Commerce	8	22	27	26	5	37	12	17	20	10	9	193	40915	
Transport	1	3	4	8	1	2	5	8	2	2	3	39	7822	
Agriculture	75	158	170	160	96	129	130	210	258	61	96	1543	133465	
Animal Workers		1										1	460	
Industries Gen	26	31	260	28	2	17	5	37	12	9	13	440	43607	
Textiles	1342	854	2878	1885	811	2807	1035	651	583	914	2302	16062	933490	
Food	39	37	60	42	16	41	23	42	26	28	37	391	57558	
Animal Substances	13					1					1	15	5570	
Veg Substances	2	31	150	6	1	6	2	3	1	5	1	208	17354	
Minerals	8	5	2	7	1	4		9	4		1	41	36850	
Labourers	13	23	21	2	3	17		3	11	2	3	98	29104	
Rank	102	194	122	149	41	114	54	157	83	30	78	1124	141693	

														Bucks LQ
MALES %														
Government	1.08	1.38	0.73	1.45	0.83	1.04	1.05	1.42	0.91	0.82	0.79	1.06	1.58	67
Defence	0.32	0.81	0.49	0.34	0.22	0.29	0.34	0.69	0.08	0.33	0.26	0.41	1.95	21
Professional	2.42	3.50	1.93	2.45	2.19	2.28	2.35	2.97	2.19	2.55	2.00	2.43	2.96	82
Personal Service	4.45	9.15	3.75	3.97	2.98	3.10	4.19	9.67	4.28	4.16	3.65	4.92	3.41	144
Commerce	2.04	1.34	1.30	2.12	1.27	1.10	1.42	0.98	1.38	1.54	1.94	1.49	3.44	43
Transport	1.17	3.98	1.68	1.94	1.40	2.45	1.84	1.52	1.41	2.78	2.73	2.13	6.84	31
Agriculture	37.66	35.68	32.47	47.53	55.95	42.46	50.37	44.06	58.03	32.00	41.35	41.75	18.48	226
Animal Workers	1.95	1.70	1.25	1.89	2.54	2.19	2.24	1.63	2.06	1.77	2.86	1.91	1.40	136
Industries Gen	11.79	13.54	23.60	10.09	8.06	13.01	8.02	11.97	7.49	21.01	9.75	13.64	15.38	89
Textiles	11.01	4.89	4.84	5.57	4.73	6.09	5.18	3.78	3.65	4.74	7.33	5.64	11.11	51
Food	5.34	6.03	6.11	5.85	5.25	5.18	5.35	7.10	5.35	5.60	7.16	5.90	5.67	104
Animal Substances	0.74	0.08	0.28	0.19	0.18	0.59	0.31	0.42	0.10	0.33	0.29	0.32	0.68	47
Veg Substances	4.86	2.34	7.20	1.70	1.18	1.20	1.25	3.28	0.89	1.41	1.74	2.94	1.96	150
Minerals	3.80	6.05	3.63	3.56	4.64	8.93	3.57	5.33	3.39	7.62	7.05	5.21	14.56	36
Labourers	11.05	8.79	10.49	11.05	8.27	9.89	12.27	4.47	8.53	13.06	10.83	9.88	10.14	97
Rank	0.34	0.73	0.25	0.30	0.31	0.21	0.25	0.71	0.26	0.29	0.26	0.36	0.43	84
All	100	100	100	100	100	100	100	100	100	100	100	100	100	100
FEMALES %														
Government	0.16	0.10	0.03	0.09	0.12	0.07	0.13	0.23	0.12	0.06	0.15	0.11	0.09	122
Professional	1.80	2.22	1.46	1.37	1.52	1.61	1.48	2.58	2.11	1.15	1.28	1.70	1.46	116
Wives	55.52	57.67	52.32	51.72	50.20	44.96	55.28	58.87	61.44	55.28	41.26	52.76	62.10	85
Personal Service	10.94	21.23	9.88	13.56	8.98	9.40	10.91	16.79	11.50	9.69	8.66	12.31	13.95	88
Commerce	0.16	0.30	0.27	0.37	0.20	0.51	0.31	0.32	0.50	0.32	0.17	0.32	0.63	50
Transport	0.02	0.04	0.04	0.12	0.04	0.03	0.13	0.15	0.05	0.06	0.06	0.06	0.12	53
Agriculture	1.45	2.18	1.67	2.30	3.85	1.79	3.31	3.98	6.41	1.94	1.84	2.54	2.06	123
Animal Workers		0.01											0.01	0
Industries Gen	0.50	0.43	2.56	0.40	0.08	0.24	0.13	0.70	0.30	0.29	0.25	0.72	0.67	107
Textiles	26.02	11.80	28.30	27.11	32.52	38.87	26.33	12.33	14.48	29.14	44.02	26.40	14.44	183
Food	0.76	0.51	0.59	0.60	0.64	0.57	0.59	0.80	0.65	0.89	0.71	0.64	0.89	72
Animal Substances	0.25	0.00	0.00	0.00	0.00	0.01	0.00	0.00	0.00	0.00	0.02	0.02	0.09	29
Veg Substances	0.04	0.43	1.47	0.09	0.04	0.08	0.05	0.06	0.02	0.16	0.02	0.34	0.27	127
Minerals	0.16	0.07	0.02	0.10	0.04	0.06	0.00	0.17	0.10	0.00	0.02	0.07	0.57	12
Labourers	0.25	0.32	0.21	0.03	0.12	0.24	0.00	0.06	0.27	0.06	0.06	0.16	0.45	36
Rank	1.98	2.68	1.20	2.14	1.64	1.58	1.37	2.97	2.06	0.96	1.49	1.85	2.19	84
All	100	100	100	100	100	100	100	100	100	100	100	100	100	100

1871 ALL AGES	Bucks Regist County			Bucks	LQ	Bucks aged 10+		
	male	female	Total	male	female	Per 10,000		
MEN & WOMEN	75,748	79,259	155007					
Aged 10+	55,473	58,751	114224			10000	10000	10000
Lace Manufacturer	29	8,077	8106	50	2953	5.2	1374.8	709.7
Labourer Undefined	3,979	31	4010	115	65	717.3	5.3	351.1
Straw Plait	112	3,412	3524	459	1124	20.2	580.8	308.5
Cabinet Maker, Upholsterer	2,264	597	2861	690	1034	408.1	101.6	250.5
Shoemaker	1,686	121	1807	126	70	303.9	20.6	158.2
Milliner	5	1,793	1798	51	89	0.9	305.2	157.4
Paper Manuf	466	255	721	677	574	84.0	43.4	63.1
Blacksmith	662	8	670	87	274	119.3	1.4	58.7
Tailor	518	44	562	68	17	93.4	7.5	49.2
Shirt Maker		550	550	-	102	-	93.6	48.2
Sawyer	479		479	252	-	86.3	-	41.9
Wheelwright	322		322	156	-	58.0	-	28.2
Brickmaker	313	2	315	127	12	56.4	0.3	27.6
Coach maker	271	3	274	176	136	48.9	0.5	24.0
Brewer	244	1	245	141	55	44.0	0.2	21.4
Miller	240	4	244	119	175	43.3	0.7	21.4
Engine & Machine Maker	236	-	236	33	-	42.5	-	20.7
Printer	150	26	176	50	523	27.0	4.4	15.4
Turner	174		174	356	-	31.4	-	15.2
Saddler	149	1	150	104	8	26.9	0.2	13.1
Brush & Broom Maker	68	47	115	117	221	12.3	8.0	10.1
French Polisher	101	10	111	234	102	18.2	1.7	9.7
Silk Manuf	17	92	109	10	27	3.1	15.7	9.5
Iron Manful	95	1	96	8	7	17.1	0.2	8.4
Engine Driver Stoker	83		83	39	-	15.0	-	7.3
Watchmaker	81	-	81	58	-	14.6	-	7.1
Maltster	66		66	95	-	11.9	-	5.8
Timber Merchant	63	3	66	77	53	11.4	0.5	5.8
Tin Plate	57		57	51	0	10.3	-	5.0
Embroiderer		54	54	-	572		9.2	4.7
Basket Maker	49	2	51	86	35	8.8	0.3	4.5
Gas Works	51		51	55	-	9.2	-	4.5
Lathmaker	48		48	235	-	8.7	-	4.2
Cooper	48		48	37	-	8.7	-	4.2
Millwright	47		47	92	-	8.5	-	4.1
Shopman	21	23	44	47	41	3.8	3.9	3.9
Whitesmith	43		43	74	-	7.8	-	3.8
Factory Labourer	32	11	43	38	18	5.8	1.9	3.8
Mechanic, Manuf, Shopmar	41		41	34	-	7.4	-	3.6
Tanner	40		40	68	-	7.2	-	3.5
Machine		40	40	-	28	-	6.8	3.5
Fancy Goods Manuf	7	31	38	36	77	1.3	5.3	3.3
Mat Maker	38		38	416	0	6.9	-	3.3
Rope	37	1	38	53	11	6.7	0.2	3.3
Furrier	25	12	37	99	76	4.5	2.0	3.2
Stone Merchant	29		29	71	-	5.2	-	2.5
Fellmonger	26		26	190	-	4.7	-	2.3
Apprentice	25	1	26	86	20	4.5	0.2	2.3
Earthenware Manuf	25		25	13	0	4.5	-	2.2
Brassfounder	24		24	17	0	4.3	-	2.1
Ag Implement Maker	23		23	94	-	4.1	-	2.0
Currier	23	-	23	24	-	4.1	-	2.0
Gas Fitter	23		23	39	-	4.1	-	2.0
Furniture Broker	13	5	18	51	96	2.3	0.9	1.6
Other Leather	16	-	16	217	-	2.9	-	1.4
Cutler	12	1	13	10	18	2.2	0.2	1.1
Hair Manufacturer	7	5	12	8	9	1.3	0.9	1.1
Shipwright	11		11	4	-	2.0	-	1.0
Manufacturing Chemist	9	2	11	12	50	1.6	0.3	1.0
Umbrella	9	2	11	43	11	1.6	0.3	1.0
Limestone Quarrier	11		11	31	-	2.0	-	1.0
Tobacco Pipe Maker	7	4	11	58	84	1.3	0.7	1.0
Water Providers	10		10	58	0	1.8	-	0.9
Goldsmith, Silversmith	9	1	10	7	5	1.6	0.2	0.9
Coppersmith	10		10	64	-	1.8	-	0.9
Dyer	8	1	9	10	10	1.4	0.2	0.8
Trimming	-	9	9	-	30	-	1.5	0.8
Toy Maker	1	7	8	12	85	0.2	1.2	0.7
Staymaker	-	8	8	-	14	-	1.4	0.7
Other Wire Etc	8		8	20	0	1.4	-	0.7

1871 ALL AGES	Bucks Regist County			Bucks	LQ	Bucks aged 10+ Per 10,000		
	male	female	Total	male	female			
Others Iron	8		8	23	0	1.4	-	0.7
Others In Carriage Making	6	1	7	38	146	1.1	0.2	0.6
Carvers & Figures	7	-	7	14	-	1.3	-	0.6
Rag Gatherer	5	2	7	32	21	0.9	0.3	0.6
Stone Quarrier	6		6	3	-	1.1	-	0.5
Musical Instrument Maker	5	-	5	10	-	0.9	-	0.4
Others Toys	4	1	5	40	304	0.7	0.2	0.4
Weaver Other	1	4	5	2	9	0.2	0.7	0.4
Haberdasher	2	3	5	7	11	0.4	0.5	0.4
Others In Bones	5		5	19	0	0.9	-	0.4
Other In Coal	5		5	116	0	0.9	-	0.4
Nail Manuf	4	1	5	5	1	0.7	0.2	0.4
Other Wood Arts	4		4	20	0	0.7	-	0.4
Pattern Designer	4		4	38	0	0.7	-	0.4
Woolen Cloth Manuf	3	1	4	1	0	0.5	0.2	0.4
Fustian	1	3	4	5	11	0.2	0.5	0.4
Glover Other	1	3	4	13	9	0.2	0.5	0.4
Sacking	4		4	83	0	0.7	-	0.4
Others In Mats	1	3	4	19	51	0.2	0.5	0.4
Oil & Colourman	4		4	17	0	0.7	-	0.4
Woodcarver	3		3	18	-	0.5	-	0.3
Other Patterns	3		3	19	0	0.5	-	0.3
Gunsmiths	3		3	4	0	0.5	-	0.3
Needle maker	3		3	17	0	0.5	-	0.3
Woolstapler	3		3	23	-	0.5	-	0.3
Glover Leather	3		3	28	0	0.5	-	0.3
Others In Dress	2	1	3	13	9	0.4	0.2	0.3
Paper Box		3	3	0	21	-	0.5	0.3
Other Paper	3		3	16	0	0.5	-	0.3
Water Others	3		3	57	-	0.5	-	0.3
Plater	3		3	33	0	0.5	-	0.3
Locksmith	3		3	6	-	0.5	-	0.3
Toolmaker	2		2	4	0	0.4	-	0.2
Others In Chemicals	2	-	2	13	-	0.4	-	0.2
Silk Dyer	2		2	18	-	0.4	-	0.2
Flax & Linen	1	1	2	2	1	0.2	0.2	0.2
Cotton Manufacturer	1	1	2	0	0	0.2	0.2	0.2
Textiles Other	1	1	2	30	32	0.2	0.2	0.2
Net	x	2	2	-	18		0.3	0.2
Canvas	2		2	37	0	0.4	-	0.2
Boxmaker	1	1	2	3	3	0.2	0.2	0.2
Cork Cutter	2		2	15	0	0.4	-	0.2
Others In Cane, Straw Etc	2		2	47	0	0.4	-	0.2
Coal Miner	2		2	0	-	0.4	-	0.2
Glass Manuf	2	-	2	2	-	0.4	-	0.2
Copper Manuf	2		2	9	0	0.4	-	0.2
Zinc Manuf	2		2	17	0	0.4	-	0.2
Wire Worker	2		2	4	0	0.4	-	0.2
Other Printer	1		1	9	-	0.2	-	0.1
Artificial Flower		1	1	-	3		0.2	0.1
Philos.Instrument Maker	1		1	5	0	0.2	-	0.1
Weighing Machine	1		1	9	-	0.2	-	0.1
Spinning Machine Maker	1		1	2	0	0.2	-	0.1
Pin Manufacture		1	1	0	37	-	0.2	0.1
Others In Tools	1		1	8	0	0.2	-	0.1
Sail Maker	1		1	4	0	0.2	-	0.1
Carpet & Rug Manuf	1	-	1	2	-	0.2	-	0.1
Ribbon		1	1	0	9	-	0.2	0.1
Hosiery	-	1	1	-	1	-	0.2	0.1
Leather Case	1	-	1	7	-	0.2	-	0.1
Floor Cloth	1		1	19	-	0.2	-	0.1
Others In Oils	1	-	1	10	-	0.2	-	0.1
Iron Miner	1		1	1	-	0.2	-	0.1
Clay	1		1	6	0	0.2	-	0.1
Other Precious Stone Work	1		1	5	0	0.2	-	0.1
Anchor-Smith	1		1	4	0	0.2	-	0.1

1881 & 1891 aged 10+

	England & Wales 1881		Bucks 1881		England & Wales 1891		Bucks 1891		Bucks Location Quotients				Bucks % change 91/81	
	Male	Fem	Male	Fem	Male	Fem	Male	Fem	M 81	M 91	F 81	F91	M	F
Total	9,313,666	9,992,513	56,316	58,629	10,591,967	11,461,890	60848	63190					8	8
Lithographer	26690	4179	16	-	23602	2928	8	-	10	-	6	-		
Map Colourer	129561	1610	387	3	175553	3536	825	3	49	32	82	15	113	
Musical Instrument Maker	9,505	10,592	13	14	11,487	14,249	50	62	23	23	76	79		
Toys & Fishing Tackle	59,088	2,202	239	30	81,959	4,527	390	100	67	232	83	401	63	233
Type Founder	5,546	135	1	-	8,636	349	1	-	3	-	2	-		
Seal Die	459	166	1	-	588	118	-	-	36	-	-	-		
Watchmaker	9,008	241	3	1	12,174	449	13	-	6	71	19	-		
Philos.Instrument Maker	2,965	1,899	21	3	3,944	2,832	17	11	117	27	75	70		
Electrical Apparatus	1,137	32	-	-	1,844	55	10	-	-	-	94	-		
Weighing Machine Maker	1,486	53	-	-	1,314	83	1	-	-	-	13	-		
Gunsmiths & Ordnance	22,576	775	76	-	22,485	1,363	83	4	56	-	64	53	9	
Engine & Machine Maker	3,385	220	-	-	4,492	350	3	1	-	-	12	52		
Ag Implement Maker	2,496	26	7	-	12,135	469	31	-	46	-	44	-		
Millwright	2,391	195	1	1	3,205	429	2	-	7	87	11	-		
Fitter, Turner	7,817	220	3	-	9,183	215	4	-	6	-	8	-		
Boiler Maker	38,180	301	61	1	46,634	757	71	-	26	57	27	-	16	
Domestic Machinery	4,066	53	27	-	3,185	72	7	-	110	-	38	-	-74	
Toolmaker	6,940	-	46	-	6,112	1	30	-	110	-	85	-	-35	
Saw Maker	64,663	-	100	-	87,510	-	138	-	26	-	27	-	38	
Cutler	26,170	-	25	-	36,726	-	15	-	16	-	7	-	-40	
Needle Maker	1,554	721	7	-	1,826	505	16	-	74	-	153	-		
Pin Manufacture	9,162	191	2	-	11,992	266	11	-	4	-	16	-		
Coach & Rail Carriage	2,016	100	4	-	2,007	126	6	-	33	-	52	-		
Wheelwright	16,651	1,583	3	1	17,734	2,258	5	-	3	11	5	-		
Bicycle Maker	2,381	2,074	1	-	2,164	1,659	-	-	7	-	-	-		
Saddler	234	495	-	-	292	605	1	-	-	-	60	-		
Ship Builder	33,167	337	434	11	41,454	531	648	19	216	556	272	649	49	
Ship Rigger	28,635	97	296	1	27,836	114	295	1	171	176	184	159	0	
Sail Maker	1,059	13	1	-	10,965	559	4	-	16	-	6	-		
Carpenter, Joiner	21,831	2,035	148	1	24,378	2,943	143	1	112	8	102	6	-3	
Painter,	21,702	39	14	-	62,599	118	34	-	11	-	9	-		
Cabinet Maker, Uphols	2,834	27	-	-	3,448	-	1	-	-	-	5	-		
Furniture Broker & Others	4,082	47	-	-	3,517	59	1	-	-	-	5	-		
Locksmith	235,017	216	1,317	-	220,661	318	1364	-	93	-	108	-	4	
Taxidermist	99676	454	376	2	123119	740	536	2	62	75	76	49	43	
Carver Gilder	59,844	10,014	2,395	25	78,217	13,144	3390	112	662	43	754	155	42	348
Woodcarver	5,075	958	20	5	-	-	-	-	65	89	-	-		
Artificial Flower	7,342	352	4	-	19,803	595	56	-	9	-	49	-		
Dye Man & Blacking	686	159	6	-	-	-	4	-	145	-	-	-		
Manufacturing Chemist	8,199	363	8	1	9,375	670	15	-	16	47	28	-		
Wool-Stapler	3,080	28	6	1	3,503	52	35	2	32	609	174	698		
Woolen Cloth Manuf	720	4,461	2	1	722	4,436	-	-	46	4	-	-		
Silk Manuf	2,715	546	6	-	3,938	607	4	-	37	-	18	-		
Lace Manufacturer	12,843	1,128	4	-	19,708	1,775	21	1	5	-	19	10		
Cotton Manufacturer	2446	28	4	-	1714	34	2	-	27	-	20	-		
Bleacher	59,048	60,445	2	-	62,119	62,476	2	-	1	-	1	-		
Factory Worker Textiles	17,655	39,694	11	85	16,071	31,811	1	1	10	36	1	1		-99
Fancy Goods Manuf	11,359	32,785	14	4,442	13,030	21,716	5	1108	20	2309	7	925		-75
Embroiderer & Trimmings	185,410	302,367	-	3	213,231	332,784	5	-	-	0	0	-		
Carpet & Rug Manuf	11,799	1,840	1	-	26,103	5,005	1	2	1	-	1	7		
Hatter	5,697	7,817	-	8	2,879	4,365	2	2	-	17	12	8		
Straw Plait	1,388	6,185	4	22	2,476	7,714	3	29	48	61	21	68		
Tailor	3,332	12,087	4	47	1,281	7,659	5	300	20	66	68	710		538
Milliner	8,795	5,190	1	-	9,232	7,375	-	-	2	-	-	-		
Shirt Maker	13,617	9,072	8	1	16,363	12,585	3	2	10	2	3	3		
Hosiery	3,001	27,983	87	1,654	3,425	14,959	27	515	479	1007	137	624	-69	-69
Haberdasher	107,668	52,980	417	59	119,496	89,224	456	68	64	19	66	14	9	15
Glover Leather	2,937	357,995	3	1,861	4,470	415,961	1	2006	17	89	4	87		8
Shoemaker & Clog	1,379	81,865	-	516	2,153	52,943	5	377	-	107	40	129		-27
Wig Maker, Hairdresser	18,862	21,510	1	6	18,200	30,887	-	2	1	5	-	1		
Button	4,879	4,686	4	6	5,677	6,804	6	3	14	22	18	8		
Umbrella	2,263	13,261	2	5	2,756	9,199	-	2	15	6	-	4		
Others In Dress	180,884	35,672	1,582	243	202,648	46,141	2002	370	145	116	172	145	27	52
Mat Maker	14,165	768	48	7	24,063	1,274	82	7	56	155	59	100	71	
Hemp Man	2,286	4,121	1	-	1,949	3,107	-	-	7	-	-	-		
Rope	4,118	4,112	9	2	5,377	4,500	5	3	36	8	16	12		
Canvas, Sacking Mats	639	1,663	-	1	1,588	3,203	2	4	-	10	22	23		
Maltster	1,800	479	19	-	2,194	548	10	3	175	-	79	99		
Brewer	1,181	2,297	4	-	1,497	2,549	6	2	56	-	70	14		
Miller	9,658	2,093	35	-	8,372	2,369	21	-	60	-	44	-	-40	
Ginger Beer	1,179	2,051	3	4	1,015	1,752	4	2	42	33	69	21		
Sugar Refiner	9,473	58	48	-	9,050	38	46	-	84	-	88	-	-4	
Manure Manufacture	24,196	371	199	3	25,918	394	181	3	136	138	122	138	-9	
Bone, Horn	23,162	300	188	1	22,369	390	184	6	134	57	143	279	-2	
Others In Bones	4,325	337	37	2	5,981	710	36	3	141	101	105	77	-3	

1881 & 1891 aged 10+	England & Wales 1881		Bucks 1881		England & Wales 1891		Bucks 1891		Bucks Location Quotients				Bucks % change 91/81	
	Male	Fem	Male	Fem	Male	Fem	Male	Fem	M 81	M 91	F 81	F 91	M	F
Currier	2951	119	-	-	3,499	234	3	-	-	-	15	-		
Tanner	1,168	55	2	-	878	53	-	-	28	-	-	-		
Furrier	1,710	155	1	-	2,090	444	2	-	10	-	17	-		
Parchment	247	95	1	-	693	223	3	-	67	-	75	-		
Hair	14,991	560	33	1	22,338	3,165	24	1	36	30	19	6	-27	
Brush & Broom Maker	10,157	91	30	-	10,279	69	22	-	49	-	37	-	-27	
Feather Dresser	4,683	3,465	21	8	5,694	4,318	58	25	74	39	177	105		
Oil Miller	407	24	25	1	313	20	13	-	1016	710	723	-		
Oil & Colourman	893	1,743	2	-	-	-	-	-	37	-	-	-		
Japanner	8,714	4,185	79	180	9,685	6,167	100	213	150	733	180	626	27	18
India Rubber	429	2,089	-	-	460	2,368	-	1	-	-	-	8		
Floor Cloth	4,428	102	1	-	3,796	62	-	-	4	-	-	-		
Waterproof	4,257	381	2	-	6,747	716	12	-	8	-	31	-		
Others In Oils	1,359	1,539	3	-	1,146	1,685	-	-	37	-	-	-		
Sawyer	3,517	1,448	-	-	6,466	4,146	1	1	-	-	3	4		
Lath Maker	1,312	22	-	-	1,528	78	7	-	-	-	80	-		
Turner	1,233	350	2	1	-	-	-	-	27	49	-	-		
Cooper	533	28	5	-	1,030	123	6	-	155	-	101	-		
Others In Wood	24,712	-	350	-	23,281	-	360	-	234	-	269	-	3	
Others In Bark	2,919	18	40	-	2,437	13	38	-	227	-	271	-	-5	
Basket Maker	11,382	2,595	279	1	12,688	1,912	281	4	405	7	386	38	1	
Straw (ex Plait)Cutter etc	18,596	103	36	2	17,143	69	31	-	32	331	31	-	-14	
Paper Manuf	-	-	-	-	-	-	34	10	-	-	-	-		
Envelope	272	40	1	-	7,475	1,233	-	-	61	-	-	-		
Card	9,017	2,525	86	619	9,860	2,469	96	497	158	4178	169	3651	12	-20
Paper Box	2,598	50	-	-	840	-	1	-	-	-	21	-		
Ticket	10,352	8,277	368	285	12,014	8,029	408	266	588	587	591	601	11	-7
Other Paper	175	1,933	-	1	289	2,458	2	43	-	9	120	317		
Coal Miner	1,209	440	1	-	1,631	814	-	-	14	-	-	-		
Iron Miner	1,187	8,718	-	1	2,121	17,178	1	14	-	2	8	15		
Mine Service	642	498	-	17	1,110	1,306	1	3	-	582	16	42		
Others In Mines	1,823	227	4	-	2,722	237	8	-	36	-	51	-		
Slate Quarrier	378,664	3,099	1	-	513,843	3,267	19	-	0	-	1	-		
Limestone Quarrier	25,879	231	-	-	18,158	73	1	-	-	-	1	-		
Clay	3,572	30	2	-	5,991	29	2	-	9	-	6	-		
Coprohte	-	-	-	-	2,401	28	2	-	-	-	15	-		
Cement	14,900	-	1	-	13,763	77	-	-	1	-	-	-		
Well Sinker	3,270	39	2	-	2,711	-	1	-	10	-	6	-		
Brickmaker	4,722	122	3	-	5,896	-	4	-	11	-	12	-		
Earthenware Manuf	686	19	4	-	-	-	-	-	96	-	-	-		
Tobacco Pipe Maker	3,634	46	6	-	5,432	-	-	-	27	-	-	-		
Glass Manuf	1,460	-	-	-	1,105	-	6	-	-	-	95	-		
Water Providers	47,337	2,738	389	3	41,022	2,666	368	-	136	19	156	-	-5	
Oth Precious Stone Work	28,719	17,877	17	1	34,828	21,772	21	2	10	1	10	2		
Copper Manuf	1,703	738	1	-	1,484	687	3	-	10	-	35	-		
Tin Manufacturer	19,938	1,692	2	-	24,055	2,105	-	-	2	-	-	-		
Zinc Manuf	2,517	8	9	-	3,819	4	9	-	59	-	41	-		
Brassfounder	588	1,977	-	-	1,772	1,857	1	-	-	-	10	-		
Lacquerer	7,298	50	2	-	8,486	52	-	-	5	-	-	-		
Pewterer	32,392	4,531	55	21	39,702	6,538	63	7	28	79	28	19	15	
Wire Worker & Others	2,241	24	-	-	3,377	171	1	-	-	-	5	-		
Screw Cutter	26,892	982	27	-	34,777	2,054	36	-	17	-	18	-	33	
Lamp	478	2,209	-	-	7,809	3,283	3	-	-	-	7	-		
Iron Manful	4,791	838	-	-	4,976	1,803	2	-	-	-	7	-		
Blacksmith & Whitesmith	8,722	521	4	-	10,196	979	7	2	8	-	12	37		
Nail Manuf	5,673	2,344	6	-	6,793	3,259	3	-	17	-	8	-		
Manufacturer Undef	2,541	503	5	-	3,111	714	10	-	33	-	56	-		
Labourer Undefined	198,786	1,891	64	-	199,853	2,553	128	1	5	-	11	7	100	
Engine Driver Stoker	120,388	388	636	7	139,524	500	696	7	87	307	87	254	9	
Factory Labourer	9,603	9,138	2	-	5,127	4,816	2	-	3	-	7	-		
Artisan	9,898	579	17	-	10,303	896	18	3	28	-	30	61		
Apprentice	556,876	2,893	4,194	29	594,128	1,947	3782	8	125	171	111	75	-10	-72
Machine	66,137	-	132	-	82,056	-	213	-	33	-	45	-	61	
Factory Labourer	16,907	4,238	77	12	28,043	10,117	110	11	75	48	68	20	43	
Artizan	28,777	2,255	128	1	52,266	6,301	106	10	74	8	35	29	-17	
Apprentice	3,825	759	8	3	-	-	-	-	35	67	-	-		
Machine	4,645	7,524	17	6	8,769	21,478	22	27	61	14	44	23		

INDUSTRIAL OCCUPATIONS IN 1901 - BUCKS ADMINISTRATIVE COUNTY

1901 was the first year when figures for the administrative county were published. This makes comparison with 1891 difficult particularly as in neither year was much local information provided. In 1901 there were three tables which provide data. The first covering the whole county was similar to those published for the registration county since 1851. The second with slightly less detail provides information by age, sex and administratively urban or rural status. The third shown below covered the four largest urban areas (Aylesbury UD, Chesham UD, Chepping Wycombe MB and Slough UD. The third and the first these are summarised below.

Class No	MALES	CONDENSED LIST OCCUPATIONS Urban Areas with population 5,000+							
		Ayle	Chesh	Wyc	Slough	Ayle	Chesh	Wyc	Slough
			Number				Percentage		
	Total aged 10+	3,269	2,680	5,780	4,267				
	Unoccupied	566	398	815	897	17.3	14.9	14.1	21.0
v.2	Clerks	42	30	85	82	1.6	1.3	1.7	2.4
VI	Transport	400	114	323	575	14.8	5.0	6.5	17.1
	Railway				347				
VII	Agriculture	162	83	66	216	6.0	3.6	1.3	6.4
X 1-7	Metal Manufacture	71	47	88	242	2.6	2.1	1.8	7.2
XII	Building	361	240	566	571	13.4	10.5	11.4	16.9
XII	Wood & Furniture	88	236	2,407	56	3.3	10.3	48.5	1.7
	(Wood Turners)		161				7.1		
	(Brush & Broom)		109				4.8		
	(Cabinet Makers)			1,543					
	(French Ploishers)			383					
	(Upholsters)			197					
	(Sawyers)			123					
XVI	Skins, Leather Furs	12	117	30	12	0.4	5.1	0.6	0.4
XVII	Paper, Printing	349	52	84	37	12.9	2.3	1.7	1.1
	(Printers)	273				10.1			
XIX	Dress	107	769	131	144	4.0	33.7	2.6	4.3
	(Shoes)		716						
XX	Food Drink Lodging	402	205	413	358	14.9	9.0	8.3	10.6
	All Other	709	389	772	1,077	26.2	17.0	15.5	32.0
	Brick Tiles				112				3.3
	Total occupied	2,703	2,282	4,965	3,370	100.0	100.0	100.0	100.0
FEMALES									
	Total aged 10+	4,099	2,892	6,184	4,721				
	Unoccupied	2,769	1,918	4,526	3,339	67.6	66.3	73.2	70.7
	Occupied Unmarried	1,027	780	1,316	1,082				
	Occupied Married	294	194	342	300				
	Married Occupied					13.6	12.4	10.3	12.1
III.4	Teaching	52	55	118	90	3.9	5.6	7.1	6.5
IV.1	Domestic Servants	392	195	441	575	29.7	20.0	26.6	41.6
IV.3	Charwomen	51	20	18	33	3.9	2.1	1.1	2.4
IV.4	Laundry	65	35	92	193	4.9	3.6	5.5	14.0
XVIII	Paper & Printing	174	16	83	4	13.2	1.6	5.0	0.3
XIX	Dress	184	104	237	184	13.9	10.7	14.3	13.3
XX	Food Drink Lodging	133	57	83	72	10.1	5.9	5.0	5.2
	All Other	270	492	586	231	20.4	50.5	35.3	16.7
	(Brush & Broom)		238				24.4		
	(Shoes)		164				16.8		
	(Willow Cane)			274					
	All Other excl ( )	270	90	586	231	20.4	9.2	35.3	16.7
	Total occupied	1,321	974	1,658	1,382	100.0	100.0	100.0	100.0
	No of Domestic servants percentage of no households					18.4	12.2	13.5	23.0

1901	Buckinghamshire		England & Wales		Bucks % E & W	
	Male	Fem	Male	Fem	Male	Fem
Not Occupied	13,640	57,142	1,977,283	9,017,834	0.690	0.634
Occupied	61,002	21,379	10,156,976	4,171,751	0.601	0.512
Government	758	217	171,687	26,500	0.442	0.819
Defence	211	-	168,238	-	0.125	
Professional	1,604	1,842	311,618	294,642	0.515	0.625
Domestic Servants	689	8,229	47,893	1,285,072	1.439	0.640
Outside Servants	3,024	78	173,908	13,350	1.739	0.584
Others In Service	33	31	50,502	12,266	0.065	0.253
Nurses Midwives	40	92	6,765	26,341	0.591	0.349
Day Servants	-	479	-	111,841	na	0.428
Laundry Workers	27	1,502	8,874	196,141	0.304	0.766
Commercial	1,152	147	530,685	59,944	0.217	0.245
Railway	2,197	6	351,911	1,441	0.624	0.416
Other Transport	2,393	20	561,894	2,028	0.426	0.986
Warehouses	20	1	115,013	1,109	0.017	0.090
Coal Merchants	258	5	49,736	1,040	0.519	0.481
Messengers	656	45	194,059	14,247	0.338	0.316
Agriculture	14,067	219	923,644	52,168	1.523	0.420
Ag Other	2,057	33	157,585	5,653	1.305	0.584
Mining	5	0	669,770	3,350	0.001	na
Quarries	76	1	103,628	535	0.073	0.187
Dealers	472	117	141,444	35,361	0.334	0.331
Steel	3	0	106,890	2,001	0.003	na
Metal	672	8	442,878	64,137	0.152	0.012
Blacksmiths	871	8	136,752	316	0.637	2.532
Engineering	736	0	355,278	1,668	0.207	0.000
Ship Yards	41	0	86,524	113	0.047	0.000
Railway Coach Wagon Makers	2,031	0	23,278	21	8.725	0.000
Vehicles	703	1	87,498	3,120	0.803	0.032
Retail	2,445	923	547,351	205,568	0.447	0.449
Building	5,978	7	945,184	672	0.632	1.042
Navies	630	0	97,680	0	0.645	na
Furniture	3,869	182	106,353	15,178	3.638	1.199
Willow, Cane Rush Workers	109	399	9,626	1,894	1.132	21.067
Woods	958	7	86,000	4,309	1.114	0.162
Brick, Plain Tile Makers	844	2	60,856	3,071	1.387	0.065
Other Cement Etc	18	1	47,644	24,492	0.038	0.004
Chemicals	36	0	84,793	18,855	0.042	0.000
Chemists	63	1	17,082	6,685	0.369	0.015
Skins	253	18	64,987	14,399	0.389	0.125
Brush Makers	163	347	9,259	7,005	1.760	4.954
Paper Manufacture	486	324	15,359	8,851	3.164	3.661
Other Paper	22	115	14,621	36,136	0.150	0.318
Printers	676	478	119,834	29,959	0.564	1.596
Textiles	43	1,123	401,936	592,732	0.011	0.189
Straw Plait	3	173	493	1,354	0.609	12.777
Clothing	2	10	15,446	21,441	0.013	0.047
Dress		146	472	48,759	0.000	0.299
Tailors	382	58	119,545	117,640	0.320	0.049
Clothes	11	2,245	16,149	455,586	0.068	0.493
Shoe	1,877	387	177,805	45,176	1.056	0.857
Creamery Workers	67	67	568	364	11.796	18.407
Food Preparation	132	18	55,585	51,314	0.237	0.035
Butchers	763	28	105,165	3,850	0.726	0.727
Millers	348	10	38,316	1,746	0.908	0.573
Bakers	847	163	102,177	46,769	0.829	0.349
Brewers	279	0	38,123	115	0.732	0.000
Public Houses	1,002	402	137,762	73,834	0.727	0.544
Lodging	97	630	34,666	96,481	0.280	0.653
Utilities	237	0	71,284	141	0.332	0.000
Sundry Industries	19	0	10,315	3,325	0.184	0.000
General Labourers	3,061	19	450,766	10,353	0.679	0.184
Miscellaneous	472	15	141,514	8,842	0.334	0.170

INDUSTRIAL OCCUPATIONS IN 1911

Major changes were introduced in 1911. For the first time an attempt was made to provide information by Industry rather than occupation. However, no industry statistics were published for Buckinghamshire. It was included as part of a group of 6 counties in the South Midlands. The information published at a local level for 1911 was considerably greater than that for 1901 although it remained limited to the largest towns that by then included Fenny Stratford. The information at a county level on occupations was copious with 394 categories with at least one person in the county.

1911	PERCENTAGE OF TOTAL OCCUPIED									LOCATION QUOTIENT							
	E & W	Bucks	Ayl	Wyc	Ches	F St	Slough	Other UDs	RDs	Bucks	Ayl	Wyc	Ches	F St	Slough	Other UDs	RDs
FEMALES																	
Civil Service & Telegraph	0.82	1.38	3.24	0.57	0.96	0.44	1.51	0.65	1.48	167	393	69	117	54	183	79	180
Local Govt & Hospital	1.26	0.88	1.47	0.18	0.35	0.66	2.07	0.58	0.89	70	116	14	28	52	163	46	70
Midwives	1.73	1.90	1.89	1.93	1.22	1.77	2.29	1.43	1.99	110	109	111	71	102	132	83	115
Teaching	3.88	5.76	3.97	7.06	5.33	5.52	6.64	4.60	5.92	149	102	182	138	142	171	119	153
Arts etc	1.07	0.91	1.16	1.10	0.52	1.77	1.73	0.82	0.77	85	109	103	49	165	162	76	72
Hotel DS	1.31	1.87	0.73	3.55	0.35	1.10	1.73	9.40	0.46	143	56	271	27	84	132	717	35
Domestic Service	26.33	41.71	28.12	26.46	20.10	33.33	37.30	40.22	48.07	158	107	100	76	127	142	153	183
Charwomen	3.11	2.38	3.79	2.54	1.75	1.99	2.46	3.34	2.08	77	122	82	56	64	79	107	67
Laundresses	3.46	5.57	5.56	4.87	7.34	2.65	10.94	5.96	4.93	161	161	141	212	77	316	172	143
Dom Service (clubs etc)	0.83	0.81	0.37	0.57	0.35	0.88	0.73	1.26	0.85	98	44	69	42	107	88	152	103
Clerks	2.56	1.29	1.34	2.37	1.22	2.21	3.96	1.12	0.82	50	53	93	48	86	155	44	32
Agriculture & Forestry	1.96	2.04	0.12	0.13	0.52	0.44	0.22	0.78	3.14	104	6	7	27	23	11	40	160
Metals	1.97	0.12	0.86	0.04	0.09	0.00	0.28	0.20	0.02	6	43	2	4	0	14	10	1
Jewellery	0.38	0.07	0.12	0.00	1.14	0.00	0.06	0.00	0.01	19	32	0	300	0	15	0	3
Wood Furniture	0.62	2.05	0.37	14.66	0.96	0.00	0.39	0.68	0.95	327	59	2346	154	0	63	109	152
Chemicals	0.76	0.22	0.06	0.18	0.00	0.00	1.01	0.03	0.21	29	8	23	0	0	132	4	28
Skins, Leather	0.37	0.07	0.06	0.04	0.44	0.22	0.00	0.03	0.06	19	17	12	118	60	0	9	16
Hair & Feathers	0.23	1.03	0.00	0.04	17.05	10.38	0.00	0.03	0.12	448	0	19	7436	4526	0	15	54
Paper excl Shops & Publis	2.03	4.45	13.88	5.40	2.53	7.06	0.17	1.26	4.48	220	685	266	125	348	8	62	221
Textiles manufacture	13.59	1.89	0.92	0.70	0.70	1.10	0.28	0.72	2.70	14	7	5	5	8	2	5	20
Drapers Etc	2.48	2.09	2.87	4.30	3.58	2.65	3.02	2.42	1.38	84	116	173	144	107	122	97	56
Tailors	2.63	0.32	0.43	0.57	0.52	0.22	0.34	0.68	0.20	12	16	22	20	8	13	26	7
Milliners	1.38	0.98	1.59	2.19	1.49	0.66	2.07	1.12	0.55	71	115	159	108	48	150	82	40
Dressmakers	7.02	7.03	8.31	7.46	4.90	9.93	8.82	8.41	6.44	100	118	106	70	141	126	120	92
Staymakers	1.94	1.01	1.28	0.88	0.87	0.22	0.89	2.18	0.83	52	66	45	45	11	46	112	43
Shoe Makers	0.92	1.43	0.00	0.09	12.24	0.00	0.11	0.10	1.43	155	0	10	1328	0	12	11	155
Others In Dress manufacture	1.03	0.38	0.31	0.31	2.97	0.00	0.11	0.27	0.27	37	30	30	290	0	11	27	26
Food Workers	1.12	0.41	3.55	0.13	0.09	0.00	0.00	0.78	0.12	36	316	12	8	0	0	70	11
Food Dealers	4.69	4.47	5.44	5.75	5.86	5.74	4.52	4.19	4.08	95	116	123	125	123	97	89	87
Coffee Shop, Lodging houses	1.89	0.94	1.77	1.05	0.61	1.10	1.40	1.60	0.67	50	94	56	32	58	74	85	35
Public Houses	2.51	2.80	2.57	2.90	2.01	5.52	2.35	2.90	2.82	112	102	115	80	220	94	115	113
All Others	4.12	1.74	3.85	1.97	1.92	2.43	2.62	2.21	1.25	42	93	48	47	59	64	54	30
	100	100	100	100	100	100	100	100	100								
Servants per 1000 Hlds	159	207	181	132	121	122	197	255	222	130	114	83	76	77	124	160	140
	E & W	Bucks	Ayl	Wyc	Ches	F St	Slough	Other UDs	RDs	Bucks	Ayl	Wyc	Ches	F St	Slough	Other UDs	RDs
MALES																	
Central / local government	2.17	1.69	3.47	1.59	1.61	3.40	2.53	2.78	1.27	78	160	73	74	156	117	128	59
Defence	1.80	0.32	0.35	0.12	0.07	0.24	0.63	0.33	0.34	18	20	7	4	13	35	18	19
Professions	3.21	3.13	4.20	2.66	2.85	2.68	3.77	5.15	2.82	97	131	83	89	84	118	160	88
Domestic indoor service	1.98	6.06	1.21	1.07	1.17	3.99	3.05	5.25	7.93	307	61	54	59	202	154	266	401
Domestic outdoor ser	1.41	1.81	1.44	0.64	0.51	1.55	2.08	2.52	1.98	129	102	46	36	110	148	179	140
Merchants	2.64	1.64	2.85	2.30	1.75	1.73	3.12	1.96	1.26	62	108	87	66	65	118	74	48
Commercial Clerks	3.15	1.15	1.79	1.94	1.57	0.95	2.80	1.72	0.73	37	57	62	50	30	89	55	23
Railway transport	3.47	4.19	4.09	1.64	1.24	28.90	12.70	3.20	3.13	121	118	47	36	832	366	92	90
Road transport	4.12	3.26	5.35	3.89	4.06	2.74	4.32	4.26	2.74	79	130	94	98	67	105	103	66
River transport	1.15	0.26	0.38	0.02	0.00	0.18	0.20	0.81	0.23	22	33	1	0	15	18	70	20
Wharf Labourers	1.18	0.17	0.15	0.15	0.00	0.66	0.27	0.27	0.14	14	12	13	0	56	23	22	12
Messengers	1.95	1.24	2.62	1.98	1.10	1.37	2.08	2.49	0.79	64	134	101	56	70	107	128	40
Other transport	0.34	0.06	0.12	0.05	0.00	0.48	0.11	0.08	0.04	18	35	13	0	140	33	24	11
Agriculture & forestry	9.96	24.53	5.17	2.70	4.28	8.82	5.54	11.42	34.62	246	52	27	43	89	56	115	348
Coal or shale mines	7.72	0.01	0.00	0.03	0.00	0.00	0.00	0.02	0.00	0	0	0	0	0	0	0	0
Others in quarrying	1.10	0.15	0.03	0.03	0.00	0.12	0.14	0.10	0.19	14	3	3	0	11	12	9	18
General engineering	5.85	2.58	2.44	1.76	1.86	3.81	5.42	2.04	2.49	44	42	30	32	65	93	35	43
Iron & steel manufacture	3.49	0.40	2.65	0.25	0.07	0.12	0.72	0.35	0.26	11	76	7	2	3	21	10	7
Electrical apparatus	0.74	0.50	0.65	0.21	0.11	0.77	1.76	0.51	0.42	67	87	29	15	105	238	69	56
Ships & boats	0.91	0.06	0.03	0.00	0.00	0.00	0.02	0.28	0.06	7	3	0	0	0	2	31	6
Cycles, coaches oth vehi	1.52	5.00	1.71	0.67	0.91	2.98	3.73	9.26	5.75	328	112	44	60	196	245	609	378
Precious metals	0.87	0.43	0.50	0.46	1.97	0.36	0.68	0.58	0.29	50	57	53	226	41	78	66	33
Building	8.26	9.42	10.32	7.76	11.04	9.48	14.24	13.36	8.49	114	125	94	134	115	172	162	103
wood furniture	2.22	7.69	2.32	46.89	8.55	2.50	1.47	2.65	3.83	347	105	2116	386	113	66	120	173
Brick tile	0.43	0.73	0.68	0.02	0.15	0.06	0.93	0.17	0.96	171	157	4	34	14	216	39	223
Earthenware, glass	0.60	0.02	0.00	0.03	0.00	0.00	0.02	0.02	0.03	4	0	5	0	0	4	3	4
Chemicals	1.18	0.45	0.59	0.54	0.18	0.30	2.49	0.35	0.26	38	50	45	15	25	211	29	22
skins, leather	0.58	0.41	0.21	0.18	0.55	0.30	0.23	0.85	0.42	72	36	32	95	52	39	147	73
Printers	1.12	1.12	11.56	0.69	2.30	0.54	0.99	0.83	0.40	100	1034	62	206	48	89	74	36
Paper excl shops & publis	0.41	1.07	1.62	1.79	0.00	0.42	0.42	0.43	1.20	257	390	432	0	101	5	104	289
Textiles	3.50	0.08	0.18	0.09	0.29	0.00	0.02	0.02	0.07	2	5	3	8	0	1	0	2
Textile printing dying	0.61	0.01	0.00	0.00	0.07	0.00	0.02	0.00	0.01	1	0	0	12	0	4	0	1
Tailors	1.07	0.62	1.06	0.60	1.17	0.36	1.33	1.54	0.37	58	99	56	109	33	125	144	35
Shoe makers	1.48	2.50	0.85	0.58	28.47	0.83	1.27	1.14	1.69	169	58	39	1928	56	86	77	114
Others in dress	0.73	0.37	0.53	0.64	0.88	0.36	0.54	0.53	0.26	51	72	88	120	49	74	72	35
Drapers etc	1.14	1	1.59	1.29	1.39	1.31	1.29	1.36		64	140	113	122	115	113	120	33
Food drink lodging	7.98	8.32	15.14	9.19	8.55	8.34	9.56	12.53	6.98	104	190	115	107	105	120	157	88
General labourers	2.65	4.34	5.97	1.98	2.70	3.10	6.04	3.86	4.60	164	226	75	102	117	228	146	174
All Others	5.32	3.48	6.20	3.57	8.55	6.26	3.84	5.00	2.61	65	117	67	161	118	72	94	49
	100	100	100	100	100	100	100	100	100	100	100	100	100	100	100	100	100

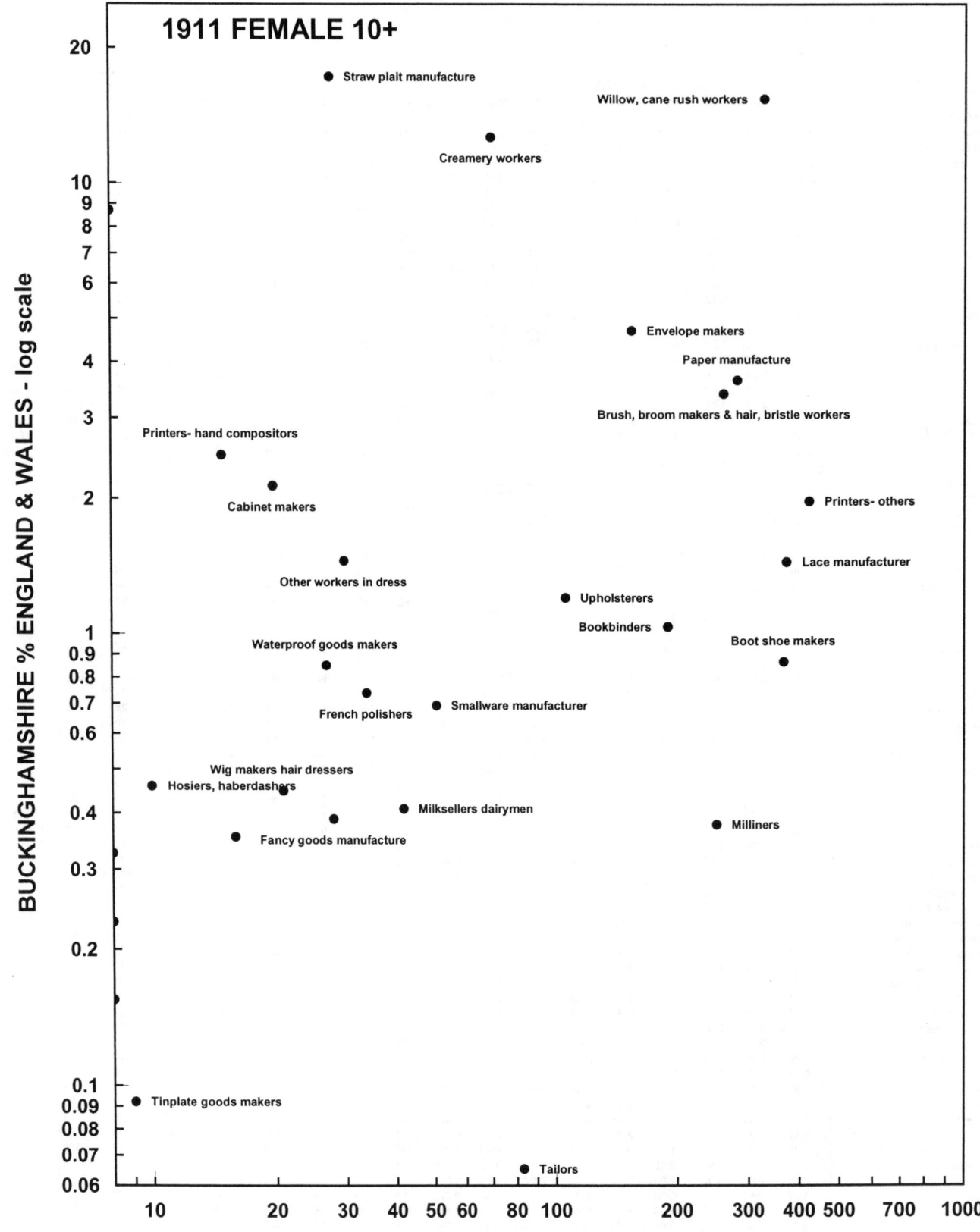

1911 FEMALE 10+

- Straw plait manufacture
- Willow, cane rush workers
- Creamery workers
- Envelope makers
- Paper manufacture
- Brush, broom makers & hair, bristle workers
- Printers- hand compositors
- Cabinet makers
- Printers- others
- Lace manufacturer
- Other workers in dress
- Upholsterers
- Bookbinders
- Boot shoe makers
- Waterproof goods makers
- French polishers
- Smallware manufacturer
- Wig makers hair dressers
- Hosiers, haberdashers
- Milksellers dairymen
- Fancy goods manufacture
- Milliners
- Tinplate goods makers
- Tailors

Y-axis: BUCKINGHAMSHIRE % ENGLAND & WALES - log scale

X-axis: NUMBER IN INDUSTRIAL OCCUPATIONS IN BUCKS - log scale

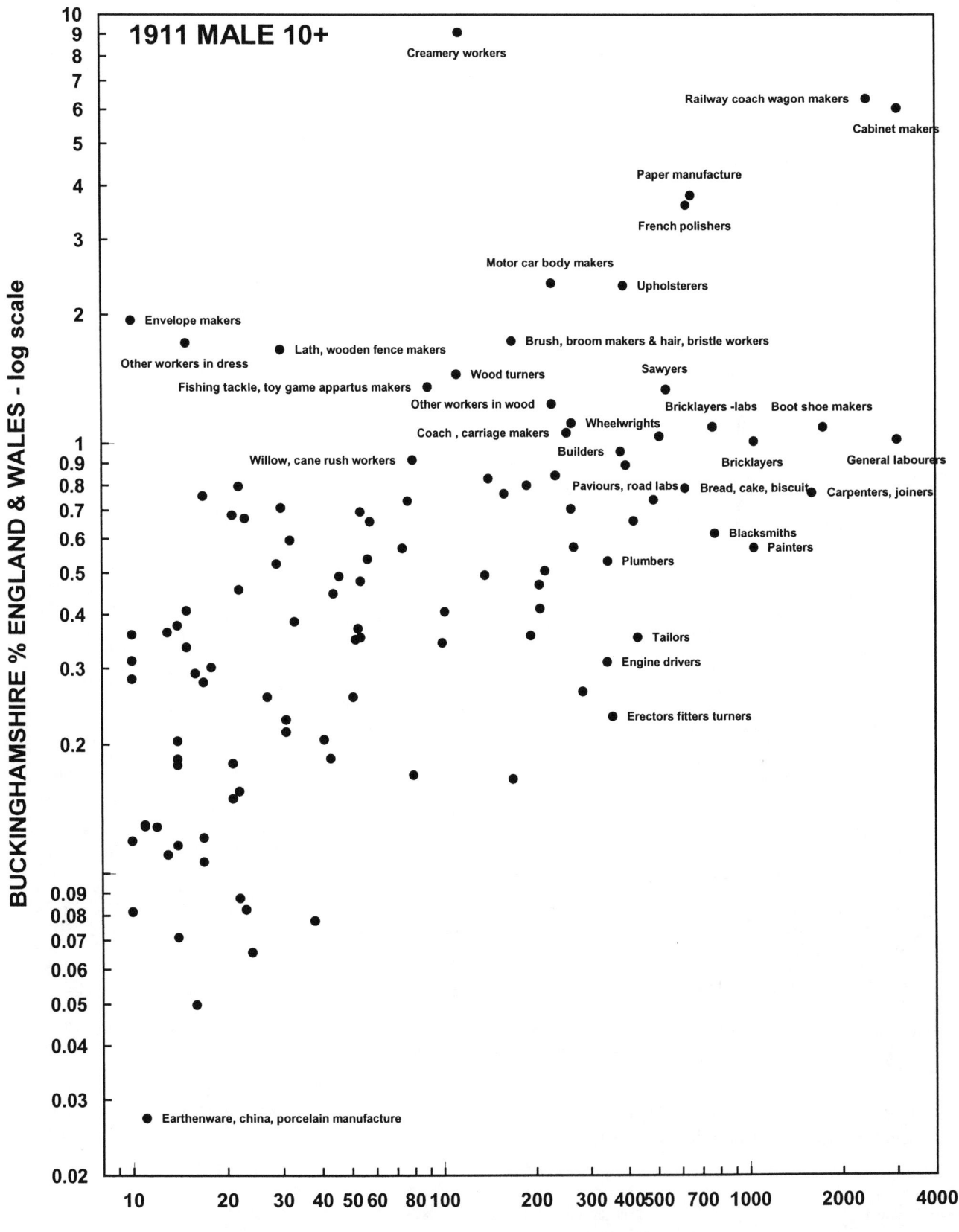

BUCKINGHAMSHIRE % ENGLAND & WALES - log scale

NUMBER IN INDUSTRIAL OCCUPATIONS IN BUCKS - log scale

1911 MALE 10+

Creamery workers

Railway coach wagon makers

Cabinet makers

Paper manufacture

French polishers

Motor car body makers

Upholsterers

Envelope makers

Other workers in dress

Lath, wooden fence makers

Brush, broom makers & hair, bristle workers

Fishing tackle, toy game appartus makers

Wood turners

Sawyers

Other workers in wood

Bricklayers -labs

Boot shoe makers

Coach , carriage makers

Wheelwrights

Willow, cane rush workers

Builders

Bricklayers

General labourers

Paviours, road labs

Bread, cake, biscuit

Carpenters, joiners

Plumbers

Blacksmiths

Painters

Tailors

Engine drivers

Erectors fitters turners

Earthenware, china, porcelain manufacture

85

1921 FIGURES FOR OCCUPATIONS AND INDUSTRY

The census for 1921 introduced a new classification of occupations and for the first time satisfactory figures for the number employed in a given industry. Using the occupation figures the county as a whole is compared with the whole country in the table below. Of the two sets of figures only the occupation ones were provided at a local level (page 87).

BUCKINGHAMSHIRE ADMINISTATIVE COUNTY - Occupations						
	Number		Percentages		Location Quotient	
Category - nb used on table on p. 87	Male	Female	Male	Female	Male	Female
Population	113,979	122,192	%		100 = national average	
Aged under 12	23,789	23,457	20.9	19.2		
Aged 12+	90,190	98,735	79.1	80.8		
Aged 12+ Occupied % Total aged 12+	77,299	27,328	85.7	27.7		
			% Occupied			
1 Fisherman	4		0.01	0.00	2	0
2 Agricultural workers	17,310	708	22.39	2.59	228	136
3 Mining & Quarrying	83	1	0.11	0.00	1	5
4 Coke, Lime, Cement makers	25	2	0.03	0.01	15	17
5 Brick, Pottery, Glass makers	489	6	0.63	0.02	82	2
6 Chemical, Paint workers	70	9	0.09	0.03	18	9
7 Metal workers	5,865	144	7.59	0.53	59	21
8 Precious Metals workers	34	2	0.04	0.01	18	2
9 Electrical Apparatus Makers	752	14	0.97	0.05	81	11
10 Watch makers	111	9	0.14	0.03	71	59
11 Skin workers, Leather makers	255	92	0.33	0.34	70	69
12 Textile makers	79	128	0.10	0.47	3	3
13 Textile Goods & Clothing makers	1,711	2,001	2.21	7.32	91	58
Shoe makers	1,013		1.31		129	
14 Food, Drink, Tobacco makers	1,320	245	1.71	0.90	105	39
15 Wood workers	9,858	761	12.75	2.78	306	455
Cabinet Makers	4,950		6.40		2040	
Coach & Carriage Builders	946		1.22		664	
16 Paper workers, Printers	1,705	1,242	2.21	4.54	156	180
Paper	677	288	0.88		583	642
Printers	993	759	1.28		109	205
17 Builders, Bricklayers	4,360	10	5.64	0.04	133	91
18 Painters & Decorators	1,748	23	2.26	0.08	132	128
19 Rubber, Bone etc workers	222	282	0.29	1.03	104	397
20 Vehicles, Ship, Musical Instrument makers	393	171	0.51	0.63	60	108
21 Gas, Water, Eleectical Utilility workers	215		0.28	0.00	69	0
22 Transport & Communication workers	6,469	268	8.37	0.98	70	67
Railway	1,832	9	2.37	0.03	90	57
Roads	3,089	40	4.00		89	117
23 Commerce & Retailing workers	5,873	2,392	7.60	8.75	85	77
Wholesale & Retail principals	2,637	631	3.41	2.31	96	83
Salesmen & Shop assistants	1,664	1,669	2.15	6.11	82	77
24 Government & Defence	4,119	541	5.33	1.98	144	120
Government	1,160	541	1.50	1.98	75	120
Defence	2,959		3.83		223	
25 Professional workers (not clerks)	2,232	2,494	2.89	9.13	112	110
26 Entertainment & Sport workers	296	109	0.38	0.40	112	125
27 Domestic & other Personal Service workers	2,502	13,509	3.24	49.43	509	107
Indoor Domestic servants	763	11,193	0.99	40.96	109	78
28 Private Sector Clerks	2,449	1,719	3.17	6.29	47	62
29 Warehousemen & Packers	666	270	0.86	0.99	113	128
30 Stationary Engine Drivers	454		0.59	0.00	193	155
31 Other Workers espically Labourers	5,630	176	7.28	0.64	66	64
32 Retired & Not Gainfully Employed	12,891	71,407			46	33

The figures were given for 184 types of 'industry', including a wide variety of service industries. Figures for the agricultural, quarrying and manufacturing types of industry are shown on graphs on page 88 (note these are the first figures for *industry* rather than *occupation* shown in this paper.

Following these a number of the more important manufacturing industries in the county are examined in 9 graphs that place Bucks relative to other individual counties and the major towns of England & Wales:

Cabinet & furniture making	Printing & binding	Rolling stock for railways
Brushes & brooms	Butter, cheese & condensed milk	Motor cars & cycles
Paper & board	Bricks tiles* + Brewing & malting *	Car bodies
* males only		

Two examples might be noted. Cabinet and furniture making accounted for 7% of all occupied males in Bucks. The Bucks total of 5,343 was only a quarter of those in London (21,280) and less than those in Lancashire. In butter, cheese and condensed milk factories, a far smaller industry, Bucks ranked only just below Wiltshire in both the proportion employed and the total numbers.

1921 - OCCUPATIONS % of ACTIVE POPULATION IN EACH OCCUPATION

MALES

	Sex	Fish	Agric	Quary	Cemt	Brick	Chem	Metl	Prec	Elect	Watch	Leath	Textl	Cloth	Food	Wood	Pppt	Build	Paint	Rubb	Vehc	Utls	Trans	Co	Re	Govt	Prof	Enter	Dom	Clerk	Ware	Sedr	Other	ALL	Act
URBAN																																			
Wycombe	m	-	2.6	0.0	0.0	0.0	0.1	5.0	-	0.6	0.3	0.2	0.1	1.1	1.4	49.3	2.0	3.1	1.6	-	0.4	0.4	6.8	8.7	1.6	2.0	0.2	2.1	2.9	1.4	0.9	-	5.2	100	90.4
Slough	m	-	5.3	0.1	-	0.8	0.4	17.7	0.0	1.8	0.1	0.2	0.1	2.2	2.4	5.3	0.8	5.3	2.8	0.1	0.5	0.4	12.0	9.8	2.6	2.5	0.5	3.0	9.2	2.2	0.8	-	10.9	100	87.5
Wolverton	m	-	3.0	0.1	-	0.0	0.1	23.8	0.0	3.1	0.2	0.6	0.0	0.7	1.2	21.7	2.2	2.3	7.3	0.0	2.5	0.7	5.5	6.8	0.7	1.4	0.7	2.1	4.1	1.1	0.9	-	7.0	100	85.6
Aylesbury	m	-	3.9	0.0	-	0.2	0.1	13.9	0.1	1.6	0.2	0.1	0.0	1.5	3.9	4.7	12.0	5.8	2.5	0.1	0.4	0.5	10.4	11.3	4.1	2.5	0.5	3.3	3.9	2.3	0.8	-	9.4	100	87.3
Chesham	m	-	5.4	0.0	0.0	-	0.0	4.2	0.1	0.5	0.3	0.5	0.3	17.5	1.9	17.9	2.7	6.9	2.4	4.3	0.7	0.4	7.3	10.0	1.6	2.2	0.4	2.5	4.4	1.3	0.5	-	4.1	100	89.1
Bletchley	m	-	9.2	0.3	-	0.2	-	9.3	-	1.6	0.2	0.2	-	0.8	1.0	6.6	0.6	8.6	1.8	1.5	0.2	0.4	33.0	8.1	1.7	2.8	0.4	2.4	3.5	0.7	0.5	-	4.5	100	87.7
Marlow	m	0.1	10.6	0.1	0.1	1.6	0.2	6.4	-	0.7	0.4	0.3	-	1.8	3.4	7.8	5.1	5.9	3.4	-	0.1	0.5	12.1	14.3	3.2	3.7	0.6	3.7	3.8	0.3	0.3	-	9.7	100	84.2
N. Pagnell	m	-	12.2	-	-	0.1	0.1	12.9	-	1.8	0.1	1.7	0.3	1.7	2.7	16.1	0.6	4.5	6.5	-	0.7	0.5	9.2	8.6	1.5	2.2	0.8	3.1	3.2	1.0	0.4	-	7.4	100	87.1
Beaconsfield	m	-	17.3	0.1	0.1	0.1	0.1	5.7	-	1.2	0.2	0.2	0.3	1.2	1.2	3.0	1.0	7.8	2.2	0.1	0.5	0.1	11.0	15.3	4.6	9.1	1.5	4.3	5.0	0.3	0.5	-	5.8	100	85.6
Buckingham	m	-	19.1	-	-	0.4	-	5.9	-	0.5	0.3	0.5	0.1	2.2	3.3	4.5	2.2	7.1	3.2	-	0.5	0.5	10.8	13.9	2.5	5.9	-	3.6	4.3	0.7	0.7	-	7.2	100	87.2
Linslade	m	-	10.9	1.1	-	0.1	-	12.3	-	0.4	0.3	0.1	0.1	1.2	1.2	9.5	1.2	5.2	4.0	0.3	1.1	0.6	19.0	10.5	1.5	2.1	0.4	2.5	5.8	0.6	0.3	-	7.7	100	84.0
Eton	m	-	3.3	-	-	0.2	-	8.8	-	0.9	0.3	0.2	-	6.7	1.4	6.8	3.2	2.1	2.9	-	0.3	0.2	11.7	9.6	2.4	14.0	1.2	12.6	3.3	0.9	0.6	-	6.4	100	36.1
RURAL																																			
Hambleden	m	0.1	52.1	-	0.1	-	-	2.6	-	0.9	-	0.1	-	0.6	1.6	8.7	-	4.4	0.4	-	-	-	6.0	4.3	1.0	2.3	-	7.5	0.6	0.4	0.4	-	5.7	100	86.9
Wycombe	m	-	25.5	0.1	0.1	0.3	0.0	4.1	0.1	0.7	0.1	0.1	0.1	0.7	1.2	21.0	5.7	6.1	1.5	0.1	0.1	0.1	6.8	6.1	2.3	2.9	0.3	3.2	1.9	0.6	0.8	-	7.4	100	86.9
Eton	m	0.0	26.8	0.1	0.1	1.3	0.1	7.5	0.1	1.0	0.1	0.1	0.1	1.2	1.6	3.4	0.9	5.2	1.6	0.4	0.5	0.3	9.1	8.3	3.2	3.9	0.6	5.2	3.4	0.8	0.6	-	12.2	100	85.8
Amersham	m	-	28.4	0.1	0.0	0.7	0.1	4.2	0.0	1.1	0.1	0.1	0.2	1.9	1.3	8.2	0.5	8.2	2.1	0.3	0.5	0.1	4.3	2.9	34.9	1.8	0.1	1.8	0.8	0.2	0.6	-	5.7	100	84.1
Aylesbury	m	-	31.2	0.1	-	0.2	0.0	3.0	0.0	0.3	0.1	0.1	0.0	0.6	1.0	2.9	-	5.5	1.2	0.1	0.1	0.2	6.6	4.4	-	2.8	0.2	2.8	1.2	0.3	0.6	-	8.7	100	86.7
Aylesbury (2)	m	-	48.0	0.1	-	0.3	0.0	4.6	0.0	0.4	0.1	0.2	0.0	1.0	1.5	4.5	0.8	8.5	1.8	0.1	0.1	0.2	6.6	4.4	-	2.8	0.2	2.8	1.2	0.3	0.6	-	8.7	100	86.7
Long Crendon	m	-	59.0	0.2	-	0.7	-	3.2	-	0.2	0.2	0.1	-	0.9	2.5	4.1	0.2	5.5	1.0	-	0.2	-	4.9	4.4	1.6	1.9	0.1	3.4	0.6	-	-	-	0.2	100	86.7
Wing	m	-	50.1	0.2	0.2	0.5	-	3.8	0.1	0.2	-	-	-	1.1	2.9	3.4	0.4	6.5	1.2	-	0.1	0.1	7.7	4.4	0.7	1.6	0.3	4.1	1.4	0.3	0.4	-	8.2	100	87.5
Winslow	m	-	54.0	0.0	-	0.5	-	2.9	-	0.4	0.1	0.3	-	1.8	1.9	3.6	0.3	6.5	1.0	-	0.0	-	7.2	2.5	1.6	1.8	0.2	3.3	0.8	0.2	0.2	-	4.5	100	85.9
Buckingham	m	-	56.8	0.4	-	4.7	-	2.6	-	0.4	-	0.0	-	0.9	1.9	2.6	0.7	6.6	0.7	-	0.0	-	7.2	2.5	1.6	1.8	0.2	3.3	0.8	0.2	0.2	-	4.5	100	85.9
N. Pagnell	m	-	41.1	0.2	-	0.9	0.0	6.0	-	0.5	0.1	2.0	0.2	6.8	1.5	6.0	0.5	6.6	2.4	0.0	0.7	0.3	5.8	5.4	1.1	2.5	0.1	2.7	1.4	0.7	0.5	-	4.0	100	87.2
County Total	m	0.0	22.4	0.1	0.0	0.6	0.1	7.6	0.0	1.0	0.1	0.3	0.1	2.2	1.7	12.8	2.2	5.6	2.3	0.3	0.5	0.3	8.4	7.6	5.3	2.9	0.4	3.2	3.2	0.9	0.6	-	7.3	100	85.7

FEMALES

	Sex	Fish	Agric	Quary	Cemt	Brick	Chem	Metl	Prec	Elect	Watch	Leath	Textl	Cloth	Food	Wood	Pppt	Build	Paint	Rubb	Vehc	Utls	Trans	Co	Re	Govt	Prof	Enter	Dom	Clerk	Ware	Sedr	Other	ALL	Act
URBAN																																			
Wycombe	f	-	0.4	-	-	-	-	0.4	-	-	0.1	0.6	0.4	10.3	0.4	18.1	4.4	-	0.4	-	0.9	-	1.0	12.8	1.0	7.3	0.3	32.5	7.8	0.3	-	-	0.8	100	27.8
Slough	f	-	1.4	-	0.1	-	0.3	0.8	-	0.1	0.1	0.2	-	7.9	2.3	1.3	1.0	-	0.1	-	1.5	-	1.3	12.6	2.1	9.4	-	39.4	14.7	2.9	-	-	0.8	100	29.0
Wolverton	f	-	0.3	-	-	-	-	0.5	-	0.1	-	0.1	-	7.4	0.3	3.2	29.4	-	0.3	0.1	0.8	-	0.7	10.7	1.7	6.2	1.1	26.5	6.0	3.9	-	-	0.5	100	25.3
Aylesbury	f	-	0.6	0.1	-	-	0.2	3.5	-	0.2	0.1	-	0.7	5.8	2.4	0.7	11.8	-	-	0.1	0.8	-	1.0	11.7	4.3	7.4	0.6	36.6	8.8	2.3	-	-	0.7	100	33.4
Chesham	f	-	0.4	-	-	-	-	0.1	-	0.1	-	4.0	1.4	15.5	0.3	3.5	3.3	-	0.1	12.6	3.4	-	0.5	13.5	2.7	6.2	0.1	23.5	6.6	1.8	-	-	0.6	100	31.0
Bletchley	f	-	1.4	-	-	-	-	-	-	-	-	-	-	5.8	-	0.8	5.1	-	-	13.1	0.4	-	1.8	14.8	1.2	9.7	1.2	36.6	6.4	0.8	-	-	1.0	100	22.9
Marlow	f	-	1.6	-	0.1	0.1	-	-	-	-	-	-	-	8.8	3.7	3.3	3.7	-	0.1	0.1	-	-	1.5	10.0	0.7	6.9	0.6	52.2	8.1	-	-	-	0.9	100	30.0
N. Pagnell	f	-	1.3	-	-	-	-	0.3	-	-	-	0.3	1.0	12.3	1.6	1.0	0.8	-	0.8	-	0.3	-	1.6	15.4	0.8	9.4	0.5	44.1	7.0	0.5	-	-	1.0	100	21.9
Beaconsfield	f	-	0.9	-	-	-	-	0.3	-	-	-	-	0.3	2.4	-	-	0.6	-	-	-	0.5	-	2.0	5.9	1.4	12.2	0.6	66.8	5.3	-	-	-	0.6	100	36.3
Buckingham	f	-	0.8	-	-	-	-	0.6	-	-	0.3	-	0.3	9.2	5.0	-	-	-	-	-	-	-	0.3	12.6	0.6	9.5	-	51.3	3.4	5.6	-	-	-	100	26.9
Linslade	f	-	0.7	-	-	-	-	0.3	-	-	-	-	-	9.6	-	2.1	10.6	-	-	-	-	-	4.1	6.5	1.0	8.9	0.7	43.8	10.3	0.3	-	-	1.0	100	28.3
Eton	f	-	0.2	-	-	-	-	-	-	-	-	-	-	4.6	0.6	0.5	0.8	-	-	-	0.2	-	0.6	7.2	0.3	4.2	0.2	75.5	4.3	-	-	-	0.9	100	55.1
RURAL																																			
Hambleden	f	-	7.3	-	-	-	-	-	-	-	-	-	-	0.5	6.4	-	1.4	-	-	-	-	-	0.5	2.7	1.4	5.9	-	73.1	0.9	-	-	-	-	100	26.9
Wycombe	f	-	3.4	-	-	0.1	-	0.1	-	-	-	0.1	0.6	5.1	0.5	4.0	6.0	-	-	0.0	0.1	-	1.2	6.6	2.3	10.1	0.4	52.6	5.6	0.4	-	-	0.7	100	25.1
Eton	f	-	5.0	-	-	0.1	0.0	0.4	-	0.2	0.1	-	0.2	4.1	0.6	0.3	1.1	-	0.1	0.1	0.7	-	0.8	5.5	1.6	7.6	0.7	63.9	5.4	0.5	-	-	0.9	100	32.2
Amersham	f	-	2.3	-	-	-	-	0.2	-	0.0	-	0.1	0.4	5.4	0.1	0.4	0.3	-	1.7	0.6	-	-	0.5	5.8	2.5	11.1	0.2	62.3	5.3	0.1	-	-	0.4	100	30.1
Aylesbury	f	-	3.8	-	-	-	-	0.7	-	-	-	-	0.3	3.4	0.6	-	0.3	-	-	0.1	-	-	0.6	9.0	2.8	12.1	0.6	60.1	1.9	-	-	-	0.3	100	20.3
Long Crendon	f	-	8.4	-	-	-	-	-	-	-	-	-	-	3.4	0.6	-	0.3	-	-	-	-	-	0.6	9.0	2.8	12.1	0.6	60.1	1.9	-	-	-	0.3	100	21.3
Wing	f	-	6.5	-	-	-	-	0.4	-	-	-	0.2	0.6	9.2	0.2	0.4	6.9	-	-	-	-	-	0.4	8.0	1.5	11.7	0.2	48.8	2.5	1.7	-	-	1.0	100	22.6
Winslow	f	-	4.7	-	-	-	-	-	-	-	-	-	-	1.4	7.0	1.1	-	0.8	-	-	0.8	-	-	1.1	8.5	2.6	9.6	0.2	59.6	1.9	0.2	-	-	0.6	100	24.3
Buckingham	f	-	7.1	-	-	-	-	-	-	-	-	-	-	0.7	3.5	3.0	-	-	-	-	-	-	-	1.2	3.9	2.3	14.1	-	62.3	1.4	0.3	-	-	0.3	100	22.2
N. Pagnell	f	-	3.6	-	-	0.1	-	0.3	-	-	-	1.5	1.3	17.5	-	0.5	2.7	-	0.1	0.5	0.3	-	0.9	7.7	1.5	9.8	0.2	46.2	4.6	0.4	-	-	0.1	100	24.1
County Total	f	-	2.6	0.0	0.0	0.0	0.0	0.5	-	0.1	0.0	0.3	0.5	7.3	0.9	2.8	4.5	-	0.1	1.0	0.6	-	1.0	8.8	2.0	9.1	0.4	49.4	6.3	1.0	-	-	0.6	100	27.7

Aykesbury RD (2) excludes military at Halton from calculations

For key to categories see text

1921 FEMALE

% ENGLAND & WALES TOTAL - log scale

AGRICULTURAL & INDUSTRIAL EMPLOYMENT IN BUCKS (log scale)

Butter, Cheese Factory · Furniture · Railway Rolling Stock · Brooms & Brushes · Paper & Board · Printing & Binding · Farming Mk Gardening · Cars & Cycles · Dressmaking · Carriage, Motor Car Bodies · Other Gardening · Other Wood & Basket Works · Toys · Bead · Other Engineering · Shoes · Tailoring · Wood Carving Bedding Etc · Building · Photography · Saddlery · Other Clothing · White Lead, Paints · Tanning · Bedsteads · Other Textiles · Maltings & Breweries · Saw Mills · Other Manufacturing · Furriers · Bolts, Nuts · Jam

1921 MALE

% ENGLAND & WALES TOTAL - log scale

AGRICULTURAL & INDUSTRIAL EMPLOYMENT IN BUCKS (log scale)

Furniture · Railway Rolling Stock · Butter, Cheese Factory · Paper & Board · Other Wood & Basket · Brooms & Brushes · Cars & Cycles · Farming Mk Gardening · Building · Carriage, Motor Car Bodies · Bricks · Other Gardening · Saw Mills · Shoes · Printing & Binding · Bead · Other Forging · Other Engineering · Toys · Bolts, Nuts · Other Agr · Grain Milling · Jobbing Carpentry · Maltings & Breweries · Tanning · Electrical Wiring & Contracting · Tailoring · Saddlery · Wood Carving · Beds etc · Photography · White Lead, Paints · Mineral Waters · Ag Engineer · House & Shop Fittings · Bedsteads · Sand, Gravel · Bacon, Meat · Rope · Aeroplanes · Other Textiles · Precious Metals · Dressmaking · Cardboard Boxes · Other Electrical · Bridge Works

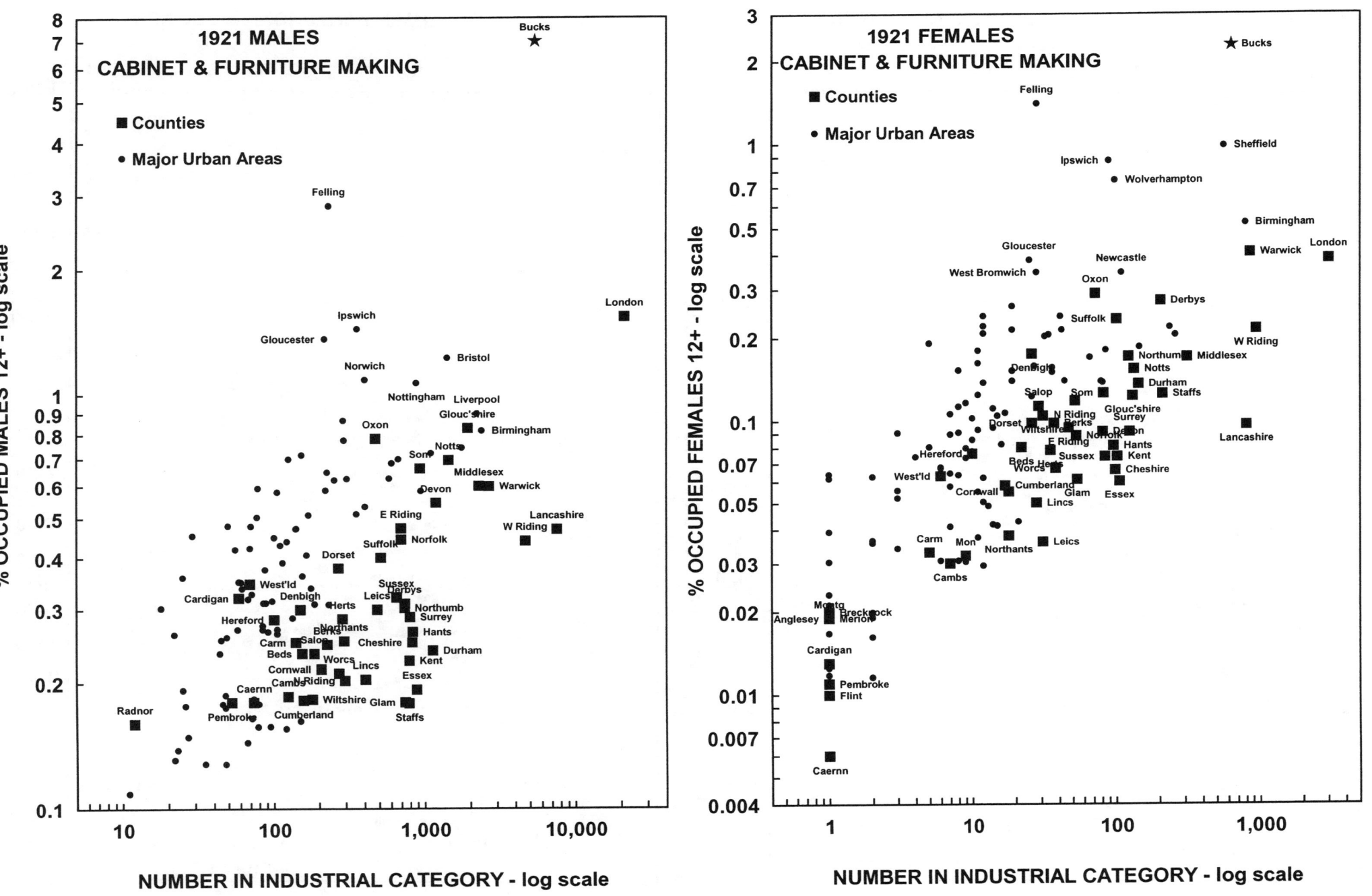

68

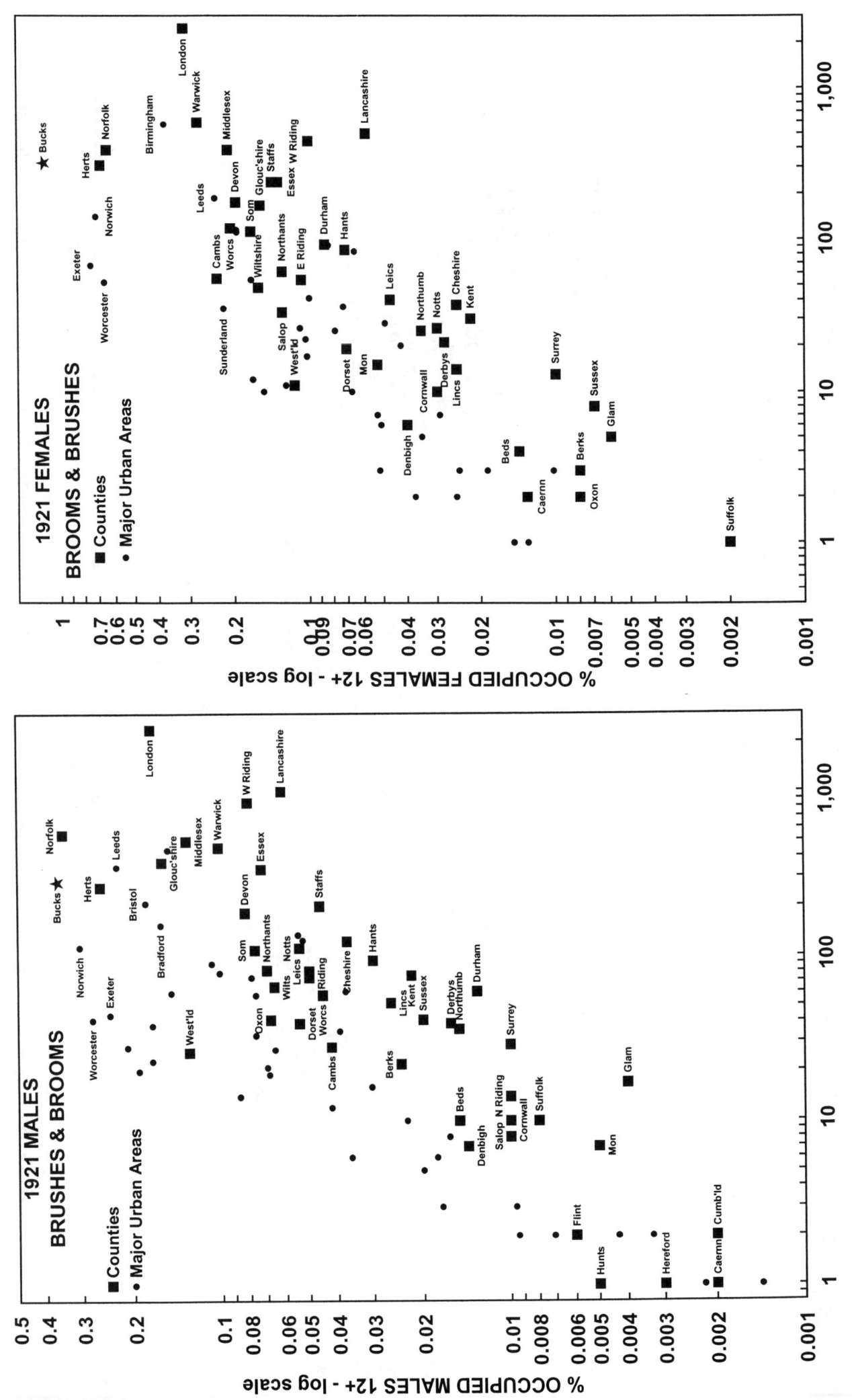

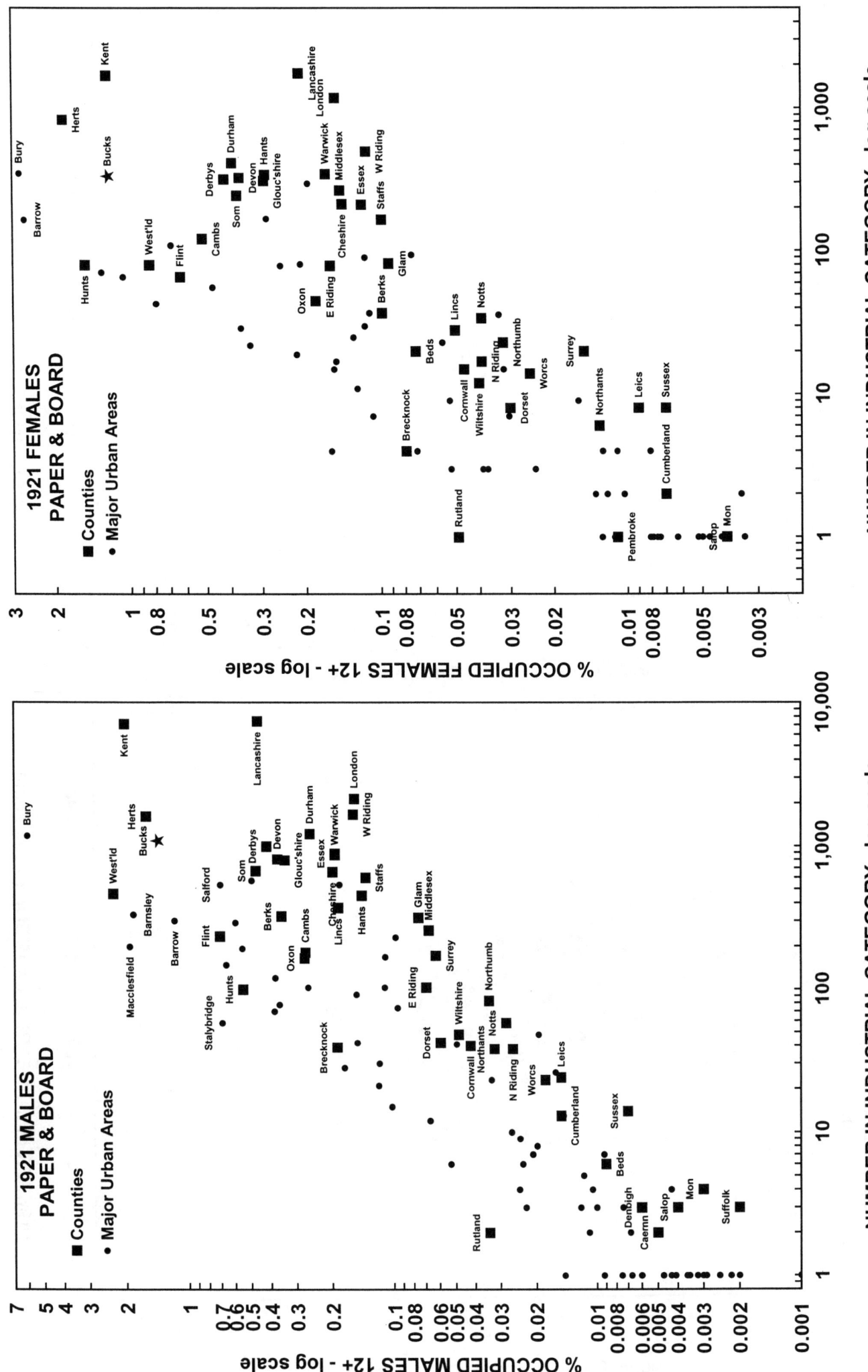

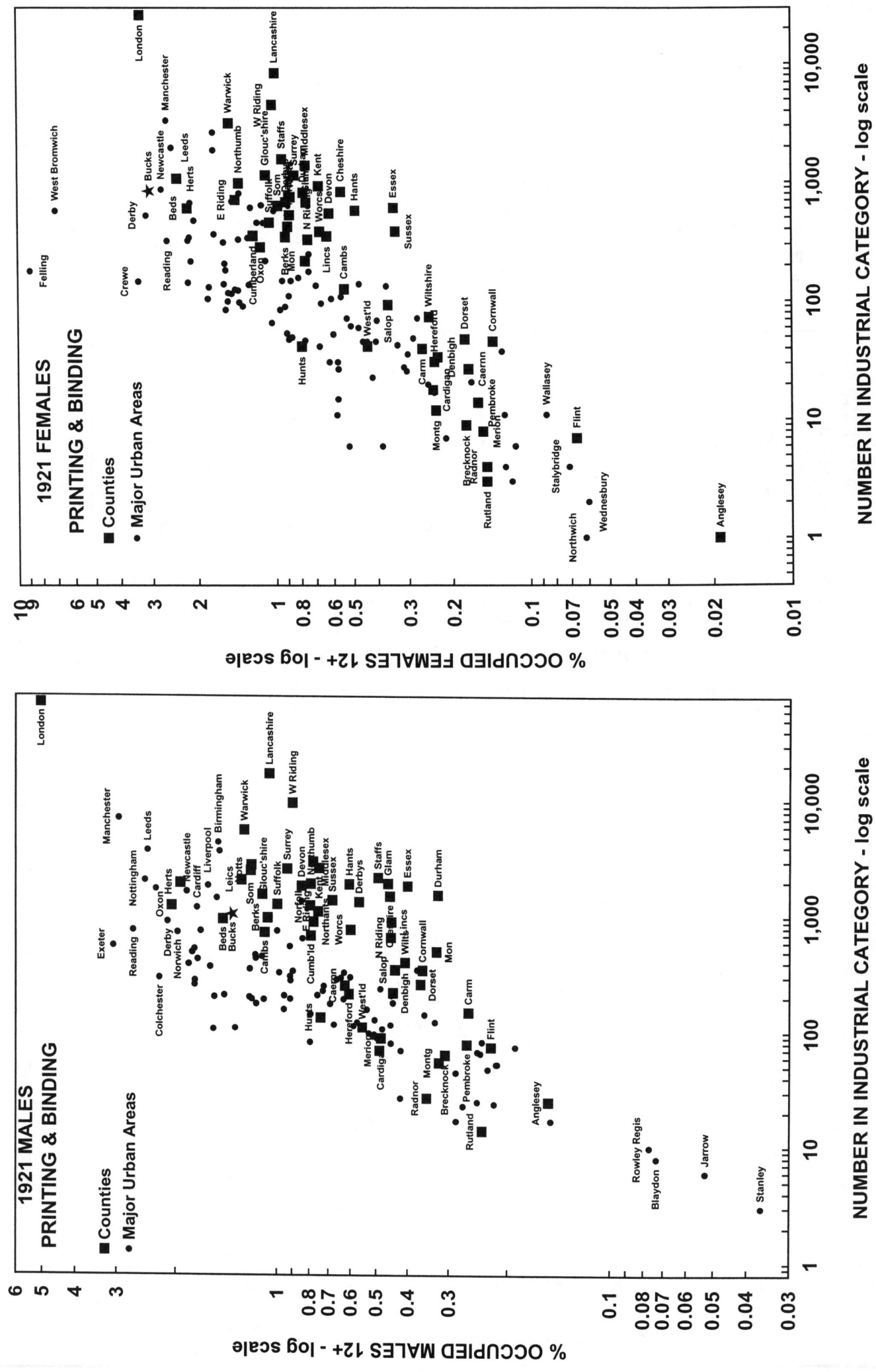

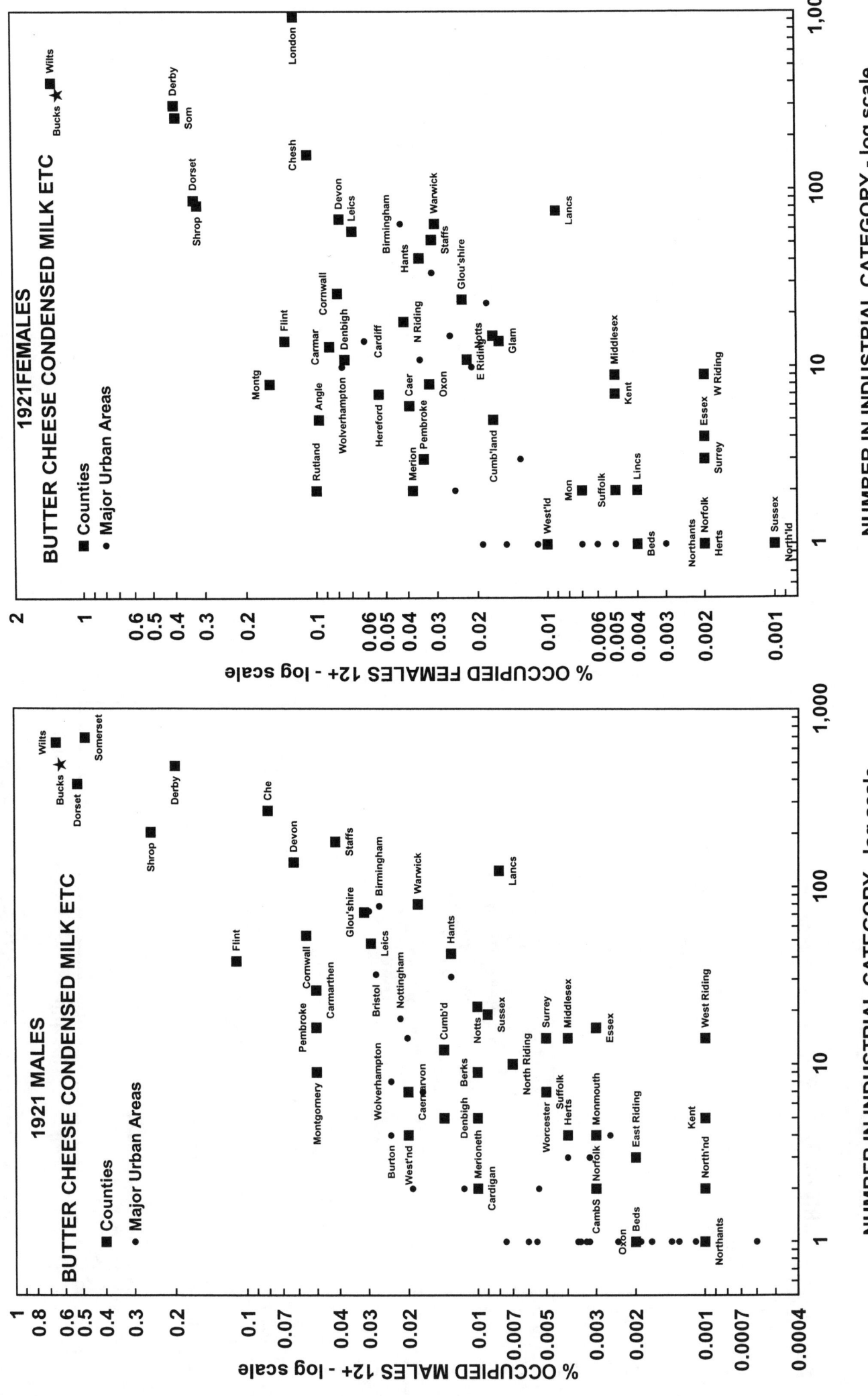

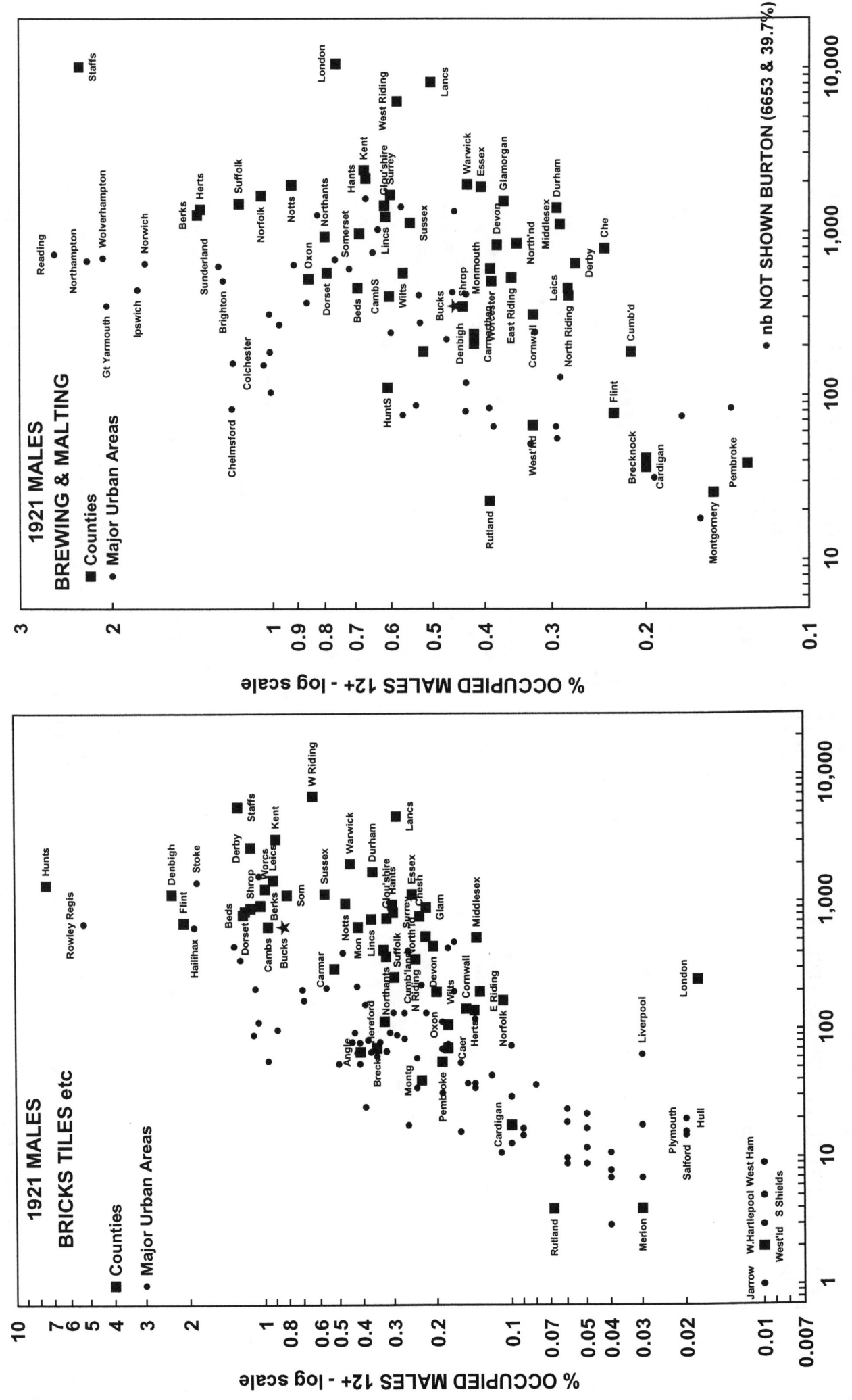

94

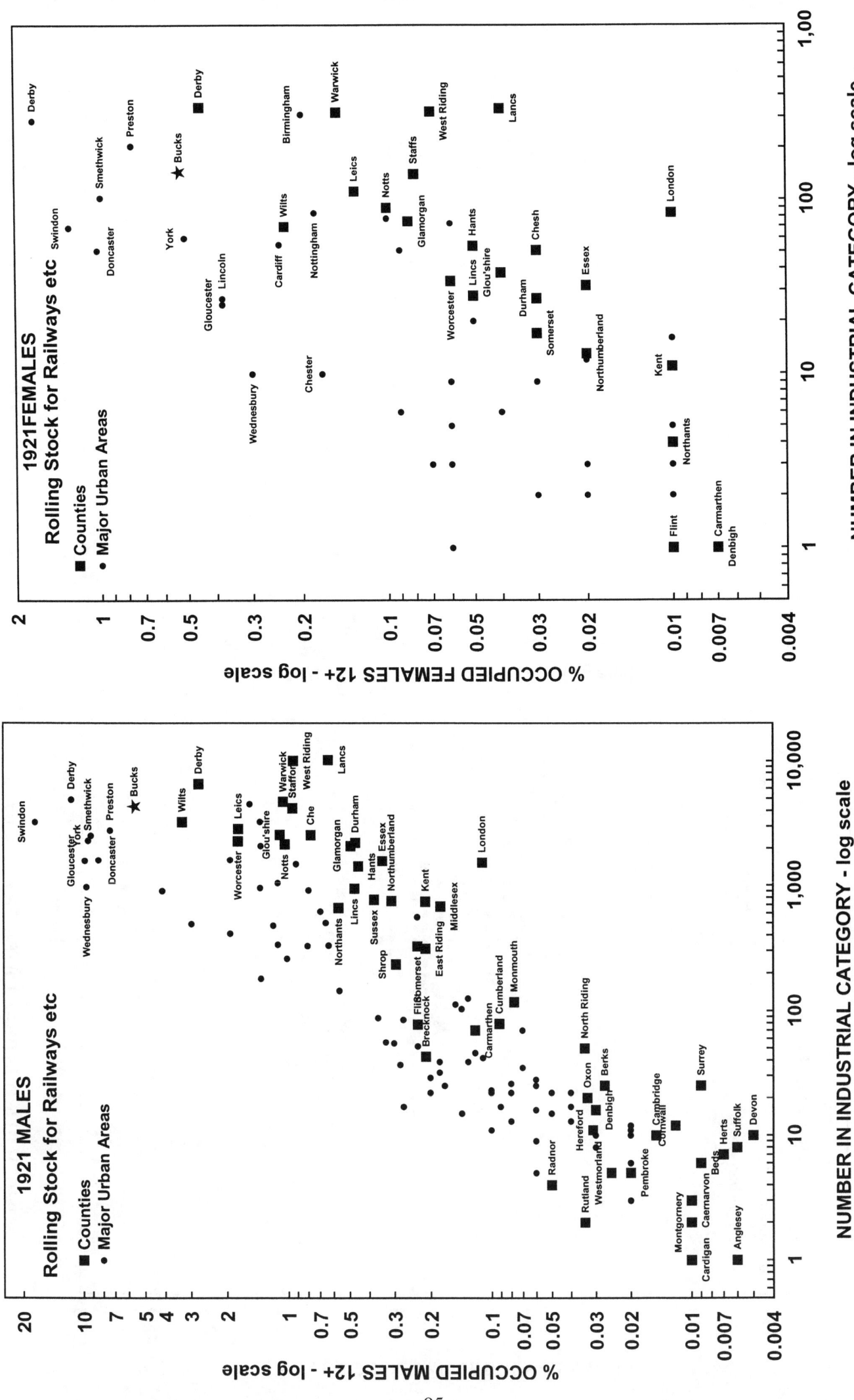

1921 MALES
MOTOR CARS & cYCLES

1921 FEMALES
MOTOR CARS & CYCLES

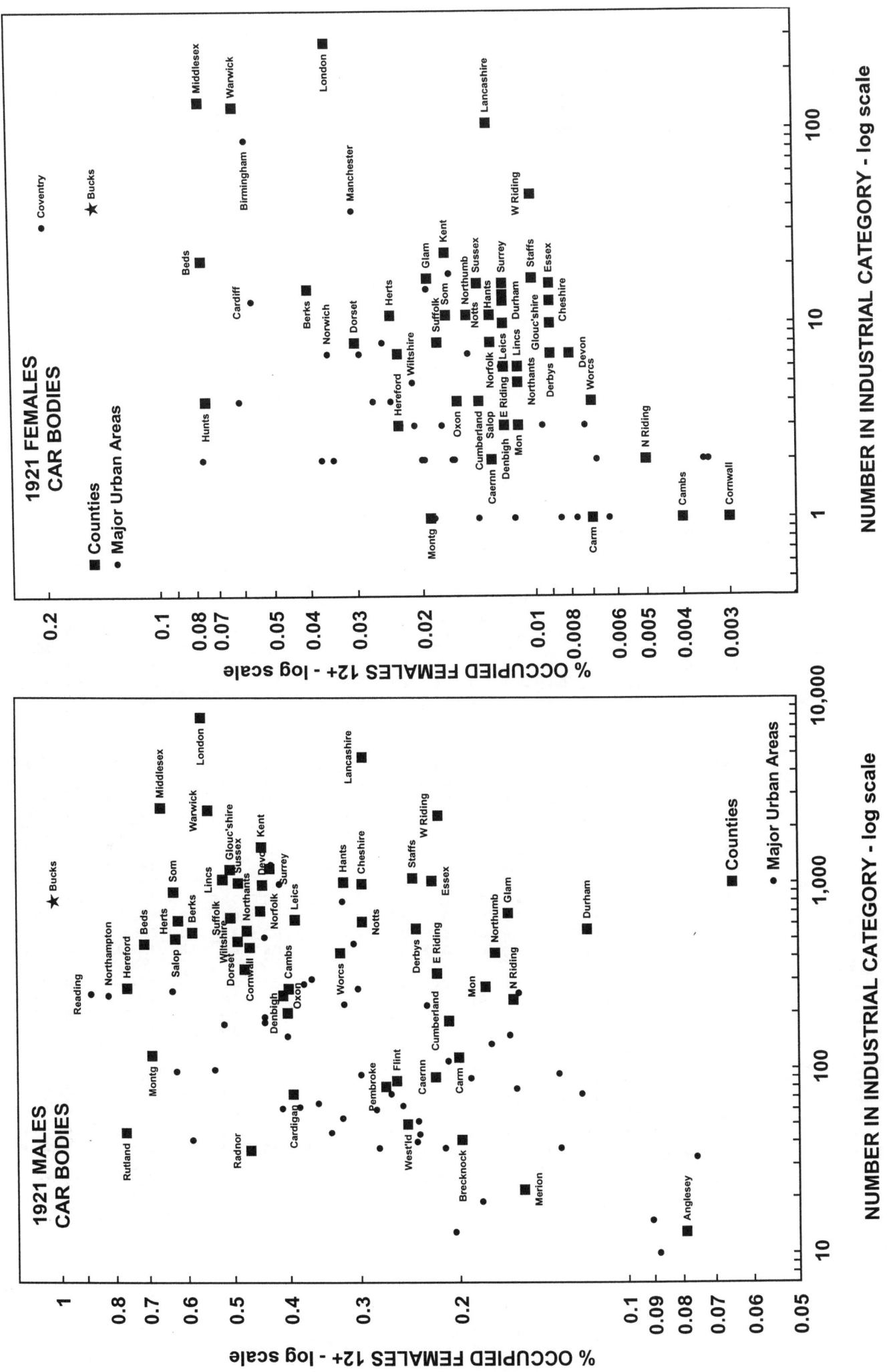

1921 MALES CAR BODIES

1921 FEMALES CAR BODIES

INDUSTRIES IN 1931

The classification used was similar to that of 1921. Of the 236 industries in Bucks 68 had less than 5 persons and a further 34 less than 10 persons (this calculation excludes service industries and agriculture).The local information was not as full as this. It was provided only for county boroughs and urban areas with a population of over 50,000. However, it was fuller than in 1921 and is used here in three tables.

1931 MALES	Pop 14-69	% Occ	% Unem	Agr	Qua rry	Manr	Util	Rail	Road	Other tran	Dist	Com mrce	Def enc	Nat Gvt	Loc Gvt	Prof	Ent	Priv serv	Other
Slough	12498	96.8	12.8	4.3	0.3	51.4	1.6	7.7	4.0	0.2	12.8	2.7	1.0	3.2	2.9	2.4	1.1	4.5	0.2
Wycombe	10414	98.2	6.2	1.1	0.1	70.7	1.1	1.4	3.1	0.1	10.8	1.6	0.2	1.4	2.6	2.2	0.8	2.8	0.1
Aylesbury	4631	96.6	6.0	2.4	0.0	44.8	2.6	4.1	4.1	0.2	16.9	2.5	2.1	3.0	8.3	2.5	0.5	5.0	0.8
Wolverton	4776	92.1	7.5	2.1	0.0	70.8	0.8	4.5	2.1	0.1	10.7	0.9	0.1	0.7	2.3	1.4	0.4	3.0	0.2
Chesham	3133	99.4	4.2	3.5	0.1	56.2	2.0	1.7	3.3	0.1	15.1	2.0	0.3	2.4	4.1	1.9	0.6	6.1	0.6
Bletchley	2214	93.6	3.3	5.2	0.6	28.8	1.7	34.0	0.9	0.1	13.9	1.5	0.1	3.9	3.2	1.3	0.4	4.8	0.1
Marlow	1750	96.8	8.5	3.6	0.6	45.5	2.6	1.9	4.4	0.8	16.7	2.6	0.3	2.1	3.1	3.2	0.5	11.9	0.8
Beaconsfield	1549	92.1	3.7	5.2	0.1	27.3	1.2	1.7	2.7	0.4	14.5	7.1	0.9	4.6	2.8	8.6	4.4	18.4	0.1
N Pagnell	1407	96.1	10.5	7.1	0.2	60.3	1.6	2.4	1.0	0.2	12.3	1.3	0.0	1.7	3.9	2.4	0.2	5.2	0.4
Buckingham	1113	93.3	10.2	14.6	0.0	33.9	3.5	1.4	3.0	0.1	17.8	2.8	0.6	2.2	5.7	5.3	0.4	8.1	0.5
Linslade	852	93.8	9.3	8.5	2.3	31.9	1.5	15.6	2.2	2.2	14.4	2.5	0.1	3.0	3.1	3.8	0.4	10.1	0.7
Eton	638	97.6	6.3	0.2	0.5	38.9	0.3	2.4	3.2	0.5	15.4	3.6	0.7	1.2	2.4	21.5	0.7	9.0	0.0
Rural Districts																			
Long Crendon	1261	96.7	8.7	42.5	0.3	20.9	0.1	3.0	2.0	0.0	9.7	1.0	0.2	2.0	3.9	2.5	0.0	11.2	0.8
Winslow	2110	95.9	6.9	41.5	0.1	21.2	1.2	3.6	1.8	0.0	10.4	1.1	0.3	1.1	4.3	2.5	0.5	9.8	0.4
Buckingham	2542	105.2	15.6	41.4	0.1	21.7	0.9	3.1	1.4	0.1	6.1	0.5	0.2	0.6	4.1	5.9	0.1	13.7	0.2
Wing	1916	96.5	5.9	35.5	0.4	19.3	0.4	5.3	1.2	3.2	6.5	2.8	0.7	0.3	5.4	2.2	0.5	16.3	0.3
Aylesbury (2)				32.9	0.1	25.8	0.5	3.4	2.7	0.1	9.4	0.9		1.5	5.8	2.0	0.3	14.2	0.4
Aylesbury	9946	94.1	4.0	18.4	0.0	14.5	0.3	1.9	1.5	0.0	5.3	0.5	44.0	0.8	3.2	1.1	0.2	8.0	0.2
N Pagnell	4855	95.4	9.4	31.7	0.4	34.9	1.2	4.6	1.7	0.1	9.6	0.8	0.1	0.9	2.9	1.7	0.3	9.4	0.1
Hambleden	702	97.9	4.2	29.1	0.0	20.5	0.2	0.2	2.1	0.3	3.6	0.9	0.3	1.1	3.6	2.7	0.2	35.1	0.2
Wycombe	9809	96.0	5.8	14.7	0.1	51.5	0.8	1.8	3.5	0.3	8.4	1.4	0.3	2.0	2.4	2.2	0.5	9.9	0.4
Eton	10106	94.7	5.6	13.3	0.8	32.0	1.3	2.9	2.6	0.6	11.8	3.8	1.6	3.0	2.6	4.5	1.8	17.9	0.3
Amersham	9921	92.2	5.4	12.1	0.2	34.6	1.2	1.9	3.4	0.5	12.8	4.3	0.8	2.5	2.9	5.0	1.1	16.4	0.5
TOTAL	98143	95.7	6.7	11.9	0.2	39.8	1.1	3.8	2.6	0.3	10.4	2.1	4.9	1.9	3.1	2.8	0.7	8.9	0.3
FEMALES																			
Slough	12368	34.3	8.5	0.6	0.0	43.4	0.1	1.9	0.3	0.1	11.8	1.4	0.1	2.6	4.3	6.0	1.0	26.4	0.0
Wycombe	10498	30.8	3.4	0.3	0.0	40.8	0.2	0.1	0.3	0.1	15.8	0.8	0.0	1.1	3.7	9.2	1.1	26.4	0.1
Aylesbury	5296	36.0	3.0	0.3	0.0	33.5	0.2	0.1	0.2	0.1	13.6	0.6	0.1	3.5	6.2	6.9	0.8	33.9	0.2
Wolverton	5008	27.2	4.4	0.2	0.1	52.5	0.0	1.3	0.2	0.0	12.4	0.2	0.0	2.0	3.7	3.6	0.4	23.6	0.0
Chesham	3440	35.2	2.1	0.4	0.0	43.3	0.3	0.3	0.0	0.1	15.1	1.2	0.1	2.5	3.2	5.1	0.1	28.4	0.0
Bletchley	2321	25.9	3.8	1.0	0.0	39.1	0.3	1.0	0.0	0.0	14.2	1.2	0.2	1.4	5.4	3.8	1.6	30.8	0.0
Marlow	1950	34.8	4.8	1.5	0.0	18.8	0.2	0.3	0.3	0.0	15.0	0.8	0.0	1.1	3.1	4.5	0.8	53.2	0.5
Beaconsfield	2245	43.0	2.6	0.6	0.0	5.5	0.0	0.6	0.0	0.0	6.1	1.2	0.0	1.5	0.6	11.3	1.4	70.8	0.4
N Pagnell	1482	25.4	6.8	0.3	0.0	14.5	0.6	0.9	0.0	0.0	16.2	0.6	0.0	1.1	10.2	7.4	0.3	48.0	0.0
Buckingham	1201	34.4	5.6	0.5	0.0	14.3	0.0	0.0	0.0	0.0	14.1	1.0	0.0	1.8	5.4	7.2	0.0	55.8	0.0
Linslade	981	32.7	4.6	1.0	0.7	32.6	0.0	0.7	0.0	2.6	12.1	0.3	0.0	2.6	3.9	4.9	2.0	37.5	0.0
Eton	907	56.1	3.5	0.2	0.0	9.8	0.0	0.2	0.2	0.0	11.4	0.8	0.0	1.2	1.6	53.5	0.6	20.5	0.0
Rural Districts																			
Long Crendon	1326	21.8	4.3	3.2	0.0	5.8	0.0	0.0	0.4	0.0	13.0	0.4	0.0	1.4	8.7	6.9	0.0	60.3	0.0
Winslow	2190	23.4	5.6	3.7	0.0	8.0	0.0	0.2	0.2	0.0	8.6	0.4	0.2	2.9	9.5	6.8	0.0	59.1	0.4
Buckingham	2653	24.4	5.2	5.4	0.0	2.9	0.0	0.2	0.0	0.0	4.2	0.0	0.0	2.4	7.0	15.4	0.0	62.3	0.2
Wing	2041	26.8	2.4	6.0	0.0	24.5	0.0	0.0	0.0	0.9	6.0	1.1	0.2	2.4	7.3	3.4	0.4	47.6	0.2
Aylesbury	7130	24.5	5.9	2.4	0.1	11.5	0.0	0.1	0.1	0.0	8.8	0.5	5.9	2.5	8.5	4.8	0.4	54.3	0.1
N Pagnell	5118	24.8	6.5	2.3	0.0	22.2	0.0	0.0	0.3	0.0	11.0	0.3	0.1	2.3	5.9	5.2	0.4	50.0	0.0
Hambleden	718	30.5	3.3	2.4	0.0	5.2	0.0	0.0	0.5	0.0	9.0	0.0	0.0	2.8	7.5	2.8	0.5	69.3	0.0
Wycombe	10183	29.4	4.6	2.0	0.0	24.0	0.1	0.2	0.4	0.1	9.0	0.5	0.0	2.5	5.6	5.7	0.6	49.0	0.3
Eton	12219	36.8	3.4	3.4	0.0	14.0	0.1	0.3	0.1	0.1	8.5	1.4	0.3	1.8	2.1	5.8	1.1	60.7	0.2
Amersham	11991	33.7	3.4	0.9	0.0	8.8	0.1	0.2	0.2	0.1	8.6	1.3	0.0	2.0	3.7	9.8	0.9	63.1	0.5
TOTAL	103266	31.6	4.5	1.5	0.0	24.9	0.1	0.5	0.2	0.1	10.9	0.9	0.4	2.1	4.5	7.6	0.8	45.4	0.2

Aylesbury (2) figures excluding De Urban areas listed in order of total population.   Rural areas listed in order of Male % in agric

1931 Male

	Bucks No	%	Slough	Wyc	Ayles	Wol	Ches	Blet	Mar	Beac	N P	Buck	Lin	Eton	Amer RD	Ayles RD	Buck RD	Eton RD	Hamb RD	L Crd RD	N P RD	Wing RD	Wins RD	Wyc RD
In industries 14+			10717	9626	4219	4092	2989	2007	1561	1375	1223	942	731	586	8675	9003	2314	9063	659	1122	4235	1745	1893	8897
% Occupied		95.7	96.8	98.2	96.6	92.1	99.4	93.6	96.8	92.1	96.1	93.3	93.8	97.6	92.2	94.1	105.2	94.7	97.9	96.7	95.4	96.5	95.9	96.0
% Unemployed		7.1	12.8	6.2	6.0	7.5	4.2	3.3	8.5	3.7	10.5	10.2	9.3	6.3	5.4	4.0	15.6	5.6	4.2	8.7	9.4	5.9	6.9	5.8
% In each industry																								
Agriculture	10976	12.5	4.3	1.1	2.4	2.1	3.5	5.2	3.6	5.2	7.1	14.6	8.5	0.2	12.1	18.4	41.4	13.3	29.1	42.5	31.7	35.5	41.5	14.7
Mining & Quarrying	221	0.3	0.3	0.1	0.0	0.0	0.1	0.6	0.6	0.1	0.2	0.0	2.3	0.5	0.2	0.0	0.1	0.8	0.0	0.3	0.4	0.4	0.1	0.1
Mine quarry prod	81	0.1	0.1	0.0	0.0	0.0	0.0	0.3	0.2	0.1	0.0	0.0	0.4	0.0	'0.1	0.1	0.0	0.1	0.0	0.5	0.1	1.3	0.0	0.0
Bricks Pottery Glass	1204	1.4	1.8	0.0	0.2	0.0	0.7	5.2	1.6	0.1	0.4	1.0	3.8	0.0	1.5	0.6	9.2	1.3	0.2	1.1	3.1	1.1	4.2	0.5
Chemicals	176	0.2	0.9	0.0	0.1	0.0	0.1	0.1	0.1	0.2	0.1	0.0	0.1	0.0	0.2	0.0	0.0	0.3	0.0	0.1	0.1	0.1	0.0	0.1
Paints	213	0.2	1.4	0.1	0.0	0.0	0.0	0.0	0.0	0.1	0.0	0.0	0.0	0.9	0.1	0.0	0.0	0.4	0.0	0.0	0.0	0.0	0.0	0.0
Glue	78	0.1	0.4	0.1	0.1	0.0	0.0	0.0	0.0	0.1	0.0	0.1	0.1	0.0	0.1	0.0	0.0	0.1	0.0	0.0	0.0	0.0	0.0	0.0
Refining Other	102	0.1	0.8	0.0	0.0	0.0	0.0	0.0	0.0	0.0	0.0	0.0	0.0	0.2	0.0	0.0	0.0	0.0	0.0	0.0	0.0	0.0	0.0	0.0
Founding	301	0.3	0.4	0.1	0.2	0.3	0.3	0.2	0.6	0.4	0.1	0.4	0.8	0.0	0.3	0.3	0.6	0.4	0.3	0.8	0.5	0.7	1.1	0.3
Engineering	965	1.1	1.9	2.3	0.9	0.4	0.6	0.3	0.8	1.2	0.7	0.6	1.9	1.7	1.1	0.2	0.2	1.3	1.1	0.5	0.3	0.7	0.1	1.3
Electrical	1225	1.4	6.6	0.4	0.8	0.3	1.4	0.3	0.4	1.1	0.1	0.4	0.7	2.6	1.2	0.2	0.3	1.6	0.0	0.3	0.2	0.2	0.2	0.4
Vehicles	5455	6.2	8.3	1.6	1.4	59.3	0.9	5.7	1.2	1.7	44.2	2.0	4.8	5.3	1.2	1.0	1.0	2.7	0.2	3.4	11.1	0.9	2.9	0.9
Ship	32	0.0	0.0	0.0	0.0	0.0	0.0	0.0	0.4	0.0	0.0	0.0	0.3	0.0	0.0	0.0	0.0	0.1	0.2	0.0	0.0	0.0	0.0	0.1
Cutlery	55	0.1	0.3	0.1	0.0	0.0	0.0	0.0	0.0	0.0	0.0	0.0	0.0	0.0	0.0	0.0	0.0	0.1	0.0	0.0	0.0	0.0	0.0	0.1
Other Metal	440	0.5	1.0	0.2	4.1	0.0	0.1	0.0	0.1	0.3	0.0	0.0	0.1	0.2	0.2	0.4	0.0	0.6	0.0	0.0	0.1	0.2	0.1	0.1
Precious	94	0.1	0.1	0.1	0.2	0.1	0.2	0.0	0.3	0.2	0.1	0.2	0.1	0.2	0.2	0.0	0.0	0.1	0.0	0.2	0.0	0.0	0.1	0.1
Cotton	119	0.1	0.8	0.0	0.0	0.0	0.0	0.0	0.0	0.0	0.0	0.0	0.0	0.2	0.0	0.0	0.0	0.2	0.0	0.0	0.0	0.0	0.0	0.0
Wool	23	0.0	0.0	0.0	0.0	0.0	0.0	0.0	0.0	0.2	0.0	0.0	0.1	0.0	0.0	0.0	0.0	0.0	0.0	0.0	0.0	0.0	0.0	0.1
Mixed Fibers	120	0.1	0.5	0.2	0.1	0.0	0.3	0.0	0.1	0.2	0.0	0.0	0.0	0.2	0.1	0.0	0.0	0.1	0.0	0.3	0.1	0.1	0.0	0.1
Furs Skins	106	0.1	0.0	0.1	0.0	0.3	0.0	0.1	0.0	0.0	1.1	0.0	0.0	0.0	0.0	0.0	0.0	0.0	0.0	0.0	1.4	0.0	0.0	0.0
Leather Goods	75	0.1	0.1	0.0	0.0	0.0	0.3	0.1	0.1	0.1	0.2	0.3	0.3	0.2	0.1	0.0	0.1	0.1	0.2	0.1	0.2	0.0	0.4	0.0
Clothing & Shoes	1402	1.6	1.4	0.7	1.2	0.8	12.2	0.5	1.1	2.0	1.5	2.3	2.1	6.0	1.6	0.5	0.9	1.1	0.5	0.8	4.6	1.1	1.4	0.4
Food	2049	2.3	4.4	1.3	7.0	1.2	1.9	3.6	1.3	2.2	2.0	9.7	2.1	3.1	1.4	1.4	2.5	1.9	2.0	2.0	1.9	2.1	1.9	1.3
Drink	326	0.4	0.3	0.1	1.3	0.0	0.9	0.1	5.4	0.1	1.3	0.2	0.3	1.0	0.2	0.1	0.0	0.3	0.0	0.0	0.5	0.3	0.0	0.1
Wood & Basket	1086	1.2	0.7	1.2	0.5	0.1	9.8	1.8	0.6	0.1	0.3	0.4	1.0	0.5	1.6	0.5	0.3	0.9	0.3	0.9	1.0	0.7	0.4	1.9
Furniture	8053	9.2	1.6	51.7	0.4	0.1	0.3	0.4	8.6	1.4	0.1	0.2	0.4	2.4	4.2	0.2	0.0	0.5	10.3	0.0	0.2	0.1	0.1	24.6
Paper & printing	2783	3.2	1.2	2.3	18.3	3.8	3.4	1.5	5.4	1.7	1.3	2.9	3.4	3.2	1.2	1.4	0.2	1.9	0.0	0.6	0.6	1.3	0.5	8.0
Building	9024	10.3	13.4	7.4	7.6	3.8	16.0	4.3	16.4	13.3	6.7	13.1	6.3	9.6	16.6	7.4	6.1	12.4	5.2	8.8	8.0	8.1	7.9	10.7
Rubber	29	0.0	0.2	0.0	0.0	0.0	0.0	0.0	0.0	0.1	0.0	0.0	0.0	0.0	0.0	0.0	0.0	0.0	0.0	0.0	0.0	0.0	0.0	0.0
Musical Instruments	320	0.4	1.8	0.0	0.0	0.1	0.0	0.0	0.0	0.0	0.1	0.0	0.1	0.9	0.1	0.0	0.0	1.0	0.0	0.2	0.1	0.0	0.1	0.0
Other	630	0.7	0.7	0.5	0.3	0.0	6.5	3.3	0.3	0.1	0.1	0.0	0.3	0.3	0.8	0.1	0.0	1.3	0.2	0.0	0.1	0.0	0.1	0.2
Gas	469	0.5	1.0	0.6	0.7	0.2	0.9	0.8	1.6	0.5	1.1	0.4	1.2	0.0	0.5	0.1	0.0	0.7	0.0	0.3	0.1	0.2	0.3	0.0
Water	99	0.1	0.0	0.1	0.2	0.0	0.1	0.0	0.3	0.1	0.1	0.0	0.1	0.0	0.3	0.1	0.0	0.2	0.0	0.1	0.0	0.1	0.0	0.1
Electricity	493	0.6	0.6	0.4	1.7	0.6	1.0	0.8	0.6	0.6	0.3	3.1	0.1	0.3	0.4	0.1	0.9	0.5	0.0	0.0	0.8	0.2	1.1	0.4
Railway	3496	4.0	7.7	1.4	4.1	4.5	1.7	34.0	1.9	1.7	2.4	1.4	15.6	2.4	1.9	1.9	3.1	2.9	0.2	3.0	4.6	5.3	3.6	1.8
Road	2451	2.8	4.0	3.1	4.1	2.1	3.3	0.9	4.4	2.7	1.0	3.0	2.2	3.2	3.4	1.5	1.4	2.6	2.1	2.0	1.7	1.2	1.8	3.5
Other	283	0.3	0.2	0.1	0.2	0.1	0.1	0.1	0.8	0.4	0.2	0.1	2.2	0.5	0.5	0.0	0.1	0.6	0.3	0.0	0.1	3.2	0.0	0.3
Distributive	9663	11.0	12.8	10.8	16.9	10.7	15.1	13.9	16.7	14.5	12.3	17.8	14.4	15.4	12.8	5.3	6.1	11.8	3.6	9.7	9.6	6.5	10.4	8.4
Other	1911	2.2	2.7	1.6	2.5	0.9	2.0	1.5	2.6	7.1	1.3	2.8	2.5	3.6	4.3	0.5	0.5	3.8	0.9	1.0	0.8	2.8	1.1	1.4
Defence	4494	5.1	1.0	0.2	2.1	0.1	0.3	0.1	0.3	0.9	0.0	0.6	0.1	0.7	0.8	44.0	0.2	1.6	0.3	0.2	0.1	0.7	0.3	0.3
National	1795	2.0	3.2	1.4	3.0	0.7	2.4	3.9	2.1	4.6	1.7	2.2	3.0	1.2	2.5	0.8	0.6	3.0	1.1	2.0	0.9	0.3	1.1	2.0
Local	2866	3.3	2.9	2.6	8.3	2.3	4.1	3.2	3.1	2.8	3.9	5.7	3.1	2.4	2.9	3.2	4.1	2.6	3.6	3.9	2.9	5.4	4.3	2.4
Professions	2599	3.0	2.4	2.2	2.5	1.4	1.9	1.3	3.2	8.6	2.4	5.3	3.8	21.5	5.0	1.1	5.9	4.5	2.7	2.5	1.7	2.2	2.5	2.2
Entert & Sport	688	0.8	1.1	0.8	0.5	0.4	0.6	0.4	0.5	4.4	0.2	0.4	0.4	0.7	1.1	0.2	0.1	1.8	0.2	0.0	0.3	0.5	0.5	0.5
Personal Service	8264	9.4	4.5	2.8	5.0	3.0	6.1	4.8	11.9	18.4	5.2	8.1	10.1	9.0	16.4	8.0	13.7	17.9	35.1	11.2	9.4	16.3	9.8	9.9
Other	283	0.3	0.2	0.1	0.8	0.2	0.6	0.1	0.8	0.1	0.4	0.5	0.7	0.0	0.5	0.2	0.2	0.3	0.2	0.8	0.1	0.3	0.4	0.4

99

1931 FEMALE

1931 FEMALE	Bucks		Slough	Wyc	Ayles	Wol	Ches	Blet	Mar	Beac	N P	Buck	Lin	Eton	Amer	Ayles	Buck	Eton	Hamb	L Crd	N P	Wing	Wins	Wyc
	No	%	RD	RD	RD	RD	RD	RD	RD	RD	RD	RD	RD	RD	RD	RD	RD	RD	RD	RD	RD	RD	RD	RD
In industries 14+	31175		3911	3125	1851	1306	1185	578	648	941	352	391	307	492	3903	1653	616	4351	212	277	1192	534	486	2864
% Occupied	31.6	31.6	34.3	30.8	36.0	27.2	35.2	25.9	34.8	43.0	25.4	34.4	32.7	56.1	33.7	24.5	24.4	36.8	30.5	21.8	24.8	26.8	23.4	29.4
% Unemployed	4.3	4.3	7.8	3.3	2.9	4.3	2.1	3.7	4.6	2.5	6.4	5.3	4.4	3.3	3.3	5.5	4.9	3.3	3.2	4.2	6.1	2.4	5.3	4.4
Agriculture	482	1.5	0.6	0.3	0.3	0.2	0.4	1.0	1.5	0.6	0.3	0.5	1.0	0.2	0.9	2.4	5.4	3.4	2.4	3.2	2.3	6.0	3.7	2.0
Bricks Pottery Glass	33	0.1	0.7	-	0.1	-	-	-	-	0.1	-	-	-	-	0.0	0.1	-	-	-	-	-	-	-	-
Chemicals	147	0.5	2.8	-	0.1	-	0.2	0.2	-	0.1	-	1.3	-	0.4	0.1	-	-	0.4	-	-	0.1	0.2	-	0.0
Paints	83	0.3	1.6	-	-	0.1	-	-	-	-	-	1.0	-	0.4	-	-	-	0.3	-	-	-	-	-	-
Glue	29	0.1	0.5	0.0	-	-	-	-	-	-	-	-	-	-	-	-	-	0.1	-	-	-	-	-	-
Founding	17	0.1	0.2	-	-	-	0.2	-	-	-	-	-	-	-	0.1	-	-	-	-	-	-	-	-	-
Engineering	87	0.3	0.7	0.8	0.2	-	0.1	-	0.2	0.1	0.3	-	0.7	-	0.1	0.2	-	0.2	0.5	-	-	-	-	-	0.2
Electrical	330	1.1	6.2	0.4	0.1	-	0.1	-	0.2	0.1	-	-	-	1.0	0.2	0.1	-	1.1	-	0.4	0.1	-	-	0.2
Vehicles	425	1.4	4.7	0.4	0.2	10.3	0.3	0.5	-	0.1	5.4	0.3	0.2	0.2	0.2	0.1	0.2	0.8	-	-	0.6	-	0.2	0.3
Cutlery	41	0.1	0.9	-	-	-	-	-	-	-	-	-	-	-	-	-	-	0.1	-	-	-	-	-	-
Other Metal	103	0.3	1.0	0.3	1.3	-	-	-	-	0.1	-	-	0.2	0.2	0.1	0.2	-	0.5	-	-	-	-	-	0.0
Cotton	101	0.3	1.8	-	0.3	-	-	-	-	-	-	-	0.2	-	-	-	-	0.6	-	-	-	-	-	-
Mixed Fibers	146	0.5	0.5	0.4	0.2	0.2	1.9	-	-	-	-	-	-	-	0.8	0.2	0.2	0.1	-	0.7	1.8	-	0.2	0.7
Furs Skins	23	0.1	0.1	0.0	-	-	-	-	-	-	-	-	-	-	0.0	0.1	-	-	-	-	1.3	-	0.2	-
Leather Goods	104	0.3	0.1	0.0	-	0.2	7.1	-	-	-	1.1	-	0.3	-	0.2	0.2	-	-	-	0.4	0.3	-	-	-
Clothing & Footwear	1324	4.2	4.9	2.6	3.5	3.1	10.3	6.6	4.0	2.4	4.8	3.8	17.6	2.6	3.3	3.8	1.6	2.8	3.3	2.2	12.5	11.8	3.7	2.6
Food	942	3.0	9.9	1.0	10.6	0.3	0.8	0.3	1.9	1.1	1.7	5.9	1.0	1.0	0.8	3.4	0.6	2.6	0.5	0.7	0.7	1.5	0.8	0.9
Drink	61	0.2	0.1	0.1	0.2	-	0.1	-	4.5	-	1.1	-	0.3	0.2	0.1	0.1	-	0.1	-	-	0.1	0.6	-	0.0
Wood Working & Basket	64	0.2	0.4	0.4	-	-	3.0	0.3	-	-	-	-	-	-	0.1	-	-	0.0	-	-	0.3	-	-	-
Furniture	1261	4.0	0.8	28.2	-	-	0.1	0.2	2.3	-	-	0.3	0.3	1.4	0.8	0.1	-	0.4	0.9	-	0.2	-	0.2	9.2
Paper & Printing	1609	5.2	1.9	3.3	16.5	38.2	3.9	4.2	5.1	0.5	0.9	1.8	10.7	1.8	0.5	2.5	0.3	1.9	-	0.4	1.9	9.6	1.9	8.4
Building	69	0.2	0.2	0.3	0.2	0.1	0.1	-	0.3	0.3	0.3	-	-	0.2	0.1	0.1	0.2	0.3	-	-	0.3	0.4	-	0.4
Rubber	20	0.1	0.4	-	-	-	-	-	-	-	-	-	-	-	0.0	-	-	0.0	-	-	-	-	-	0.0
Musical Instruments	113	0.4	1.7	0.1	-	-	0.1	-	-	-	-	-	-	-	0.1	-	-	0.9	-	-	-	-	-	-
Other	590	1.9	1.3	2.5	0.1	-	15.2	26.8	0.5	0.1	-	-	0.3	0.2	1.2	0.1	-	0.5	-	0.4	1.5	0.6	0.8	0.8
Electricity	16	0.1	0.0	0.2	0.1	0.3	0.3	0.2	0.2	-	-	-	-	-	0.0	-	-	0.3	-	-	-	0.1	0.4	0.1
Railway	146	0.5	1.9	0.1	0.1	1.3	0.3	1.0	0.3	0.9	-	-	0.7	0.2	0.2	0.1	0.2	0.1	-	-	-	-	0.2	0.2
Road	58	0.2	0.3	0.3	0.2	0.2	-	-	0.3	-	0.9	-	-	0.2	0.2	0.1	-	0.1	0.5	0.4	0.3	-	0.2	0.4
Other	29	0.1	0.1	0.1	0.1	-	0.1	-	-	-	-	-	2.6	-	0.1	-	-	0.1	-	-	-	0.9	-	0.1
Distributive	3385	10.9	11.8	15.8	13.6	12.4	15.1	14.2	15.0	6.1	16.2	14.1	12.1	11.4	8.6	8.8	4.2	8.5	9.0	13.0	11.0	6.0	8.6	9.0
Other	292	0.9	1.4	0.8	0.6	1.2	1.2	1.2	0.8	1.2	0.6	1.0	0.3	0.8	1.3	0.5	-	1.4	-	0.4	0.3	1.1	0.4	0.5
Defence	123	0.4	0.1	-	0.1	-	0.1	0.2	-	-	-	-	-	0.2	0.0	5.9	-	0.3	-	-	0.1	0.2	0.2	0.0
National	659	2.1	2.6	1.1	3.5	2.0	2.5	1.4	1.1	1.5	1.1	1.8	2.6	1.2	2.0	2.5	2.4	1.8	2.8	1.4	2.3	2.4	2.9	2.5
Local	1397	4.5	4.3	3.7	6.2	3.7	3.2	5.4	3.1	0.6	10.2	5.4	3.9	1.6	3.7	8.5	7.0	2.1	7.5	8.7	5.9	7.3	9.5	5.6
Professions	2354	7.6	6.0	9.2	6.9	3.6	5.1	3.8	4.5	11.3	7.4	7.2	4.9	53.5	9.8	4.8	15.4	5.8	2.8	6.9	5.2	3.4	6.8	5.7
Entertainments & Sport	245	0.8	1.0	1.1	0.8	0.4	0.1	1.6	0.8	1.4	0.3	-	2.0	0.6	0.9	0.4	-	1.1	0.5	-	0.4	0.4	-	0.6
Personal Service	14164	45.4	26.4	26.4	33.9	23.6	28.4	30.8	53.2	70.8	48.0	55.8	37.5	20.5	63.1	54.3	62.3	60.7	69.3	60.3	50.0	47.6	59.1	49.0
Other	55	0.2	0.0	0.1	0.2	-	-	-	0.5	0.4	-	-	-	-	-	0.5	0.1	0.2	0.2	-	-	-	0.2	0.4	0.3

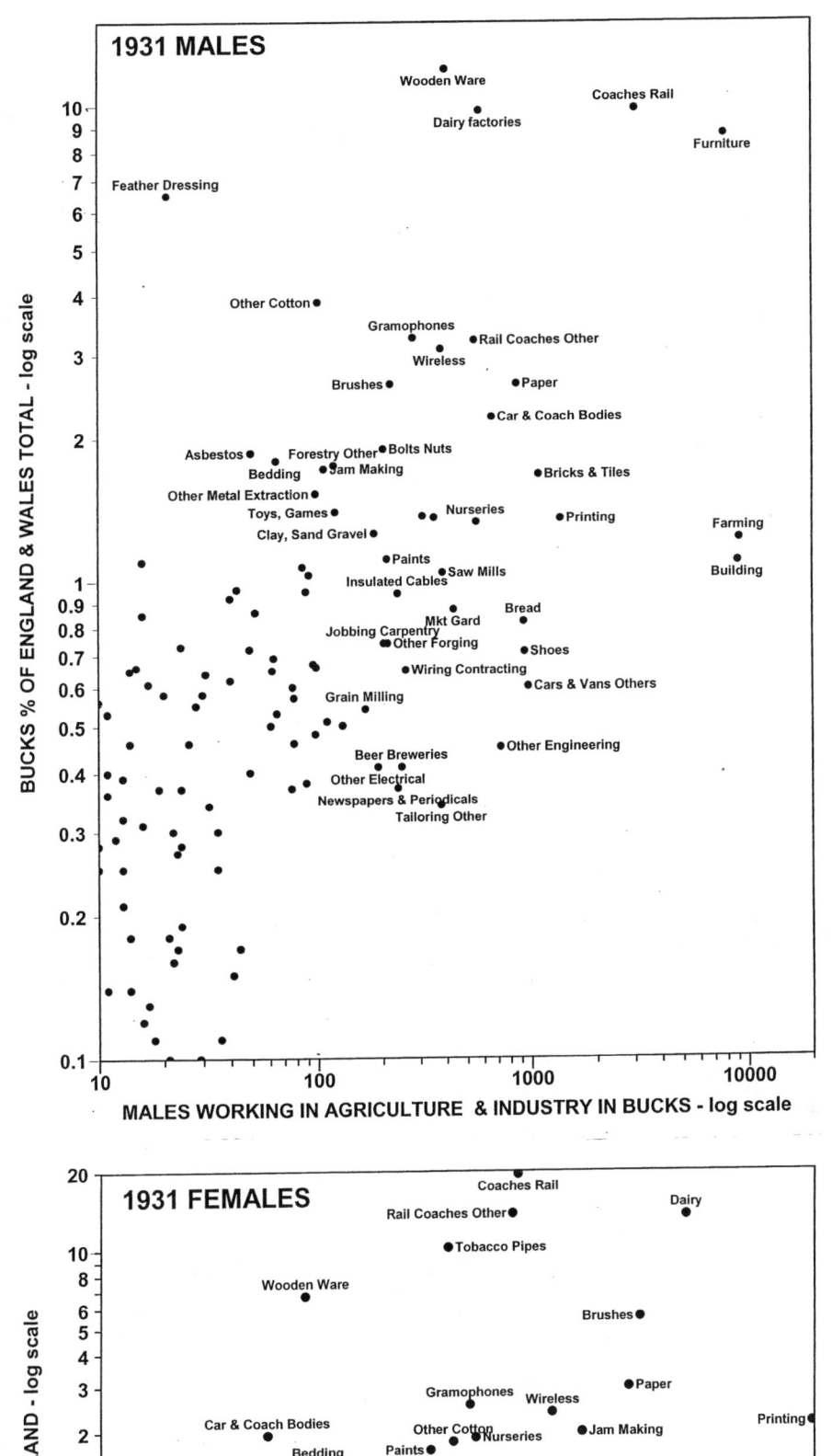

1931 MALES

BUCKS % OF ENGLAND & WALES TOTAL - log scale

MALES WORKING IN AGRICULTURE & INDUSTRY IN BUCKS - log scale

1931 FEMALES

BUCKS % OF ENGLAND - log scale

FEMALES WORKING IN AGRICULTURE & INDUSTRY IN BUCKS - log scale

INDUSTRIES AND INDUSTRIAL OCCUPATIONS IN 1951

A new classification was introduced for this Census for both Industries and Occupations. The Census in many ways marked the high water mark of census procedures. The detail it contains shows a remarkable progress from the early years of the Nineteenth century. The final table here for occupations in the various administrative units of the county is a reflection of this (see Vision of Britain).

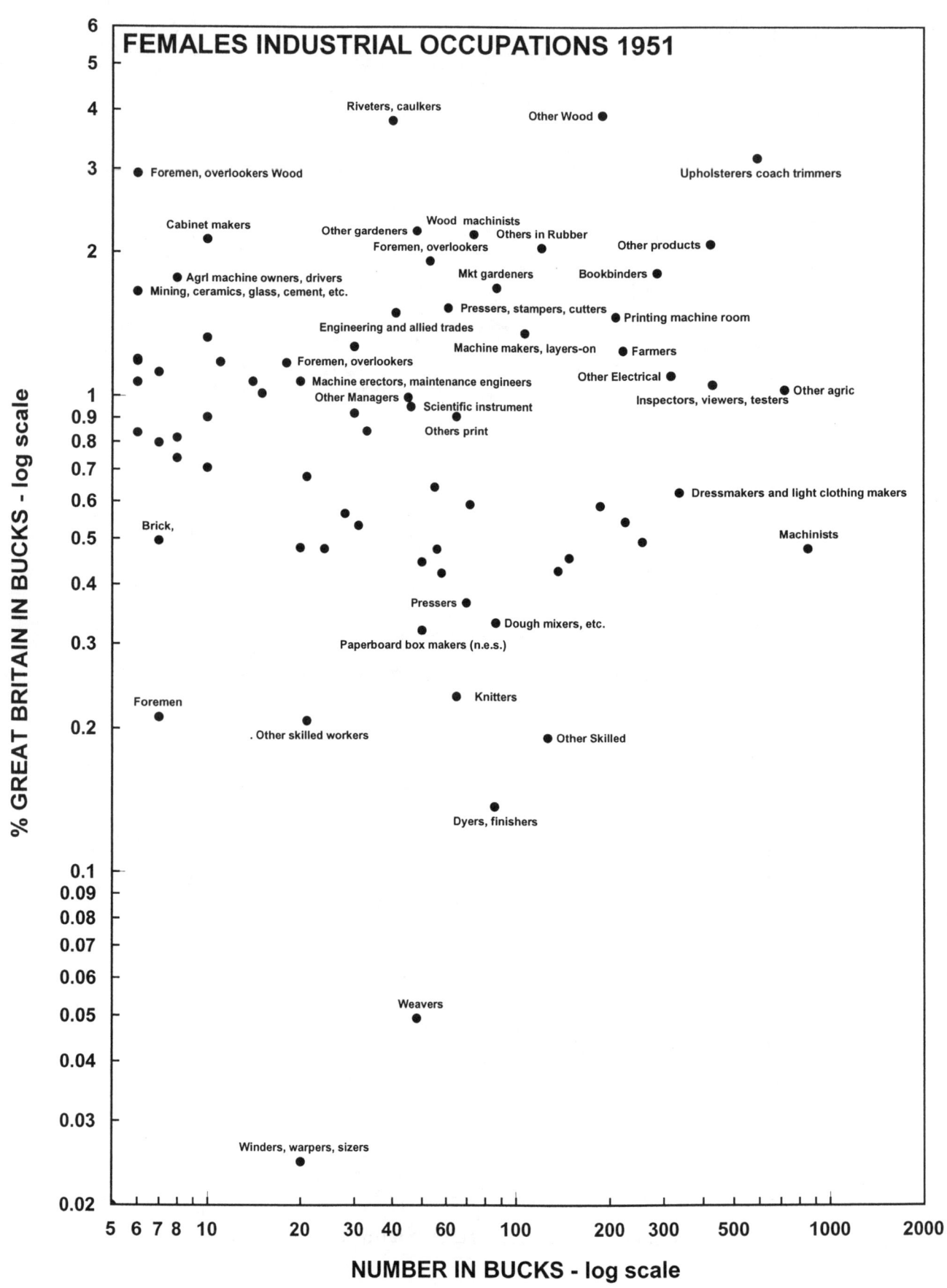

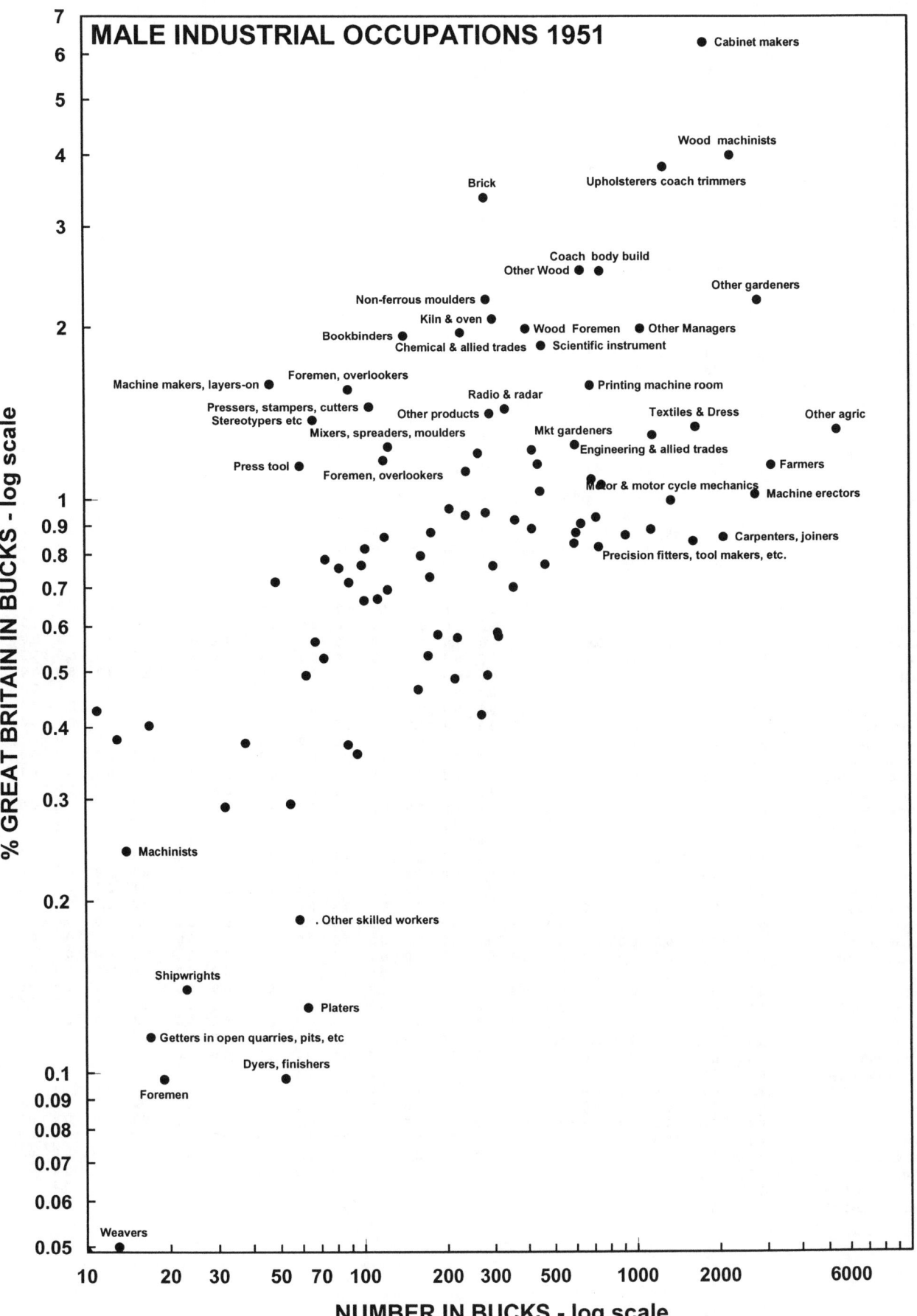

MALE INDUSTRIAL OCCUPATIONS 1951

Chart plotting % GREAT BRITAIN IN BUCKS (log scale, y-axis) against NUMBER IN BUCKS (log scale, x-axis).

Labelled data points include: Cabinet makers, Wood machinists, Upholsterers coach trimmers, Brick, Coach body build, Other Wood, Other gardeners, Non-ferrous moulders, Kiln & oven, Wood Foremen, Other Managers, Bookbinders, Chemical & allied trades, Scientific instrument, Foremen overlookers, Machine makers layers-on, Printing machine room, Pressers stampers cutters, Other products, Radio & radar, Textiles & Dress, Other agric, Stereotypers etc, Mixers spreaders moulders, Mkt gardeners, Engineering & allied trades, Press tool, Foremen overlookers, Motor & motor cycle mechanics, Farmers, Machine erectors, Precision fitters tool makers etc, Carpenters joiners, Machinists, Other skilled workers, Shipwrights, Platers, Getters in open quarries pits etc, Dyers finishers, Foremen, Weavers.

INDUSTRIES - Urban Areas in size order then Rural Districts

MALE 1951

	Total	Slough	Wycmbe	AylBury	Wolvert	Bletley	ChesHam	Beacfld	Marlow	Bucking	NPagnel	Linslade	Eton	Amer RD	Ayle RD	Buck RD	Eton RD	NPa RD	Wing RD	Wsl RD	Wy RD
ALL	123005	27722	16582	7650	5654	4584	3239	2367	1367	1243	1112	896	812	7706	10252	4186	10911	2931	1823	2101	9867
Agriculture	10392	329	79	130	66	121	176	84	35	136	79	38	34	1039	1767	960	1214	1152	769	750	1434
Coal mining	7	1		1				1						2							
Other mining quarry	185	5	3		1	1			13	1	2	9	1	6	4		104	19	7		9
Bricks	1831			2	4	337	25		7			5		114	39	762	8	8		503	17
Cement	130	4									1	1		3			11		110		
Coke ovens, chem	472	325	39	3		15	5	2			2			3	3		58	2	1		14
Metal manufacture	2948	2309	49	356		2	5	3		3	2	26		107	2	1	75	1	1		22
Shipbuilding	164	114	1	1			10		1		1	2	3				8			1	22
Machine tools	627	314	77	82		3	1	2	1		40			17	1	1	32			1	55
Textile machinery	10	6	1												1		1				1
Constructional engin	374	224	95	2	1	5		6	1			1		3	19	1	8		2	3	3
Other mech engin	5085	2517	1201	212	10	12	38	39	8	54	44	222	7	87	33	14	152	28	6	9	392
Electrical machinery	540	164	5			122	2							243	2						1
Wireless apparatus	1002	333	208	28	5	5	66	6	3	1	1		1	15	3		117	18	1	1	190
Other electrical	2296	547	603	57	3	157	4	394	1	5	1	4		16	4		486	7			7
Motor cars	1476	958	37	38	9	5	12	8	17	6	280	6	1	53	5		24	4		1	12
Aircraft	2134	1128	108	96	3	41	3	3		17		1		11	256	8	375	29	1		54
Other metal goods	1727	803	157	465	5	8	37	3	5	2	2	4	3	84	20	3	62	8	4	6	46
Preci instr jewelery	1767	903	135	54	11	2	144	4	6	3	3	3	3	42	40	2	388	5	1	3	15
Cotton spinning	2	0						1									1				
Cotton waving	99	56	7														36				
Woolen worsted	29	3	3						1		1	1					17			1	2
Rayon etc	56	9	1		4		1										41				
Hosiery	188	178	2									1									7
Textile finishing	71	4	2					1						50			14				
Leather goods	252	4	41	3	19		11		3	2	10	20	2	1	3		4	125		1	3
Tailoring	336	85	64	11	4	30	15	8	7	3	6		53	10	1		15	12		9	4
Dressmaking	23	6	7		1			1	1					1			2				4
Shoe making repair	479	63	45	22	14	10	169	7	8	4	2	5	11	24	8	11	21	24	4	6	21
Food	3519	1892	294	251	46	105	94	27	23	139	39	10	13	172	62	21	177	36	22	17	79
Drink	262	12	21	55			43		116		7	3	2	1	1		2	1			3
Timber	774	104	192	7	3	63	20	12	52		3	2		52	21		88	1		4	150
Furniture	8295	973	6117	22		11	16	7	43		4	1	12	295	18	1	50	66		3	656
Paper & board	1558	9	182				1	2	1			6	1	1	4	1	104	1			1245
Printing	2288	304	351	1113	180	35	104	16	16	19	9	14	20	47	6	2	20	2	2	1	27
Other manufacturing	3213	834	281	6	16	126	275	83	16	2		8	3	39	7	1	1453	1	1	5	56

percentages of each area's total

	Total	Slough	Wycmbe	AylBury	Wolvert	Bletley	ChesHam	Beacfld	Marlow	Bucking	NPagnel	Linslade	Eton	Amer RD	Ayle RD	Buck RD	Eton RD	NPa RD	Wing RD	Wsl RD	Wy RD
Agriculture	8.4	1.2	0.5	1.7	1.2	2.6	5.4	3.5	2.6	10.9	7.1	4.2	4.2	13.5	17.2	22.9	11.1	39.3	42.2	35.7	14.5
Coal mining	0.0	0.0	0.0	0.0	0.0	0.0	0.0	0.0	0.0	0.0	0.0	0.0	0.0	0.0	0.0	0.0	0.0	0.0	0.0	0.0	0.0
Other mining quarry	0.2	0.0	0.0	0.0	0.0	0.0	0.0	0.0	1.0	0.1	0.2	1.0	0.1	0.1	0.0	0.0	1.0	0.6	0.4	0.0	0.1
Bricks	1.5	0.0	0.0	0.0	0.1	7.4	0.8	0.0	0.5	0.0	0.0	0.6	0.0	1.5	0.4	18.2	0.1	0.3	0.0	23.9	0.2
Cement	0.1	0.0	0.0	0.0	0.0	0.0	0.0	0.0	0.0	0.0	0.1	0.1	0.0	0.0	0.0	0.0	0.1	0.0	6.0	0.0	0.0
Coke ovens, chem	0.4	1.2	0.2	0.0	0.0	0.3	0.2	0.1	0.0	0.0	0.2	0.0	0.0	0.0	0.0	0.0	0.5	0.1	0.1	0.0	0.1
Metal manufacture	2.4	8.3	0.3	4.7	0.0	0.0	0.2	0.1	0.0	0.2	0.2	2.9	0.0	1.4	0.0	0.0	0.7	0.0	0.1	0.0	0.1
Shipbuilding	0.1	0.4	0.0	0.0	0.0	0.0	0.3	0.0	0.1	0.0	0.1	0.2	0.4	0.0	0.0	0.0	0.1	0.0	0.0	0.0	0.6
Machine tools	0.5	1.1	0.5	1.1	0.0	0.1	0.0	0.1	0.1	0.0	3.6	0.0	0.0	0.2	0.0	0.0	0.3	0.0	0.0	0.0	0.6
Textile machinery	0.0	0.0	0.0	0.0	0.0	0.0	0.0	0.0	0.0	0.0	0.0	0.0	0.0	0.0	0.0	0.0	0.0	0.0	0.0	0.0	0.0
Constructional engin	0.3	0.8	0.6	0.0	0.0	0.1	0.0	0.3	0.1	0.0	0.0	0.1	0.0	0.0	0.2	0.0	0.1	0.0	0.1	0.1	0.0
Other mech engin	4.1	9.1	7.2	2.8	0.2	0.3	1.2	1.6	0.6	4.3	4.0	24.8	0.9	1.1	0.3	0.3	1.4	1.0	0.3	0.4	4.0
Electrical machinery	0.4	0.6	0.0	0.0	0.0	2.7	0.1	0.0	0.0	0.0	0.0	0.0	0.0	3.2	0.0	0.0	0.0	0.0	0.0	0.0	0.0
Wireless apparatus	0.8	1.2	1.3	0.4	0.1	0.1	2.0	0.3	0.2	0.1	0.1	0.0	0.1	0.2	0.0	0.0	1.1	0.6	0.1	0.0	1.9
Other electrical	1.9	2.0	3.6	0.7	0.1	3.4	0.1	16.6	0.1	0.4	0.1	0.4	0.0	0.2	0.0	0.0	4.5	0.2	0.0	0.0	0.1
Motor cars	1.2	3.5	0.2	0.5	0.2	0.1	0.4	0.3	1.2	0.5	25.2	0.7	0.1	0.7	0.0	0.0	0.2	0.1	0.0	0.0	0.1
Aircraft	1.7	4.1	0.7	1.3	0.1	0.9	0.1	0.1	0.0	1.4	0.0	0.1	0.0	0.1	2.5	0.2	3.4	1.0	0.1	0.0	0.5
Other metal goods	1.4	2.9	0.9	6.1	0.1	0.2	1.1	0.1	0.4	0.2	0.2	0.4	0.4	1.1	0.2	0.1	0.6	0.3	0.2	0.3	0.5
Preci instr jewelery	1.4	3.3	0.8	0.7	0.2	0.0	4.4	0.2	0.4	0.2	0.3	0.3	0.4	0.5	0.4	0.0	3.6	0.2	0.1	0.1	0.2
Cotton spinning	0.0	0.0	0.0	0.0	0.0	0.0	0.0	0.0	0.0	0.0	0.0	0.0	0.0	0.0	0.0	0.0	0.0	0.0	0.0	0.0	0.0
Cotton waving	0.1	0.2	0.0	0.0	0.0	0.0	0.0	0.0	0.0	0.0	0.0	0.0	0.0	0.0	0.0	0.0	0.3	0.0	0.0	0.0	0.0
Woolen worsted	0.0	0.0	0.0	0.0	0.0	0.0	0.0	0.0	0.1	0.0	0.1	0.1	0.0	0.0	0.0	0.0	0.2	0.0	0.0	0.0	0.0
Rayon etc	0.0	0.0	0.0	0.0	0.1	0.0	0.0	0.0	0.0	0.0	0.0	0.0	0.0	0.0	0.0	0.0	0.4	0.0	0.0	0.0	0.0
Hosiery	0.2	0.6	0.0	0.0	0.0	0.0	0.0	0.0	0.0	0.0	0.0	0.1	0.0	0.0	0.0	0.0	0.0	0.0	0.0	0.0	0.1
Textile finishing	0.1	0.0	0.0	0.0	0.0	0.0	0.0	0.0	0.0	0.0	0.0	0.0	0.0	0.6	0.0	0.0	0.1	0.0	0.0	0.0	0.0
Leather goods	0.2	0.0	0.2	0.0	0.3	0.0	0.3	0.0	0.2	0.2	0.9	2.2	0.2	0.0	0.0	0.0	0.0	4.3	0.0	0.0	0.0
Tailoring	0.3	0.3	0.4	0.1	0.1	0.7	0.5	0.3	0.5	0.2	0.5	0.0	6.5	0.1	0.0	0.0	0.1	0.4	0.0	0.4	0.0
Dressmaking	0.0	0.0	0.0	0.0	0.0	0.0	0.0	0.0	0.0	0.0	0.0	0.0	0.0	0.0	0.0	0.0	0.0	0.0	0.0	0.0	0.0
Shoe making repair	0.4	0.2	0.3	0.3	0.2	0.2	5.2	0.3	0.6	0.3	0.2	0.6	1.4	0.3	0.1	0.3	0.2	0.8	0.2	0.3	0.2
Food	2.9	6.8	1.8	3.3	0.8	2.3	2.9	1.1	1.7	11.2	3.5	1.1	1.6	2.2	0.6	0.5	1.6	1.2	1.2	0.8	0.8
Drink	0.2	0.0	0.1	0.7	0.0	0.0	1.3	0.0	8.5	0.0	0.6	0.0	0.0	0.0	0.0	0.0	0.0	0.0	0.0	0.0	0.0
Timber	0.6	0.4	1.2	0.1	0.1	1.4	0.6	0.5	3.8	0.0	0.3	0.2	0.0	0.7	0.2	0.0	0.8	0.0	0.0	0.2	1.5
Furniture	6.7	3.5	36.9	0.3	0.0	0.2	0.5	0.3	3.1	0.0	0.4	0.1	1.5	3.8	0.2	0.0	0.5	2.3	0.0	0.1	6.6
Paper & board	1.3	0.0	1.1	0.0	0.0	0.0	0.0	0.1	0.0	0.0	0.0	0.7	0.1	0.0	0.0	0.0	1.0	0.0	0.0	0.0	12.6
Printing	1.9	1.1	2.1	14.5	3.2	0.8	3.2	0.7	1.2	1.5	0.8	1.6	2.5	0.6	0.1	0.0	0.2	0.1	0.1	0.0	0.3
Other manufacturing	2.6	3.0	1.7	0.1	0.3	2.7	8.5	3.5	1.2	0.2	0.0	0.9	0.4	0.5	0.1	0.0	13.3	0.0	0.1	0.2	0.6
All Manufacture	35.9	54.8	62.3	37.7	6.0	23.9	34.0	26.9	25.5	21.0	41.6	38.7	16.7	19.4	5.5	19.9	36.2	13.5	8.9	27.4	31.4

FEMALE 1951

	Bucks	Slough	Wycmbe	Ayl Bury	Wol vert	Blet ley	Ches Ham	Bea cfld	Mar low	Buck ing	N Pa gnel	Lins lade	Eton	Amer RD	Ayle RD	Buck RD	Eton RD	N Pa RD	Wing RD	Wsl RD	Wy RD
ALL	49721	13564	6661	4134	1544	1500	1771	1158	683	530	434	285	586	3857	1939	693	4932	951	413	443	3643
Agriculture	1164	87	26	7	12	13	24	15	6	7	17	5	0	137	147	65	224	88	58	51	175
Other mining quarry	9																8				1
Bricks	35	2				2	1					1		5	1	13	1	1		8	
Cement	3	1																	2		
Coke ovens, chem	396	329	21	2		2	6							1	1		22	1	1		11
Metal manufacture	529	396	12	54			5							42	2		15				3
Shipbuilding	9	5					4														
Machine tools	102	45	12	22					1		4						13	1			4
Textile machinery	2	1													1						
Constructional engin	28	24	4																		
Other mech engin	976	535	187	57	1		12	1	1	23	4	20		7	5	9	23	7	1		83
Electrical machinery	153	27				96								29			1				
Wireless apparatus	1110	277	144	9		3	146							5	1		75	9		1	440
Other electrical	870	200	178	78		79	2	167	4	2				2		1	143	9		1	4
Motor cars	179	139	4	5				1			23			2			3				2
Aircraft	678	385	19	36	1	18	1	1		3		1		5	71	3	40	76			18
Other metal goods	733	459	112	86	1		4		3					38	1	1	16	1	1		10
Preci instr jewelery	716	554	26	1	2		34			1		1		12	15		64	5	1		
Cotton spinning	2	0					1										1				
Cotton waving	84	50	3					1									30				
Woolen worsted	21			1								5					12			1	2
Rayon etc	41	4	1				4										32				
Hosiery	350	316	2						9	1			1	5			1	1			14
Textile finishing	24	3	2											17			2				
Leather goods	173	4	82	1	1		39				1	33						11		1	
Tailoring	896	156	365	17		161	69	3	1	2	2		14	20	3		3	72	2		6
Dressmaking	456	106	66	6	84	4	10	11	8	5	2	2	3	35	5	1	32	5	3	6	62
Shoe making repair	277	3	8	2	1	1	52		1		1	1	1	2	1	100	3	99			1
Food	2112	1384	207	141	13	18	104	2	24	36	7	1	6	86	10	2	38	11	7	7	10
Drink	60	10	10	6		1			20		11			1							1
Timber	86	3	45	1		1	4		1				5	3	6	1	7				9
Furniture	1224	104	966	3	1	1	1	4	8	2	1		5	22			17	1		1	87
Paper & board	348	5	58				1		1					1	18	1	23				240
Printing	1216	109	185	422	318	7	51	13	7	7	3	18	10	22	2		11	1		1	29
Other manufacturing	1857	619	221	25	19	195	269	33	22			1	2	30	5		355	3	3	1	54

Percentages of each area's total

	Bucks	Slough	Wycmbe	Ayl Bury	Wol vert	Blet ley	Ches Ham	Bea cfld	Mar low	Buck ing	N Pa gnel	Lins lade	Eton	Amer RD	Ayle RD	Buck RD	Eton RD	N Pa RD	Wing RD	Wsl RD	Wy RD
Agriculture	2.3	0.6	0.4	0.2	0.8	0.9	1.4	1.3	0.9	1.3	3.9	1.8	0.0	3.6	7.6	9.4	4.5	9.3	14.0	11.5	4.8
Other mining quarry	0.0	0.0	0.0	0.0	0.0	0.0	0.0	0.0	0.0	0.0	0.0	0.0	0.0	0.0	0.0	0.0	0.2	0.0	0.0	0.0	0.0
Bricks	0.1	0.0	0.0	0.0	0.0	0.1	0.1	0.0	0.0	0.0	0.0	0.4	0.0	0.1	0.1	1.9	0.0	0.1	0.0	1.8	0.0
Cement	0.0	0.0	0.0	0.0	0.0	0.0	0.0	0.0	0.0	0.0	0.0	0.0	0.0	0.0	0.0	0.0	0.0	0.0	0.5	0.0	0.0
Coke ovens, chem	0.8	2.4	0.3	0.0	0.0	0.1	0.3	0.0	0.0	0.0	0.0	0.0	0.0	0.0	0.1	0.0	0.4	0.1	0.2	0.0	0.3
Metal manufacture	1.1	2.9	0.2	1.3	0.0	0.0	0.3	0.0	0.0	0.0	0.0	0.0	0.0	1.1	0.1	0.0	0.3	0.0	0.0	0.0	0.1
Shipbuilding	0.0	0.0	0.0	0.0	0.0	0.0	0.2	0.0	0.0	0.0	0.0	0.0	0.0	0.0	0.0	0.0	0.0	0.0	0.0	0.0	0.0
Machine tools	0.2	0.3	0.2	0.5	0.0	0.0	0.0	0.0	0.1	0.0	0.9	0.0	0.0	0.0	0.0	0.0	0.3	0.0	0.0	0.0	0.1
Textile machinery	0.0	0.0	0.0	0.0	0.0	0.0	0.0	0.0	0.0	0.0	0.0	0.0	0.0	0.0	0.0	0.0	0.0	0.0	0.0	0.0	0.0
Constructional engin	0.1	0.2	0.1	0.0	0.0	0.0	0.0	0.0	0.0	0.0	0.0	0.0	0.0	0.0	0.0	0.0	0.0	0.0	0.0	0.0	0.0
Other mech engin	2.0	3.9	2.8	1.4	0.1	0.0	0.7	0.1	0.1	4.3	0.9	7.0	0.0	0.2	0.3	1.3	0.5	0.7	0.2	0.0	2.3
Electrical machinery	0.3	0.2	0.0	0.0	0.0	6.4	0.0	0.0	0.0	0.0	0.0	0.0	0.0	0.8	0.0	0.0	0.0	0.0	0.0	0.0	0.0
Wireless apparatus	2.2	2.0	2.2	0.2	0.0	0.2	8.2	0.0	0.0	0.0	0.0	0.0	0.0	0.1	0.1	0.0	1.5	0.9	0.0	0.2	12.1
Other electrical	1.7	1.5	2.7	1.9	0.0	5.3	0.1	14.4	0.6	0.4	0.0	0.0	0.0	0.1	0.0	0.1	2.9	0.9	0.0	0.2	0.1
Motor cars	0.4	1.0	0.1	0.1	0.0	0.0	0.0	0.1	0.0	0.0	5.3	0.0	0.0	0.1	0.0	0.0	0.1	0.0	0.0	0.0	0.1
Aircraft	1.4	2.8	0.3	0.9	0.1	1.2	0.1	0.1	0.0	0.6	0.0	0.4	0.0	0.1	3.7	0.4	0.8	8.0	0.0	0.0	0.5
Other metal goods	1.5	3.4	1.7	2.1	0.1	0.0	0.2	0.0	0.4	0.0	0.0	0.0	0.0	1.0	0.1	0.1	0.3	0.1	0.2	0.0	0.3
Preci instr jewelery	1.4	4.1	0.4	0.0	0.1	0.0	1.9	0.0	0.0	0.2	0.0	0.0	0.0	0.3	0.8	0.0	1.3	0.5	0.2	0.0	0.0
Cotton spinning	0.0	0.0	0.0	0.0	0.0	0.0	0.1	0.0	0.0	0.0	0.0	0.0	0.0	0.0	0.0	0.0	0.0	0.0	0.0	0.0	0.0
Cotton waving	0.2	0.4	0.0	0.0	0.0	0.0	0.0	0.1	0.0	0.0	0.0	0.0	0.0	0.0	0.0	0.0	0.6	0.0	0.0	0.0	0.0
Woolen worsted	0.0	0.0	0.0	0.0	0.0	0.0	0.0	0.0	0.0	0.0	1.8	0.0	0.0	0.0	0.0	0.0	0.2	0.0	0.0	0.2	0.1
Rayon etc	0.1	0.0	0.0	0.0	0.0	0.0	0.2	0.0	0.0	0.0	0.0	0.0	0.0	0.0	0.0	0.0	0.6	0.0	0.0	0.0	0.0
Hosiery	0.7	2.3	0.0	0.0	0.0	0.0	0.0	0.0	1.3	0.2	0.0	0.0	0.2	0.1	0.0	0.0	0.0	0.1	0.0	0.0	0.4
Textile finishing	0.0	0.0	0.0	0.0	0.0	0.0	0.0	0.0	0.0	0.0	0.0	0.0	0.0	0.4	0.0	0.0	0.0	0.0	0.0	0.2	0.0
Leather goods	0.3	0.0	1.2	0.0	0.1	0.0	2.2	0.0	0.0	0.0	0.2	11.6	0.0	0.0	0.0	0.0	0.0	1.2	0.0	0.2	0.0
Tailoring	1.8	1.2	5.5	0.4	0.0	10.7	3.9	0.3	0.1	0.4	0.5	0.0	2.4	0.5	0.2	0.0	0.1	7.6	0.5	0.0	0.2
Dressmaking	0.9	0.8	1.0	0.1	5.4	0.3	0.6	0.9	1.2	0.9	0.5	0.7	0.5	0.9	0.3	0.1	0.6	0.5	0.7	1.4	1.7
Shoe making repair	0.6	0.0	0.1	0.0	0.1	0.1	2.9	0.0	0.1	0.0	0.2	0.4	0.2	0.1	0.1	14.4	0.1	10.4	0.0	0.0	0.0
Food	4.2	10.2	3.1	3.4	0.8	1.2	5.9	0.2	3.5	6.8	1.6	0.4	1.0	2.2	0.5	0.3	0.8	1.2	1.7	1.6	0.3
Drink	0.1	0.1	0.2	0.1	0.0	0.1	0.0	0.0	2.9	0.0	2.5	0.0	0.0	0.0	0.0	0.0	0.0	0.0	0.0	0.0	0.0
Timber	0.2	0.0	0.7	0.0	0.0	0.1	0.2	0.0	0.1	0.0	0.0	0.0	0.9	0.1	0.3	0.1	0.1	0.0	0.0	0.0	0.2
Furniture	2.5	0.8	14.5	0.1	0.1	0.1	0.1	0.3	1.2	0.4	0.2	0.0	0.9	0.6	0.0	0.0	0.3	0.1	0.0	0.2	2.4
Paper & board	0.7	0.0	0.9	0.0	0.0	0.0	0.1	0.0	0.1	0.0	0.0	0.0	0.0	0.0	0.9	0.1	0.5	0.0	0.0	0.0	6.6
Printing	2.4	0.8	2.8	10.2	20.6	0.5	2.9	1.1	1.0	1.3	0.7	6.3	1.7	0.6	0.1	0.0	0.2	0.1	0.0	0.2	0.8
Other manufacturing	3.7	4.6	3.3	0.6	1.2	13.0	15.2	2.8	3.2	0.0	0.0	0.4	0.3	0.8	0.3	0.0	7.2	0.3	0.7	0.2	1.5
All Manufacture	31.7	46.1	44.1	23.6	28.6	39.3	46.3	20.5	16.3	15.5	13.6	29.1	8.2	10.2	7.6	19.0	20.1	33.0	5.1	6.3	29.9

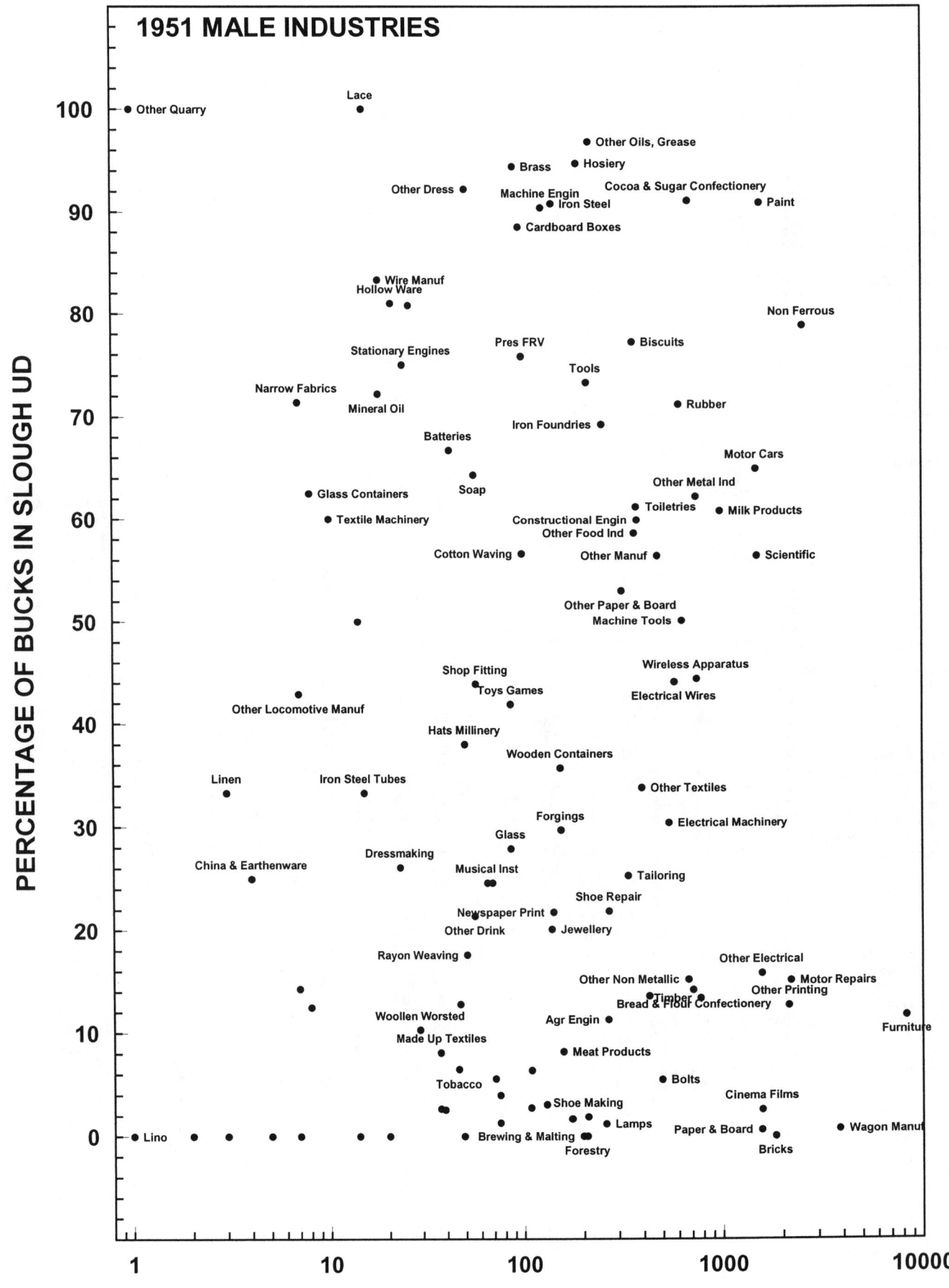

1951 MALE INDUSTRIES

NUMBER IN BUCKINGHAMSHIRE - log scale

PERCENTAGE OF BUCKS IN SLOUGH UD

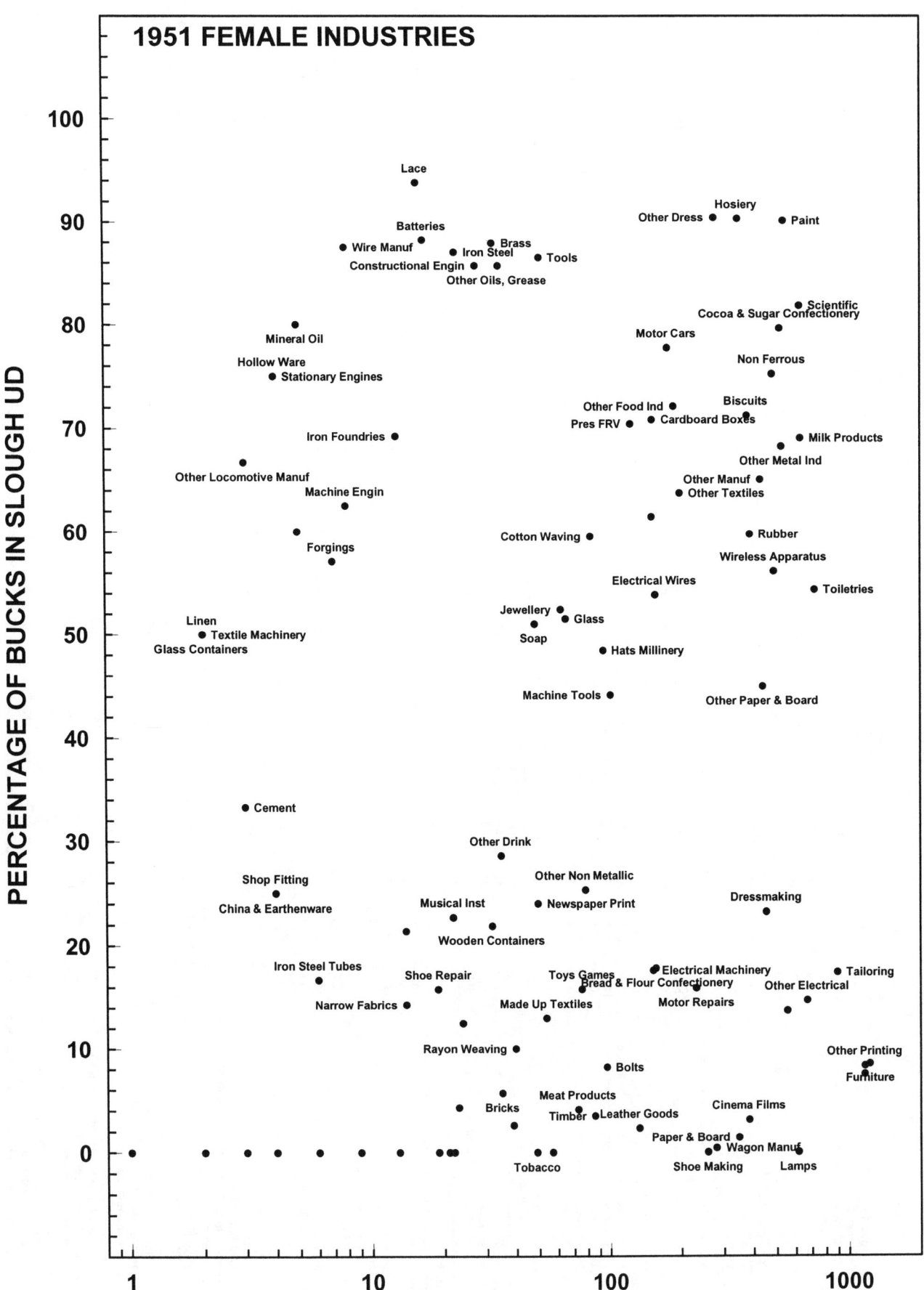

1951 FEMALE INDUSTRIES

PERCENTAGE OF BUCKS IN SLOUGH UD

NUMBER IN BUCKINGHAMSHIRE - log scale

INDUSTRIAL & CERTAIN OTHER OCCUPATIONS - Urban Areas in size order then Rural Districts - LOCATION QUOTIENTS

MALE 1951	BUCKS %'s 188457	Slo ugh 32179	Wyc mbe 19697	Ayl Bury 10061	Wol vert 6505	Blet ley 5769	Ches Ham 5386	Bea cfld 3845	Mar low 3031	Buck ing 1900	N Pa gnel 2100	Lins lade 1517	Eton 1476	Amer RD 19215	Ayle RD 15668	Buck RD 5275	Eton RD 20407	N Pa RD 6736	Wing RD 4728	Wsl RD 3615	Wy RD 19347
Population aged 15 + % tOTAL	77.26	98	100	99	100	104	100	100	99	99	101	100	98	99	105	105	99	100	102	103	99
I - XXVII Occupied % pop 15+	88.18	104	103	101	92	102	99	100	100	98	94	98	102	96	99	102	99	96	101	96	101
XXVIII. Retired and unoccupied % Pop 15+	11.82	72	79	94	163	83	104	102	101	111	142	112	83	129	107	85	106	129	95	128	96
% Occupied Population																					
Employers	3.02	44	80	67	66	51	97	111	121	152	134	101	86	141	122	167	116	165	124	195	109
Managers	5.59	98	92	69	46	61	111	167	107	71	54	104	87	167	46	32	187	51	55	45	97
Operatives	83.74	105	103	103	109	108	100	95	96	98	102	98	102	91	103	103	93	97	99	90	99
Working on own account	6.50	59	82	72	60	60	95	108	133	147	94	128	98	139	100	105	107	157	130	244	118
Out of work	1.15	119	102	252	36	29	64	90	123	14	109	60	43	100	66	41	125	44	137	50	90
I. Fishermen	0.00	0	0	0	0	0	0	2451	3133	0	0	0	0	0	0	0	0	0	0	0	0
II. Agricultural, etc. occupations	10.19	22	15	26	19	31	62	73	54	114	68	52	55	139	172	262	113	276	255	336	140
1. Agricultural and horticultural occupations	8.98	0	15	25	20	33	64	77	57	118	69	47	55	145	180	261	121	285	262	359	146
010, 011 Farmers, farm foremen, etc.	2.45	7	10	16	22	42	41	31	26	97	66	52	61	109	208	341	68	309	293	565	148
013, 014 Market gardeners, etc. & foremen	0.47	47	20	22	16	71	87	24	72	17	78	42	84	102	84	61	284	432	242	43	85
015 Other gardeners	2.18	30	27	22	10	16	92	210	141	69	54	45	59	265	85	92	177	94	84	95	166
III. Mining and quarring occupations	0.10	13	22	102	0	72	54	76	340	79	73	688	0	64	63	493	110	158	810	81	61
IV. Wkers in ceramics, glass, cement, etc.	0.66	40	37	7	4	267	128	0	37	167	66	223	45	61	42	413	61	99	944	690	20
V. Coal gas, etc. makers, workers in chemicals	0.46	337	33	64	81	84	24	75	21	191	48	43	109	26	12	80	100	50	40	72	25
VI. Workers in metal manuf, engineering	14.58	173	96	112	193	88	83	68	86	84	150	97	112	68	47	37	106	80	63	58	69
1. Foremen, overlookers	0.84	208	107	119	135	123	62	32	70	85	87	106	95	65	33	37	114	38	36	15	60
4. Foundry workers (excl pattern makers)	0.79	340	118	76	62	6	35	15	6	0	56	163	76	19	8	0	82	35	54	31	36
9. Metal machinists	1.38	208	108	180	183	45	26	122	81	34	101	107	165	38	22	8	109	62	54	41	57
10. Fitters, machine erectors	5.31	164	98	100	187	81	72	55	80	106	146	91	101	66	54	49	110	85	68	69	82
184 Motor and motor cycle mechanics	1.06	90	109	106	58	104	101	123	69	180	118	121	66	128	79	67	106	112	108	108	95
12. Plumbers, pipe fitters, etc.	0.87	119	74	114	104	82	182	136	179	145	160	79	251	129	73	54	91	68	48	61	79
16. Electrical apparatus makers, etc. (n.e.s.)	2.24	102	86	134	243	202	101	84	111	127	151	97	106	100	50	56	106	103	63	104	65
Others Metal	2.10	233	87	85	340	23	106	27	82	-30	263	71	95	26	38	0	106	76	52	-6	44
VII. Textile workers	0.18	248	91	59	0	14	172	44	56	45	84	113	0	110	10	30	101	13	52	0	96
VIII. Leather workers, fur dressers	0.54	46	74	49	118	31	685	35	109	88	191	201	92	67	27	29	45	834	39	61	42
2. Boot and Shoe makers	0.38	61	75	66	78	45	955	51	117	63	39	131	132	82	34	42	59	429	40	65	53
Others leather	0.16	11	71	9	210	0	67	0	90	145	538	362	0	35	11	0	13	1763	37	50	19
IX. Makers of textile goods and articles of dress	1.30	48	411	42	195	52	40	38	79	12	232	122	123	57	18	4	40	28	30	32	155
1. Garment workers	0.26	124	130	80	57	187	128	149	152	62	172	270	504	129	11	10	95	27	94	159	45
383 Tailors	0.15	113	113	130	100	212	93	156	166	108	299	67	675	110	12	18	90	31	41	250	41
Other Garment	0.11	140	152	13	0	154	176	140	134	0	0	543	273	155	8	0	101	21	166	37	49
Other Textile	1.04	29	480	32	229	18	18	11	61	0	247	85	29	40	20	3	27	28	14	0	182
X. Makers of foods, drinks and tobacco	1.00	152	94	127	86	84	164	72	160	213	124	157	109	85	59	49	86	84	78	65	71
1. Makers of foods	0.69	0	121	173	122	108	216	84	114	312	171	216	145	124	86	68	117	123	110	95	101
Drinks Tobacco	0.32	478	34	28	8	30	52	48	260	0	23	31	31	3	3	8	18	0	9	0	5
XI. Workers wood, cane and cork	6.32	71	274	30	228	46	146	52	104	33	172	42	71	83	33	19	53	93	39	39	155
472 Carpenters, joiners	1.63	91	63	86	119	66	166	91	144	117	126	109	140	133	97	61	111	128	114	130	88
Other Wood	4.69	64	348	10	266	39	139	38	91	3	188	19	47	65	11	4	33	81	13	8	179
XII. Makers of, workers in, paper; printers	1.89	64	109	504	108	55	142	75	165	50	39	105	126	40	46	8	46	32	57	9	182
3. Printers, bookbinders	1.35	70	106	663	122	71	188	23	51	70	49	131	132	51	62	12	47	39	49	12	65
Others Paper	0.54	48	117	101	73	13	26	207	456	0	14	37	111	11	5	0	43	17	79	0	477
XIII. Makers of products (n.e.s.)	0.75	199	159	49	36	92	338	86	45	42	10	197	53	74	31	14	82	18	52	22	56
XIV. Workers in building and contracting	5.73	68	52	117	70	82	129	111	134	177	82	86	125	122	143	102	80	132	200	197	98
583 Bricklayers	1.16	70	58	75	76	85	173	89	160	172	89	137	138	125	131	95	78	167	136	159	113
Others Building	4.58	68	50	128	68	82	118	116	127	179	80	73	122	122	146	104	80	124	216	206	94
XV. Painters and decorators	2.75	88	207	76	230	49	122	81	140	69	198	97	98	95	54	32	59	111	54	48	105
XVI. Admin/tors, directors, managers(n.e.s.)	3.86	104	105	80	34	61	108	154	88	78	59	133	54	164	42	19	180	43	38	29	103
620-629 Managers in industrial undertakings	2.50	106	117	52	25	45	106	165	86	63	35	115	52	165	33	22	193	42	41	26	109
XVII. Persons employed in transport, etc.	7.50	94	100	112	69	285	109	58	119	151	92	196	119	97	68	72	94	103	96	95	90
1. Railway transport workers	1.41	115	49	99	123	790	70	27	38	39	88	356	63	40	50	66	54	207	77	87	54
2. Road transport workers	4.55	89	127	114	54	82	119	60	148	190	103	148	122	112	79	89	95	83	89	101	106
655-658 Powered passenger vehicle drivers	0.87	37	159	121	65	33	147	127	179	109	50	91	182	193	64	45	95	62	59	66	127
659 Drivers of goods vehicles	2.60	95	116	110	55	117	104	44	135	268	113	175	111	84	86	118	92	97	102	134	100
3. Water transport workers	0.16	66	56	85	47	123	70	49	63	102	0	634	510	145	41	17	207	29	174	52	117
681 Dock labourers	0.01	144	0	236	0	384	0	0	0	0	0	1584	0	0	145	418	118	0	0	0	0
5. Other workers in communications, etc.	1.24	99	71	139	73	506	128	80	111	148	77	160	105	90	55	30	82	70	144	99	63
702 Postmen, post office sorters	0.46	99	65	161	81	237	216	101	150	226	161	195	0	111	67	23	84	80	46	99	89

Note Roman Numerals indicate a GROUP of occupations, Arabic Numerals under 20 without a leading' 0' a SUB GROUP, other Arabic Numerals an individual type. Those without any numeral a residual in the Group or sub group. The original figures for these and 'types' are included in groups and sub groups

108

INDUSTRIAL & OTHER OCCUPATIONS* - Urban Areas in size order then Rural Districts - LOCATION QUOTIENTS

FEMALE 1951	BUCKS %'s	Slo ugh	Wyc mbe	Ayl Bury	Wol vert	Blet ley	Ches Ham	Bea cfld	Mar low	Buck ing	N Pa gnel	Lins lade	Eton	Amer RD	Ayle RD	Buck RD	Eton RD	N Pa RD	Wing RD	Wsl RD	Wy RD
	197834	34292	21005	10989	6921	5150	6047	4068	3450	2042	2277	1753	1771	22222	13877	4147	22736	7087	4319	3653	20028
Population aged 15 + % TOTAL	79.3	98	100	100	102	99	103	102	98	98	103	101	102	102	99	97	101	100	100	101	99
I - XXVII Occupied % pop 15+	32.7	129	106	107	73	98	107	100	100	84	81	93	122	90	81	71	108	73	83	64	92
XXVIII. Retired and unoccupied % Pop 15+	67.3	86	97	97	113	101	97	100	100	108	109	103	89	105	109	114	96	113	108	118	104
% Occupied Population																					
Employers	1.0	46	67	58	78	72	43	164	154	120	127	98	91	146	141	253	136	139	134	187	123
Managers	2.6	77	69	99	93	66	77	115	119	99	158	128	102	135	121	152	103	116	104	146	123
Operatives	91.6	103	102	101	100	103	102	98	97	97	98	99	100	97	98	96	98	99	99	92	97
Working on own account	3.4	49	83	73	122	79	92	111	150	209	119	103	108	136	126	119	109	135	125	220	135
Out of work	1.4	79	72	130	67	48	73	116	79	32	70	81	97	114	103	94	156	57	104	158	122
II. Agricultural, etc. occupations	2.1	35	23	15	42	43	49	48	64	54	209	22	0	115	224	353	148	267	319	366	162
1. Agricultural and horticultural occupations	2.0	0	25	13	42	47	51	52	70	59	229	24	0	125	244	387	160	293	344	392	176
VI. Workers in metal manufacture, engineering	3.0	170	141	37	52	69	97	90	68	38	81	55	29	45	20	0	98	99	93	16	116
16. Electrical apparatus makers, etc. (n.e.s.)	0.7	98	183	14	76	111	84	201	148	0	88	136	25	47	5	0	122	161	62	24	156
VII. Textile workers	0.5	152	80	112	0	0	70	74	69	46	41	0	141	27	132	54	176	15	107	66	81
VIII. Leather workers, fur dressers	0.6	4	119	16	60	0	618	0	37	481	229	452	0	36	0	586	3	1277	69	52	41
IX. Makers of textile goods and articles of dress	5.2	81	252	35	118	149	73	43	83	35	125	284	94	61	32	23	78	79	267	82	96
1. Garment workers	3.4	97	162	32	123	218	102	51	92	40	130	306	97	64	27	35	94	101	350	109	84
383 Tailoresses	0.5	60	133	78	59	591	126	55	45	91	240	463	69	78	48	27	43	29	590	257	63
385 Dressmakers and light clothing makers	0.7	82	86	69	236	70	35	181	154	104	123	71	53	114	57	102	92	168	193	148	127
386 Machinists	1.7	105	206	8	99	139	116	6	96	0	147	269	85	47	13	16	112	76	393	59	78
X. Makers of foods, drinks and tobacco	0.7	127	157	61	95	76	116	39	273	0	144	0	149	110	44	57	51	74	60	185	84
1. Makers of foods	0.4	0	146	98	149	134	203	23	226	0	202	0	262	193	77	101	89	129	106	325	89
XII. Makers of, workers in, paper; printers	2.0	57	92	252	612	64	85	23	44	146	89	149	103	18	135	66	45	138	136	96	139
3. Printers, bookbinders	1.3	33	81	386	668	67	134	37	27	55	129	149	56	22	167	21	42	171	59	142	84
other Paper	0.8	94	110	38	522	59	7	0	72	293	26	149	178	10	84	137	50	85	258	21	229
XVI. Administrators, directors, mangeresses	0.8	83	106	52	27	57	64	193	98	56	150	58	86	188	47	17	134	55	65	120	111
XVII. Persons employed in transport, etc.	2.4	84	80	80	94	352	86	70	72	58	85	118	81	89	106	187	100	112	130	165	109
5. Other workers in communications, etc.	1.8	92	61	93	54	432	78	72	89	26	68	91	78	76	112	195	104	91	161	191	107
XVIII. Commercial, finance, etc.(exc. clerical)	10.4	85	113	113	130	113	120	89	174	130	171	119	116	105	111	94	81	100	70	98	87
1. Commercial occupations	10.3	85	113	114	129	114	118	89	175	131	173	120	117	104	111	94	82	100	70	99	86
720-729 Owners, etc. of retail businesses	1.7	0	124	117	206	102	144	117	215	159	257	121	121	137	141	109	110	132	86	159	103
730-739 Saleswomen, shop assistants	7.7	90	115	120	122	121	122	79	180	125	166	122	125	98	112	98	75	98	65	95	87
2. Persons employed in finance and insurance	0.1	44	119	32	221	76	230	182	112	0	0	0	0	186	102	133	31	146	0	0	208
XIX. Professional and technical (exc. clerical)	9.8	61	74	170	71	51	57	140	79	104	108	108	41	147	134	144	129	90	88	132	96
770-772 Nurses and midwives	3.7	114	56	283	38	29	35	120	59	50	94	38	14	119	143	88	107	68	52	75	55
780,785 Teachers	3.4	65	94	81	100	77	73	121	98	116	145	209	42	147	122	148	96	139	117	194	110
XXII. Persons engaged in personal service	26.0	71	80	109	77	86	76	153	124	124	88	78	167	130	114	146	118	96	111	132	101
862-865 Owners, etc. of cafes, hotels, etc.	1.5	82	75	87	107	94	52	113	116	172	124	64	143	117	122	110	120	121	102	122	111
867 Waitresses, still room hands	0.9	81	110	198	119	148	66	116	245	131	69	27	60	90	71	77	96	42	61	19	118
876 Charwomen, office cleaners	1.9	150	143	132	145	202	55	73	132	182	139	111	147	35	60	107	47	31	17	137	66
877-878 Laundry workers, dry cleaners	1.6	91	97	138	14	5	241	113	270	337	25	129	181	84	185	148	65	32	98	60	71
882 Cooks	3.0	47	64	66	37	43	46	196	132	92	101	78	238	167	123	179	150	113	145	151	113
883-885 Other domestic servants (indoor)	12.1	11	78	108	75	88	76	201	120	97	82	60	205	166	135	183	148	118	142	168	123
XXIII. Clerks, typists, etc.	20.3	129	103	92	108	69	97	83	86	101	82	118	79	90	75	61	109	76	53	73	89
890-895 Costing, estimating, other clerks	10.9	125	102	100	139	82	92	67	95	135	97	129	70	84	80	62	97	94	60	82	92
891-892 Typists, secretaries	8.5	126	107	85	64	50	107	107	79	68	60	113	88	100	72	57	125	55	45	67	88
XXIV. Warehousewomen, storekeepers, packers, etc.	3.4	188	83	85	53	50	204	46	70	61	60	34	57	93	60	67	66	50	82	48	54
XXVI. Workers in unskilled occupations (n.e.s.)	8.0	165	97	83	98	148	119	68	78	92	86	59	90	46	60	44	63	104	93	35	113
I,III-V,XI,XIII-XV,XX,XXI,XXV,XXVII Others	4.8	151	81	65	76	245	190	63	45	0	42	19	65	75	206	25	1	65	62	41	140

* These are all for which figures were given. See Vision of Britain Website 1951 Census

109